THE DEVIL IN SILICON VALLEY

THE DEVIL
IN SILICON VALLEY

Northern California, Race,

and Mexican Americans

PRINCETON UNIVERSITY PRESS Princeton and Oxford

Published by Princeton University Press, 41 William Street, Princeton, New Jersey 08540
In the United Kingdom: Princeton University Press, 3 Market Place, Woodstock,
Oxfordshire OX20 1SY

Library of Congress Cataloging-in-Publication Data

Pitti, Stephen J., 1969–
The devil in Silicon Valley : Northern California, race, and Mexican Americans /
Stephen J. Pitti.
p. cm.
Includes bibliographical references and index.
ISBN 0-691-09287-7 (alk. paper)
1. Santa Clara Valley (Santa Clara County, Calif.)—History.   2. Santa Clara Valley
(Santa Clara County, Calif.)—Race relations.   3. Santa Clara Valley (Santa Clara
County, Calif.)—Social conditions.   4. Mexican Americans—California—Santa Clara
Valley (Santa Clara County)—History.   5. Mexican Americans—California—Santa
Clara Valley (Santa Clara County)—Politics and government.   6. Mexican Americans—
California—Santa Clara Valley (Santa Clara County)—Social conditions.   I. Title.

F868.S25 P68 2003
305.868'72079473–dc21   2002029278

British Library Cataloging-in-Publication Data is available

This book has been composed in Minion

Printed on acid-free paper. ∞

www.pupress.princeton.edu

Printed in the United States of America

10 9 8 7 6 5 4 3 2 1

For Alicia, Antonio Malik, and Thalia María

Contents

Illustrations

Acknowledgments

This study of Santa Clara County's Mexican community stands as a marker of my debts to the local residents who helped me understand the region and its history. I hope that the dozens who provided access to their personal archives or narrated their memories of past events will recognize themselves in the history told here. I have accumulated weighty academic debts, as well. Albert Camarillo's fine reputation as mentor, scholar, and friend to his graduate students is richly deserved, and his interest and faith in nurturing this project from its early stages made its completion possible. Gordon Chang, George Fredrickson, and Ramón Saldívar also gave of their time and energy, and David Gutiérrez played a special role as a project muse. Special thanks to friends and fellow students Jon Schoenwald, Sam Truett, Martín Valadez, and John González for frequent bursts of inspiration. My Yale colleagues Jean-Christophe Agnew, Jennifer Baszile, Graham Boyd, Jon Butler, Hazel Carby, Vilashini Cooppan, Nancy Cott, Michael Denning, John Mack Faragher, Jonathan Holloway, Matthew Jacobson, Robert Johnston, Gilbert Joseph, Diana Paulin, Patricia Pessar, Victorine Shepherd, Laura Wexler, and Bryan Wolf have been terrific intellectual companions and supportive friends. An exciting group of students, including Mark Overmyer Velázquez, Brian Herrera, Ben Johnson, Manuel Berrelez, Angelica Jongco, Jordan Gonzales, and Wendy Montoya, have animated this project, and the staff and residents of Trumbull College—Janet Henrich, Victor Henrich, Peter Novak, Curtis Lee, Laura King, Debbie Rueb, and Peggy Lee—have provided a warm residential community. In Sacramento, Scott Flodin, Kim Johnson, Mark Kornweibel, and Paul Schmitz provided rich wisdom and relief.

A number of programs and institutions also assisted in the completion of this project. The Mellon Foundation, Ford Foundation/National Research Council, Morse Junior Faculty Fellowship at Yale, Irvine Fellows Program at Stanford, Stanford Humanities Center, Stanford Center for Chicano Research, Dorothy Compton Foundation, Whiting Foundation, California State

University Doctoral Incentive Program, Julian Samora Research Institute, and Yale University Council for International and Area Studies provided much appreciated resources for this study. The staff of the Department of Special Collections at Stanford's Green Library helped to shape and animate this study from its conception until its completion. As curator and archivist, Roberto Trujillo energetically assisted me in finding primary and secondary sources relevant to this project. Special thanks also go to the staffs of the Beinecke Library at Yale University, Walter Reuther Library at Wayne State University, Bancroft Library at U.C. Berkeley, Holt-Atherton Department of Special Collections at the University of the Pacific, Santa Clara University Archives, and California State Archives. Jeff Paul at San Jose State University's Chicano Resource Library has been a particularly invaluable source of local knowledge and a great supporter of this project for several years. David Bacon, Jesús M. Garza, and Jesús Angel Peña encouraged this book by offering their stunning visual representations of Silicon Valley's development. Thomas LeBien at Princeton University Press worked the editorial magic for which he is famous, and Maura Roessner, Anne Reifsnyder, and Anita O'Brien provided generous and professional help

This has been a family enterprise, and the generosity, patience, and scholarly expertise of my parents, Edith and Joseph Pitti, made this a much better book. Their line editing, help with selecting images, and deep knowledge of California history were indispensable. My sisters, Catherine Pitti and Gina Marie Pitti, along with my brother-in-law, Michael Friedman, have delivered well-timed jokes, helped with local transportation, and made visits to Northern California a family reunion. Gina's expertise in postwar Chicano history set a standard that I endeavored to follow. Arthur Schmidt, Aurora Camacho de Schmidt, Genevieve Schmidt Camacho, and Tom Quinn—all committed teachers and activists—gave sustenance and support while spurring my interest in baseball, good food, and other pleasant diversions.

My greatest thrills over the course of the last ten years have come from spending time with Alicia Schmidt Camacho, compañera in this and other projects, and from witnessing the birth and growth of our twins, Antonio Malik and Thalia María. My dedication and greatest love remains with them.

THE DEVIL IN SILICON VALLEY

Prologue

The Devil Defined

This book explores the historical experiences of California's residents of Mexican origin, the state's largest "minority" population, in one of the world's most influential but least understood locales, the region commonly known today as Silicon Valley. It might be understood as a sort of counter-history, in the sense that its trajectory runs against common myths about the Valley's development. *The Devil in Silicon Valley* contends that Northern California must be understood as a place shaped by deeply entrenched, although changing, labor and race relations from the early nineteenth century forward. Rather than focusing on the region simply as a high-tech fantasy zone for computer software designers, these pages argue for the importance of remembering that ethnic Mexicans and other racialized communities have lived in the area for a long time, and that these populations have laid claims to the Valley for many generations. Latinos have helped to shape this region of California for more than two hundred years, shaping in turn national and international developments since the nineteenth century.

The Devil of this book's title is drawn from an anecdote told to a University of California at Berkeley anthropologist. In the form of a donkey, the Devil is said to have walked into the San José Mission. Several native Ohlone neophytes there climbed up for a ride, the donkey wondrously elongating to accommodate them. One Indian, spying the fact that the donkey had three cloven feet and one rooster's foot, warned the others; the donkey tossed them and vanished. There are a number of interpretations of this tale, but I prefer the simplest: beginning in the late eighteenth century, a new understanding of racial difference infiltrated the Valley, bringing with it patterns of conquest and violence, which in turn begged patterns of accommodation and resistance. Over the two hundred years with which this book is concerned, ideologies of race, like the Devil, took on different forms, assumed different guises, and extracted varying costs, but the manifestations of violence, which always attend racism, were its most constant feature. And the simplest lessons learned from the two-hundred-year history of this storied Valley are two: that the label Silicon Valley—which follows on the heels of the region's fame as an entrepot for Gold Rush hopefuls, then as home to one of the world's largest mercury mines, then as an Edenic spot for the cultivation of perishable cash crops—will be replaced by something else is a near certainty; almost as certain as the second lesson, that race will continue to delineate the Valley's economic, social, and political possibilities, regardless of a booster's moniker.

The advent of Silicon Valley has drawn forth some of the most enthusiastic boosterism in a valley and state famous for the genre. My interests lie elsewhere. Ideologies of racism were imported into the valley by the Spanish, and a graduating scale of political and labor practices whose most consistent motif was violence and its threat became the norm. In the mid-nineteenth century it became the Anglo American community's fortune, born of force, to place itself squarely atop this pre-existing, nascent hierarchy of race. Americans didn't force their way up a ladder so much as they grafted a new top rung to a pre-existing one, and the circumstances and consequences of the racial assumptions they imposed from that height put in sharp relief the declining fortunes of Mexican Americans, Mexican immigrants, and the then vanishing Native population. But nonwhites were not simply victims. For decades, migration and transnational beliefs informed Latino strategies of accommodation and resistance, strategies that subtly, then dramatically, shifted as the constant movement of people occurred around an increasingly settled population. My interest is not in a valley of silicon, or fruit, or mercury, or gold; my interest is in a valley of people, shaped by race for centuries.

I first envisioned specific elements of this project while standing on a San José rooftop with a pair of elderly *Mexicanos* in the mid-1990s. Never a roofer and none too handy with a hammer, I'd been summoned up a long ladder to help these two 84-year-old immigrants carry the pail of tar they needed to cover some holes in one of the Silicon Valley's longstanding community centers. Ray Salazar and Lino Covarrubias had each volunteered at this aging site for four decades, ever since leaving agricultural work in the San Joaquin Valley and settling permanently in Santa Clara County during the area's boom years in the 1950s. Prior to climbing that ladder, I'd spent several terrific hours in their company hearing personal stories of immigration, home-buying, political activism, and discrimination at the hands of local *gueros*, "whites." Because Latinos have left at best a scattered written record of their many activities in the region, these and other extensive oral histories play a prominent role in my reconstruction of the Valley's neglected past. My subsequent offer of assistance to these two "informants" was an effort to thank them for their time, my way of trying to give them back something in exchange for the valuable stories they had shared. The rest of the afternoon I marveled at Ray and Lino's strength and dexterity, grew embarrassed by my own clumsiness, and became increasingly aware of the nuanced story I had set myself the task of writing.

Climbing that ladder helped me begin to think more clearly about the history of Mexican immigrants and Mexican Americans in this Northern California valley. Despite years of research, when I looked around from my rooftop vantage point it became evident that I had only begun to see the patterns of local Latino life and politics for myself. As I focused on the distant rooftops of the area surrounding "the Alameda," an important thoroughfare designed by Spanish colonists and built by Indian workers in the late eighteenth century, it became increasingly clear that I would need to reckon with the broad patterns of Northern California's Mexican American history, which remained largely unwritten. Taking my cue from the long presence of Mexican-origin residents, the following chapters explore the historical development of the San José area from the late eighteenth century forward. But while I argue for the critical importance of native residents, early European colonial efforts, and the legacies of their interactions, it remains visibly obvious that the "Silicon Valley" has undergone a series of startling changes since those early years. It would be foolish to contend otherwise. To take but one example, as I tried to follow Ray and Lino's directions on how to stir and apply tar, I noticed that the building on which we stood was located almost directly beneath one of the many freeways that have cut through the area since World War II. These concrete symbols of national spending and economic growth helped make San José the capital of the semiconductor and microelectronic industries in the United States by the early 1970s.

The presence of that freeway also promoted the ongoing movements of people in and out of the Santa Clara Valley, a constant process of renewal and growth. The region—like other parts of the American West—has not only been an important place in its own right, it has also served as a space through which people have traveled in search of work. I argue in the following chapters that migration has been a dynamic force in the Valley, a social process that shaped imperial institutions, native resistance, working-class political activism, and new forms of cultural politics over generations. In the decades before Lino and Ray's arrival, the local Mexican immigrant community had grown dramatically as a result of the development of railroads, a pattern mirrored in Los Angeles, El Paso, San Antonio, and other southwestern cities, and a phenomenon that illustrated the importance of broader, national political and economic forces in shaping modern San José. From my perch underneath the freeway, I could begin to see the effects of World War II–era migrations on the region, movements that had made San José a critically important demographic center for Mexicans and Mexican Americans in Northern California by 1950. Lino and Ray were part of that migrant history, two members of one of the state's largest Latino communities that would number some 403,401 county residents by the year 2000.[1]

Not surprisingly, my rooftop perch also afforded me the chance to see the Valley's often forgotten poverty. Migrants who settled in the area during the twentieth century rarely enjoyed much immediate economic prosperity, and my engagement with San José's long history began to contend with the persistence of real hardship among many local Latinos. The neighborhood surrounding the community center where I spoke with Ray and Lino was largely ethnic Mexican and mostly poor, facts evident from the Spanish we could hear spoken over the roar of freeway traffic, and from the presence of middle-aged *Mexicanas* across the street waiting for buses to take them to their low-wage domestic and assembly jobs across town. *The Devil in Silicon Valley* illustrates that Mexican-origin residents, often clustering at the lowest rungs of the local economy, have been integral to the emergence of modern San José, a "new western city" characterized by a variety of racial and ethnic communities, the prevalence of both high-tech skilled jobs and blue-collar employment, and pockets of neighborhood poverty in the midst of urban wealth.[2] Stories abound in the following pages that illustrate how the labor of Mexican Americans and Mexican immigrants built the region from its early foundations as a European settlement to its recent, digital-age glory. And, as Ray and Lino knew well, the area has kept many Latino residents confined to menial occupations in ways long dictated by ideologies of race. From the nineteenth century forward, a variety of discriminatory forces limited Latino economic opportunities and settlement patterns in the area, and an early death became an all too common consequence for many workers.

The area now known as Silicon Valley has in fact seen more than its fair share of violence, a topic raised by Lino and Ray when they turned to discuss memories of police brutality in Northern California. They also recalled jobs that took a severe physical toll. For these two men whose health had been impaired due to the nature of available work; whose children had suffered from labor accidents, an inconsistent diet, unsanitary neighborhoods, and restricted educational opportunities; whose families were granted limited access to health care, education, and employment; whose recourse to government for the safeguarding of basic human and legal rights was nebulous, the violence of the policeman's club sat only at the extreme of a long continuum of hardship. I encountered countless similar stories from other Latinos during the course of my research, and the history of San José that I undertook began to illustrate that, for those facing dangerous living and working conditions, the leap between a beating and the sight of a hungry child has never appeared so great.

These difficulties shaped settlement and local politics, and devilish manifestations of powerful racial hierarchies often prompted Latinos to emigrate from a Valley that many white Americans considered the promised land. Thousands of ethnic Mexicans left to build permanent residences elsewhere during the nineteenth and twentieth centuries, and Lino and Ray told me about their frequent visits to Mexico over the course of the last forty years. Like other Latinos, they expressed an uneasy attachment to Northern California, and their ties to distant places shaped how San Joseans made political demands on local employers, labor unions, and government officials. Matters of work and residency were of paramount importance in local ethnic politics, and forging transnational connections with Mexico remained a core concern for Ray, Lino, and many other Latinos. As the following chapters contend, all this assured that the Santa Clara Valley would play host to some of the most creative political activism in the West, and many local residents, concerned about labor issues and connections with Mexico, influenced the course of social movements in regions beyond San José. Some, including César Chávez and Ernesto Galarza, even took their place on an international stage.

The Devil in Silicon Valley interprets the history of these Latinos in Northern California for the first time. I make the case throughout that developments in the San José area captured and in many cases predated general trends in the broader history of Mexican Americans in the United States. Migrations, the advent of low-wage work, and the development of unions and other political organizations have played a key role in San José's history and make the place central for any consideration of the Latino past. The area now known as Silicon Valley has in fact been a fulcrum around which some of the most compelling developments of modern times have played out. Northern California witnessed a transition from European imperialism to American nationalism, from precapitalist relations to a capitalist society in which new extractive industries—particularly mining and agriculture— shaped the fates of the region's working class. Large-scale movements of people to and from the area during the twentieth century transformed the Valley, and local immigrants bore the brunt of the social dislocations caused by new economic and political shifts in twentieth-century California. By the late twentieth century, however, San José would also be home to a vibrant civil rights movement based in many ways on imagined connections to faraway homes in Mexico.

As those matters suggest, the region's diverse communities have long played a critical role in the area's development, and some readers may find in the following chapters not only the broad contours of Mexican American history but also a few contemporary lessons. One might be the importance of admitting that historical writing inevitably emerges in dialogue with an author's own political context. Contemporary developments certainly honed my passion for writing this book, and I should be clear about some of the biases that shaped its content from the start. I was no doubt influenced above all by the highly charged decade of the 1990s in which many Californians scorched Mexican immigrants like Ray and Lino for supposedly contributing too little to the state's development. I decided early on that I would try to uncover local ethnic Mexican perspectives in part to confound anti-immigrant propagandists. I have maintained openly Luddite sensibilities about the virtues of the region's high-technology economy, bristling when regional pundits celebrate Silicon Valley notables like Hewlett and Packard. I'll take my stand with Ray and Lino, and I'll take inspiration from immigrant artists like Jesús Pérez, whose menacing image of a Bay Area *taquería* graces the cover of this book. It's my strongest belief that they and other working-class Latinos tell the most revealing stories about California, but readers will decide for themselves whether accounts of Silicon Valley require a greater love for computer programmers and other high-technology "whiz kids" than I can muster. I have instead thrown my energies into bringing the Devil of race to judgment for the trouble he has caused Latino residents in the area.

❑   ❑   ❑

A note on usage: I have attempted to use terms in this study that carefully illustrate both the changing nature of social relations in the area and the diversity of the Mexican-origin community in the Santa Clara Valley. Other scholars have used a variety of categories to describe Mexican neighborhoods, households, and workplaces, although none can adequately capture the complexity of these places and the many (at times contradictory) ways in which residents have named themselves. These terms of self-description have changed significantly over time. Neither "Hispanic" nor "Latino," for example, would have been recognized as terms for self-description in the area just thirty years ago. But since impishly slippery ethnic and racial categories must be defined, I use "ethnic Mexican" to refer broadly to all residents of Mexican background. In this regard, "the ethnic Mexican community," "ethnic Mexican people," and "ethnic Mexicans in San José" are the umbrella terms intended to represent a wide cross-section of local residents. At times I also use "Latino" in the same way, particularly when discussing the nineteenth-century community of Chileans and ethnic Mexicans at the New Almadén mine. I prefer that term to "Hispanic" because the former seems to be in wider use among many ethnic Mexicans, Puerto Ricans, and other Latinos who are today attempting to consider and reimagine their common pan-ethnic ties in the United States "from below." I use two other descriptors as subcategories to capture the diversity of the Latino community. "Mexican Americans," on the one hand, refers to residents of Mexican descent who were born in the United States or who became naturalized U.S. citizens.

"Mexicanos" and "Mexicanas," "Mexican immigrants," or simply "Mexicans," on the other, refer to immigrant men and women from Mexico. While I consider this a work of Chicano history and I am myself a Chicano historian, the terms "Chicana" and "Chicano" are not utilized here until the study turns to consider the years after 1960. "Chicano" as an analytical term does little to clarify the internal dynamics within the ethnic Mexican community until recently, and since it was not commonly used by Mexican-origin residents as a self-descriptor until the late-1960s, I am uncomfortable with using it to describe, for example, "local Chicanas/os in the 1800s."

As important as these words are, residents of the Santa Clara Valley have also invested equally extraordinary meaning in terms like "American" and "white," a subject taken up in other chapters. "Americans" refers to citizens of the United States unless otherwise noted. I remain uncomfortable with that term since the United States has never been synonymous with "America," but more accurate neologisms like "Unitedstatesian" are too cumbersome and distracting. Frequent mention is made over the following pages of "white Americans," a term designating those of European descent. The meanings of that term certainly also have changed over time. In general I use "white" instead of "Anglo" because many San José residents hailed from southern Europe rather than England during the early twentieth century, and because Latinos in the area more often have used that term to describe the dominant population. Throughout the period covered here, ethnic Mexicans also labeled them "gringo" or "yanqui" or "bolillo" ("white bread"), far more derisive and scathing language that ought to remind readers yet again of the longstanding racial tensions endemic to this celebrated valley.

Chapter 1

Devil's Destiny

Father Narciso was accused of baptizing Indians by force.
When punished they protested, "Father, it hurts!"
"Of course," agreed the missionary, "but the pains of
hell hurt worse."
—Mrs. Fremont Older, *California Missions and Their Romances*

In the early spring of 1786, three native residents of Mission Santa Clara
issued a startling accusation: the mission's Father Tomás de la Peña had
murdered four local Indians two years before. The testimonies of Plácido
Ortiz, Anecelto Valdez, and the local headman Antonio about the priest's
activities soon prompted extensive investigations by Spanish colonial officials. As those efforts developed, another native resident of the area reported
that he had seen the friar give "many blows with the iron of a hoe to someone who was watering the crops." The priest for his part claimed that he had
only been teaching that man how to use the hoe properly, and that the
deceased had died instead from "a serious epidemic illness," an all too common problem in the late-eighteenth-century Santa Clara Valley. In defending
himself, Peña argued that local Spanish soldiers and not Catholic priests were
the violent actors often guilty of punishing native people too severely. He
wrote that "On occasion soldiers have used their weapons against the pagans
without having encountered resistance. At times the pagans have been left
abused by the cruel punishment of being hung from a tree by one foot, by
scarifying their buttocks with swords. The same soldiers hang them and then
beat them with staves, each one taking his turn." Despite Peña's emphatic
pleas, Alta California's Governor Pedro Fages initially decided that the friar
had been too severe in his treatment of local natives, and that several had
likely died as a result of the cleric's practice of corporal punishment. But

Fages then abruptly changed his mind; he "concluded that the three main accusers among the Indians had manufactured the whole thing" and sent the native perjurers to be incarcerated at the Monterey Presidio for ten years. In the following months, several witnesses in the case admitted that they had lied to investigators about the Franciscan's activities, pressured to do so by Plácido and Antonio.

The actions and reactions of priest, perjurers, and governor illustrate the messy set of social relations that had developed in the Santa Clara Valley since the arrival of the Spanish in the previous decade. Peña had founded the mission only a few years before, and he defended himself by attacking the colonial soldiers there to support the Catholic settlement. Government officials at times worried about Franciscan behavior, and Indians reacted in a variety of ways to the Spanish presence. Both friars and military officials increasingly believed that many Indians acted from untrustworthy motives: Plácido, the leader of the three accusers, seems to have been driven by anger about his declining political authority in the region. One of several natives of Baja California drawn to the area to work at the local mission, Plácido had managed the friars' storehouse, distributing food to local residents with the help of Anecleto and Antonio, until Father Peña removed him from that prestigious position because of apparent graft. The three accusers apparently hoped that their verbal assault on Peña would lead to the priest's removal and would help them regain their lost authority at the mission.

The lines of continuity running between Peña's valley and the more modern Silicon Valley are few and hard to trace. Like later elites, Spanish colonists manipulated work and opportunity to shore up their political control. While colonial social categories that differentiated Europeans from Indians were not hard and fast during the late eighteenth and early nineteenth centuries, they appeared more and more determining as the decades passed. As these categories became more rigid, they did so along racial lines; in short, the Devil began making trouble by the late eighteenth century. Even by 1786, residents of northern Alta California had begun to identify themselves in ethno-racial terms as either indigenous, mixed-race, or European. Such racial thinking prompted Peña and other colonial authorities to define their own more European and "civilized" practices in opposition to Alta California's heathen Indians, even as native people with diverse cultural traditions and linguistic backgrounds came together in struggles against the Spaniards. These developments had parallels in many places where European colonists controlled new territories, but they remain largely forgotten in Northern California.

Expressing new ideas about race, residents such as Antonio and Father Peña watched changing cultural practices reshape the Valley and give birth to new social conflicts during the 1780s. Among other things, colonial policies in Alta California shaped the project of Spanish settlement, created new divisions among native inhabitants, reframed political aspirations, and helped define concepts such as "freedom." Natives like Plácido were clearly interested in the contents of the mission's storehouses and valued access to them. For their part, Franciscans emphasized that those repositories would help to acculturate the region's natives to Catholic and European practices. Soldiers and settlers, on the other hand, viewed commodities with a different eye, and they frequently valued Indian men as workers and Indian women as wives or sexual conquests. In partial response, native residents such as Plácido, Anecelto, and Antonio developed fresh tactics of political resistance and accommodation.

The determining force of race and the rapid pace of native acculturation could already be seen in Peña's encounter with Antonio and the other accusers, which, in turn, revealed two other changes that would reshape Valley society over the next sixty years. First, as Peña's own testimony about monitoring the "proper" use of a hoe made clear, the Spaniards introduced new ways of understanding and controlling productive work in the Valley. Prior to the arrival of these Europeans, as we shall see, no Valley resident regulated the labor of another in this way, and conflicts and debates about work persisted through the early 1840s and beyond. Second, new migrations began to restructure Valley society. The late eighteenth and early nineteenth centuries saw the influx of people, goods, and ideas into the region as Alta California was increasingly linked to Europe, central Mexico, and eventually the eastern United States. By contrast, many native residents increasingly chose to leave the region for other parts of the province.

This was imperial Alta California, an area and an epoch shaped by political conflicts, labor struggles, rapid cultural change, and new migrations. Together these developments laid a foundation upon which white Americans would establish themselves by the 1840s. Valley communities developed more fiercely racialized allegiances after the United States claimed the territory in 1848, but the origins of such thinking lay in this earlier era. While often celebrated as an arcadia, the San José area witnessed new struggles for political power by the early nineteenth century that would persist for over a century. Some Indians planned militant revolts, while others joined mission society or worked for European colonists. In this "contested Eden," diverse communities continued to compete against a backdrop of mythmaking about the Valley's peace and prosperity.[1]

RACE IN THE VALLEY

Long before Plácido, Anacleto, and Antonio ever met Father Peña, their forebears had established extensive village settlements, trade networks, and social organizations based on gathering acorns, fennel, and other plants through-

San José and Northern California. Map by Scott Flodin.

out the region. The Ohlone had inhabited the area for at least six thousand years prior to Spanish explorations, existing amidst an atmosphere of political rivalries and occasional violence, and patterns of their social organization remained intact well into the nineteenth century. Like many native residents elsewhere in northern Alta California, Valley inhabitants continued to hunt tule elk, antelope, deer, and other animals, to harvest clams, to fish in local streams, and to burn grasslands in order to encourage the annual growth of herbs, grasses, and other plants.[2]

As the Peña episode makes clear, social relations in Alta California became more complex and marked by often bloody conflicts after the arrival of the Spanish. The settlers who entered the Valley in the late eighteenth century did not find a "virgin land" devoid of human settlement, of course, but Spanish commander Pedro Fages's first visit to the region in 1770 did set the stage for subsequent colonial projects to "civilize" local "savages." Race functioned as a governing principle of political identity, used to determine the distribution of land, labor, and other resources, but racial categories were less hard and fixed than they would later become. Religiosity proved a more determining force, at least in the early years of Spanish control. The Santa Clara Valley encountered Europe in the Age of Enlightenment, and Fages and his compatriots spoke openly about the heathens residing in the region. In the aftermath of heated sixteenth- and seventeenth-century debates about human rationality, universalism, and political equality, Europeans struggled to understand local natives and assert their own power in the region.

To emphasize that their arrival in northern Alta California heralded a new social order, José Joaquín Moraga and other representatives of the Spanish crown, most from the Mexican regions of Sonora and Sinaloa, constructed a new colonial settlement in 1777 on the ruins of an abandoned native village, naming it San José de Guadalupe after Moraga's patron saint.[3] In building this first *pueblo* (Spanish civilian town) in Alta California, the Spanish government hoped that colonial settlers from Europe and central New Spain (Mexico) would grow enough wheat to support the *presidios* (garrisons or fortresses) at nearby San Francisco and Monterey. They also intended to extend "the Catholic Religion to the numerous Gentiles who live in these lands." The pueblo and the two missions assured Spanish dominance by 1780, making the Valley a hub of colonial society in northern Alta California, one integrally dependent on both indigenous residents of the region and ongoing ties to other parts of New Spain.[4]

Challenging the economic and cultural practices of the region's native demographic majority, the pueblo of San José grew at a rapid rate in the early nineteenth century, doubling in size every twenty-five years (see table 1). But in this remote region surrounded by thousands of native Californians, colonists reckoned repeatedly with indigenous peoples and the very meaning of "Spanishness." At times *pobladores* (settlers) argued for militant vigilance and affirmed stark contrasts between themselves and California Indians. Responding in 1782 to Indian raids on Mission Santa Clara livestock, Lieutenant José Joaquín Moraga declared that "we should consider them

TABLE 1

Estimated Population of San José Pueblo, 1790–1848

Year	Estimated Population
1790	80
1800	165
1810	125
1820	240
1828	415
1846	700

Source: Daniel Garr, "A Frontier Agrarian Settlement: San José de Guadelupe [*sic*], 1777–1850," *San José Studies* 2:3 (November 1976), 98; Hubert Howe Bancroft, *History of California* (San Francisco: The History Company, 1888), 2:133, 377; Bancroft, *History of California* (San Francisco: The History Company, 1888), 6:4.

A depiction of the Ohlone Indians who lived around Mission San José. BancPic 1963:001:1023:FR, Bancroft Library, University of California, Berkeley.

enemies, all the more because we are surrounded by a great number of pagans. At any hour they could turn ugly, come to realize what they could do as a united group, and direct their will against our work." Franciscan friars at Mission San José asserted in 1813 that the area's native people had little in common with enlightened Europeans, observing that these native residents were "the poorest, most backward, and most stupid of the peoples of America." Other chroniclers reported that the Ohlone were somehow less than human, as when the artist Louis Choris suggested in 1816 that "I have never seen one laugh. I have never seen one look one in the face."[5]

But impressions of the region's "uncivilized" Indians remained complicated by local religious, political, and demographic factors. Like their counterparts in many other Spanish frontier settlements, Santa Clara Valley colonists often did make room for the Ohlone and other indigenous groups on their social ladder, and unlike most English colonists elsewhere in North America, Alta Californians witnessed significant intermarriage between Europeans and local Indians. The children of *pobladores* and native residents often became full members of colonial society and enjoyed significant social status. Geographic isolation from other parts of the Spanish empire demanded such openness. The region's distance from the rest of Mexico led few recognizably "Spanish" colonists to arrive in the Valley prior to the 1830s, and it was natural increase rather than immigration that accounted for most of the pueblo's demographic growth throughout the early nineteenth century. The ethnic diversity of the small settler population also complicated local social divisions, and in strict blood quantum terms, most were in fact *castas*, mixed-blooded *mestizos* and *mulatos* who shared a Spanish, Indian, and African heritage. Pueblo San José residents were many-hued, and only one of seventy-one adult males living in the pueblo between 1786 and 1799 had been born in Spain and could accurately claim *pureza de sangre* (pure Spanish blood).[6]

This phenotypical and cultural diversity complicated the ways *pobladores* thought about native people. Catholic proselytizing offered Indian equality under God, muted some overt conflicts between the settler and indigenous populations, and created new opportunities for many Ohlone. Catholic friars in the Santa Clara Valley and other parts of Alta California struggled to change the religious practices and world-view of the recently converted Indians in their charge by promising salvation in Heaven and material benefits on Earth. Like other missionaries throughout Latin America, they established catechism classes to teach Catholic doctrine in both Spanish and native languages, attempted to eradicate "heathen" customs and traditions, and stressed the importance of sexual abstinence before marriage. In the early nineteenth century, the Franciscans also attempted to put an end to native abortion practices, which had continued at Mission Santa Clara. As agents of cultural change, colonial religious authorities over the next twenty years extended their spiritual influence over many local Indians. Priests such as Fray Magín Catalá, who arrived at Santa Clara in 1794, conducted exorcisms to remove the evil he believed haunted neophyte communities, speaking directly to natives' longstanding spiritual concerns about evil spirits. As Catalá cultivated his prestige as one especially knowledgable about Catholic teaching and the worship of Christ, rumors abounded that the padre had foretold numerous deaths among the local neophytes, even sowing hardship among his enemies.[7]

From the time of Mission Santa Clara's establishment in 1777 and Mission San José's founding in 1797, the two local missions lured numerous native residents into the Valley's colonial settlements by offering food, spiritual rewards, and prestige. Boasting the largest group of neophytes in northern Alta California, Mission San José soon grew larger than the nearby pueblo. Friars became involved in local power struggles within and between *rancherías*, and they did their best to play politics to their own advantage. In the early years of Mission Santa Clara's existence, the Franciscans had baptized four children of the prominent local Ohlone headman Aqui to connect themselves to the Valley's indigenous power structure. These spiritual conquests reaffirmed the leadership of the local headman, and signs of Franciscan success quickly became clear.[8] In baptizing thousands more, the friars assured converts that they might one day become self-supporting, contributing members of Spanish society.[9]

While social divisions remained, belying that promise, the local missions and the pueblo of San José did eventually provide some real opportunities to Alta California natives, and other *indios* also held positions of prestige in colonial society. Most notably, a farm worker and native of Chihuahua named Manuel González became *alcalde* (mayor) of San José pueblo in the 1780s. The possibility that indios might advance undoubtedly reinforced the colonial system, but the friars also resorted to more brutal tactics to entice non-Christians to join the mission communities. Colonial violence determined the ways in which California natives responded to the rapid changes underway during the late eighteenth and early nineteenth centuries, prompted new patterns of migration throughout Alta California, and shaped the stories Indians would subsequently tell about the Spanish colonists. Both Indians and soldiers in the area later remembered, for instance, that Mission Santa Clara's Father Manuel Fernández had once traveled to nearby rancherías and "severely threatened the Indians who refused to become Christians, and with some he even went beyond threats to actual punishment." The priest purportedly horsewhipped an Indian slow to respond to his call, and some native people in the Santa Clara Valley, affirming that friars were often agents of violence, spread the news that Franciscans purposefully burnt the rancherías of non-Christians.[10]

In part because of Franciscan strong-arm tactics, many native people living in Valley missions defiantly retained their existing cultural and political practices well into the nineteenth century.[11] Even at the missions, many parents gave their newborn children clandestine Ohlone names such as Kaknu, and Christian Indians performed the dances that had been their "main form of communal religious expression" prior to their settlement at the missions.[12] The Ohlone's indigenous trade network also remained in operation, local tribelets in the Bay Area continued to speak "dialects of five mutually unintelligible languages," and each village still represented "an independent, landholding religious congregation" that retold its own myths and practiced its own ceremonies. Interranchería ties depended on a longstanding system of shell money that enabled residents to trade with one another, though conflicts over commerce as well as territorial boundaries erupted among them both before and after the arrival of Spanish colonists. Indigenous headmen in Valley towns continued to resolve conflicts within their own settlements, and established modes of political resolution—particularly commerce and intermarriage—still provided ways to mediate intervillage conflict. The colonial intrusion did change affiliations among native people, however, and local residents of Valley missions forged new relations with ranchería residents with whom they often had only limited prior contact. As they congregated in the area surrounding San José pueblo, former residents of distant villages now married and formed political ties, and a new lingua franca apparently emerged, "an amalgamation" of the dialects spoken by the diverse neophyte population.[13]

In the mission context, new social lines marked insiders from outsiders, the lowly from the more powerful. Acts of violence against "barbaric" Indians in the area soon became a critical way to define those categories. And while always unsteady and qualified by religious promises of inclusion, race clearly drew fateful and clear distinctions. Most obviously, newcomers to California imported microbes to the area that attacked natives regardless of cultural or ideological orientation. Lacking natural immunities to smallpox and other threats, many who flocked to Valley missions seeking "baptism and other rituals that might protect them from disease" found that the poor sanitation, close living quarters, and stressful conditions of the missions "increased morbidity and mortality" significantly during the early 1800s. In response, ranchería and mission inhabitants called upon their own shamans to cleanse them of these new diseases, and their ties to home communities only led to greater devastation when returning Christians unwittingly spread microbes further into the interior of California. Between 1802 and 1833 at least 6,565 Indians died at Mission Santa Clara from measles, smallpox, and other diseases, and the four northern Alta California missions would bury some 10,812 inhabitants by 1840.[14]

For those who survived, culture and religion went far in distinguishing social position. The Valley's distance from central Mexico led many local mestizos and settled indios to affirm more vehemently by the early nineteenth century that they were culturally "Spanish." Reinforcing their distance from the *indios bárbaros* ("barbarous Indians") in the area, pueblo denizens called themselves *vecinos*, or residents, of Valley settlements. Both before and after Mexico's independence from Spain in 1821, local natives who did not settle at the missions, become Christians, speak Spanish, and adopt other Spanish-Mexican cultural practices remained defined as threatening outsiders, *bárbaros* in the eyes of these "people of reason" (*gente de razón*), acculturated persons of African, Indian, and Spanish descent. A traveler in the Valley during the 1820s noted that these inhabitants "style themselves *Gente de Razón* to distinguish themselves from the Indians," and that they berated the "heathens" whose "intellectual qualities are frequent subjects of animadversion amongst these enlightened communities." Neophytes and their children could become people of reason and advance in the colonial context. As in other parts of New Spain, residency in the missions or pueblo at times allowed some Indians to "declare themselves *mestizos*." To add to the fluidity of social categories, by the 1820s and 1830s, the Santa Clara Valley and other parts of Alta California would witness the emergence of a "Californio" identity based on an affirmation of the region's Castillian heritage.[15]

As *gente de razón* defined their own privileges and the boundaries between civilized and uncivilized communities, and as Franciscan missionaries encouraged native acculturation and settlement, many Indian peoples launched a defiant opposition to the colonial order. Neophytes fleeing Valley missions to return to their rancherías began by the early nineteenth century to plot collaborative raids on those Spanish settlements, plans that no doubt helped to shape a new sense of pan-Indian affiliation. Their overt and at times violent efforts to resist Spain's colonial presence further contributed to a belief among *gente de razón* that true barbarians lived just beyond the reach of the Spanish colonists. Franciscan friars at Mission San José literally mapped these fears onto the local landscape in 1824 when they drew a picture that marked surrounding regions as the home of *indios bárbaros*. Colonists argued for stricter controls over fugitive neophytes and concerns about depredations led friars and soldiers to band together by the early nineteenth century to subdue those Indian communities once again. *Gente de razón* from the missions and the pueblo often worked together to defend their settlements against Indian raids, and in typical fashion Sergeant Luis Peralta led a retaliatory expedition in 1805 against a ranchería that had attacked two Valley colonists. His party killed ten and sent twenty-nine others to live at Mission San José.[16]

Brutal as this was, violence did not only break out between Spaniards and Indians. In fact, neophytes often engaged Alta California's so-called *bárbaros* during the early nineteenth century in violent military conflicts. Those confrontations often reflected older political tensions between rancherías, longstanding regional dynamics that the Franciscans manipulated to their own advantage. In one such case in 1823, Father Pedro José Altamira of Mission San Francisco Solano accused Father Narciso Durán of Mission San José of ordering Indians under his direction to attack, kill, and capture native rebels from surrounding communities. Again in 1831, when a Mission Santa Clara neophyte named Yóscolo rebelled against the Franciscans and raided their supplies, other neophytes were sent to capture him. Successful in their venture, they helped to nail Yóscolo's "head . . . to a post near the church door as an object lesson." The messy politics of imperial Alta California became most clear in such moments when colonial politics pitted Indian against Indian.[17]

LABOR TROUBLES

Neophytes who took up arms helped to maintain the power and strength of Spanish settlements, and colonists developed a new labor system in the Valley to harness the work of these Indians and others. Believing that native Californians had gathered acorns and done little else prior to the Europeans' arrival, officials enforced new approaches to labor and offered new rewards to encourage agricultural production. Most Spanish policymakers had assumed since the 1760s that native Californians would labor in Franciscan missions, and the ecological disruptions wrought by the arrival of European cattle and agricultural practices pushed many native residents to do so. An interest in trade goods prompted others to seek out the friars, and many young Ohlone flocked to the missions in quest of material items never before seen in California. As Father Francisco Palóu explained it, Franciscans were well aware that local residents could "be conquered first only by their interest in being fed and clothed, and afterwards they gradually acquire knowledge of what is spiritually good and evil. If the missionaries had nothing to give them, they could not be won over." To acquire these riches, however, California natives had to submit to the Franciscans' labor requirements, and the missions began to instruct Indians to work in a European fashion. One historian has suggested that some 60 to 70 percent of the male population at the missions worked under the friars' immediate direction, while roughly 30 percent labored in agriculture, and the remaining 10 percent tended the Franciscans' large herds of cattle. *Mayordomos*, drawn from the military, supervised neophyte farm workers and *vaqueros* (cowhands). Only male neophytes worked in these sorts of tasks, and the friars reproduced the division of work familiar in Europe by directing native women to "engage in tasks fitted to their sex."[18]

As in other parts of Alta California, bells rang throughout the day to mark the rhythms of daily life at Santa Clara and San José missions and to remind residents of the developing economic system. They announced the beginning of work shifts, the end of mealtimes, and the singing of vespers, and Indians lived with an ear to those chimes. From the vantage point of the friars, there was much work to be done in this newly settled Valley. Mission bells reinforced their authority and helped guide regional developments. In 1799, for instance, Santa Clara's Fray Magin Catalá directed those in his charge to build a road connecting his mission to the San José pueblo. The Alameda, as it became known, would serve as the major thoroughfare in the area throughout the course of the nineteenth century. (The road survives and remains an important landmark today.) Gangs of Indian workers also performed other chores. The resident Nasario Galindo recalled that Mission San José neophytes processed grain and carried fifty-pound loads of wheat collected from local fields during the Mexican period. Other converts helped transport local products to market, and when hides could not be moved by cart from the Santa Clara Mission to the docks nine miles away because of winter rains one year, "about a thousand Indians were loaded each with a hide, and carried them to the embarcadero."[19]

To guide these projects, soldiers and colonists managed and controlled, surveyed and tutored native laborers. Craftsmen from Mexico arrived to teach neophytes skills useful to the mission economy. Franciscans appointed trusted natives to monitor their fellow neophytes, yet another example of the intra-ethnic divisions developing in the Valley, and these powerful Indian go-betweens often enforced Franciscan authority. Under the direction of those local overseers, neophytes labored not for wages but rather under a system of Franciscan paternalism that rewarded these so-called children with food and clothing. The missions were a collective enterprise, and native workers sustained the community, but converts felt a damaging toll on their bodies when Franciscans, *alcaldes*, and *mayordomos* made use of corporal punishments to control their labor. Economic changes shaped both individual aspirations and new social conflicts. Clearly, those like Antonio, who charged Father Peña with murder in 1786, saw work for the friars as a means to increase their own power and prestige in the mission system. For their part, Peña and other friars viewed the work of Indians as their "way to salvation, and if it could be directed towards increasing the wealth of the mission and acquiring religious articles for the church, then so much the better."[20]

Colonial society also offered Indian laborers work opportunities outside the mission boundaries. Pueblo residents coveted Indian laborers for themselves, and the town's colonial elite eventually defined its own economic and social privileges in relation to the tasks performed for them by local Indians. Native Californians who lived in pueblo San José escaped Franciscan supervision and often could more easily preserve their religion and independence. Many who did so became vaqueros and took quickly to horse culture, becoming extraordinarily adept at breaking and riding the wild mares and stallions that congregated near the San José pueblo. By the 1830s they worked for local elites who depended on these skills and others acquired in and around the missions. One Valley resident recalled how "many [neophyte] shepherds" counted Mission Santa Clara's sheep in their native language ("1-Imefen; 2-Uchigin; 3-Capagan," etc.) by marking a stick "as to account for the flock." Native Californians took domestic jobs, as well, and because local pueblo families desired household servants, approximately 150 native servants, most of them women, made up one-sixth of San José's population by the 1820s. Indian residents clearly dominated these and other lower rungs of Valley society.[21]

Colonial San José and its adjacent missions had done much to create new economic and cultural practices, but emerging labor systems also resulted from ongoing dynamics among Indians of different rancherías. Native peoples remained agents of their own history. Colonists took advantage of inter-rancheria disputes to purchase captives when warfare between kin groups erupted in the San Joaquín Valley. Similarly, indigenous inhabitants at times helped Santa Clara Valley colonists secure workers by acquiring other Indians for the missions and pueblo. In the 1840s, for example, Máximo, a headman of a Miwok ranchería who had become a military captain in John A. Sutter's Sacramento Valley settlement of New Helvetia, sent captured Miwok laborers to the secularized Mission San José. Another ex-neophyte from Mission Santa Clara who had rebelled in the 1830s also trafficked in Indian workers by 1848. Eager to make peace with the San José pueblo from which he had stolen many horses, and ready to become a labor contractor in the new period of American rule, he offered the local alcalde gifts of captured native people, promising they "would be useful workers."[22]

With Indian labor assured, friars and pueblo residents in the Santa Clara Valley participated in new patterns of trade during the early nineteenth century, linking the San José area to more distant economies as capitalism developed worldwide. While Valley residents did not witness the "market revolution" experienced by contemporary New Englanders, their orientation toward outside commerce impressed newcomers. When in 1806 Count Nikolai Petrovich Rezanov and his entourage from Sitka purchased food in the area, for example, a member of the Russian expedition noted that Father Uria of the San José Mission already knew how to obtain "business advantages" in the negotiations. The Russian observed that "it was by no means the first time" that Padre Pedro de la Cueva "had engaged in trade." Most importantly, a vital commerce soon developed in Alta California that sent local cow hides and tallow to New England in exchange for manufactured goods. The market economies of missions San José and Santa Clara developed rapidly as a result of these activities, with the latter raising approximately 18,000 head of cattle, 1,500 sheep, and 1,100 horses during the 1820s alone. Rather than backwater traditionalists—as Franciscan missionaries would later be portrayed by Americans arriving in California—foreign traders saw the priests at missions San José and Santa Clara as "first-class merchants" and "shrewd partners" in business, and more than one historian has since contended that these clerical entrepreneurs became more interested in these economic activities than in the spiritual conversion of their Indian wards.[23] The business acumen of local missionaries in fact foreshadowed that of later settlers in the Valley.

The hide and tallow trade also accelerated the development of a mestizo bourgeoisie in the Valley. By 1819 there were forty-five rancheros living in the pueblo of San José, and an American observer noted soon thereafter that residents "who had any wealth, had it in cattle, at their ranches in the vicinity." The hide and tallow agent Faxon Dean Atherton expressed his certainty in 1836 that it was "their chief pride . . . to see who can cheat a foreigner the most." To capitalize on these emerging trade networks linking California to world markets, the Valley's newly established Mexican elite—residents such as Antonio Pico, Selvis Pacheco, Dolores Pacheco, Jose Noriega, and Antonio Suñol—took full advantage of Indian workers. Since 1769 California Indians had provided the sweat and muscle that developed Valley commerce, but during the 1820s friars began to worry about their dwindling influence with native residents. From the early years of the Spanish occupation of the Valley, the friars had struggled to keep local Indians away from the corrupting influence of San José pueblo where settlers offered neophytes valued trade goods in exchange for their work. Stymied by the difficulties of controlling native labor in the Valley, Fray Narciso Durán, the longtime Mission San José priest, would complain in 1845 that "the Indians, in my opinion, do not deserve to be directed by a missionary. A slavedriver is what they ought to have."[24]

Broader political changes frustrated Durán and other clerics. As Valley residents became tied to distant markets, Alta California lost its colonial ties to Spain and became "Mexican" national territory for the first time in 1821. Mexican independence accelerated other economic transformations already underway and threatened Franciscan authority. A new national framework began to play an important role in governing local intergroup relations, and discussions of republican citizenship would shape Valley politics for decades. Most importantly, Mexico's governing authorities emphasized that Indians would be truly equal citizens of the new nation, included to a degree unknown in the colonial period. Officials sought to do away with the corporate property holdings of the Church, now at odds with the ideals of secular nationalism and a society of yeomen farmers. Under the rule of Mexican President Valentín Gómez Farias, the national government in 1833 announced that the missions would be "secularized"—that is, converted into parishes—and that Franciscan lands would be broken into thirty-three-acre parcels that individual neophytes might own. Many in California and central Mexico supported this attack on Church power as a way both to teach Indians the value of private property and to limit the influence of missionaries, still loyal to their *patria* (motherland) of Spain. But because natives were deemed unfit for the privileges of landowning, nascent elites in places like the Santa Clara Valley acquired mission properties and established methods of debt peonage to retain control over legions of Indian workers.[25]

Enterprising mestizo sons of presidio soldiers acquired enormous tracts of land in the Santa Clara Valley during the 1830s, and critics charged that those inhabitants supported mission secularization as a poorly veiled property grab. Liberal rhetoric about neophytes' common Mexican citizenship also conveniently justified the exploitation of Indians no longer "productively" attached to the missions and ensured enormous profits in an expanded hide and tallow trade. Mission San José's Fray Narciso Durán contended in 1831 that local *gente de razón* adamantly believed that when it came to difficult work,

> The INDIAN must do it. Does the wheat need to be cut? Bring in the INDIAN. You need to . . . build a house, make a coral, carry firewood [or] water for the kitchen, etc? Let the INDIAN do it. . . . They rely upon the INDIAN as if the INDIAN alone were the son of Adam and everyone else didn't have arms. . . . In this way it actually seems as if nature had destined the Indian to be the slave of the *gente de razón*.

As elite rancheros replaced the padres as the region's new labor brokers, most neophytes remained propertyless and could take little solace in the once powerful paternalism of the Franciscans. Few gained ownership of Alta

California's redistributed mission lands, and only seven of the more than one thousand former inhabitants of Santa Clara Mission received such property.[26] The liberal rhetoric of Mexican independence in the end meant few material gains for native residents of northern Alta California.

But while assumptions about Indian inferiority survived in San José pueblo, national debates about mission secularization exposed some of the contradictions in contemporary liberal thinking about political rights. *Gente de razón* promised Indian neophytes new freedoms but insisted that they were not yet ready for full equality with landed mestizos, and these pronouncements prompted many native peoples to redefine their interests. Indians influenced by liberal notions of social equality declared their own sense of purpose in Alta California. On a practical side, some engaged in military resistance or stole settlers' livestock. A handful filed formal petitions with the new government to request freedom from Franciscan control, and others fled the missions to return to ancestral rancherías. Four hundred neophytes at Mission San José did so in May 1827, and the population of Mission Santa Clara would soon decline from 1,125 converts in 1832 to just 291 in 1839. By 1842 the number of mission residents in Alta California had likely declined to a third of what it had been in 1834. Government official Antonio María Osio recognized that these revolts and movements developed in part from liberal efforts to "inst[ill] republican ideals in the Indians' minds." While Osio believed that native residents "did not understand" the complex political questions of the day, he acknowledged that former neophytes now "deemed themselves important persons and took to calling each other 'sovereign,' since they wanted to give themselves the full treatment to which citizens were entitled." Responding to Indian depredations, he and others lamented that the Franciscans could no longer "supervise the Indians' conduct and punish them appropriately when they deserved it."[27]

Other political conflicts also became critical to Valley residents after 1821, and some of these developments anticipated future Valley struggles over national identity. Many Mexican citizens in Alta California expressed growing resentment about their own lack of participation in local and national decision making. Their strong sense of regional identity, nurtured by Alta California's long isolation from Mexico City, now came into conflict with the emergent nationalism articulated in central Mexico. Local attachments developed among Alta California's *gente de razón*, and many San Joséans during the 1820s and 1830s increasingly thought of themselves as "Californios" rather than "Mexicans," thereby trumpeting their distinctiveness. Residents emphasized "a sense of reciprocity and obligation, at least with respect to other *gente de razón*," and their growing interest in blood purity shaped an insistence that, unlike Mexicans to the south, Californios had remained racially pure in far northern New Spain, "descendents of pure Spaniards."[28]

Arguments that the region remained more Spanish than mestizo, more

Californio than Mexican, also gave rise to new calls for Alta California's political separation from Mexico City. Californios launched a number of failed revolts against the central government during the 1830s and 1840s. Not surprisingly, Mexican government officials expressed concern about such dissent within their new nation and feared that Russia, but especially the United States, might take control of Alta California. To deter foreign threats, Mexican officials therefore passed a Colonization Act in 1824 to populate the nation's far northern provinces with new citizens. While Alta California remained an isolated outpost in the eyes of most Mexican officials over the next two decades, this new policy encouraged a gradual influx of American and European immigrants into the Santa Clara Valley, foreigners who could naturalize as Mexicanos if they embraced Catholicism. Empowered to grant property, the governors of Alta California made forty-one land grants in the Santa Clara County area after 1821, including several to immigrant Europeans and Anglo-Americans. This right to own land and establish a settled community would prove critical to the Valley's subsequent history, as residency eventually led white settlers to claim the Valley for themselves in the name of their own racial supremacy.[29]

But in the short term, relations between the region's small number of incoming American settlers and its already-established Mexican citizens remained mostly harmonious. As late as 1845 only about 150 Americans resided in the pueblo, compared with 750 Mexicans, and a U.S. takeover of Mexico still seemed anything but inevitable. Few American settlers showed disdain for Mexican culture prior to 1845, and many instead entered Alta California society, learned the Spanish language, accepted Mexican citizenship, and sometimes even took Spanish surnames.[30] A few served in the *diputación*, or territorial legislature. Roughly two-thirds of the Anglo male population in San José married Mexican women between 1821 and 1846, and many American settlers also joined Californios in their grievances against the Mexican government.[31] Common economic interests also united Mexicans and white Americans. Joining propertied Alta Californians, men such as Robert Livermore and Henry Bee, like many Mexican rancheros, used California Indians as laborers, relying on former neophytes to work the Valley soil. Together, Americans and Mexicans sold produce and cattle to hide and tallow traders visiting San Francisco Bay, to Russian soldiers who lived at Fort Ross, and to residents of the Hawaiian Islands.[32]

But race relations began to change during the 1830s, and the Devil infiltrated the Valley in new ways. White Americans brought with them the disdain for Indian "savages" central to American racial thought during this period, and these incoming settlers shared with local Californios a common desire to subdue the "barbarous Indians" nearby. Settlers like William Heath Davis approved the "good discipline" that Catholic priests continued to demand of the few converted neophytes still living at the nearby missions, for instance. After the German immigrant Charles Weber arrived in the area in 1843, he negotiated a pact with the native leader José Jesús, a former Mission Santa Clara neophyte and now chief of the Siakumne (Yokuts), "to ensure the security of [his] rancho" from native attacks. When Locolumne Indians did raid Valley ranchos four years later, José Jesús provided Weber "most of the two hundred men who formed the expedition" that set out to fight the invaders from the San Joaquín Valley. Anglo-native sexual relations at times turned into violent conquests.[33] On other occasions, Indian men facilitated the sexual adventures of white Americans. The young entrepreneur Faxon Dean Atherton, later considered one of California's finest residents, described in 1836 how he had spent the night at Mission San José, writing in his journal that "All the young girls of the Mision [sic] are kept locked up nights by themselves, to keep them from mischievous pranks. They are under the charge of a man who is called an Alcalde, but I found that he knew the value of a 4 real piece, and understood what he received it for. There are some pretty fair girls amongst them, and what is more, devilish neat and clean."[34] The chilling cooperation between Atherton and the Indian alcalde showed the growing vulnerability of Indian women in this era.

Race and labor, ideologies of difference and economic change, all continued to transform the Valley in dramatic ways after 1821. The Indian revolt led by Estanislao provides another case in point. A product of the Franciscan mission system, this former vaquero and alcalde, who had directed native workers at Mission San José, returned to his ranchería in 1828 and began to lead raids against the area's Mexican settlements. The revolt reflected new political ideologies current in Mexico as well as new patterns of violence evident throughout Alta California. The rebels sought to achieve the political equality promised them under national independence. After skillfully ambushing a Mexican militia unit, Estanislao and his group celebrated with a festival at which "the bodies of the soldiers were put on display so that the neighboring tribes, who were invited to the festivities, would admire the natives' great valor and prowess." But just as interranchería conflicts shaped Estanislao's show of strength, they also led to the rebel's eventual defeat. After the militia's first failed venture against him, another armed contingent left San Francisco and Mission San José that included both "inhabitants of the pueblo of San José and some allied Indians who were longstanding enemies of Estanislao's ranchería." Only too "anxious to avenge long-standing grievances . . . they had been awaiting the right moment to attack Estanislao and his people," and they now killed most of the rebel band. The former neophyte soon gave himself up, unable to survive the web of enemies conspiring against him.[35]

While making clear the conflicts between Mexican citizens and Indians during the 1820s, Estanislao's revolt and surrender illustrated again that political struggles were not simply defined as Californios versus Indians in the

Mexican period. These episodes also displayed the near impossibility of armed military resistance by the Valley's native populations, even by 1828. Racial inequalities soon became more entrenched. The Santa Clara Valley witnessed the ongoing political development of the Mexican nation, conflicts between rancherías, the depredations of California natives targeting local ranchos, the resulting punitive expeditions by both *gente de razón* and mission neophytes, the consuming political conflicts among local Californios over the fate of the province, and the arrival in California of new American and European immigrants.[36]

MANIFEST DESTINY

It was that last process that would transform Alta California in most dramatic fashion. Although many of San José's Americans and Europeans seem to have welcomed assimilation into the Valley's Mexican society in the 1830s, new political pressures soon changed the delicate balance between white Americans and Mexicans. By 1845 several different national governments had announced their designs on the region, and Mexico was but one of these countries. Alta Californians had long complained that federal policymakers paid them little attention. Officials in Mexico City now increasingly proclaimed their fears about their future claim to California, and prominent writers such as Tadeo Ortiz de Ayala reminded his readers that Russians lived just seventy-eight miles north of San Francisco Bay. National leaders also expressed suspicions that Americans had established their own colony north of San Francisco, while others noted greater concerns about apparent British designs on the territory. In 1835, in fact, the first English-language book written exclusively about California, the Scottish merchant Alexander Forbes's *California: A History of Upper and Lower California*, professed the hope that Mexico would resolve its foreign debts to the English by giving up California. Noting "how little progress [Alta California's] population has made in this country," Forbes argued on racial grounds that "It is obvious that it is from the free white and creole races and from the introduction of fresh colonists, the future population of California must proceed; for the enslaved Indians are already on the decline, and, on the dissolution of the missionary system, they will dwindle away and soon become almost extinguished."[37] Calls in Central Mexico to improve communication networks and military routes between northern Alta California and the new nation's interior regions soon followed, and Mexicans renewed demands that Russia withdraw from California entirely.[38]

Russia did so in 1841, but American citizens arriving in northern Mexico began by the mid-1840s to express their own distinct hope that Mexico would then follow suit and also retreat from the region. Many held racist perceptions of California's native and Mexican populations shaped by a long history of anti-Hispanic sentiment and by recent English-language writers such as Thomas Jefferson Farnham and Alfred Robinson, whose published accounts reinforced notions of white racial superiority and the providential westward march of the United States. Farnham asserted that the Californios were "in every way a poor apology of European extraction," and he denounced their slothful approach to work in Alta California:

> Destitute of industry themselves, they compel the poor Indian to labor for them, affording him a bare savage existence for his toil, upon their plantations and the fields of the Missions. In a word, the Californians are an imbecile, pusillanimous, race of men, and unfit to control the destinies of that beautiful country.

> No one acquainted with the indolent, mixed race of California, will ever believe that they will populate, much less, for any length of time, govern the country. . . . They must fade away.[39]

Among American immigrants, notions of Manifest Destiny became increasingly influential by the early 1840s, a worldview stressing that settlers would help bring about "the domination of civilization over nature, Christianity over heathenism, progress over backwardness, and, most importantly, of white Americans over the Mexican and Indian populations that stood in their path." This, at long last, was the Devil's language. Mexican government officials had hoped that these settlers would become loyal subjects of Mexico, but the bellicose attitudes of the migrants led policymakers in Mexico City to attempt new measures that might bring the country's northern provinces under greater central control. In response, Americans began to call for the military takeover of the Mexican north, an imperial spirit that became an animating cause of the Mexican War, which broke out in 1846.[40]

Astute Mexican observers had long worried about Americans' declarations of their national and racial superiority, and such political tensions had been evident even before Estanislao's rebellion when Jedidiah Smith passed through the area in 1826. A trapper seeking lucrative beaver pelts, Smith and his followers became the first Americans to enter California by land from the east; embodying the period's American nationalism, then approaching high tide, Smith openly praised "that restless enterprise that . . . is now leading our countrymen to all parts of the world" and proudly announced that "it can now be said there is not a breeze of heaven but spreads an American flag." Considered a threat by government officials, Smith's presence provoked new fears in and around San José. Military authorities suspected that the trappers were U.S. spies, and American activities certainly encouraged that conclusion. A short time earlier, the group had arrived unannounced and without Mexico's permission. When Governor José María Echeandía detained the trappers at Mission San Gabriel and ordered them to leave the province, the group instead headed north through the Central Valley and camped on the Stanislaus River. Soon thereafter, San Joaquín Valley natives, including neophytes who had lived in Santa Clara Valley missions, visited the San José area and informed local friars about the Americans' encampment. Native stories that the trappers were "making a map" of the area further confirmed Mexican officials' fears that the Americans had imperial ambitions.[41]

In an unlikely coincidence, four hundred neophytes then left Mission San José for the San Joaquín Valley in May, no doubt prompted to do so by liberal rhetoric about freedom, but government representatives feared that Smith had recruited the Indians to make war against the Mexicans. The often-harsh inequalities of local missions could not explain their exodus, according to Alta California's former governor Luis Antonio Arguello, it was instead the trappers' efforts "to win the goodwill of these natives" that threatened to corrupt Indians "well satisfied with the law that incorporates them into the Mexican nation." The threat of an Indian-American alliance worried Mexican authorities. Arrested and incarcerated at Mission San José for two months, Smith continued to insist that he was only an eager trapper. When released and given specific instructions about how to travel east to the United States, he and his fellow travelers defied the Mexican government's marching orders and followed their own route out of California, but not before writing the United States Minister in Mexico City to complain "as an American citizen" that "Spanish [sic] impositions" had left him "intirely [sic] destitute of money."[42]

Smith's arrival and imprisonment made clear that new national competitions for control of California were clearly changing the area by 1830. Despite Smith's claim to the contrary, former governor Arguello believed for certain that the trapper was no American innocent. While likely not a spy of the United States, Smith and his compatriots assumed Mexico's national inferiority and expressed their own hopes that the American flag would one day fly over San José. Just as Smith mapped the province's rivers and other resources, many Americans and Europeans arriving subsequently found in the territory other impressive "natural advantages" that would yield profitable returns when a progressive nation seized control of the region. This was the essence of Manifest Destiny. Lamenting that so many Mexican mestizos had already settled in San José and other parts of the province, a Frenchman noted in the late 1820s that while San Joséans "own[ed] herds and harvest[ed] grain . . . the natural laziness of these creoles, and other things . . . have arrested the development of, and brought decay to, this establishment." Among the American visitors who followed Jedidiah Smith, advocates of a U.S. takeover became all the more excited in 1845 when Andrés Castillero, a Mexican army officer sent to counter U.S. influence among residents of

California, spread news about a rich quicksilver discovery a few miles south of San José. American government officials quickly took interest. Thomas Larkin, the U.S. consul at Monterey, immediately informed Senator Thomas Hart Benton and Secretary of State James Buchanan of this development, and John C. Frémont, an officer in the Army Corps of Topographical Engineers, subsequently offered to purchase the mineral rights to the Santa Clara Valley from the Mexican government.[43]

More concerned about developing the region's agriculture, many American settlers who arrived in the 1840s expressed shock at the rancheros' "baronial estates" and apparent dependency on the pueblo's communal lands. Affirmations of white American supremacy drew strength from an aversion to the economy established by mission and pueblo residents. Those from the United States expressed certainty that Californio decisions to allow their livestock to wander together on unfenced territory betrayed a disinterest in private property, and many dreamed about what a more "civilized" American society might create in the Santa Clara Valley. In effect sticking a new top rung on a preexisting social ladder, Americans like Josiah Belden compared the "rude state" of local Mexican society with what American settlers might one day build in the region. In suggesting that Indians and Mexicans had produced little during the years they controlled the Valley, these newcomers began to call for replacing Mexican indolence with Anglo American "industry," the peonage established at Valley missions with "free white labor," and "superstitious" Catholicism with rational Protestantism.[44]

New ethnic conflicts took center stage by the mid-1840s that reflected these devilish American attitudes towards race and labor. While earlier groups of American settlers had attempted to adapt to local Mexican society, freshly arrived immigrants took a more confrontational stance toward the region's inhabitants, taking their cues from Texans who had wrested control of that northern Mexican state by asserting their own cultural distinctiveness as white Americans. Contending that California Mexicans, including those around San José, were equally unworthy of holding political power, American travelers and settlers suggested that, as Catholics, Mexicans were incapable of democratic governance and unable to recognize the value of hard work. Descriptions of nonwhites unfit to govern themselves or prosper in the capitalist market were twin hallmarks of republican ideology in the United States of the 1830s and 1840s, and as westward migrants found their way to the Santa Clara Valley, some dismissed Californio "religious ceremonies [as] very grotesque and amusing." Migrants scrambled to join other Protestants in creating new churches intended to make clear their differences from Mexican residents, and one resident recalled that "The people that came there in '47 organized a body of Christians and had regular service every Sabbath. . . . Some of us were Cumberland Presbyterians, some Methodists[,] some Baptists, and we had a Methodist preacher at first."[45]

After 1841 American immigrants increasingly dispossessed San José Californios of their property, killed their cattle for food, and stole their horses running loose on the pueblo's communal lands. Incoming settlers acted in the name of acquiring private property to establish a more familiar community of independent white farmers. Mexicans in the Valley reacted to these attacks with great anger. Longtime resident Secundino Robles attributed Californio participation in the War of 1846 to this "scandalous stealing of property," and Charles White, the first American alcalde of San José, blamed "runaway sailors [and] volunteers from the [U.S.] army" for the violence and criminal plunderings in the area. To further complicate the situation, native raiders—prompted to steal Californio horses by white trappers who had arrived in the state—also increased their attacks on Valley ranchos during the mid-1840s. Ethnic Mexicans now felt threatened by both Indians and white settlers, and new rounds of violence soon altered the lives of local Californios forever.[46]

Alta Californians learned that the United States and Mexico were at war in July 1846, but by that time white settlers, the so-called Bear-Flaggers, under the command of U.S. Army officer John C. Frémont had already declared the region independent from Mexico. Fighting raged between Californios and U.S. forces in Southern California, and while many San Joseans remained unsure about whether to fight on behalf of Mexico, white Americans almost unanimously rallied behind their country's providential mission to expand west to the Pacific Coast. Their sense of national and racial affiliation proved a powerful force. In January 1847 Californios agreed to lay down their arms in return for a guarantee that they would enjoy the rights of U.S. citizens. War sealed the political fate of San José and all California residents, and the conflict's conclusion in 1848 led Mexico to cede half of its territory to the United States, including the coveted settlements of the San Francisco Bay Area.[47]

Longtime Mexican residents could only speculate about their futures under U.S. rule. As they soon discovered, American settlers would revolutionize patterns of residency and attendant meanings of race, ultimately creating such a violent society in the San José region that the very existence of conquered Californios and Indians would be threatened. In the short sixty years since Plácido, Anecelto, and Antonio had accused Father Tomás de la Peña of murder, colonial settlements and work regimes in this Northern California valley had become firmly established, local missionaries and *pobladores* had made violence a constant threat, and dissidents like Yóscolo had suffered death at the hands of Spaniards and converted neophytes. With the coming of American rule in 1848, discerning Californios and Indians must have seen the shadow of the devil standing behind their new white neighbors.

Chapter 2

The Golden State

> It is without doubt that . . . the population of the pueblo
> will grow, and the space which separates it from
> [Mission] Santa Clara will be filled with houses, the
> location being extremely favorable for the establishment
> of a great city.
> —Eugene Duflot de Mofras, *Exploration de l'Orégon, des
> Californies, et de la Mer Vermeille* (1844)

The image of Yóscolo's head nailed to a local mission post provides a particularly gruesome illustration of the violent nature of Valley race relations after Mexico's national independence in 1821. Subsequent developments were to prove just as pernicious for local Indians and ethnic Mexicans. By the early 1840s, as Mexico, the United States, and other nations jockeyed for control of California, Manifest Destiny began to transform the region. Contemporary observers struggled to explain what was happening to native people, why the town of San José grew so dramatically, how the Valley became "filled with houses" and new settlers, and what "the establishment of this great city" would mean for its current and future denizens. In the 1840s and 1850s, American ideologies of race grouped Mexicans with Indians as nonwhites and fostered new ways of thinking about the political fate of the conquered. In this single most important period in the political history of California, white settlers celebrated their new family farms and small towns, all the while seizing Valley resources and redistributing them to other arriving Americans. The Devil was at work in the service of U.S. national expansion, and he was busy.

For many migrants, San José's location at the foot of San Francisco Bay assured its providential success under American rule. Starry-eyed observers

An overhead view of San José in 1858. This artist and others emphasized the industry of the region's Gold Rush–era settlers. Notice the prominent American flag above the city skyline. BancPic 1963:002:0659:C, Bancroft Library.

contended that the arrival of hardworking Americans would lead to the development of regional agriculture for the first time, and Bayard Taylor and others anticipated that the advent of the United States heralded the triumph of "culture, plenty, peace, happiness, everywhere." Conquest, Taylor believed, would put "a more beautiful race in possession of this paradise—a race in which the lost symmetry and grace of the Greek was partially restored; the rough, harsh features of the Oriental type gone; milder manners, better regulated impulses, and a keen appreciation of the arts which enrich and embellish life." When the era of Mexico City's control over Alta California ended, American settlers in the region fashioned a vision of their own racial supremacy based on tales of traditional Californio indolence, and a new racial system, sanctioning varied and in some ways more sublimated violence, began to replace the one developed under Spain and Mexico. Californios who had previously considered themselves *gente de razón* were now often villified as papists and feudal lords, condemned because the blood of "barbarous" natives presumably coursed in them as well. In the face of dramatic demographic and ideological change, the local economy based on Indian labor began to crumble, as did fears of so-called *índios bárbaros* and the established power of the mestizo elite. As Americans took up permanent residence in the Valley, the long-term consequences for the dispossessed and displaced population, and the migrants who would follow, was hinted at and then confirmed.[1]

Few white Americans worried about the toll exacted on the region's conquered residents. And certainly the Valley's Californios and Indians sang no paeans to the foresight and judicious character of white settlers; instead, they cried out about new manifestations of racial violence and disfranchisement.

Witnessing the economic and political consequences of American statehood, conquered inhabitants knew firsthand that the Golden State rested on a foundation of racial discrimination, a truth that Mexican Americans in Southern California would come to learn only in later decades. In the wake of American takeover, these local residents began to define a "Mexican American" identity for the very first time, prompted to do so by wicked and often violent conflicts over race, property, and labor. The Treaty of Guadalupe Hidalgo had ended the war in 1848, defined the future of the roughly 100,000 resident Mexicans in the new Southwest, and established the new boundary line between the United States and Mexico. Assured full rights of U.S. citizenship if they remained in the territory, Californios in San José and elsewhere would appeal again and again to that international agreement to counter the activities of rapacious white settlers during the 1850s. In the process of insisting that their own residency in California conferred treaty rights, these Mexican Americans, often bitter about their declining social position and fearing for their lives, now forged a new sense of identity for themselves.

RACE AND WHEAT

While the American conquest in 1848 inscribed new sorts of power relations on San José and other parts of Alta California, it was the California Gold Rush immediately following the war that had the greatest impact on local politics. The victors of war approached the Valley more in the spirit of subjugation than of integration. The area underwent dramatic demographic and economic transformations: "In 1848, before the discovery of gold, perhaps 165,000 people lived in California. The vast majority of them—approximately 150,000—were Indians, most of whom lived autonomously in what came to be known as the mother lode and other isolated regions away from Mexican settlements. . . . Then James Marshall discovered gold, word leaked out, and the rush to California was on."[2] As battle smoke cleared and the ink dried on the Treaty of Guadalupe Hidalgo, many of the Americans who flooded into the state anticipated the sharp decline of Mexican Americans' cultural and political influence. While more distant Southern California towns such as Santa Barbara, Los Angeles, and San Diego certainly experienced tumult as a result of the mineral discoveries in the Northern California foothills, many more gold-seekers passed through the San Francisco Bay Area, including San José, on their way to the Mother Lode, speculated about the region's agricultural potential, and hoped to settle in the Santa Clara Valley after leaving the mines. They predicted that San José would soon flourish. Cornelius Cox, for example, who had traveled overland from Tucson and arrived in California in January 1850, called the area around San

José "a very pretty inland town and situated in the heart of a rich and beautiful Country. As an agricultural district, it is superior to any part of the State that we have passed through." Similarly, a San Francisco newspaper correspondent recommended the area in 1848, noting that "upon the whole, I cannot conceive of a richer spot, both in regard to agriculture and mineral wealth, than this valley." Commodore Robert Stockton agreed, purchasing two thousand acres of land in the Santa Clara Valley in 1847 after witnessing the surrender of the Californios in the Mexican War. Many migrants assumed that local lands were there for the taking, and squatters commonly expressed little compunction about stealing Californio properties.[3]

Thanks to nascent boosterism and San José's proximity to the mines, the European and American population of San José grew quickly during the Gold Rush years. No other California locale of comparable importance to Mexican Americans experienced such an immediate change following the Mexican War. Indeed, while most regions of Southern California remained home to a Mexican American demographic majority for more than two decades after statehood in 1850, San José's non-Mexican population grew from approximately 150 in the year before the Mexican War to 3,673 by 1860 and 12,509 by 1870. Nearby townships in the Valley also developed, expanding the total population of the county to 6,664 in 1852, to 11,912 in 1860, and to 25,269 in 1870. Especially after 1865, San José promoters sought to attract working-class white residents eager to own their own small plots of land in the area, promising that "Every workingman, by taking a Share in this Homestead, can, with the same money he would pay away for rent, have a house and lot of his own." More quickly than other Mexican Americans in the state, Californios residing in the Santa Clara Valley found that their "Mexican pueblo" had become an "American town."[4]

Neighborhoods and institutions in San José changed dramatically as American settlers imported republican ideologies already popular in other parts of the United States. Working-class Americans were susceptible to the lure of white supremacy during the 1850s thanks to political and economic turmoil in the United States. In many ways an antislavery call for equality among white workers in the East, republican ideologies often activated frontier racism in the American West, where Mexicans, Indians, and Asians seemed to threaten settlers' aspirations. One observer happily noted that the Presbyterian church established on Second Street greeted Americans and proved "refreshing to the eye of civilization." Declaring their intentions to create a society of small farmers and economic opportunity, many opposed anything that smacked of slavery. San Joseans stressed that their commitment to "free soilism" distinguished them from San Francisco's "southern gentlemen . . . unaccustomed to manual labor." Clearly an expression of working-class pride, this was hardly an unequivocal declaration of newfound enlightenment on questions of racial equality. Reflecting the racist biases implicit in

Wheat farming became prominent in the Santa Clara Valley soon after California statehood, and many newly arrived residents took part in the Gold Rush mentality that reshaped that local industry. "Harvesting Near San José," BancPic 1963:002:0670:A, Bancroft Library.

"free soilism" and the anti-Catholic bigotry of the so-called Know Nothing political party, many Gold Rush–era settlers welcomed only newcomers whom they considered racially white to hold land in the area. Notions of working-class political rights, as David Roediger and others have noted, "could not be raceless" in the heated climate of the antebellum United States. As a result, European immigrants, even Catholics, enjoyed a warmer welcome in the region than did Mexicans or African Americans. Despite some opposition to their presence, many of the Irish who settled in the Santa Clara Valley after the Mexican War in fact took important positions in local government and other civic institutions.[5]

In the demographic and political context of the 1850s, Mexicans suffered stunning new patterns of disfranchisement and discrimination. White settlers

TABLE 2

Total Population of Santa Clara and Other California Counties, 1860–1870

	Year	
County	1860	1870
Santa Clara	11,912	25,269
Los Angeles	4,385	8,504
San Bernardino	940	3,064
Santa Barbara	2,351	2,640

Source: Federal Census of the United States, 1860 and 1870. Camarillo, *Chicanos in a Changing Society*, 116–117.

easily conflated Californios, Mexican immigrants, and local Indians in ways that must have offended *gente de razón* who had long defined their own civility in contrast to *indios bárbaros*. According to new settlers, a common inferiority linked those groups because Californios carried the blood of the much-reviled "digger Indians." Whites assumed that Californios were also racially indistinguishable from Mexican and Chilean immigrants arriving in the state, all of whom were considered "interlopers and greasers." Local newspaper reporters emphasized the contrasts between "whites" arriving from Europe and the United States and the "natives"—both Indians and Californios—of this newly conquered territory. The editor of the *Santa Clara Register* wrote in 1853 that "the Spanish races and American Indian tribes are distinguished by the great abundance and coarseness" of body hair, and he asked readers if "the beasts, whether wild or domesticated, are hairy." Certain that the more evolved "Anglo-American branch of man" was engaged in a struggle with "the Spanish races," he concluded that while Mexicans in the Santa Clara Valley possessed the "natural good" of animals, they were clearly unable "to elevate themselves to the same degree reached by the Anglo Saxon race." One recently arrived American similarly claimed that the Mexicans' adobe architecture made it clear that Californios were "but little removed above the savages from whom he is in part descended."[6]

White supremacy not only defined Californios and Indians as inferior, it also compelled settlers to shape a new political economy around agriculture and other "civilized" practices. Hoping to preserve the region for free white laborers, white San Joseans intended to prohibit the settlement of Mexicans and other Latin Americans. Local officials passed a vagrancy law in 1855 to discourage the arrival of those "peons," and one Bay Area newspaper reported that "All that is wanted here now is an immigration of the right sort of men, viz: farmers, to make this one of the richest counties on the face of the globe."[7] In California, the term "farmer," beyond indicating obvious permanent residency, became a racial codeword signifying whiteness during the Gold Rush. Editors of San Francisco's *Californian* expressed a sentiment that would become dominant in the Valley by the early 1850s: "We desire only a White population in California; even the Indians among us, as far as we have seen, are more a nuisance than a benefit to the country, we would love to get rid of them. . . . [W]e dearly love the country, but declare our positive preference for an independent condition of California to the establishment of any degree of slavery, or even the importation of free blacks."[8] By employing the rhetoric of Manifest Destiny, white Americans contrasted the Valley's so-called half-caste races with the superior yeoman farmers they associated with the United States. The Yale-educated surveyor Chester S. Lyman, hired by San José officials to subdivide the ranchos granted before 1848, was but one local American during the Gold Rush era who compared the "indolence" of the area's Mexicans with the triumph of "Yankee ingenuity."[9]

Eager to distinguish themselves from adobe-dwellers in the region, Americans such as Naval Commander Robert Stockton arranged for "regular old-styled Eastern" homes to be sent by ship from New England to San José, and William Brewer and others soon contended that "the very houses [in San José] show the decay and decline of one race and the coming in of a superior one." These homes suggested that San José was fast becoming a republican haven, and signs of such domesticity went hand in glove with the new economy. As the Valley became overwhelmingly non-Mexican, its new residents envisioned a society based primarily on the cultivation of wheat, a crop that would require relatively little hired labor to plant and harvest. Wheat grown in California promised fantastic profits, miners paid $20 to $50 for a barrel of Chilean flour in the Sierras, and many settlers hoped to turn former Californio estates into producers of that golden crop. According to San José's William Fisher, farmers needed only to "scratch up the surface of the ground" in order to reap these bushels. "Grain fields laid off in squares by fences" dramatically illustrated the region's new political economy and personified American eagerness to create a booming and distinctly American agriculture. Hoping to replace Mexicans' ranchos and communal grazing lands with a more familiar system of private property and commercial agriculture, new farmers erected fences around fifty thousand acres by 1855, almost twenty-six thousand of which were devoted to the cultivation of wheat, barley, and other grains. They developed other boom crops as well, extending the cultivation of fruit begun by Californios before 1848. Celebrated later as founders of Valley agriculture, Joshua Redman and Charles Clayton grew apples and other produce on lands formerly owned by Mission Santa Clara and sold them to San Francisco retailers. When the immigrant Louis Pellier inaugurated the planting of French prunes in 1856, he made the Valley into the prune capital of the world, a title it retained into the mid-twentieth century.[10]

Many Californios in the Santa Clara Valley also hoped to capitalize on this climate of speculative investment and huge profits. Although less experienced with the American economy, Mexican Americans attempted to use their lands to expand their power and prestige in the years after 1848. San Joseans formerly had experienced the vagaries of the hide and tallow market, and the *Alta California* reported that "a number of rancheros" sold their Santa Clara Valley produce to San Francisco residents, undoubtedly at a highly inflated price. Several hundred Californios from the San José area also rushed to the foothills in search of ore in the summer of 1848, and some took their Indian servants still bound by relations of peonage. Others remained to lease Valley lands to incoming settlers.[11]

But despite Mexican American efforts to profit off the Gold Rush, racial ideologies gave white Americans dramatic advantages in this speculative economy. Cloaked in discussions of property and work, white supremacy

A hay-baling scene from the late nineteenth century in Santa Clara Valley. Alice Hare Collection, 04950, Bancroft Library.

was a guiding principle of local development. New entrepreneurs saw themselves doing something radically different with Valley lands, replacing the "feudal" Mexican society that had preceded American democracy with a more productive system. In these pronouncements, Americans paid little attention to the work long performed by Mexicans and Indians in and around San José, and they declared that Californios had few rightful claims to area properties. According to republican ways of thinking, Mexican and Indian men had never learned how to make California lands productive before 1848, and this neglect justified American demands for a complete takeover of the state's resources. The editor of *The Santa Clara Register* opined in 1853, for instance, that the United States had conquered California and other regions owned by Mexico because "an imperative law of nature, and of nature's God" had directed those events. He then argued that other areas of that country, particularly Sonora and Baja California, also "ought to belong to us" because that "nation of drones" had refused to "drive the plough" and develop its resources. Many new settlers agreed with such imperial thinking. After being evicted from a Californio's land near Mountain View, for instance, the squatter E. A. Van Court stressed that, unlike Mexican Americans, she and her husband had actually improved the estate on which they had lived.[12]

Mexican Americans hoped that the American courts might protect them from Gold Rush scoundrels. On paper, the Treaty of Guadalupe Hidalgo did just that, and Californios in San José frequently appealed to that international agreement as well as to the regional Land Claims Boards created by the U.S. Congress in 1851 to rule on the validity of their Spanish-Mexican grants. But leading government officials in the Valley rejected the spirit of the treaty and transferred county resources to new white residents. Tellingly, the first American survey of San José, drawn in May 1847, ignored the existing land claims of Californios and early American settlers in the pueblo. William J. Lewis, who arrived in California during the Gold Rush and who, as the official surveyor for Santa Clara County from 1849 to 1856, judged the legitimacy of Mexican-era land grants and their stated boundaries, did as much as anyone to expedite the transfer of property in the local area. Although charged with interpreting Spanish-language documents, Lewis later admitted in court that he was unable to speak much Spanish and had little interest in learning the names given by Californios to local hills, trees, and rivers, critical landmarks often cited as boundary markers on Mexican *diseños* (the topographical sketches of land grants drawn in the Mexican period). Indeed, Lewis expressed little regard for the Mexican documents upon which Californios staked their legal claims. Instead, he believed that many *diseños* had actually been drawn up since the Mexican War to cheat his American compatriots; even documents that clearly dated to the era of Mexican rule were "of course inaccurate and merely rough sketches" and therefore subject to his own "interpretation."[13]

Lawyers representing the federal government on land cases in the Santa Clara Valley and other parts of California also struggled to prove that Californio properties belonged in the public domain and could be claimed by white settlers. By the late 1850s, when the U.S. District Court heard many of those claims, American attorneys framed their legal cases as a contest between the honest work of settlers interested in the public good, on the one hand, and the greed of established Mexican elites, on the other. These battles pitted republican citizenship against the interests of landed barons, and the attorney general of the United States added his support in 1858 to the cause championed by white settlers. Arguing that these "squatters" were actually among "the worthiest citizens of America," he insisted that Californio claimants were the real criminals, "perverting the machinery of the law to the purposes of private plunder."[14] Mexican Americans suffered through long and costly legal battles as a result of those suits—the average case took seventeen years—and even when opposing lawyers saw no hope of winning, as in the claims against Valley residents Manuel Alviso, Antonio Suñol, Agustín Bernal, and Juana Briones, Californios still hired attorneys and arrived prepared for trial. Ultimately, federal attorneys might offer no argument on behalf of the prosecution, but Mexican Americans in the area were forced to pay high legal fees and surveyor's costs accrued on behalf of their own defense.[15]

With assistance from government officials and lawyers, white settlers rapidly acquired Santa Clara Valley properties. Observers noted that arriving

Americans and Europeans scrambled "with avidity" to purchase city lots and county lands, and that they crafted a number of ways to defraud Mexican Americans in the process. In one common pattern, José Domingo Peralta and other landowners inadvertently signed away their titles, thinking that they were only leasing their lands to local settlers. Trying to avoid this problem, Mariano Castro and other Californios granted power of attorney to settlers like Peter Davidson, entrusting these lawyers "to use, cultivate, rent, bargain, sell and convey, or otherwise dispose of" their property. Perhaps not surprisingly, these men and others made enormous personal profits from such agreements, in part by leasing the grazing rights to other Americans. As San José became an important supply center for the state's mining communities, merchants also took advantage of cash-poor Mexican Americans by issuing them loans. Californios commonly attached their lands to guarantee repayment and sold their cattle at below market prices to speculators such as Martin Murphy, Jr., to pay their rising debts.[16]

In short, white Americans controlled the legal process and the buying and selling of goods in the town, developments that over the course of the 1850s led to most local Californios being dispossessed of their Valley properties. Regardless of the protections guaranteed by the Treaty of Guadalupe Hidalgo, the twin ideologies of Manifest Destiny and republican citizenship asserted a hold on Valley politics, and the widespread conviction that Mexicans had never actually labored upon the land prompted farmers, merchants, politicians, and lawyers to justify disfranchising Californios in the region. By 1860 only twenty men and six women in San José's ethnic Mexican community of over nine hundred held property in the county. While that small, elite group of Californios maintained some of their lands, and at times their Indian servants, most continued to experience a dramatic economic decline. The deleterious effects of economic, legal, and other changes in the Valley were broadly visible, and they anticipated developments that would soon engulf Southern California. The number of Mexican American residents who reported a "personal estate" on the Santa Clara County census of 1860 dropped dramatically over the following decade, from 129 to 63, and the total value of the personal estates owned by the entire community declined by more than 50 percent during those years. By contrast, the county's richest resident in 1870, the Irish immigrant James Murphy, claimed a personal estate valued at almost twice the combined amount claimed by all of the ethnic Mexicans who resided in San José.[17]

The destruction of Californios' land base helped to create a new low-wage labor force in the Santa Clara Valley. In the turbulent 1850s many Spanish-speaking residents entered low-paying jobs, often laboring in seasonal agriculture for the same white settlers who had recently acquired their former Valley lands. By 1860, 55 percent of the Mexican men in San José had become day laborers, and another 20 percent toiled as farm workers. Elite

Californio families—the Alvisos, Berryessas, Bernals, Pachecos, and others—moved in rather dramatic fashion into occupations that had previously been filled by neophytes and other reviled Indian employees. The Gold Rush forced these proud *gente de razón* to survive as wage workers at the margins of Valley society. A small number did exert greater control over this process, capitalizing on skills developed in Alta California since the 1820s. Almost 10 percent of all Mexican men found work as either teamsters or saddle makers in 1860, and nearly 40 percent of women wage workers who declared an occupation in that year were either dressmakers or seamstresses, no doubt the best available occupations in a time of diminishing economic freedom for the ethnic Mexican community. Most local Mexican women worked as servants in the homes of white residents by that year, while others earned wages as milliners, blanket makers, and prostitutes. Many men and women struggled to find year-round work, and while many incoming American settlers prided themselves on their newfound economic success after 1850, no significant Mexican American middle class would develop in the county for roughly a century. No Californio or Mexican resident entered a professional position in the county between 1860 and 1900, and few completed more than six years of school in the five decades following the California Gold Rush.[18]

MIGRANTS AND DISSIDENTS

Along with conquered Californios, other groups of Latinos also labored in county agriculture during these years. While the framers of the Treaty of Guadalupe Hidalgo had never anticipated that new groups of Mexicans would move to these territories won by war—they assumed that the Far West would be home to white Americans—immigrant Mexicanos did come to populate the American Southwest. The Gold Rush drove that development. Between ten and twenty thousand moved into California in search of the ore after 1848, and, escaping from outbreaks of discrimination and racial violence in Northern California mining regions, thousands took refuge in Santa Clara County thereafter. While most stayed for only a short time, some settled permanently, causing the Chilean Pedro Isidoro Coubet to note in 1850 that "the new city of San José was the focal point of all the miners who had become disillusioned" in the foothills of the Sierra Nevada. Because of heightened racial warfare in the mines, moving to San José and other nearby communities often constituted an act of survival. According to census enumerators, the Spanish-surnamed population of San José grew by at least 150 between 1845 and 1860. As the following chapter illustrates, many hundreds more sought wage work at the New Almadén mine located a few miles south of the town. Observers estimated that some two thousand Mexicans and

Chileans comprised the New Almadén community during the latter part of the 1850s, a group almost equal in size to the entire Mexican population of Los Angeles County. By 1860, in fact, Santa Clara County likely boasted the largest Latino immigrant population in the United States.[19]

As in other parts of the region during the nineteenth century, the size of that group grew as a result of contemporary thinking about the natural skills and abilities that nonwhites would supposedly contribute to capitalist agriculture. In San José and other parts of California, American commentators commonly assumed that Mexicans were particularly suited for low-wage, manual work. If conquered Californios and immigrant Mexicans, they imagined, could provide the routine, least-remunerative labor, incoming white Americans would be available for more rewarding industries. All this seemed natural. "You will want these hardy [Mexican] men," one white settler wrote using biblical language, who "will become the hewers of wood and the drawers of water to American capital and enterprise." In building new labor regimes, white settlers relied on vestiges of the old Mexican economic system based on the debt peonage of native workers. The town council thus ruled in 1850 that "any Indian found drunk or loitering" could be detained and hired out to an employer willing to pay enough money to purchase "clothes for said Indian."[20]

Not all white San Joseans were pleased with the idea of debt peonage or the arrival of Mexican immigrants from the state of Sonora, and racial violence erupted in part as a response to the presence of these nonwhites thought to exhibit innate traits of criminality. In his diary entry of February 1852, Alfred Doten, a future resident of the San José area, recorded his animosity toward those he had first encountered in the Mother Lode: "God damn their thieving Mexican souls eternally to the hottest corner of hell and may every sack of the dirt which they have stolen from me turn into brimstone to help roast their damned infernal carcasses. Amen."[21] Doten wrote in response to the apparent presence of Mexican bandits in the region, and in truth white residents were not the only ones who precipitated racial violence in the 1850s. During an era marked by many overt conflicts, Mexican highwaymen such as Joaquín Murrieta preyed on white and Chinese settlers, often with the support of Californios angry about their declining social and economic positions. "Social bandits" of a sort, these criminals voiced the concerns of their dominated community, just as Estanislao and Yóscolo had articulated Indian resentment toward missions San José and Santa Clara prior to 1846. During the decade after the Mexican War, Mexican outlaws aggravated existing racial tensions and encouraged settlers' fears that dangerous cutthroats lurked in the Valley, a threat to public safety and economic prosperity.

In part because Californios and Sonorans were thought to be governed more by "passions" than by "reason," white settlers emphasized that, "when excited[,] the [Mexican] men were impulsive, rash and cruel, fearless and brave, with no fear for a knife or pistol." Another settler proposed that Californios and Mexicans showed such tendencies because they had lived "under a government but a little removed from a state of anarchy, in which the strong oppressed the weak, and the rapacious plundered the defenceless without punishment." These republican expressions of white racial superiority fostered new rounds of anti-Mexican violence throughout the state, as the Berryessa household learned firsthand in the Santa Clara Valley. The family had been eminent members of the provincial elite prior to 1846. Journalists in San José contended thereafter that members of that Californio clan were "bad citizens and dangerous men," notable for being "violent, brutal, revengeful, and bloodthirsty," and the Berryessas would be among the first Mexican Americans in the state to witness the power of those racial labels.[22]

The family first felt the sting of racial violence during the war between the United States and Mexico. In 1846, members of the California Battalion murdered José de los Reyes Berryessa and his twin sons on the road to Sonoma, and the German-born Charles Weber, later the founder of the town of Stockton, then set out to steal Nicolás Berryessa's large herd of horses. A "cruel and bloodthirsty" man, in Antonio Berryessa's view, Weber and his company of armed men rounded up thirty-five or forty horses from the Californios' corral; grabbed saddles, bridles, and rifles; threatened to kill the women inside the house; opened doors and trunks by force; and committed "thousands of other outrages" before departing. Over the next few years, the spooked Berryessa clan faced the daunting challenges that confronted many other local Mexican Americans. Squatters built houses on the family lands and shot the Californios' horses and cattle. A dishonest surveyor apportioned most of the Berryessa tract to the public domain, family lawyers proved untrustworthy, and a San José mob descended on the estate in 1854 and rode away with Demesio Berryessa, accusing him of murdering a white settler. They lynched him later that year. Remembering the horrifying Gold Rush era, Antonio Berryessa lamented in 1877 that "Of all the California families, perhaps ours can most justly complain about the bad faith of adventurers and squatters and about the illegal activities of the American lawyers."[23]

Retributions against Californios like the Berryessas became a frequent source of news and pride among white San Joseans, and this violence proved enormously consequential for thwarting the integration of ethnic Mexicans in California. White Americans commonly marked ethnic Mexicans with the badge of blackness, as when San José residents in 1855 called a Mexican immigrant, considered the leader of a "gang of outlaws," "the Negro García." Concerns about phenotype and blood purity determined racial violence. After a white laborer was found shot and mutilated about ten miles from San

José in 1853, local settlers charged that "a gang of persons of Spanish blood, who are suspected of having murdered a number of Americans," had begun a race war against American settlers and squatters, and they set out to find the culprits. Against the vindictive backdrop of the recent war with Mexico and inspired by surging nationalism and a desire to protect the political economy of the Valley, white Americans and Europeans banded together in the name of self-preservation. Newspapers in the Santa Clara Valley drew attention, for example, to the Texans' mythic stand at the Alamo, where, it was said, Davey Crockett had single-handedly killed twenty-six Mexican soldiers before dying with the words "I am an American" on his lips. A history of the Santa Clara Valley written in 1881 reminded readers that, since the early 1850s, suspected Mexican criminals—"dark" men likened to "monsters," "tigers," and "assassins"—had threatened American men traveling alone and had been ready to "brutally murder" a white woman left at home without her husband's protection.[24]

While white vigilantes shot or hanged suspected ethnic Mexican criminals in the San José area, local settlers took even more extreme measures to cleanse Northern California of its profligate Indian communities, a sort of final solution to race problems in the state. Before the discovery of gold in Northern California, San José's American alcalde authorized pueblo residents to shoot suspected Indian horse thieves on sight. In early November 1847 natives employed by whites or Californios were also forced to carry work certificates to distinguish them from Indians who had no proper business in the pueblo, and those not employed by San Joseans were allowed to visit the town only after securing a special pass from the Indian subagent. As one early twentieth-century historian suggested, such "measures bear close resemblance to the black codes of the south," and when a cholera outbreak killed many of the Valley's indigenous residents in the fall of 1850, more than one San Josean blamed the dead for having been "improvident in their habits and mode of living." Convinced that California's progress depended on the elimination of "diggers," San José newspaper columns demanded that Indians "be exterminated," and settlers openly expressed fantasies about killing Indians. Many native residents fled to other parts of the state, often only to encounter even more extreme anti-Indian violence. Disease, flight, and violence took their toll; census enumerators counted 450 Indian residents in Santa Clara County in 1852, and only 29 eight years later. In the late 1850s an elderly Ohlone man who had lived in the Valley for decades sadly recalled that "when he was a little boy, his tribe was numerous about here—but all have died, and he is the only one left."[25]

While the vast majority of Mexican Americans did not suffer from that degree of racial violence, most Latinos did experience patterns of rapid economic and political disfranchisement in the decade following the Treaty of Guadalupe Hidalgo. Not pogroms, these were systematic efforts to reduce the

Mexican American population to a landless, powerless minority. The police and courts quickly established a legal double-standard assuring that non-white residents would receive much harsher punishments than did white settlers facing similar crimes. Between 1850 and 1864, therefore, all but one of the accused criminals executed in the county were ethnic Mexicans, while white settlers, such as Henry Dietzman, accused of killing "a Spaniard named Pedro" in 1862, were simply sent to prison on manslaughter charges. Even the *Santa Clara Register* noted in 1853 that "it is seldom that an American convict is hung by the neck on conviction of [a] crime." The legal process also turned against conquered Californios in other ways. No Mexican American served as a member of the first jury that met in San José in 1848, and none would sit on a county grand jury throughout the rest of the nineteenth century. Between 1848 and 1900 only white settlers became local sheriffs, justices of the peace, and police officers, a pattern witnessed in other cities, such as Los Angeles, during the nineteenth century. Racism also gave rise to informal mechanisms of justice, and committees of vigilance, which Valley settlers established after 1850 around San José, enlisted over a thousand county residents by 1851.[26]

In ways devastating to Mexican Americans, racial violence and discriminatory public policies defined both the political economy of the region and local white identities during the Gold Rush. Residents later spoke with pride of the ways in which this second conquest of Mexicans shaped a new Santa Clara Valley. In historical narratives and other festive visions of white superiority, settlers and their children continued to justify Mexicans' disfranchisement by making references to the dramatic progress inaugurated by American rule in 1848. Even decades later, the influential citizen Thomas Fallon and others expressed little remorse about the retributive violence they had witnessed. In Fallon's account and most others, thievery and violence were essential Mexican traits that threatened local prosperity, and white Americans likened violations of the "public trust" to the depredations of a Mexican bandit. Fallon wrote angrily, for instance, about the San José water company "that charges us to drink," concluding only that "we hung [*sic*] Tiburcio Vásquez for lesser crimes." As late as 1904 a celebratory local history written by prominent white women near San José fondly recalled other nearly forgotten episodes of vigilantism. According to their account, a white posse had arrested four Mexicans accused of cattle theft in November 1855, lynching two of the men from a local bridge. The most eminent families staked their own prestige to having participated in such peacekeeping; if vigilance committee membership lists were ever discovered, the women who authored the 1904 history reported, "doubtless the names written there would have a familiar sound to many old settlers."[27]

While white residents proudly told stories of anti-Mexican violence in the

Valley, Californios and Mexicans expressed their own perspectives on this
racial terror. Having lived for years in Alta California, and having controlled
local lands and native workers under Mexican rule, Californios no doubt
were shocked, not to say affronted, by the way many Americans and European immigrants arrogantly defined their own superiority. Mexican Americans bitterly excoriated the activities of Gold Rush settlers. Antonio Berreyesa
and others furiously detailed the violent and unscrupulous actions of white
Americans, and the *Santa Clara Register* warned readers in 1853 that a "very
dangerous feeling" had already developed among ethnic Mexicans in the Valley. According to the newspaper's editors, "the history of modern times will
fail to give a parallel case of wrong and oppression, systematically practised
and often under the color of law, on the part of the conquerors against a
subjugated race."[28] Local Latinos made heroes of California residents, including highwaymen, who seemed to fight back against such subjugation. Well
into the 1930s and 1940s, ethnic Mexicans in San José and other parts of the
Southwest sang the "Corrido de Joaquín Murrieta" that narrated a decidedly
different perspective on nineteenth-century banditry from the one promoted
by white celebrants of the Gold Rush. As Latinos remembered that hero of
the 1850s, Murrieta proclaimed that

> I am not an American
> But I do understand English
> I learned it with my brother
> Forward and backward
> And any American
> I make tremble at my feet.

> When I was barely a child
> I was left an orphan.
> No one gave me any love,
> They killed my brother,
> And my wife Carmelita,
> The cowards assassinated her.

> I came from Hermosillo
> In search of gold and riches.
> The Indian poor and simple
> I defended with fierceness
> And a good price the sheriffs
> Would pay for my head.

> From the greedy rich,
> I took away their money.
> With the humble and poor

I took off my hat.
Oh, what unjust laws
To call me a highwayman. . . .

My career began
Because of a terrible scene.
When I got to seven hundred (killed)
Then my name was dreaded.
When I got to twelve hundred
Then my name was terrible. . . .

I'm neither a Chilean nor a stranger
On this soil which I tread.
California comes from Mexico
Because God wanted it that way.
And in my stitched serape,
I carry my baptismal certificate.[29]

The irredentist perspective offered by this ballad certainly drew strength by defining Mexican Americans as a conquered people, by stressing that California was former Mexican soil, and by emphasizing that the origins of racial violence lay in the unwarranted attacks on Mexicans by white Americans.

While it became a matter of common sense among white Americans that Mexicans rightly constituted a "subjugated race," many ethnic Mexicans living on Valley soil struggled against that assumption, finding increased strength in their common heritage and shared experiences of violence and subjugation. Cultural activities took on new importance in the face of Gold Rush–era threats to ethnic Mexican communities. Attendance at bull and bear fights, which remained popular in Mexico throughout the late nineteenth century, linked San Joseans to both California's Mexican past and contemporary Mexico. Religious practices were understood in light of the American conquest, as the local priest José Pinero sermonized in 1850 about "the temptations and seductions they were going to be exposed to because of the coming of Americans and Protestantism." But the Catholic Church was an unsteady base of support. While for a time, at least, membership in that institution likely confirmed some Mexican residents' sense of identity and strength, local churches suffered from impoverished Californios' inability to tithe.[30]

San Joseans expressed a range of other responses as they became the first in the state after 1848 to lose their long-held property and political prestige. No small number supported "social bandits" such as Murrieta (and later Tiburcio Vásquez) who complained that "we were unjustly and wrongfully deprived of the social rights that belonged to us." A minority insisted that as "people of reason," their common whiteness instead united them with newly arrived Americans and Europeans. Other Valley residents no doubt embraced the perspective offered by Santa Barbara's Pablo de la Guerra, who argued in 1849 that

> it should be perfectly understood in the first place, what is the true signifi-cance of the word "White." Many citizens of California have received from nature a very dark skin; nevertheless, there are among them men who have heretofore been allowed to vote, and not only that, but to fill the highest public offices. It would be very unjust to deprive them of the privilege of citizens merely because nature had not made them White.[31]

Confronted by a flood of American and European immigrants who believed otherwise, Californios sought to hold onto their shrinking Valley estates and to retain some political influence after the Mexican War. María Trinidad Peralta de Castro, for example, unsuccessfully attempted to gain some con-cessions from the San Francisco–San José Railroad in the early 1860s before allowing the company to run its line through her family's land near Moun-tain View. Dozens of others appealed to the courts to maintain their prop-erty and prestige.[32]

These efforts suggest Californios' willingness to adapt to changing condi-tions, to demand the guarantees promised in the Treaty of Guadalupe Hidalgo, and to utilize the American judicial system to protect their interests. But the 1861 case of local resident Antonio Chabolla illustrated that, even when Californios won court battles to maintain their lands, as many eventu-ally did, legal decisions alone would not confer rights. Chabolla had first taken his claim to the California Land Commission in the early 1850s after squatters settled on his property, and he had continued to fight for that land until the Third Judicial District Court of California in April 1861 finally confirmed his title to the rancho. He did not feel relief for long, however, because the widespread support for "free labor" and "free soil" rendered the court's verdict impossible to enforce. When the sheriff of San José attempted to organize a posse to evict squatters from Chabolla's land in May 1861, he found not a single county resident willing to join the deputized group on Chabolla's behalf. Rather, a public display of force and a declaration of "squatters' rights," designed to send a strong message to other Mexican claimants around the region, followed the *Chabolla* decision.[33]

By early afternoon on the day the sheriff first attempted to organize a posse, nearly a thousand American settlers descended on San José from Santa Clara and surrounding counties, "some on horses, some on wagons, some on foot, and nearly all armed." One group brought a small cannon with them, and together the large group of settlers rode to the Chabolla ranch, six miles away. Already encamped, others had formed a "battle array" and were clearly willing to fight any sheriff attempting to move them. By late after-noon, two thousand settlers had joined the rally, and together they agreed

The cultivation of strawberries and other fruit boomed in the decades after
California statehood thanks to racial segmentation in the labor market. Here a
white boss directs Chinese workers near San José while other white Americans
lounge in a small boat in the background. BancPic 1963:002:1364:FR, Bancroft
Library.

"to just march the entire squatter army right through the streets" of San José
"in order to reduce all adversely disposed persons to a proper state of sub-
mission." Led by a brass band, "two or three farm wagons filled with women
and girls, some carrying guns," and Colonel Hopper, a Mexican War veteran
"mounted on a fine white mustang, and with a drawn sword in his hand,"
the group encountered the sheriff who attempted to stop their march on the
road into town. They passed him easily and celebrated their arrival at San
José's Washington Square Park with gunshots and speeches, including one
declamation by Hopper that the crowd "remember the occasion of their now
being in arms in defence of their rights, their homes, and their firesides,
against fraud, oppression, and wrong, and to be ready at all times to shoul-
der their guns and be on hand as they were on the present occasion." Once
again, settlers' bullets enforced white America's political and economic hegemony in the area, and the sheriff made no further effort to enforce the court
order in the *Chabolla* case. Having witnessed the threat of mob violence
under the leadership of a Mexican War officer, the once-sympathetic judge
agreed justice was hopeless. Chabolla had won his court case but lost his
property.[34]

By 1861 most San José Californios had exhausted their legal recourses to

keep their lands away from white settlers. Witnessing extraordinary and de-
structive changes in the Valley, families such as the Berreyesas had experienced systematic disfranchisement at the hands of squatters, lawyers, and
surveyors since the late 1840s. Others suffered from the discriminatory legal
system and from violent assaults by Northern California vigilantes.[35] Transformed into a low-wage labor force, absorbed and discarded by white
farmers as seasonal needs dictated, Californios and other ethnic Mexicans
became a veritable "internal colony" in Northern California. Those who took
Californio lands profited from racial violence in the Valley, and many Mexican Americans felt they had no choice but to work within the American legal
system to protect their rights under the Treaty of Guadalupe Hidalgo. Others
developed different ways to counter those changes. Nicolás Berreyesa apparently wrote frequently to former Mexican politicians still living in California,
hoping that one-time elites might still be able to protect his interests. Some
left the state entirely, most for Mexico. A few became highwaymen, took up
arms, and preyed on whites and Chinese in the gold mining region and
other parts of Northern California.[36]

In the range of their responses, settler violence and the "contentious,
racialized struggles . . . over land ownership [and] labor-market position"
during the 1850s summoned the first articulations of Mexican American
identity in California.[37] Conquered residents remained critical of the recent
United States takeover of the Southwest, and Mariano Vallejo, Antonio María
Osio, and other former elites gave interviews and wrote personal accounts
documenting the atrocities committed by white settlers. Telling the truth
about California history seemed one of the only ways to force other local
residents to recognize the violence of California statehood. More than one
countered local boosters by arguing that the Gold Rush years replaced a far
more idyllic society, an era that in effect had not known the devilish power
of white racism. In the face of white settlers' denigrating accounts of the lazy
days preceding American rule, Californios posited that all residents had then
been happier and more content. Mexican immigrants arriving from Sonora
called California and its adjacent states "El Norte" [the north] and "terri-
torio perdido" [lost land] to remember the region as former Mexican national territory. Those monikers added to the ongoing critiques of the Mexican War and its aftermath.[38]

In spite of acute instability brought on by land loss, the arrival of new
immigrants from Mexico, rampant racial discrimination by the Valley's legal
system, and the changing position of ethnic Mexicans within the labor market, local Latinos created an important new community near San José. The
largest concentration of Spanish-speakers in California congregated around
the mercury mine located south of the town by the early 1860s, and that new
company pueblo enjoyed booming profits after the Mexican War thanks to
the presence of numerous low-wage industrial laborers. Along with some of

the most overt instances of anti-Mexican discrimination in the nineteenth century, Santa Clara County witnessed another far-reaching transformation. Here, for the first time in the state's history, Californios, Mexican immigrants, and other Latin Americans banded together to defend their residency and work. Animated by transnational political developments, they defied the insidious logic of Manifest Destiny and the menacing perspectives of white settlers on contemporary race relations. Their new mining community and political activities, the subject of the next chapter, would serve as a harbinger of the future for many ethnic Mexican communities throughout the Southwest.

Chapter 3

Transnational Industries

I often think, as I stoop to pick a cluster of white-petaled
flowers, that seem the very expression of the freshness
and briefness of the morning, how, in some shadowy
"labor" a thousand feet below, a gang of Mexicans,
finishing their night-shift, may be passing the "barrilito"
from one grimy mouth to another.
—Mary Halleck Foote, "A California Mining Camp" (1878)

As in other regions of the American West, capital-intensive industries played
an important role in the development of Northern California in the late
nineteenth century, and mining led the way. After 1848 the rapid political
and economic disfranchisement of the Valley's Californio elite was matched
by the steady movement of Latinos into wage work; white residents took
over the Valley's best lands and dominated the political system, and many
displaced local residents—members of the Berryessa, Alviso, and Suñol families, for example—joined new immigrants from Latin America seeking work
at the New Almadén mercury mine located some fifteen miles south of San
José. The Devil drove ethnic Mexicans underground, and these Californios,
Mexican immigrants, and Chileans became the first Latino industrial workers in the United States, a class that by the early twentieth century would
become dominant in communities from south Florida to southern Colorado.
The dramatic events that unfolded at the New Almadén mine over the 1850s
and 1860s heralded and foretold the general contours of subsequent Latino
history in the United States.

As the previous chapter suggested, many related political struggles played
themselves out in Santa Clara County and elsewhere after the Mexican War
as contests to control the land itself, and Mexican Americans' inability to

retain those holdings often translated into a fundamental loss of political power by the early 1860s. But while historians of California have paid considerable attention to the so-called decline of the Californios, Latino industrial workers in the state have received far less attention. In passageways far below the Valley's celebrated wheat fields and fruit orchards, these Californios and Mexican immigrants were experiencing wage labor in one of the world's largest mercury mines. While the area became home to new American settlers during the 1850s and 1860s, it also soon became the second largest producer of mercury in the world, sending ships and railroad cars loaded with "quicksilver" to Asia, Latin America, Europe, and other parts of the United States. An extremely valuable commodity, mercury amalgamates gold and silver, allowing miners to remove valuable ores from surrounding rock and sand with far greater ease. The mercury unearthed at New Almadén helped to fuel excavations worldwide. Hundreds of employees experienced the rhythms of mining work near San José after the Treaty of Guadalupe Hidalgo, and new patterns of immigration from Latin America during the Gold Rush brought many directly from established mining communities in Mexico to labor in Northern California. As one Mexican American resident of New Almadén told a local newspaper, these Latinos resident at the mine were "industrious people whose work has contributed greatly to the progress of San José and its surroundings."[1]

This chapter offers several new contentions about Latinos and Northern California. First, it argues that Latinos at the New Almadén mine played an important role in the industrial history of the American West. Second, it focuses on this industrial site to suggest a new reckoning with post-1848 ethnic politics in the American Southwest. Mexican residents of New Almadén loudly protested the social conditions they experienced in the aftermath of the Mexican War, leading local Latinos to make important connections between their own circumstances and broader national developments in the United States and Mexico. In responding to industrialization and life at New Almadén, Santa Clara County's Mexican-origin mine workers in fact paid great attention to the political crises facing the Mexican nation during the 1850s and 1860s. Consequently, this chapter's third contention is that Latinos at New Almadén exhibited patterns of transnational involvement in the mid-nineteenth century that would be common of Mexicans, Dominicans, Cubans, and other Latinos in the twentieth-century United States.

THE MINE AND ITS WORKFORCE

The development of New Almadén clearly reflected the broader political shifts in mid-nineteenth-century California. As most American settlers after the Mexican War continued to imagine the Valley as a sort of "virgin land" open to the "free labor" of white Americans, industrial mining boomed by capitalizing on established patterns of racial disfrancishment and the availability of low-wage workers. As with the gold that prompted the great rush to the state after 1848, residents of Northern California had known for decades about the existence of cinnabar in the area; even prior to the arrival of Spanish settlers, local Ohlone had used this ore as a decorative paint. In 1824 two Mexican residents, Secundino Robles and Andrés Chabolla, became the first non-Indians to find these "quicksilver" deposits. Seeking silver, the disappointed pueblo residents did not recognize the considerable market value of what they had in fact discovered, and decades passed before a Mexican army officer interested in metallurgy, Andrés Castillero, correctly identified the ore in 1845. He established a business partnership with the Robles brothers of San José, with Father José María Real of the Santa Clara Mission, and with General José Castro, who also lived in the area. They directed local Indians to work the mine until, much to Castillero's regret, the outbreak of war with the United States forced him return to Mexico and to lease and then sell New Almadén's mineral rights to the Barron and Forbes Company, a British firm that already had mining interests in Nayarit, Mexico. The Mexican War therefore brought about not only a transfer of the Valley's land to the United States, but also the sale of local mining rights to an international corporation. The latter was specifically celebrated as a sign of the progressive "whitening" of California. A writer in *Hutchings Magazine* opined that while the mine's Mexican owners had been "too timid to avail himself of its gifts," the new white proprietors understood exactly what to do with nature's abundance.[2]

The British owners of New Almadén rapidly set about creating a society distinct from the one that most of the Valley's white settlers hoped to fashion. Beginning in the late 1840s, Barron and Forbes became the first corporate employer in California to bring hundreds of Mexicans together as wage workers. Hundreds of disfranchised Californios and Sonorans sought work at New Almadén, the only employer in the state that favored the retention of a year-round Mexican workforce during the 1850s. The local labor system relegated Mexicans to the lowest economic status in the region, however, quite literally driving them underground into the sort of low-wage employment that local white residents sought to avoid. Yet even as Mexicans' economic status diminished, native Indians were further displaced. Finding California's natives so "indolent" that "you will never be able to do anything with such labourers," Barron and Forbes seized the opportunity to replace them, hiring Mexicans and Chileans who already had expertise as miners in Latin America. Inaugurating a regional pattern in the American West of importing immigrants as low-wage workers, the company also recruited Sonorans, transporting them to the county as early as 1847. By 1851 all but two of the approximately seven hundred employees were either Mexican or Chilean.[3]

Few Americans arriving in California after 1848 had anticipated the

existence of an industrial Mexican workforce in the region, and the seemingly contradictory desires of these "free soilers" and those of corporate
mining interests created new social conflicts. Fearing that the mine harbored
bandidos and degenerates, settlers like Judge A. C. Innes told stories of the
"bizarre and unbelievable orgies" that immigrant and Californio "scum" enjoyed with "the female of their species" in the passageways beneath the
county soil. Something disturbing, it seemed, was happening under the Valley's seemingly pastoral landscape, something at odds with efforts to develop
a settler paradise based on "Yankee ingenuity" above ground. The region's
Mexican labor force therefore engendered new anxieties among settlers about
the working-class "greasers" in their midst, although the San José press and
government officials generally ignored the presence of subterranean Mexicans and Chileans in the Valley.[4]

As Californios and Sonorans encountered more and more violence and
disfranchisement throughout California, New Almadén's owners were able to
attract Latino miners displaced from other parts of the state. Because racial
discrimination drove many Mexicans and Chileans from nearby gold mines,
New Almadén soon found it unnecessary to import its laborers directly from
Mexico. Beginning in September 1849, for instance, the company simply
advertised in the nascent California press for "Hispanic-Americans of good
conduct" who were interested in becoming wage laborers. The mine's early
success rested on the skill and physical dexterity of transplanted Sonorans.
The critical technology at New Almadén was Mexican, imported from the
mining regions of Northern Mexico, which had already developed methods
for extracting ores from deep underground. Workers familiar with these
practices quickly built a maze of underground tunnels and caverns in the
hills south of San José, leaving at least one visitor astonished that Mexicans
could find their way "as readily as we do the streets of a city." Travelers and
other newcomers in the 1850s agreed that only Mexican workers knew how
to negotiate the dangerous paths and ladders underneath this section of the
pastoral Valley and that less experienced workers risked deadly falls from the
notched, single-beam ladders extending down the deep shafts.[5]

The Gold Rush marked Latinos' induction into California's industrial labor force. New Almadén's workers encountered the rigid routines of capitalist industry by 1850, and the ethnic Mexican men who found employment
underground heard the sounds of hammers, explosions, and drills, and later
of rail carts, which filled the dark passageways. These miners worked in
teams of six to eight and rotated tasks to maintain their energy throughout
their ten-hour workdays. As they toiled, ethnic Mexican men uttered their
own rhythmic cries, noises that sounded to one observer like "something
between a grunt and a groan." Climbing with up to three hundred pounds
of ore on their backs, their loads held "in place by a strap over [their]
forehead[s]" so that their hands would be free to move up the ladder, two

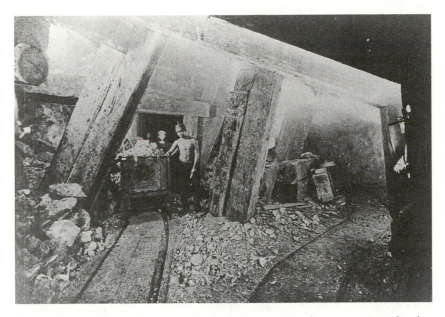

Unidentified workers at New Almadén in the late nineteenth century. New Almadén Mine Papers, box 119, folder 8, Department of Special Collections, Stanford University.

shifts of miners worked night and day, six days a week in the New Almadén mine. These *tanateros* (haulers) each made thirty trips a day carrying the rock that others had dislodged, and together workers built hundreds of miles of passageways.[6]

This difficult and dangerous work did not result in high wages. Instead, a contract labor system developed at New Almadén during the decade after American conquest in which earnings remained low as teams of workers attempted to underbid one another to gain weekly or monthly contracts. Employees tabulated their earnings on a piece-rate basis, and foremen measured the linear feet of rock each miner excavated and the number of *cargas* (a 300-pound load) each *tanatero* carried. Mine owners found these systems of measurement and payment extremely profitable, and an observer noted in 1854 that the contract and piece-rate systems were "preferred by the proprietors," in part because they created an ongoing competition among workers to maintain their jobs. A woman who described a payday in 1876 also concluded that the piece-rate system encouraged foremen to underpay miners, haulers, and teamsters. According to her observations, the miners "always think they have done more than actual measurement shown" when the foremen paid his workers. A company superintendent reiterated in 1886 the Darwinian results of the contract system: "there is natural selection and

Spanishtown in the 1860s with local children in the foreground. New Almadén
Mine Papers, box 120, folder 14.

weeding out going on among the employees, the less competent miners and
dissolute miners not being able to compete with the more skilled and better
class of miners."[7]

While labor relations in the county were being reorganized below ground,
the owners of New Almadén created new patterns of racial segregation on
the Valley floor. Barron and Forbes segregated its Latin American laborers
from its "white" employees, thereby assuring that Chilenos and Mexicanos,
frequently given the mine's most dangerous jobs, rarely worked alongside
New Almadén's Cornish or Irish residents in the 1850s and 1860s. The company also established a segregated *colonia* called "Spanishtown" after the outbreak of the Mexican War. Just as New Almadén's more dangerous underground tunnels were considered the natural workplaces of Mexicans, these
segregated residences at the top of Mine Hill were seen as their natural
homes; and when they emerged dirty and exhausted from their shifts underground, Mexican wage workers walked home to friends and families in one
of the most isolated sections of the county. White workers, on the other
hand, were welcome residents farther down the hill at either "Englishtown,"
in the case of laborers, or "the Hacienda," in the case of superintendents and
managers. Later residents remembered that "lines were rigidly drawn, and no
Mexican was permitted to live in English camp." After walking through all

three residential sections, one observer reported that "the Mexican camp was the home of a more barren and hopeless poverty."[8]

The physical environment of the Mexican *colonia* did not offer any of the advantages enjoyed by whites living down the road, in part because most of Spanishtown's buildings were constructed of wood, a material more vulnerable to the fires that twice decimated the Mexican *colonia* during the 1870s. Segregation also made it difficult for local Mexican residents to meet their basic needs, particularly since the neighborhood's nearest source of water was located a mile away near the Hacienda, an eleven-hundred-foot descent that forced Mexican teamsters to traverse the long hill each day until the company installed pipes in Spanishtown in 1881. Mexicans also watched as the company scattered piles of discarded stones from inside the mine between the houses of Spanishtown. The presence of these "tailings" killed nearly all of the neighborhood's trees and other vegetation. As a result, Spanishtowners had little shade to protect them from the sun during the hot summer months and struggled to till the rocky soil manifestly unsuited for growing most crops.[9]

The *colonia's* segregation, geographic isolation, and poor farming conditions made these residents even more dependent on mine owners in many ways. Since the company exclusively hired men to mine, haul, sort, and process the local ore, Spanishtown's lack of "natural advantages" likely had the greatest effect on the lives of local women who spent their days washing clothing, tending to chickens and small animals kept in their yards, and attempting to grow corn and other crops. Ethnic Mexican women at New Almadén often had a difficult time cultivating small gardens in the area, and many Spanishtowners had little choice but to purchase their food from local merchants. But local residents faced more than geographical segregation, limited educational opportunity, and debt to the company store; mine workers and their families experienced the physical punishments of industrial labor, as well. Along with the lynchings and other forms of violence described in chapter 1, the experience of underground work highlighted the often deleterious impact of Manifest Destiny, American conquest, and capitalist development on ethnic Mexicans' bodies during this period. Explosions, cave-ins, and equipment failures injured and killed hundreds, causing the mine's superintendent to tell one visitor in the 1850s that he did not expect workers to live past the age of forty-five. Another visitor described how the carrying of mercury proved "fatal work to the poor Mexicans who had to do it, the terrible muscular strain soon producing disease and death."[10]

Two independent investigators in 1855 helped quantify the dangers that Mexican miners faced in the years following American conquest of the state. Their survey of 7,748 local residents given medical treatment by the company's doctor between 1851 and 1855 revealed that 558 of those had died, or

7.2 percent. The most common injuries occurred when miners fell down ladders or were struck by falling rocks. Because of the "great muscular effort" exerted in climbing the mine's ladders, hauling mercury ore also took a severe physical toll in the form of "grave wounds or [bone] fractures." Between 1851 and 1854 at least 248 workers were injured ascending and descending those vertical passageways, and many of these *tanateros* suffered from "grave heart diseases, caused by the muscular strength" their jobs required. Other tasks proved even more fatal, however. Fire was a great danger, and underground explosions accounted for 20 deaths and 547 injuries during these years. In one typical incident in October 1887, three Sonorans—Agustín Alvarez, Ysidro Castro, and Marcelino Soto—lit a charge at the bottom of a shaft and unexpectedly encountered "some remnant of [a] giant powder cartridge, left unexploded in the debris." What had been left from that older cartridge caught fire, filling the shaft with a blast powerful enough to kill the men instantly. Although records on industrial accidents at the New Almadén mine remain incomplete, physicians' reports from 1891 show at least 51 major accidents above and below ground in that year alone. A federal government report from 1892 noted that Mexicans had a much higher rate of fatalities in the mine—nearly four times greater—than did "Anglo Americans." According to the report, while only 8.5 whites per one thousand died at New Almadén, Mexicans suffered from a death rate of 30.5 per thousand.[11]

An even more serious hazard jeopardized the health of all Spanishtown residents throughout the nineteenth century. More than gold or silver mining, mercury excavation and processing had tremendously deleterious effects on the local ecosystem, and residents' most serious ailments resulted not from underground explosions or other industrial accidents but rather from mercury poisoning. Beginning in the early 1850s, investigators in the Valley found that Mexicans at the mine were experiencing severe health problems. An observer noted with both optimism and horror in 1852, for example, that "The mine is inexaustable [*sic*]. The only difficulty is in getting men to work around the furnace. The foreman had only been engaged about four months when we saw him, and he was so saturated with Mercury that he shook like an aspen Leaf, and could scarcely carry on a conversation. Even the Horses about the Yard were salivated, and where the vapor from the Chimneys settles upon the hill sides for any time Vegitation [*sic*] is destroyed."[12] Neurological conditions such as "mercurial trembling" and "obstufecation or imbecility" became ghastly reminders of the new industrial system's consequences for ethnic Mexicans and others who labored in the Santa Clara Valley quicksilver mine. The ore caused deadly bouts of dysentery and diarrhea, as well as painful "rheumatic pains," and vapors from the mine often made breathing and perspiration difficult for those below and above ground. Miners who waded through shallow mercury-polluted pools of water at the bottom of New Almadén shafts often developed ulcers on

TABLE 3
Nonfatal Injuries Related to Mercury Gases at New Almadén, 1851–1854

Description	Number of Injuries	Number of Deaths
Pulmonary diseases caused by bad gases in different atmospheres	812	220
Asphyxia from said gases or bad ventilation	90	7
Phthisis, by above cause and humidity	87	87
Asthmatic affections from same causes	308	49
Ulcers in mouth or throat from mercurial gases	704	2
Extensive cutaneous eruptions from sulfurous gases	86	3
Totals	2,006	368

Source: Fernando Bernaldez and Ramón Rua Figueroa, "Memoirs of the Mines of Almadén and Almadéneos" (booklet, 1861).

their legs, and airborne mercury killed at least 368 and injured at least 2,006 in the first six years of American rule.[13]

Spanishtown's proximity to the mine's furnace, which "reduced" mercury from the minerals that surrounded it, assured that mercury fumes would have particularly devastating effects on the resident Mexican women and children. As the metal's poisons traveled beyond the mine's shafts, the non-miners in the community spent their days surrounded by the mine's toxic gases. The 1880 census counted dozens of local women and children among the sick, and in 1891 Joe Underwood, the Quicksilver Company doctor, reported the deaths of eleven individuals not employed by the mine. Of these deaths reported during a twelve-month period, nine were Mexican residents of Spanishtown, and six of those had suffered from pulmonalis, rheumatism, tubercular meningitis, and other ailments associated with mercury poisoning. Local Mexican children under the age of thirteen suffered disproportionately according to the doctor's 1891 tabulation, with the deaths of one-year-old Ana Guerra, two-year-old Santos Espinoza, eight-year-old Felix Marrijo, ten-year-old Maria Herrera, and thirteen-year-old Frank Gombia.[14]

While Mexican men remained prized for their sturdy backs and dexterity underground, managers and superintendents apparently gave little thought to the industry's effects on resident women and children. Although the company provided medical care to miners and their families by the 1860s, doctors such as W. S. Thorne often followed the company line in blaming wage workers for contracting mercury poisoning. In one instance in 1886, Thorne testified in court that "I have seen some very bad cases of salivation here; very bad; the worst that I ever saw; but in those cases which I treated they were cases where the men had done things that they were not required to do, and foolish things, and in fact things that they knew they ought not to do, and we put a stop to it."[15] While the deaths and injuries of local Mexican workers might have dramatized the enormous costs of the new economic and racial system, the declining health of Spanishtown residents instead served only to illustrate to white observers their triumph as the fittest Valley settlers. For most Californians, the harsh conditions at New Almadén did little to dull the glitter of the Gold Rush. But they did prompt mine employees to make new political demands and hone a sense of Latino identity for the first time in U.S. history.

THE POLITICAL CULTURE OF ETHNIC MEXICAN MINE WORKERS

Memories of the recent U.S. conquest of the Mexican north shaped the contemporary thinking of these residents. The Chilean Vicente Pérez Rosales expressed surprise at "the candor with which these people talked about the invasion and take-over of their country by the Yankees." Among the large Mexican community developing in the Valley arose a new political culture grounded, in part, in an identification with and concern about their home country. Viewing a fractured Mexico attempting to reconstruct itself after conquest by the United States, many Mexicans in California hoped for the emergence of a stronger central government in Mexico and consequently supported Benito Juárez and the liberalism of his Plan de Ayutla. Editorials in San Francisco's *La Crónica* and Los Angeles's *Clamor Público* expressed anger at both countries for agreeing to the Gadsden Purchase; and Latino residents around the state vehemently opposed the filibustering of U.S. citizens who invaded Latin American nations throughout the nineteenth century, particularly William Walker's 1855 expedition, which, the *San Francisco Chronicle* reported, had the effect of making "the entire Spanish race . . . antagonistic towards Americans." At New Almadén and in other ethnic Mexican communities throughout California, residents of Latin American descent at times used the term la Raza ("the race") both to describe their distinction from local whites and to emphasize their opposition to U.S. military interventions in the hemisphere. While certainly indicative of the "racial pride" that emerged to counter the anti-"greaser" racism of the 1850s and 1860s, the racial discourse about la Raza also reflected immigrants' concerns about the sovereignty and strength of their home countries.[16]

Other practices reinforced workers' ties to Mexico and Latin America. The challenge of surviving New Almadén's treacherous ladders and explosives prompted many to turn the Valley's mineshafts into sacred spaces by giving each underground passageway they built the name of a saint and by constructing a small altar to the Virgen de Guadalupe at the top of the main

Mexican and Chilean workers gathering to venerate a Catholic shrine at the top
of one of New Almadén's shafts, a sign of both persistent Latin American religious
practices and the felt dangers of mine work. BancPic 1963:002:1360:FR, Bancroft
Library.

shaft. At the beginning of each shift, according to one source, each worker
would "fall on his knees, and say his prayers, invoking the protection of the
saint during the day." In making such religious observances, Spanishtowners
also retained a sense of their own connections to Mexico and to Mexican
national citizenship as it had been defined since independence in 1821. Few
of these residents at New Almadén became naturalized U.S. citizens from the
1850s through the early 1880s, and available records document only two
such cases by 1860. Company statistics confirmed that the vast majority
(73%) of these men remained Mexicanos into the 1880s, and that only 13
percent had naturalized as U.S. citizens.[17]

Some of these residents were concerned about the fate of the United
States and its national government during the Civil War, as well. Prominent
Californios such as J. R. Pico visited the area to encourage naturalization and
voting in the 1860s, and José Ramón Pico, the nephew of the eminent Californio Andrés Pico, recruited locally for the Union's California Lancers in
March 1863. Speaking in downtown San José and summoning other "Sons
of California," he urged ethnic Mexicans to recognize that "Our country
calls, and we must obey! This rebellion of the southern states must be
crushed; they must come back into the union and pay obedience to the stars
and stripes. United, we will, by the force of circumstances become the freest
and mightiest republic on earth!" Instead of battling Confederate troops,

however, these Latino residents found themselves fighting Indians that December when the Lancers in "Company A sailed north by steamer to Humboldt Bay" to join the "ongoing campaign against the Hupa, Wintun, and other Indians in the northern region of the state." Thus continued Californios' longstanding role of suppressing native rebellions in the region.[18]

In addition to following these broader political developments, Sonorans and Californios at New Almadén developed local community institutions, social organizations, and cultural practices in response to local conditions. From the 1840s until its decline in the 1890s, Spanishtown boasted its own school, saloon, butcher shop, cemeteries, mutual aid societies, and recreational activities, many of which emerged because Mexicans were excluded from their counterparts in Englishtown. Access to many Spanishtown institutions was often restricted to male residents, and those at New Almadén—unlike some other ethnic Mexican communities in Northern California, including San Francisco and Nevada City—denied local women the opportunity to participate as members of mutual-aid and patriotic organizations.[19] Forged through segregation and committed to the male workers, Latinos in the area could rely on few other community institutions. For example, while residents of Englishtown enjoyed a school described as "the pride of Santa Clara County," Mexican boys and girls congregated in a small, poorly constructed one-room building. No high school for Mexicans existed at the mine, and in the fifty years after 1848 no Spanishtown student attended the high school in San José, located over an hour away.[20]

This racial segregation and geographical isolation helped forge common cultural practices among local residents in the 1850s and 1860s. Many Spanishtowners clearly felt attachments to their *colonia* similar to those expressed by ethnic Mexicans in Southern California neighborhoods during this period, and a sense of mutualism developed at the mine in the sharing of popular religious celebrations and the formation of Mexican patriotic societies. Chileans and Mexicans interacted with few conflicts, and the three Mexican-led mutual-aid organizations admitted Chilean workers as members.[21] Chilean men residing in the neighborhood were also clearly "Mexicanized." By 1860 nearly half of the resident Chilenos at New Almadén had married Mexicanas or Californianas, and the Chilean Pedro Ruíz Aldea, who traveled in the county in 1860, described how South Americans there had adapted themselves to the more numerically dominant Sonoran population. "In spite of being Chileans," he wrote with a tone of amazement, "a good part of the talk was over my head because they used Mexican words whose meanings I did not know." His account of life in Santa Clara County included translations of local phrases for the benefit of Chilean readers. In this changing context of transculturation, segregation, and physical danger in the years after 1848, local residents often placed great hope in returning to their *patrias*. San José's Jesús Islas led perhaps the most important effort of this sort by traveling throughout the state to gain support for his plan for re-patriation among *Mexicanos* and Californios disenchanted with racial discrimination and vigilante violence in the territory. Many of these residents living *en el extranjero* ("outside their country") wanted both to live in a safer political environment and to strengthen the recently threatened Mexican nation, although ideologies of race also shaped their motivations. Reflecting currents of anti-Indian racism that then strongly defined Mexican nationalism, Jesús Islas wrote in 1855 that "Now is the time to populate our frontiers with our useful, energetic population." Confronted with mounting Anglo racism, Mexicanos sought a measure of safety and empowerment through appeals to their transnational resources, whether local or back in Mexico.[22]

QUICKSILVER'S REFORMS

In 1863 New Almadén underwent another dramatic transformation, and as before the change was most sharply felt by the Valley's Latinos. In that year, Barron and Forbes sold its controlling interest in the mine to the Quicksilver Management Company of Pennsylvania. The new administration, led by former U.S. District Attorney Samuel L. Butterworth, took charge that November and slowly began to inaugurate new policies directed at controlling its workers living in Spanishtown. Mercury mining in the county had already proven enormously productive, and the changes instituted by corporate management emerged not as a reaction to economic crisis, but rather to assure that no labor troubles would stand in the way of New Almadén's continued success. The reforms that targeted Latin American residents were designed to maximize profits while imposing a greater degree of social order.[23]

Spanishtowners angrily responded to these developments, particularly those that seemed to threaten the health and safety of local residents. The physical dangers of living and working at New Almadén had reinforced miners' belief that they deserved greater respect from the recently arrived company officials. When an underground explosion severely wounded a miner named Gregorio in September 1864, residents expressed outrage that the Quicksilver Company, which had hired a doctor, required workers to pay a monthly fee to support his services. Further, despite the promise of quality care, Gregorio had received entirely unsatisfactory medical treatment, a fact, his neighbors insisted, that threatened the well-being of the entire community. An angry miner wrote *Nuevo Mundo* to complain that the doctor "gave [Gregorio] no immediate attention as was promised, and as a result the patient has gotten worse and will perhaps lose his life. What's this doctor for? Only to be ready to charge each worker $4. How wonderful!" According to residents, while the mine's previous owners had known enough "not to scorn the expectations and hopes of those [workers] who, abandoning their nation, family, and comforts, came drawn by jobs and industry to establish themselves in this mine," the new company had chosen instead to violate "serious and solemn promises" already made by Barron and Forbes. Most important, residents suggested repeatedly that while officials were "well within their rights" to control the actual operation of the mine, industrial workers and their families "owned" the segregated town. Responsibility for overseeing the administration of Spanishtown quickly became a cause of escalating conflict.[24]

The establishment of a company store became a key focal point of community anger. In late 1864 the company attempted to regulate Spanishtown's established "informal economy" of itinerant peddlers, water carriers, and other merchants in order to require residents to purchase all of their food and personal items at a "company store in which the whole community must buy their goods with a 75% commission added to the prices." To this, a newspaper correspondent reported, residents were ready to say "No, a thousand times no." Mexican peddlers traveling house to house had sold meat, corn, water, and other products in Spanishtown for more than fifteen years. Now company officials were treating this commerce in basic necessities as a "privilege" rather than a right long held by local people. Describing the company store, local Latinos protested in the pages of *Nuevo Mundo* about the sale of rotten meat, vegetables "that are 8 or 15 days old," and other items sold "at the most expensive price they can." Residents bristled not only at the low quality and high price of company goods, but at the very idea of a monopoly in their community. The location of the store itself near Englishtown required Mexican residents to walk far down the hill to reach it. In consequence, miners could no longer do simple things like buy supplies in the morning and still hope to work that day. Some bypassed the company store and walked fifteen miles to San José to purchase less expensive food and clothing on their free days. Some even smuggled items into Mine Hill to share with their neighbors, causing Quicksilver officials to station guards at the entrance of the company's property in late 1864. Indeed, to discourage travel to and from San José, mine officials established a toll road that charged residents a fee every time they entered or left Quicksilver property.[25]

The Quicksilver Company also announced that Mexican residents would no longer be allowed to operate small taverns and restaurants out of their homes, another practice that had thrived since the mine's inception. Selling liquor and food to miners had become a primary source of income for some residents, and the practice allowed workers to congregate together after their ten-hour shifts underground. Eager to control when and where these products were sold and intent on making a profit, company officials established a new neighborhood *cantina* designed to monopolize the sale of liquor. For male workers who had forged a leisure culture centered around drinking together after work, this attack on the neighborhood's public spaces seemed invasive. Incensed at this further intrusion, and charging the company's cantina with selling expensive rotgut, one resident speculated, "Who knows why many who drink there have not died."[26]

Such company reforms left a bitter taste in part because Spanishtowners believed that residents of this longstanding Mexican enclave had made significant sacrifices to California's industrial development. While transnational in their cultural orientation, local residents felt a strong claim on their own small corner of Northern California, their own beleaguered neighborhood. One miner suggested that Spanishtown residents could at any time in the past have decided to return to Mexico, and that only their "expectations and hopes" kept them from leaving an often hostile California environment. Others bristled that the company's reforms threatened the community's most marginal members. Basilio Nuñez, a seventy-year-old Mexican who had recently retired from company work after a ten-year stint, was one of many older residents no longer able to work underground who relied on peddling. He had long planned to survive during his later years by selling firewood to Spanishtown residents, and he had begun to spend his off days cutting timber on surrounding hillsides before quitting his job at the mine. Because Barron and Forbes officials had encouraged this practice and allowed their workers to chop wood on company land at no expense, Núñez had accumulated and hidden "40 or 50 loads" of firewood near the entrance to the company's property after more than a year of work, but when in 1864 he began to drive a small mule team uphill from his hidden piles to the homes in Spanishtown, the Quicksilver Company superintendent stopped him and told him that the wood in fact belonged to the new mine owners. In order to continue peddling, Núñez thereafter had to leave half of each load outside the superintendent's door every morning on his way up the hill to Spanishtown.[27]

As the matter of Núñez's wood suggests, company plans to establish ownership of all the natural resources within its territorial boundaries posed perhaps the most profound threat to Spanishtown residents. In January 1865 the superintendent informed the neighborhood that the company was the sole proprietor of all local real estate, even those buildings that employees had constructed since 1847. This marked an important change in New Almadén's development. Under the sixteen-year administration of Barron and Forbes, many local Mexicans had built their own wood homes, porches, fences, and gardens, turning Spanishtown into something of a haven for those who had earlier experienced racial discrimination and violence in other parts of the state. Although they may have known that the company legally owned the surrounding lands and the mines, Mexicans had reached an informal arrangement with Barron and Forbes during the 1850s that each house and its surrounding garden was the property of the residents who had labored to improve and maintain it. As the San José *Patriot* reported, "The owners and occupants of the homes at the mine made these improvements with the verbal consent, in some cases, and in other cases with the written consent of the previous owners of the mines who did not ask for rent." Now, the Quicksilver Company declared that they were entitled to these properties. In January 1865 the new managers asked residents to make a monthly rental payment that acknowledged this arrangement.[28]

Ethnic Mexicans reacted to this apparent effort to "steal" back Spanishtown with deep anger. Told by officials that "the land is ours—it's our place—those who don't like it should leave," most residents at first apparently refused either to pay rent or to abandon the homes they had built on Mine Hill. In the minds of at least some Spanishtowners, Quicksilver Company schemes to establish its ownership of their homes proved that officials would stop at nothing to inhibit the honest advancement of working people. One resident warned *Nuevo Mundo* that Mexicans who "live by the product of their labor" were under attack at the New Almadén mine, while another told of the "egotism, avarice, and unlimited rapacity" of mine officials.[29]

Conflicts over who owned Spanishtown were exacerbated by a final important policy change ushered in by the new company. In late 1864 the Quicksilver Company reformed the way it paid its employees. While Barron and Forbes had recompensed workers twice each month, giving workers greater control over their finances and the opportunity to settle personal debts and make purchases with cash on hand, the new management now decided to do so only once every thirty days. Moreover, underground miners would no longer be paid by the length of the shaft they excavated on a given day, but rather by the weight of the rock that they separated or hauled to the surface. As a result of these reforms, miners knew that they would not be able to measure their daily output for themselves and that they would have to trust their managers to calculate the wages honestly. Some employees began to whisper that their bosses were crooks. The *barateros* who crushed solid rock and separated its mercury also complained about new changes. Hired by Barron and Forbes on a more remunerative piece-rate system, their below-ground compatriots (the *tanateros*) had been the ones to measure each 300-pound unit before presenting it to be crushed above ground. But in early 1865, when Quicksilver officials instructed *tanateros* to carry the unprocessed ore in a series of much smaller wheelbarrows, the *barateros* complained that they could no longer keep track of how many pounds of rock they were receiving. They soon suspected that they were being cheated out of their pay, perhaps by half.[30]

As a result of the changes in the wage system and payment of rents, as well as the establishment of a monopolistic company store, many employees expressed concern about their economic livelihood and the very social structure of Spanishtown. Residents were often forced to borrow money from usurious company officials to purchase food at the end of each month since the various deductions meant "that the amount [of their paychecks] is not enough for them to support their families." Because residents paid high interest rates for such loans, one newspaper correspondent speculated that members of the community who had borrowed to pay for funerals had contributed richly to Quicksilver company coffers. With the high mortality rates at the mine, the writer wondered if "the child of a worker dies, and he needs $10 for the burial expenses, and not having it he borrows $20 [from the company store] and is obliged to give the owners $16 more in return, can this be legal?" An 1876 observer of arguments between local workers and mine officials noted that Spanishtowners uttered "murmurs not loud but deep" when they encountered such injustices.[31]

TRANSNATIONAL RESPONSES

New Almadén residents responded to Quicksilver Company reforms in a variety of ways during the 1860s. Spanishtowners viewed their changing world through a transnational lens, and both Mexican nationalism and a loyalty to their neighborhood animated political activities. More than two-thirds of the community's residents had been born in Mexico, most maintained their citizenship, and nearly all of them remained tied to their *patria* through the continuous movements of people, information, and culture between the two countries. Certainly many were shaped by memories of their participation in labor strikes and other political conflicts at Mexico's silver and copper mines. For many reasons, then, Spanishtowners paid close attention to the international events described in California's Spanish-language newspapers such as *La Voz de Méjico*, *Eco del Pácifico*, and San Francisco's *El Nuevo Mundo*. The latter reported receiving "many letters from New Almadén which announce that our favorable coverage of the hispano-american population in that place has been received with enthusiasm and thanks by every good Mexican patriot." Often read aloud in public to groups of Spanishtowners, the Spanish-language press remained critically important to local Latinos. As late as 1887 a store clerk at New Almadén reported the arrival of "about 100 copies of the weekly papers . . . in Spanish, besides many monthly papers and pamphlets, and books and so forth."[32]

The most pressing crisis in Mexico's brief history as a republic proved a remarkable catalyst to New Almadén's ethnic Mexicans. In 1862 French forces supported by Great Britain and Spain invaded Mexico to establish monarchical rule. As war raged between Mexican national forces and French armies over the next five years, the vast majority of Mexican citizens on both sides of the *frontera* put aside their political differences in a common effort to drive out the Europeans. Declarations of national unity and national sovereignty were strongly felt in northern Alta California, and the French occupation, which lasted until 1867, became a defining event that shaped Spanishtown politics. Cultural gatherings illustrated far more community concern for this crisis than for the U.S. Civil War. Local people sponsored fireworks, dances, and parades to assist Mexico in its nationalist struggle, and one correspondent predicted "that the union which exists here [between Mexicans] will be eternal."[33]

Expressions of Mexican nationalist sentiment became more heated among California's Sonoran population when the French occupied their home state during 1864 and 1865; many Mexican communities in Northern California then organized *juntas patrióticas* (patriotic committees) for the first time. Sonorans now saw "a foreign power trespassing on the venerable graves" of deceased parents and forebears in their home state. In this atmosphere, a local ethnic Mexican teacher instructed Spanishtown's children about the history of independent Mexico and the recent European occupation, and the pupils under his direction memorized patriotic editorials written in San Francisco's Spanish-language newspapers. Other residents sponsored theatrical productions, bullfights, and similar festivals to raise money for the military resistance in their *patria*, and speakers such as Ramón López used these occasions to urge Mexicans to "cease the fighting among brothers." At the encouragement of public speakers on September 16, residents of Spanishtown marched in Mexican independence celebrations under both the Mexican and Chilean flags. They enthusiastically adopted the anti-French *cinco de mayo* fiesta begun in 1863, a holiday soon celebrated in places as distant as California's Napa and Calaveras counties, Nevada's Reese River area, and the Oregon town of Umatilla. California's *juntas patrióticas* formed a statewide treasury, sending cash to Juarez's military forces, and immigrant Mexicanos in the Bay Area even ferried their own company of troops to Mexico in 1865.[34]

Concerns about Mexican politics also reflected and in turn shaped gender relations as nationalist demands and rhetorical symbols articulated a patriarchal interest in protecting Mexican women and restoring the "violated" Mexican nation to its prior state of well-being. In his 1865 call to "Los Mejicanos en la Alta California," Ignacio Manuel Altamirano urged "the beautiful daughters of Mexico [to] unite their enthusiasm with that of their husbands and fathers." Mexicanos in California exhorted one another to political action by developing a nationalist vision based on highly sexualized representations of Mexican history. These men referred to one another interchangeably as "sons of Mexico," "fellow citizens," "brothers," "valient Mexicans," and "fellow patriots." The spectacle of three young Spanishtown girls "capriciously dressed" in the colors of the Mexican flag at an independence celebration in September 1864 pointed to the idealization of female sexuality upon which this brotherhood of protectors was based, and Ramón López's September 1865 speech in San Francisco made more explicit the connection between a Mexican nationalist project and the recent loss of Mexico's female

Cinco de Mayo celebration in Spanishtown, late nineteenth century. These celebrants gathered around a large Mexican flag and carried paintings of Mexican President Benito Juárez as well as the Virgen de Guadalupe. New Almadén Mine Papers, box 117, folder 23.

purity under the French. As he reminded Northern California Mexican residents, "that beautiful soil on which you were born, is today watered with the blood of our brothers and the tears of the Mexican virgins who cry endlessly for the loss of their sons, brothers, husbands."[35]

While emphatically patriarchal in its structure and approach, the political culture at New Almadén was neither backward-looking nor simply "romantic." Valley residents in fact used a discourse of *Mexicanidad* to argue against the Quicksilver Company's reforms. One commentator likened their struggle in Spanishtown to a "holy cause" not unlike the one being fought against the French in Mexico. Another criticized mine officials for acting like imperialists who "oppress an entire population" and "dictate laws like one government inside another government." As Mexicans at New Almadén developed one of the most active *juntas patrióticas* in Alta California in 1863 and 1864, Ignacio Altamirano and other Mexicans in California noted angrily that, as national subjects, they had been twice conquered, first by the United States in 1848 and more recently by the French, and that the economic prosperity of California during the 1850s only accentuated Mexico's tragic loss of land, power, and prestige. And as these Valley residents worked to build regional industries such as New Almadén, Altamirano wrote, "Mexicans only know that this land is no longer theirs and that their sweat and their tears do not water the flowers of their own country."[36]

Antislavery rhetoric provided a language for expressing their dissatisfaction with conditions in Mexico and at New Almadén. Spurred in part by "the hunger which afflicts the people," as one letter writer put it, Mexican workers at New Almadén made constant use of antislavery symbols to compare their own fate at the hands of the mine owners with the efforts of the imperial French to "enslave" Mexico. Correspondents in *Nuevo Mundo* expressed anger that "the slaves for this establishment" had not been given the freedoms they deserved. A miner contrasted local conditions with the antislavery pronouncements of U.S. government officials in 1865, asking rhetorically whether "it is possible that in this land of liberty our unhappy brothers can be submerged underground in the most ignominious slavery?" *Nuevo Mundo* announced in November 1864 that the newspaper would cover the labor trouble developing in Santa Clara County "so that the government and people of the state will know that a great number of Mexicans are suffering the horrors of slavery." In a letter published in January 1863, as well, one worker rhetorically asked readers to consider "those who oppress labor, those who consider the proletariat slaves and cannot heed these orphans' emphatic cries of misery. . . . What do they deserve?" Consistently used to express outrage at the Quicksilver Company's new reforms, Spanishtowners used antislavery rhetoric to link their local demands to broader discussions of free labor and the French occupation of Mexico. In a speech given on May 5, 1865, Julio Barrio declared that "Mexico will never be a slave!" while other orators contended that the French, like the mine owners, had violated Enlightenment principles of "freedom" and "the will of the people." Likening such enemies to savages, Filomeno Ibarra, president of the Los Angeles *junta patriótica*, told Spanishtowners in September 1865 that "the barbarous Apaches and Comanches are more human than the civilized French."[37]

As Spanishtowners denounced the French occupation and cheered the anti-imperial, nation-building struggle in Mexico, they equated the Quicksilver Company to an imperial power and suggested that the company was somehow sympathetic to the French. Complaints about the dangers of mine work and the lack of medical care for Spanishtowners became another opportunity to remind residents of the presence of French invaders in Mexico. Just as they conflated the Quicksilver Company with imperial France, Spanishtowners complained that mine officials were guilty of clear racial discrimination. In discussions of the "despotic treatment" they received in both the United States and Mexico, workers complained in particular about the manager who oversaw the *barateros*, accusing the boss of "many acts of oppression" and "open hatred of all the *raza española*." One miner notified other ethnic Mexican residents of the state that the good reputation of all Latin Americans in the region was under attack, that "the new owners of the [New Almadén] mine have . . . called our neighbors at the mine assassins, indolent, gamblers." Residents responded that they were neither "greasers" or "gamblers," but rather "honorable," "industrious," "hardworking and patriotic." Ethnic Mexicans familiar with antigreaser racism in California not surprisingly believed that company officials had instituted their "avaricious" reforms at the mine in ways that took "advantage of [Mexicans'] situation and the difficulties presented everywhere in this country in finding work."[38]

Frustrated about a number of local and international matters by late 1864, Mexicans at the New Almadén mine reacted to the reorganization of labor relations and community life, the ongoing anti-imperial struggles against the French, racial discrimination directed at nonwhite workers, and the increased segregation of Spanishtown resulting from the establishment of the toll road dividing the community from San José. Writers at San Francisco's *Nuevo Mundo* argued that one chapter of the Mexican national struggle for "freedom" was being played out in Spanishtown, and residents believed that struggling against the mine owners was centrally important to "the Mexican cause." "As breezes from the Pacific arrive to fill our hearts with news of Republican triumphs by our national forces," *Nuevo Mundo* agreed in January 1865, "these enthusiastic patriots [at New Almadén], eminently republican, cannot throw themselves into the celebration because they are fighting the inequalities which victimize them, and are now passing through a period of trial the result of which cannot yet be guessed."[39]

This "period of trial" led Spanishtowners to launch what may have been the earliest ethnic Mexican–organized labor activities in U.S. history.[40] Outright protests against Quicksilver management began in November 1864 after mine workers who had complained to their foremen and supervisors about various problems were evicted from Mine Hill by a hired police force. After further discussions—probably during meetings of the local mutual aid society—Spanishtown residents asked Quicksilver management to remove the

toll gate separating them from San José and unsuccessfully lobbied the
County Board of Supervisors to build a public road connecting the mine to
that town. They also briefly investigated the possibility of bringing a legal
suit against the Quicksilver Company over the issue of who owned the
homes built by Spanishtowners. As these efforts were rebuffed or thwarted,
anger in the Spanishtown community grew to a crescendo. Finally, in January 1865 at least six hundred Mexican workers banded together with a small
group of Cornish employees to organize the Valley's first documented work
stoppage. They warned company representatives that they were prepared to
"resist from now on and forever working for that company in any capacity."[41]
Concerned about the payment of rent, the decrease in their wages, the location and prices of goods at the company store, and other issues, between
eight hundred and a thousand workers gathered to read their petition aloud
to the mine owners on January 21, stressing:

1. That [residents] can buy their provisions in San José or wherever they
    please, and that these provisions will be carried [up the road] from the
    Hacienda in the carts owned by the company, free. . . .

2. That [the owners] will inform them of the prices in San José so that the
    monopolists will comply with their contracts.

3. That the metal of the *barreteros* [*sic*] will be measured en *romana* [by
    the earlier method] and not brought in by the cartload.

4. That checks will be paid every eight or fifteen days, as the operators
    wish.

Motivated by the long national struggle in Mexico, striking workers presented themselves as a "community demanding justice," making a series of
impassioned speeches and crowding more closely together around the mine
officials as the day progressed. In response, frightened company officials
promised to comply with the terms of the petition.[42]

Three days later "most of the community" congregated in Spanishtown's
Catholic church to sign an agreement with the company superintendent. A
Nuevo Mundo correspondent noted that as workers stepped forward to add
their names to the list placed on an altar lit with candles, an image of "a
bleeding Christ" stood behind them. The apparent resolution of this "holy
cause" was, he reported, "a powerful moment which visibly moved everyone
present." Local Mexican men at the mine felt great pride at that event, vindi-
cated as protectors of their wives and families. But after another week, the
vast majority of residents felt compelled to launch a one-day walkout to
protest what they saw as "a new abuse," the mine director's announcement
that the company would in fact enforce its regulation prohibiting the sale of
liquor and the renting of homes by residents to others living in Spanishtown.

Residents soon returned to the mine, unsuccessful in their efforts to per-suade Quicksilver management to abandon this reform immediately, but having received new assurances that residents would be able to bring mer-chandise from San José, and that the company would transport items pur-chased there by cart up the long hill to Spanishtown free of charge.[43]

Caught by surprise, the company never intended to concede to the de-mands of the miners. Within days after the supposed agreement with work-ers, mine officials struck back. First, the company superintendent fired the workers' spokesperson, José Garne, and ordered him and an unnamed *Nuevo Mundo* correspondent to leave New Almadén. Next, the Mexican cantinas were shut down and the toll road was patrolled with greater vigilance. More ominously, the Quicksilver Company then persuaded both the county sheriff and the state militia to become involved; when the company learned that the miners planned to strike on January 30, officials summoned County Sheriff Adams and informed him that Mexican "greasers" in Spanishtown hoped to steal "some $30,000 intended for the payment of the men." Believing that Mexicans' natural criminality was behind the trouble, Adams feared that if he did not intervene "the Mexicans at Almadén might assassinate me." He contacted the Northern California regiment of the Union Army, and its commander General McDonnell agreed to provide support to the Quick-silver Company if local miners did not return to work on the thirtieth of that month. Infantrymen camped ready "to quell the anticipated outbreak" of trouble for an entire week, apparently intimidating the mine workers enough to keep them at their jobs for the remainder of 1865.[44]

While workers apparently remained quiescent over the next thirteen months, the high level of community organization and interest in Mexican and Latin American politics continued to focus and mold discontent. In November 1865 Spanishtowners sent the Mexican consul more money for the Juaristas than any other *junta patriótica* in Northern California. And when Spain invaded Chile following the work stoppage in January 1865, Chilenos at New Almadén formed their own patriotic associations, sent do-nations to their national military, and helped bring local Chileans and Mexi-cans—the *raza española*—even closer together by the end of the year. One Chilean at the mine announced at a Mexican patriotic fiesta that "the sons of South America gathered here cannot see you as anything but brothers . . . our destiny has been the same." In the months after the January 1865 labor conflicts, then, Spanishtown residents emphasized that their common ideals of brotherhood and fair play set them apart from the "scandalous acts" com-mitted by French invaders, Spanish armies, and mine officials. Proud of their antislavery allegiances, one letter writer reported that when Spanishtown re-ceived the news that Lincoln had been killed, for example, "we felt just as if [Mexico's former President] Benito Juárez had been the victim." After lower-ing their Mexican flags to half-mast, Spanishtowners registered shock at the "audacity" of company police agents who had mockingly raised and half-lowered an Austrian flag of their own above a company-approved tavern. When these company representatives then "crowned [the banner] in flowers" for all to see, ethnic Mexican observers were certain that they had witnessed another attempt to honor the Austrian Emperor Maximilian, an act of mockery in which, the miner suggested, the police "validat[ed] the oppression in which they keep the Mexicans in this mine."[45]

The escalating efforts to defeat occupying European armies in their homelands reinforced intense interest in local and international politics among New Almadén's Latin American residents. Workers remained angry that Quicksilver officials had almost immediately begun to violate the promises made in early 1865, and when homeowners in Spanishtown agreed to acknowledge company ownership by paying rent, these residents complained that the required amount proved difficult to pay. Furthermore, despite the company's stated commitment to set prices at its store consistent with those in San José, in practice local rates remained higher. Finally, while the company had acceded to paying workers more often and returning to the older system of weighing their output, the Quicksilver Company still managed to lower workers' wages by changing the amount it agreed to pay miners and barateros for each unit of work performed.[46]

In March 1866, fourteen months after the first strike in January 1865, Spanishtown residents launched another work stoppage. After an initial strike that lasted just four days, residents reopened their lawsuit against the company. When they learned that the district court would probably reject their arguments, however, they struck again on April 10 and this time remained off their jobs for eleven days. As tempers flared, a Nuevo Mundo correspondent called it not a strike but an "insurrection," and public opinion within the local Mexican community supported calls for dramatic change in the administration of the mine. The journalist noted that "the insurrectionists are for the most part Mexicans; they have taken over the mine and they will not let anyone work. They complain of the same offenses which they pointed to last year. . . . As of yet they have committed no act of violence." Spanishtown's junta patriótica mexicana, which had just been revived under new leadership a month before to collect monthly donations "dedicated to the republican army of Mexico," took the lead. New junta President Francisco Lauterio, Secretary Jesús Posada, and the other fifty-seven men who formed the core of the group provided leadership in the strike and wrote José Godoy, the Mexican consul in San Francisco, to request his help in ending the conflict with Quicksilver management. In early April, after Godoy had visited the area to inspect conditions and speak with residents, the consul wrote the Quicksilver Company a letter supporting the demands of Spanishtown residents "in the name of all the Mexicans of New Almadén."[47]

Mine officials responded that the consul had "assumed an authority which did not correspond to his own" and angrily denied that Mexicans had the right to make appeals for help to another national government. Jedidiah Smith had written the U.S. consulate in 1827 to complain about what was happening to him in the Valley, and New Almadén's mine workers turned to an embattled Mexico for help with their problems. Quicksilver officials, in an attempt to subvert workers' demands, capitalized on Gold Rush racism to brand Mexicans as "criminals" and to charge that "fifty Chileans and Mexicans, gamblers and bandits" had begun striking to "depriv[e] the industrious miners of their savings." When the mine's owners attempted to send these so-called undesirable residents away, officials claimed, troublemakers had "formed a confederation," threatening that, unless the Quicksilver management allowed them to stay, "they would not allow anyone to work in the mine, and in order to carry out their threat they have taken up arms." Claiming that they were protecting the "honest" majority of workers who resented the Mexican criminal element, mine officials summoned the county sheriff as they had in 1865. Sheriff Adams promptly arrested five strikers and threatened others, but nearly all of the mine's Mexican workers joined the walkout and maintained their strike until April 21. Ramón Tirado and Jesús Alari, members of the local *junta patriótica mexicana*, both defended the Mexican consul's right to advocate on behalf of local immigrants and made clear that members of their community, "mostly Mexicans, are neither bandits nor vagrants, nor have they aligned themselves with thieves in order to reclaim their rights."[48]

THE AFTERMATH

Although the courts soon settled the workers' legal case about Spanishtown properties in favor of the Quicksilver Company, the eleven-day strike brought these New Almadén residents considerable short-term success. Mine officials signed an agreement written by the strikers on April 19 that addressed their longstanding complaints. In addition to establishing specific guidelines outlining the limited terms under which the company could purchase workers' homes, this new contract established a lower rental rate of two dollars paid every six months and guarded against fraud in the payment of wages. According to the contract, "it has been agreed that the company or its agents will not weigh the metal that has been extracted from the mines by those on contract . . . unless the owners of the metal [the workers] are present in person or in the person of one empowered by them if they cannot be found after a zealous search." In an apparent victory for striking Mexican workers in California, the company president also signed a personal guarantee assuring residents that they could continue to shop for their personal items in San José.[49]

But while that contract included guarantees for twenty years, most local ethnic Mexican residents enjoyed these new terms for only a brief period of time. In part as retaliation against a Latino community thought to be unruly and demanding, Superintendent Randol set out to replace Mexican and Chilean workers with Cornish and other white workers in the 1870s. In language that echoed the "racial fault lines" of late-nineteenth-century Anglo-Saxonism, high-ranking mine employees of the Quicksilver Company supported the bleaching of the labor force, arguing that Mexicans were nonwhites, "greasers," "renegades of justice," and "slaves who lowered the standards of non-Mexicans in the County." As these remarks make evident, explanations for this new policy rarely pointed to Mexicans' recent political activities. Or, if they did so, it was done obliquely. Schoolmaster and Justice of the Peace G. E. Lighthall contended that lawless Mexicans had given the New Almadén mines a reputation "as one of the bad places in the state" to live, "one of the worst" regions of California and an embarrassment to Santa Clara County. Tales told by mine officials that Spanishtown had long been "a rendez-vous for Mexican banditti," particularly "the notorious [Tiburcio] Vásquez," echoed white settlers' ongoing opposition to Mexicans in Santa Clara County. Although some ethnic Mexican workers remained after Randol took over the administration of the mine in 1870, hundreds of others left against their will during Randol's tenure, and only 115 "Mexicans, Chileans, etc." remained as company employees by 1886.[50]

While de facto ownership of Spanishtown therefore passed out of ethnic Mexican hands during the 1870s, those who remained continued to experience a dual wage system into the twentieth century, another critical legacy of the Gold Rush era. Corporate pay records from 1881, the best available data on company wages and deductions, profile a system in which Mexicans labored for lower pay, were hired for fewer days each month, and usually kept a smaller proportion of their paychecks than did non-Mexicans. Forced to make purchases at inflated prices and often on credit at the company store, those who remained found that "this rule amounted to peonage," as one non-Mexican observer put it.[51]

The aftermath of the strike therefore signaled both continuity and change. Although there is no evidence that Mexicans participated in any other local labor strikes, residents of the Santa Clara Valley did maintain their interest in Mexican political affairs over the following decades. Indeed, it was this transnational loyalty that proved defining. Ideas of "slavery" and "freedom," the development of political demands, definitions of gender relations, and interactions with non-Mexicans continued to be shaped by events and discourses originating outside of the United States. When asked about Mexican electoral practices in Spanishtown in a 1886 court hearing, the Los Angeles–born Adolfo Banales told the jury that, when they voted in local elections, Mexican-origin residents always cast their ballots for the Republican Party be-

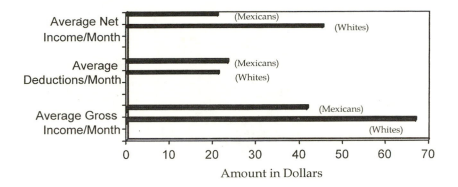

Income and deductions of mine workers in Santa Clara County in 1881.

cause "The Republican Party in this country corresponds somewhat to what is called the Liberal Party [of Benito Juárez] in Mexico, which holds a large majority there." Andreas López agreed, noting that the twenty-eight Mexican-origin voters living at the mine all preferred the Republicans "on account of that being the same as the Liberal Party in Mexico."[52]

Along with a political interest in Mexico, deeply rooted cultural practices based in the maintenance and politicization of *mexicanidad* also survived well into the 1890s. In this regard, the Santa Clara Valley's mercury miners certainly anticipated some of the interests and efforts of later residents of the San José area, although the history of nineteenth-century labor activities would be little remembered by the early 1900s. In part that disconnection with the past resulted from the fact that most residents of New Almadén left the mine soon after the strikes ended. California saw a virtual cessation of Mexican immigration from the 1860s until the 1890s, but Mexican patriotic celebrations and religious traditions still survived as cultural practices. Local institutions such as mutual aid societies, *juntas patrióticas*, and the Mexican brass band continued to develop over those decades, latent forms of social protest that remained unconnected to organized political movements for the remainder of the nineteenth century. The resurgence of Mexican immigration to California in the twentieth century ushered in a new era for the Santa Clara Valley. What followed was a revolution in local agriculture, regional politics, and urban ethnic relations, developments that would rock the state for generations.[53]

Chapter 4

Residence in Revolution

> We came to pick apricots for the first time in 1926 or so.
> I was small but I was out there, too, because my mother
> wanted my help. Not that there was really anywhere else
> for me to go when my parents were working. . . .
>
> We lived on the East Side in barrio *piojo* with the
> others who came from Texas, Mexico, and everywhere
> else. The people worked in the fields, in the canneries,
> and in other jobs. It wasn't heaven, I can tell you that.
> —Lydia Ramírez (1995)

The stories of two San Joseans encapsulate many of the struggles over residency, race, and work that remade the Santa Clara Valley after the New Almadén strikes. The first belongs to Sarah Winchester, heiress to the Winchester Repeating Rifle fortune. Prior to her 1884 move to Northern California, this American widow began in paranoid fashion to fear the vengeful retribution of Indians and Mexicans, the ghosts killed by her family's rifles. Other Californians also tried to make sense of "the closing of the frontier," the presumed end to the sort of violent race relations emblematic of the Gold Rush. But Winchester grappled with the past in extraordinary ways. She visited a spiritual medium and decided to build a house that would confuse those evil spirits, seeking her security in late-nineteenth-century San José. Few of the white Americans and European immigrants arriving in the state during the late nineteenth century showed a similar anxiety about the violent past of the American West. Fearful of frontier vengeance even from beyond the grave, Winchester employed scores of working-class San Joseans, carpenters, craftsmen, and others, in her mad hope that constant construction would frustrate wrathful ghosts. The scheme proved successful enough until 1922. With her death, Winchester left behind both a mansion and a city dramatically changed since the 1880s, her chaotic home a bizarre parody of the region's late-nineteenth- and early twentieth-century growth, a pathetic gesture to racial violence, and a strange memorial to the past.[1]

A second individual experienced life in the Santa Clara Valley in radically different ways. Lydia Ramírez, an immigrant woman who first arrived in the area during the 1920s, just after the death of Sarah Winchester, was a migrant refugee of the Mexican Revolution, one of hundreds of thousands who moved into the United States as a result of that conflict. As the following pages suggest, her local story calls attention to a set of transformations that would dramatically reshape California during the 1910s and 1920s. The emerging agricultural economy defined the fortunes of ethnic Mexicans like Ramírez, and the San José area became just one of her family's many stops on their seasonal labor circuit. Thousands like her became acquainted with the South Bay as migrant farmworkers in the early twentieth century, and their arrival initiated a sort of "demographic reconquest" of a territory that Mexico had lost in war some seventy years before. Many of these new immigrants felt unwelcome or confined to the county's least hospitable neighborhoods. Permanent residency remained a difficult achievement for most, and few found year-round security in the Valley. Seasonal labor defined their daily lives, and the majority entered the local economy near the bottom and stayed there. These new immigrants found no California dream on the streets of San José. Instead, Ramírez and other children attended school only episodically, and immigrant parents discovered that nineteenth-century racism had established tangible barriers to local employment and settlement.[2]

Few white San Joseans recognized the struggles of their ethnic Mexican contemporaries. While historians have long described colorful San Joseans like Sarah Winchester, most have skipped quickly over mention of poor workers like Ramírez. Even fewer hint of ethnic Mexican perspectives on Valley society prior to World War II, although their movements, work lives, and political activities defined the early twentieth-century Valley. Rewriting the California past requires listening to residents long ignored by official state chroniclers. Oral testimonies with Ramírez and her contemporaries illuminate the segregated shadows of local barrios and low-wage labor. They focus on obstacles to good employment and clean housing, they recall the vitality of Mexican immigrant culture, and they remember challenges to local racism and its often violent political and economic consequences. Ramírez and other immigrants confronted the ghosts of the past, and they set the stage for later generations who would make the Valley more like heaven than hell. By the 1930s Mexicanos would begin to revolutionize this Valley long haunted by repeating rifles and damning divisions of race.

FRUITS OF REVOLUTION

Transformations in the local economy guided the ethnic Mexican community's modern foundations after 1900. Production at New Almadén had dropped off considerably, making that large industrial mining center at best a secondary industry in Santa Clara County. Six municipalities in California boasted more industries than San José in 1930, the urbanization of San Francisco and Oakland clearly outpaced that of the Valley, and despite the efforts of boosters to promote San José's industrial capacity, the county remained primarily agricultural during the first three decades of the twentieth century. Wheat production, which had dominated local agriculture and required little year-round labor, gave way by 1900 to the cultivation of fruits, profitable perishables that demanded larger numbers of seasonal workers for Valley crops to be picked on time.[3]

Given its profit potential, the fruit industry quickly became the dominant agricultural industry in the Santa Clara Valley, and developers urged new white settlers "to secure small orchard farms that pay." Similar calls guided the planting of fruit groves in Orange County and other parts of Southern California during these years. In making orchards of fields, growers by 1930 devoted 65 percent of Santa Clara County land to fruit trees; only 10 percent had been used for this purpose in 1890. Prunes became the dominant local cash crop, transforming the Santa Clara Valley into the nation's leading exporter of the fruit during the 1920s and contributing to the establishment in San José of numerous packing sheds and canneries. A national center of fruit production, the Santa Clara Valley gained fame among consumers throughout the United States as an Edenic land of peaches, apricots, and prunes, fruits increasingly picked and processed by Latino hands.[4]

The majority of these ethnic Mexican workers in the 1910s and 1920s were recent arrivals, and broad political and economic changes governed the movements of the more than one million who immigrated to the United States during these years. Few descendants of conquered Californios or mid-nineteenth-century Sonoran miners remained in the San José area or other parts of California, but the labor demands of the state's urban industries and irrigated agriculture proved a powerful draw to new groups of Mexicanos. Limits placed on European and Asian immigration to the United States assured labor shortages in these sectors of the economy, and as new transportation systems made travel both from Mexico and within the United States more convenient, railroads enabled Mexicans to flee the political turmoil that engulfed their country. From 1876, a short nine years after the departure of French imperial armies, until 1911, Mexico had been ruled by the dictator Porfirio Díaz. Bent on promoting foreign investment in his country's mines and other industries, he came under ever more heated attacks, many

An elderly Mexican woman picking tomatoes in the Santa Clara Valley during the 1930s. Farm Service Administration Papers, box 3, folder 152, Bancroft Library.

launched by Mexican expatriates living in Texas and California, and revolutionary armies soon gathered against him to contest Mexico's future. The subsequent violence touched virtually every corner of that country over the following thirty years, contributing to political instability and economic poverty.

As they left towns and villages in central Mexico for points north, many followed family members who had sent news about the United States. Migration triggered processes of cultural change, as future Northern Californians came into contact with other parts of Mexico for the first time when they left their local communities behind. On a long train ride to Mexico City in the 1920s, for instance, María Soto was taught to play guitar and sing the popular songs of Jalisco by a fellow passenger. Leaving his hometown gripped by political debates about national development, Robert Montalvo met and married Josefa Camacho, and the two subsequently departed together for Cananea, Sonora. "It impressed me a great deal," he wrote in a half-finished

memoir in 1957, "to see everyone going from place to place. We were all
Mexicans, all searching for something. I carried the images of us all on
trains, in carts, on horses when I crossed the border into the United States."
Strong allegiances to home villages and states remained, and political conflicts within Mexico—between liberals and conservatives, between church
and state, and between Mexico City and other regions, to name a few—
retained a strong influence on those migrants. But there can also be no
doubt that migration changed the worldview of many.[5]

Those who fled into the United States founded new barrios, reshaped
existing communities, and took jobs in Pennsylvania steel mills, Detroit auto
factories, Chicago meatpacking plants, and California agriculture. Along the
Pacific coast, many traveled a thousand miles each year as migrant farm
laborers, moving from Imperial Valley pea fields in February, to Santa Clara
County apricots every June, to Fresno County grapes each August. Unlike
those who put down roots in Los Angeles, San Antonio, Houston, and other
urban U.S. locales, the vast majority of ethnic Mexicans who lived in the San
José area worked in agriculture. Orchards and canneries dominated the local
economy, hiring thousands of workers during peak seasons, and throughout
the state the rural farm labor force became Latinized. Orchardists profited
from the new immigration. During the 1920s local agriculturalists like
Charles C. Derby easily found summer crews to pick his produce, having
only to erect tents to attract those migrants. Such employment proved relatively enticing to Mexicanos already familiar with low-wage field work and
rigid racial segmentation in other parts of the United States. Many arrived
from Texas, from the Pacific Northwest, and from California's Imperial Valley; and while their jobs remained at the bottom of Santa Clara county's pay
scale during the 1920s, these migrants could still earn wages slightly higher
than their counterparts elsewhere.[6]

As in other parts of the Southwest, racial ideologies defined the Santa
Clara Valley labor market, and most local ethnic Mexican men and women
remained bound within restricted employment sectors. Policymakers and
journalists frequently affirmed that Mexicans were naturally suited to back-
breaking agricultural work. Few Mexicanos entered skilled and professional
positions between 1900 and 1940, and San José claimed its first Mexican
American public employee only in the mid-1920s when the former barber
and messenger service operator Manuel Castillo joined the city's police department. Castillo's was an exceptional case. Approximately 82 percent of all
ethnic Mexicans worked in unskilled and seasonal occupations by 1920,
common laborers who shared little of the economic prosperity enjoyed by
the "Valley of Heart's Delight," as local boosters had begun to call the San
José area. Work experiences shaped ethnic Mexican identities. Performing a
variety of tasks, the local resident Ray Salazar insisted that he and other
Mexican American men were simply "Jacks-of-all-trades, masters of none,"

TABLE 4

Permanent Mexico-Born and U.S.-Born Mexican Residents of Santa Clara County, 1910 and 1920

Year	# Born in Mexico	# Born in U.S.	% of Mexicans Born in Mexico
1900	65	489	13.3
1910	89	538	14.2
1920	261	651	28.6

Source: Federal Manuscript Census, Santa Clara County, 1900, 1910, and 1920.

experienced in mixing tar for construction sites, picking cotton in Central Valley fields, pruning fruit trees in the Santa Clara Valley, and performing other, similar labor at low pay. A writer from San Francisco's *La Crónica* called these jobs "punishing" occupations, tasks often dangerous and sometimes fatal to employees. Injuries were common, and just as many had suffered death or disability at New Almadén in earlier decades, ethnic Mexicans now frequently fell from ladders, were maimed by machines, or developed maladies related to pesticide exposure or unsanitary work conditions. By the 1950s the rural and cannery workforce annually reported more than four hundred disabling accidents each year, many of them suffered by children under the age of seventeen. And sadly, as agriculture boomed, orchardists and politicians affirmed that ethnic Mexicans belonged on these low and often dangerous rungs of the regional economic ladder.[7]

Many European immigrants had occupied similar positions as common laborers in the Valley in the late nineteenth century, but rhetoric about their natural skills had not restrained them for long. Comparisons of Italian, Spanish, and Portuguese immigrants to blacks, though infrequent, underwent processes of alchemic change throughout the country as notions of whiteness were redefined around the turn of the century. Broadening the boundaries of that racial category to include "swarthy" southern Europeans, the nativist *San Jose Letter*, for a time the organ of the local Populist Party, illustrated this complex transmutation. At first, its editors called upon local "white Americans" to oppose the settlement of racially suspect Portuguese immigrants, advising that "it would be well for employers to try the experiment of giving men of their own color and nationality the preference over Chinese and imported European paupers, particularly when the white Americans are willing to work for the same wages as their Asiatic and European brethren."[8] The distinction made between "white Americans" and others in 1896, and the parallel drawn between "Chinese" and "European paupers," indicated that opposition to southern and eastern European immigrants remained very much alive. But the editors changed their tone over the following year. Criticizing the county's four dollar poll tax for its maltreatment of

Workers in a Valley pear orchard during the early twentieth century. European immigrants had worked in county fruit orchards before Mexicans came to dominate the industry by the 1920s, but those Portuguese and Italian residents also enjoyed greater opportunity to move into more remunerative work. Alice Hare Collection, 04984, Bancroft Library.

"free white men eligible for naturalization," the journalists now worried that European immigrants and other poor whites would no longer vote. Discussing the place of those residents in California, the *San Jose Letter* urged readers to see, after all, that "we are considering white men—not Chinamen or negroes."[9]

While apparent for a time in the late nineteenth century, anti-Italian and anti-Portuguese nativism did not dominate political concerns for long in Santa Clara County, and the widespread acceptance of European immigrants and their U.S.-born children as "white Americans" emerged hand in hand with more salient hostilities toward those considered to be nonwhite. Along with other images of black primitivism, minstrel shows shaped a sense of whiteness among local European immigrants and their children by the 1920s. Northern Californians also invented other ways to urge one another to oppose the arrival of less desirable settlers. Hoping to contrast the rural South with his own Valley of Heart's Delight, one local merchant hired a young African American boy to pretend to fish in a muddy San José street hole after a heavy rainstorm, thereby dramatizing the need for new urban improvements by warning that unpaved sidewalks might attract black migrants.[10]

Even more important to the formation of white racism in the Valley was contemporary thinking about the "Asian menace," as opposition to immigrants from that part of the world had a long history in the area. Nearby San Francisco was an important hotbed for anti-Asian movements, mid-nineteenth-century Chinese immigrants had experienced intense discrimination and violence at the hands of white San Joseans (including the burning of the city's segregated Chinatown in 1870 and 1887), and local Japanese immigrants, who began to arrive in the Valley just prior to 1900, were met with similar attacks. The American Federation of Labor's national policy rejected Asians as members of unions. San José followed that lead. European immigrants by the early twentieth century complained about sharing jobs and living space with Asians, and AFL officials in San José affirmed during the 1920s that "whites won't mix" with Asians on the job site. Hortense DiMercurio, who grew up in the area during the 1930s, remembered that "many Italians were more prejudiced" toward nonwhites than were native-born residents of the area.[11]

Throughout California, boosters tried during the 1910s and 1920s to recruit "white families from the Eastern states" as permanent residents, appealing "to the Jeffersonian ideal of yeoman farmers living in autonomous rectitude on the land" in their advertisements about the virtues of the Golden State. Many white residents of the county experienced significant upward mobility in the early twentieth century, as congressional limits on immigration from Europe helped to boost the fortunes of those immigrants and their children. Local labor unions and the Italian American political machine assisted many co-ethnics to leave field work for urban employment, while other residents moved into professional positions in the city, profiting from ties with already established Italian American residents such as the wealthy, San José–born A. P. Giannini, founder of the Bank of Italy, or the Murphy family, descendants of an Irish settler who had been the Valley's wealthiest resident in the nineteenth century. During periods of extended unemployment, European immigrants and native-born whites also began to monopolize access to local welfare services. San Jose's Associated Charities, the area's most important employment service after its establishment in 1893, often channeled needy Italians, Portuguese, and other residents of European descent into local jobs, helping to assure that those denizens would not depart the region. The organization rarely offered assistance to Mexicans or other nonwhites into the 1920s, however, and unionists repeatedly expressed concern that the provision of county welfare would encourage Mexicans to stay permanently.[12]

Agriculture in the Valley provided many white San Joseans the opportunity to obtain orchards in the booming new fruit economy. Ethnic Italians,

Portuguese, and Spaniards, along with native-born Americans, accumulated new tracts devoted to the cultivation of those perishables, and property-holding in the Valley appeared democratic on the surface, available to immigrants and nonimmigrants alike. Most farms remained small, family-owned concerns, averaging just eighty-two acres in 1930. While there were few large-scale "factories in the field" like those found in many other agricultural regions of California, landed residents of the Valley were rarely amenable to Mexican immigrants as permanent residents and potential citizens; instead, they were more likely only to value Mexicanos as a naturally mobile, low-wage labor force. Most vocal was San José's Congressman Arthur M. Free, a member of the House Immigration Committee, who argued in 1930 that California needed "Mexican labor for harvesting crops and doing work under desert suns that white men could not be found to do."[13] Similar rhetoric dominated discussions of Mexican immigration at the national level, and proponents of Mexican immigrant workers in the Valley went so far as to claim that the temporary residency of Mexican laborers provided a unique and enlightened means of cultural uplift. Promoting a vision predicated on the understanding that ethnic Mexicans wouldn't settle in the region, some argued that their employment in California fields would have the effect of modernizing Mexico, "lift[ing] from bondage the peon, this vast, undeveloped, primitive group," when these workers returned to that country. San Joseans often affirmed that Mexicans had no real capacity for assimilation into the United States. As C. N. Thomas, director general of the International Council for Education Progress, stressed: "90%" of Mexico was not "Spanish" but Indian. Mexican peons, added Thomas, were "like children" and not "our equals intellectually and culturally."[14]

While they welcomed Mexicans as temporary workers, the Valley's white residents often contended that any permanent settlement by that population would threaten the region. Ethnic Mexicans, they claimed, had a high birth rate ("the greatest of any race on earth"), lived in "squalid quarters," earned "wages 30 to 50 percent lower than the American workman gets," and either spent their money "with Mexican shopkeepers" or sent their cash back to Mexico. Some noted the increased size of Mexican immigrant communities and feared that these workers might advance into the Valley's construction and urban trade jobs. Indeed, AFL unionists charged that San José's business elite was actively importing Mexicans as part of a deliberate union-busting campaign.[15] Many working-class San Joseans feared that big business would turn their city into another Los Angeles, complete with resident "underpaid and non-citizen Mexicans" who force "home-loving Americans [to] tramp the streets looking for work." Pointing to the recently built Hotel Sainte Claire, a modern structure designed to attract business travelers and tourists "constructed, decorated, and furnished by men long resident in this city," AFL members in 1926 maintained that such projects offered proof that San

José would benefit by denying Mexicans any opportunity to secure year-round Valley employment. National citizenship became a defining trope in assertions that Mexicans ought to be treated as "aliens" ineligible for local jobs and understood as racially distinct from whites. Pointing to recent Supreme Court decisions in the *Thind* and *Ozawa* cases, which confirmed during the 1920s that Asians could not be naturalized, Bay Area unionists labeled Mexicans "Indian peons . . . not even eligible for American citizenship." Some white San Joseans compared Latino "peons" to the "Chinese menace" and the "yellow peril," and they protested that Mexicans would depress wages to "oriental levels" if allowed to stay in the region. And as in the nineteenth century, U.S.- and European-born whites also represented ethnic Mexicans as criminals, noting, for instance, that Mexicans had already "made quite a mark in criminal cases in our Superior Courts" and that "when you read the paper, the police column was filled with Mexican drunks and stabbings."[16]

This rhetoric brought ugly consequences for ethnic Mexicans who worked and lived in the Valley after the outbreak of the Mexican Revolution in 1910. San José unionists helped write a local resolution that guaranteed that public jobs would be awarded only to U.S. citizens, and a committee of AFL unionists within Santa Clara County's Central Labor Council considered a repatriation campaign against Mexicans in 1931, modeled on a similar program in Los Angeles County. As the Valley's labor press continued vocally to support such actions, the racialization of labor kept ethnic Mexicans out of key industries. Ethnic Italians and Portuguese women employees fiercely guarded the food processing jobs they had entered before World War I, and Italian and native-born American owners of local canneries required a six-month residency period "to limit job applications by Blacks, Asians, and Hispanics." As a result, only 382 of the county's 11,231 cannery workers were ethnic Mexicans in 1930, and Mexican women would only take over the cannery workforce when ethnic Italian and Portuguese women moved into more lucrative work during World War II. Prior to the 1940s, racial violence also frequently reared its head in work conflicts. San Francisco's *Hispano-America* reported in 1931 that a "ferocious" farm manager, attempting to evict all the Mexican workers from his ranch, shot Timoteo Aldana twice without provocation. And when local sheriffs throughout Northern California jailed vagrant Mexicanos unable to make ends meet, San Francisco's Mexican Consul Ramón P. de Negri and that city's newspaper *Hispano-America* protested the thirty-day sentences to the governor of the state.[17]

Often enforced by violence, the racialization of labor and residency offered ethnic Mexicans a narrow range of local opportunities. One white resident made the prescient case that, when it came to employment, "there was a distinction between us white people in San José and those Mexicans. For one thing, they had the unskilled jobs, being the hod carriers and not the brick-

layers, the carpenters' helpers but not the carpenters, never the road contractors but the team drivers who delivered road gravel and spread it." Public
rhetoric and government activities solidified their position as common construction workers and seasonal fruit pickers, and employers and city fathers
overwhelmingly supported calls by the late 1910s to use Mexicans only in
these roles. While many ethnic Mexicans hoped to stay year-round in the
region, to raise families apart from the migrant labor cycle, and to establish
new homes, white residents responded with antipathy to those prospects and
feared that visible ethnic Mexicans settlements would spoil their Valley of
Heart's Delight. W. K. Roberts, the justice of the peace in Sunnyvale (located
just north of San José), was one of many who voiced this common concern.
Arguing for the need to restrict Mexican immigration and fearing an end to
the region's "Edenic" conditions, he complained that Mexican immigrants
"form colonies, and when they do the white people move out. . . . I want to
put in my plea for the white man and against any colored race." Other San
Joseans worried that Mexican settlement threatened local property values;
one resident referred to the dangers of Mexican immigration by suggesting
that "Nothing will so effectively kill the real estate market as the importation
of a lot of cheap and poorly paid labor." Still more fretted that an open U.S.-
Mexico border would mean the arrival of political radicals fleeing the Mexican Revolution. Charging that immigrant Mexican farmworkers were in fact
"trained organizers of the Industrial Workers of the World," Fred Marvin
warned a San José audience that "the Mexican immigrant came to America
not to seek work, but to transmit the socialistic theories with which he was
satiated to the minds of American working men."[18]

These were the commonly held opinions of San Joseans during and after
the Mexican Revolution, even those who stressed that the Valley's fruit orchards required the presence of nonwhites every harvest season. Some tried
to deter the development of permanent *colonias* by drafting real estate deeds
that included explicit restrictions on selling or renting property to "nonwhites," "Chinese or Japanese," or "Mexicans." In this way, established residents hoped to deny ethnic Mexicans the opportunity to establish permanent
homes in the Valley, and they ensured that those migrants who tried would
not do so in white neighborhoods. Restrictive covenants became particularly
rampant between 1920 and 1945 as native-born and European immigrant
residents began to move to new middle-class subdivisions to the south and
west of downtown San José. At the same time, others from those groups
made Palo Alto and municipalities to the north into residential suburbs of
San Francisco. A study of local race relations conducted just after World War
II found that "all the subdivisions [of San José] opened within the last five or
six years have written restrictions barring property from occupancy or use by
all non-Caucasians except those who are working as domestics in the area."
Until such agreements were attacked in *Shelley v. Kramer* by the U.S. Su-

TABLE 5

Racial Covenants in Santa Clara County, 1920–1945

	Number of Racial Covenants Recorded (of 2,000 real estate deeds surveyed each year)	*Percentage of 2,000 Real Estate Deeds Surveyed That Contained Restrictions by Race*
1920	188	9.4
1925	242	12.1
1930	698	34.9
1935	518	25.9
1940	529	26.5
1945	497	24.9

Source: San José Real Estate Deeds, 1920–1945, in Santa Clara County Real Estate Records, Office of the County Recorder, San José, California.

preme Court in 1948, these restrictive racial covenants guaranteed that properties in many other areas of the county would not be sold or rented to ethnic Mexicans.[19]

Racial segregation in the housing and labor markets defined stark limits on ethnic Mexican settlement. The formation and growth of Latino barrios occurred statewide in the first three decades of the twentieth century, but in Santa Barbara and other parts of Southern California, lines of urban segregation could be traced more directly to much earlier decades. San José boasted no Mexican barrio prior to the 1920s, and the Spanishtown located at New Almadén had long since disappeared. Those arriving in the Valley through the 1910s found few longstanding Mexican American residents, no established Mexican American middle class, and no identifiable Mexican neighborhood. Limited year-round job opportunities prompted many to leave local fields for work in distant Washington State or the Imperial Valley, and the novelist José Villarreal remembers small, fractured groups of immigrants "scattered throughout the far reaches of the Valley," living in tents on small farms. A state inspector admitted in 1920 that the "housing and sanitary conditions" provided by local orchardists did not "average up to the standards of other counties." Despite the many decades of ongoing ethnic Mexican residency in the region, arriving Mexicans encountered few established residents who worked outside of low-wage construction or agricultural employment.[20]

The almost invisible nature of these settlements certainly fit the longstanding hopes of many non-Mexicans in the area, but it vexed Mexican immigrants. Brief weekend excursions to shop or visit the post office in San José often provided the only opportunities to meet other ethnic Mexicans, and few community institutions or businesses developed to serve migrants. Asked about the differences between agricultural work in California's Central

Valley and Santa Clara Valley, long-time resident Joaquín Andrade responded that, in the state's booming cotton-growing regions, known for enormous corporate landholdings, "you saw Mexicans everywhere." He recalled that, in the state's Central Valley, "Even after all the whites started coming in for jobs [during the 1930s] there were still Mexicans living all over. It was segregated . . . with all Mexican towns. Here [in the Santa Clara Valley] it was people living everywhere, but out in the middle of nowhere someplace. Families who came from somewhere else and spent a couple months living on some *gabacho's* [white man's] ranch and never saw nobody else."[21] Some Mexican community institutions were slow to develop in the Santa Clara Valley. While nearby San Francisco had several Spanish-language papers and a Latino business elite by the 1920s, and while Los Angeles became Mexico's "second city" by 1930, San Joseans established neither a Spanish-language press nor a business sector catering to that population prior to the late 1930s.[22]

Nevertheless, as greater numbers of ethnic Mexican arrived for agricultural and construction work, several stable ethnic Mexican neighborhoods did form after 1920 in Santa Clara County on lands free from restrictive covenants. Migrants displayed remarkable resourcefulness and perseverance in placing their hearts and homes in the county, and in confronting other residents' hostility to their presence. Settlement in these barrios changed the lives of many ethnic Mexicans. Far more stable than the migrant labor camps scattered around the Valley, these new neighborhoods located in East San José remained intimately linked to the Valley's fruit economy and surrounded by residential areas off-limits to most ethnic Mexicans. Living a short distance from downtown, virtually every wage-earning "Eastsider" labored in an agricultural job prior to World War II, and their barrios retained a strong rural character. The area's unpaved, dusty streets and crowded houses seemed more like those of other small, rural California towns than the central districts of Los Angeles or other California cities.[23]

Most San Joseans considered this section of the county a rural backwater. Abandoned before World War I by white farmers who rejected the area's poor soils, East San José had first been home to Puerto Ricans arriving during World War I from the Hawaiian cane fields; Mexicans settled there by the early 1920s in part to be near other Spanish-speakers. The longtime Mexican resident María Sarinara later remembered that the area "had no sewers, no sidewalks, no services, no lights," while her neighbor recalled that the Mayfair district (as East San José was also known) was "no different" than poor agricultural towns in the state's Central Valley, full of "shabby shacks and old houses with outside privies in the back." A migrant worker named César Chávez, later famous as a co-founder of the United Farm Workers, remembered that in 1939 his family had "stopped on Jackson Street by an isolated but crowded barrio where many farm workers lived . . . just two unpaved dead-end streets running into Jackson and bordered on three sides by fields,

TABLE 6

Estimated Population of Permanent Mexicano and Mexican American Residents of
San José, 1930–1950

	Mexicans and Mexican Americans in San José	Total Population of San José	Mexicans as Percentage of Total City Population
1930	2,689–4,239	57,651	4.7–7.4
1940	3,337–6,687	68,457	4.9–9.8
1950	12,874–16,074	95,280	13.5–16.9

Sources: Federal Manuscript Census, Santa Clara County, 1900, 1910, 1920; *Fifteenth Census of the United States: 1930. Population.* Vol. 3, Part 1: Alabama-Mississippi (Washington, D.C.: Government Printing Office, 1932), 266; *Polk's San José City Directory* (1930, 1940, 1950).

and pastures."[24] Lacking urban services and tied to the agricultural labor market, the East Side shared much with the Valley's Spanishtown of an earlier era. Economic prosperity remained elusive, work dominated, and the Mayfair Packing Company's less-than-elegant sump pump sent a stench throughout the East Side, attracting hordes of rats into the late 1950s. As in decades past, the Valley's largest ethnic Mexican settlement again developed outside of San José proper in ways that reflected the power of residential discrimination along lines of race.

The East Side became the demographic center of the Valley's ethnic Mexican community well before World War II, and it would continue to be the home of the largest number of Mexicans and Mexican Americans in the county into the late twentieth century.[25] As ethnic Mexicans struggled to put down roots, a variety of small barrios on the East Side—with names like Piojo (lice) and Posole (stew)—developed separate reputations for themselves by 1928, each defined in part by the number of temporary migrants who spent time there. The migrants' ambivalence toward permanent residency in these barrios became clear in the name of the East Side's largest neighborhood, widely known into the late 1950s as Sal Si Puedes (Get out if you can). Mayfair residents continued to tell stories about the meaning of that name in the years before World War II and thereafter, and these stories reveal something more about social dynamics between ethnic Mexicans on the East Side. Puerto Rican residents probably gave the area its name as a mock tribute to its economic underdevelopment and the lack of attention given it by city and county officials. The neighborhood's unpaved roads made walking difficult, and when local streets became muddy during periods of intense rain, automobile traffic halted. It was therefore said at times that the barrio's name referred to the challenge of moving cars that had sunk into the muck of East Side streets. While residents derisively counseled each other to *sal si puedes* from these difficult conditions, some Eastsiders instead

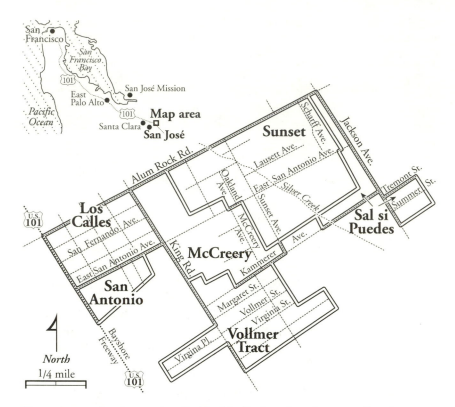

Home to many local canneries, the Mayfair district—later known as East San José—became an ethnic Mexican enclave in the years before World War II. Map by Scott Flodin.

claimed that the name pointed ironically to residents' difficulty actually getting into the neighborhood. Not only could many not find stable employment, but, thanks to a severe housing shortage, most faced great difficulties finding affordable lodgings. Incoming residents fortunate enough to locate space in the area often found themselves sharing a single ten-by-twelve-foot room with up to eleven other migrants or pitching tents in residents' backyards.[26] The elderly Nellie Hurtado recalled that in 1931, for instance, she and her family "could find no place to go, no place to live. We went from one friend's room to another friend's, and all were living very crowded already. Eventually we left and went across the [San Francisco] Bay to Oakland in search of work up there. We could find no place to live that took Mexicans." In the opinion of Hurtado and others, Sal Si Puedes might just as easily have been called Ven Si Puedes, "Come in if you can."[27]

HEARTS ELSEWHERE

Although forced by circumstances to reside in these East Side barrios, ethnic Mexicans retained affiliations and activities that connected them to more distant places. Theirs was a community that spanned state and international boundaries, and new roots in the segregated Valley did not mean the abandonment of far-flung relationships. As with their compatriots in Los Angeles, most who settled around San José had traveled extensively within their home country before entering the United States, and a considerable number had lived in Mexico's metropolitan areas or border towns before crossing the *frontera*. Records of county naturalization proceedings offer some clues about ethnic Mexican residents' earlier movements and indicate that approximately 60 percent had lived for a time in at least one Mexican city or town other than their birthplace. Knowing that they could easily reenter without sanction from the U.S. government, local Mexicans remained linked to border communities through patterns of return migration, and many hoped to return to Mexico once and for all in the near term. While eventually settling into a permanent home in Northern California, for instance, Dolores Andrade and other migrants seem to have understood their initial departures from Mexico as temporary ventures, treks in search of work that would be followed by a foreseeable return home under better conditions. "I did not want to make the trip," she later recalled, "but we had no money and life was very hard in Herreras. I just wanted to get back soon." Others fled Mexico because of military hostilities in their home region and anticipated returning at the end of the revolution.[28]

The establishment of the Border Patrol in 1924, together with crossing tolls and other regulatory efforts, certainly complicated back-and-forth trafficking, but these government activities did little to deter Mexicans' movements well into the mid-twentieth century.[29] Single men and entire families continued to cross back and forth to Mexico, traversing routes first laid down by mid-nineteenth-century Sonorans, and it seemed as if someone was always leaving East San José to visit family and friends in Mexico. Songs popular throughout California urged immigrants to repatriate. Typical was "Life, Trial, and Death of Aurelio Pompa," a ballad that described one Sonoran's travel to the state, his eventual execution by the California criminal justice system, and his final words of advice to other Mexicanos:

> Farewell, my friends, farewell, my village;
> Dear mother, cry no more.
> Tell my race not to come here,
> For here they will suffer; there is no pity here.[30]

TABLE 7
Mexican Towns and Cities Previously Inhabited by Mexican Immigrants
Resident in Santa Clara County, 1900–1945

City and State	Times Mentioned in Naturalization Testimony
Cananea, Sonora	44
Nogales, Sonora	39
Zacatecas, Zacatecas	36
Mexico City, Distrito Federal	32
Guadalajara, Jalisco	28
Saltillo, Coahuila	25
Irapuato, Guanajuato	22
Torreón, Coahuila	19
Aguascalientes, Aguascalientes	19

Source: Santa Clara County Petitions for Naturalization 1900–1945. 47 vols. Santa
Clara Courthouse.

Immigrant capital also found its way back to Mexico. Many Eastsiders
sent money earned in the Valley to other communities, prompted to do so
by limited opportunities in Northern California and expectations of eventual
return to Mexico or relocation to other parts of the United States. Rather
than using their wages to settle permanently in San José, Lorena Castillo,
who arrived in 1928 from Yuma, Arizona, with her parents and two sisters,
remembered that "few of the working families, the single men and the families, thought about staying here in the time when we first arrived. The hope
of most people was to make as much money as you could and spend very
little. Then you could take money back to where you were from to buy a
house or eat for the rest of the year." Into the 1950s, in fact, thousands of
ethnic Mexicans from Southern California, Arizona, and Texas migrated to
the San José area and labored temporarily in local fields and canneries to
afford homes and cars elsewhere. The Calles family, the Aldamas, and the
Gutiérrez brothers during the 1920s routinely sent wages earned in the Valley
to Southern California, South Texas, and Michoacán, respectively. The East
Side was packed with residents who looked forward to leaving the Valley.
Paydays sparked animated discussions of distant kin. The practice of "going
down to Western Union" to wire money to relatives became an important
translocal ritual in East San José, a foundation of many Eastsiders' identities
before World War II.[31]

Others put down firm roots. Those who decided to stay in the Santa Clara
Valley encouraged family members to join them and spent greater sums of
money in the county. Scattered work opportunities during canning seasons
convinced many to pin their hopes on these more lucrative jobs usually

denied Mexicans, and a Gold Rush mentality developed among the fortunate residents who worked long hours and made considerable wages in that industry. The experiences of Joaquín and Rosenda Enríques, recorded in county naturalization records, illustrate how complex processes of migration linked places like San José to Mexico between the world wars, and how some migrants began to settle permanently into life in the Santa Clara Valley. In the midst of the Mexican Revolution, the two had met and married in Chihuahua in 1915 and had raised two children there before moving to the town of Mocqui, Sonora, where Rosenda had given birth to another baby. Six years after their marriage, Joaquín entered the United States for the first time to work in El Paso. While there are no records of whether he traveled elsewhere within the United States, he seems to have crossed back into Mexico without notifying U.S. agents at least once since the couple's fourth child was born there two years later. The international border bent but did not break family networks, and Rosenda and the couple's four children entered the United States in 1924 to join Joaquín in Calexico, California, hundreds of miles from his original point of entry in El Paso. By 1934 they had settled on North 12th Street in San José, permanent residents of the Valley after nearly twenty years of on-and-off migration.[32]

While economic fortune remained elusive, Mexican immigrants like the Enriques family struggled to make cultural sense of their migrant lives, to manage the relatively open international border, and to forge translocal connections with loved ones elsewhere. In similar fashion, though a bit later, Higinio Meza Pérez and Guadalupe Figueroa Pérez also crossed and recrossed the U.S.-Mexico border several times throughout this period. Although it is impossible to determine from available records precisely when the couple first arrived in the United States, two of their four children, born in Colorado in the late 1930s, were U.S. citizens by birth. After the couple returned to Mexico, their third child was born in 1939 in Guadalupe's hometown of Villa Aldama, Chihuahua, and their fourth arrived in 1943 in Ciudad Juárez. Higinio and Guadalupe subsequently registered with federal agents to cross the border legally later that year, and this family of U.S. and Mexican citizens moved to the Santa Clara Valley where Higinio obtained work as a laborer. Like other ethnic Mexicans, members of the Pérez clan might have defined themselves with a number of different terms: men and women; San Joseans and Chihuahuenses; Mexican and U.S. citizens, and working people.[33]

The travels of Anselmo Andrade and Dolores Gámez echo those of many other families but illustrate more about ongoing loyalties to the *patrias chicas* (small homelands) of home villages left behind. Dolores recalls that Anselmo's departure from the village of Herreras, Durango, in the late 1910s first brought him, like thousands of other Mexicanos, to work in Texas cotton fields. Andrade subsequently engaged in migratory agricultural work throughout the United States, spending months at a time in New Jersey, Louisiana, Colorado, Minnesota, and other distant regions before returning to Durango to marry Dolores Gámez and help raise their first child, Joaquín, in 1924. Andrade left again in 1926, traveling from El Paso to the Salt River Valley in Arizona, to the Imperial Valley in California, and finally to the San José area. His first experiences in the Valley were apparently marked by violence, as a fight with a foreman on a family orchard left him with a large scar across his face. More than a year after leaving his family, Andrade returned to Durango in order to take them to Northern California, where he believed permanent work awaited in one of Santa Clara County's canneries. Pregnant with their second child, Dolores agreed, and in early 1929 the group arrived in San José. The canneries rejected Andrade's application. Frustrated by their inability to find year-round employment there, Anselmo and Dolores joined other Mexicanos in California's Central Valley, returning to the area around San José in the 1930s only to work in the annual prune harvest. They returned by train to Durango every few years during this period, making their last trip to Herreras around 1947.[34]

While immigrant work histories and contemporary concerns are notoriously difficult to trace, several themes clearly emerge in the stories of the Enriques, Pérez, and Andrade families. First, of course, is the importance of agricultural and industrial labor in drawing individuals north across the border. Smelters in El Paso, beet fields in Colorado, the cotton economy in Texas, and other labor-intensive sectors of the U.S. economy attracted thousands of Mexicanos during these years, often solicited by labor contractors (*enganchadores*) who recruited in Mexico. Second, Mexicans commonly traveled remarkable distances during these years, settling down in temporary and semipermanent homes in many locales. Many had children born in different states and on different sides of the international border, and neither city nor county boundaries defined the limits of their social worlds. Finally, ongoing events in Mexico continued to exert a hold on these residents and others. Living in what social scientists have called a transnational social field, Mexicans maintained affective ties across the U.S.-Mexico border even as they established residency in specific locales. Denied settlement opportunities in places like San José, some stayed in touch over long distances, leaving family members to maintain more permanent households in Mexico, and sending money and postcards from the United States.[35]

While Mexicanos often pined for other locales during the 1920s and 1930s, Spanish-speaking Eastsiders also established new community organizations that began to compete with one another for the time, loyalty, and resources of local residents. Informal neighborhood networks developed. Women cooked for other families, charged a small fee to babysit the children of parents working in local orchards, and shared information about job opportunities elsewhere in the county. Sundays became important days for many, and while no Catholic church developed to serve the district until the early 1950s, many worshipped with Portuguese and Italian congregations nearby. Others attended non-Catholic services with other Mexicans in the Mayfair district. Among these was the Mexican Pentecostal Church, built by Pastor Pedro Vandanos and his assistant Moises Osuna on San Antonio and 32nd streets, the development of which in 1929 reflected the strong anti-Roman Catholic sentiments sweeping through Mexico and southwestern Mexican communities. As the Mexican Pentecostal Church's thirty members attempted to convince farmworkers and their families to cut their ties with Catholicism, other San José residents who labored in 1931 to establish a small Mexican Baptist Church on Summer Avenue did so with a similar purpose. By the 1930s residents would also establish mutual-aid societies and labor unions that would serve as important bases for political organizing during the Depression decade.[36]

None of this spelled assimilation into the San José mainstream. As they adapted and created new community responses to life in the Santa Clara Valley, residents increasingly began to view themselves as members of a larger community of Mexican "nationals" living outside of Mexico. For many, feelings of national pride became more acute as a result of out-migration, and Mexican government officials urged their citizens to consider themselves a *México de afuera*, literally another "Mexico outside the nation." Residency honed nationalist sentiments as Eastsiders encountered discriminatory treatment that made clear their racialization as non-whites in U.S. society. Lydia Ramírez recalled her father's anger at being denied the right to buy property in certain areas of the county, Estela Ramírez recollected discussions at the local Baptist church of white mistreatment of the *raza Mexicana*, while Ray Salazar proudly remembered that "the whites wanted the Mexicans around because we knew how to work. We would teach the bosses how to do things in this Valley." Interactions with other ethnic Mexicans also shaped residents' sense of ethnic difference. Neighbors and co-workers hailed from many regions of Mexico, and Lydia Ramírez recalled that her family had "never thought of ourselves as Mexicans until we lived with people from all over that country." Dolores Andrade remembered groups of men and women sitting on East San José stoops, comparing stories about hometown politics.[37]

Mexican immigrants throughout the United States grappled with the meanings of national identity during this turbulent period. In the 1920s the pioneering Mexican social scientist Manuel Gamio noted that emigration helped to *forjar patria*, creating a sense of nationhood by teaching immigrants "what their mother country means, and they think of it and speak with love of it. Indeed, it can be said that there is hardly an immigrant home where the Mexican flag is not found in a place of honor, as well as pictures of national Mexican heroes. Love of country sometimes goes so far that little altars are made for flag or hero, or both, giving patriotism thus a religious quality." Mexican flags flew in homes throughout the Southwest during the 1920s, symbols of residents' ongoing concerns about conflicts in the *patria*, and inhabitants of East San José and countless other barrios threw their hearts into celebrations of Mexico's national holidays. In back pockets of their work jeans some Eastsiders carried newspapers describing Mexican politics, and others gathered to discuss their homeland every September 16 in small banquets held in barrio homes. Arguments about Mexican national politics, local race relations, and memories of specific hometowns ensued, providing a glimpse into the many shifting concerns of ethnic Mexicans in Northern California during the 1920s.[38]

THE FANTASY HERITAGE

While ethnic Mexicans reimagined their identities and their residency during the 1920s and 1930s, white residents of the Valley also struggled to make sense of the demographic turmoil wrought by the Mexican Revolution. Unlike the identities articulated on the East Side, the rhetoric of many native-born whites and European immigrants often sought to solidify the social order. These San Joseans staked their claims to the region through references to the Gold Rush and other key moments in the nineteenth-century past. Their racial rhetoric preserved and encouraged discriminatory treatment toward nonwhites, particularly when Valley government, business, and union leaders attempted to celebrate the region's "pioneer heritage." Some artists took up the project of painting public murals with this in mind, and politicians made flowery references to Northern California's Manifest Destiny. In 1929 Paul Shoup, president of the Southern Pacific Railroad, told listeners that "Bayard Taylor said, more than a half century ago, that this valley was more suited to the intellectual, moral, and physical development of a great race than any valley he had seen in the old world. . . . My travels have only impressed upon me the truth of this statement." Many native-born and European immigrants showed great interest in seeing themselves as the inheritors of this "pioneer spirit" by the mid-1920s, and theatrical performances, meetings of newly established Pioneer Societies, and gatherings of "old settlers" fostered memories of Manifest Destiny first celebrated during the 1850s.[39]

Boosters emphasized the long history of white settlement in the region, reminded denizens about the past struggles of pioneers against nonwhite incursions, and reinforced the racial and class structure of the contemporary period. Inaccurate as it was, such rhetoric did important ideological work in the early twentieth century. Replaying the triumph of white political hegemony in past decades, residents remembered places throughout the county where mid-nineteenth-century settlers had killed suspected Mexican bandits, keeping notions of Mexican criminality alive. In a departure from previous booster rhetoric, local historians now sometimes claimed the region's earlier Spanish colonists as the white forebears of twentieth-century San Joseans, a development encouraged by civic promoters and railroad advertisers in many parts of the state. Living in a region with few descendants of those conquered ethnic Mexicans, many white San Joseans eagerly identified with Californios' struggles to establish European "civilization" in the Northern California "wilderness." A few aging Californios in the state, such as Santa Clara's Encarnación Pinedo, contributed to this myth in the early twentieth century by remembering that "the overruling providence of God had selected" Spanish and Mexican settlers to be "the pioneers of that Christian civilization." But the voices of old-time Californios seemed only to accelerate processes already underway. By 1932 the San José Chamber of Commerce would publish brief histories of the city's and county's Spanish past designed to attract additional white settlers to the area, and boosters would stress into the 1940s that local European settlements and the government of the United States had been "founded in the same year."[40]

This "Spanish fantasy heritage," as Carey McWilliams described it, made contemporary society seem consistent with a glorified past, describing race relations as a natural continuation of the longstanding hegemony of white Californians. Dramatic productions, public celebrations, and local holidays reiterated that the inevitable domination of Spaniards over passive Indians, and of American settlers over inferior Californios, had made for peace and prosperity during the nineteenth century. Such events attracted a broad cross-section of California society. In the county's first performance of a "Mission Play" in 1915, college student Roy Emerson, dressed as a "gay young caballero," stepped before a packed audience at Santa Clara University and invited residents "to step back into the past when all California was young and gay and the people used to sing and dance and laugh in the sunshine." The script then narrated the "coming of the Gringo" and the "peace and happiness" that Indians and Spaniards enjoyed in the years immediately following the Mexican War.[41]

Discussions of race inevitably also became meditations on gender and sexuality. Theatrical events performed in the late 1920s and early 1930s defined the common whiteness of Spaniards and American settlers by emphasizing longstanding concerns about racial miscegenation in the region, a prominent matter of debate in contemporary discussions of immigration. In May 1927 the *Union Gazette* recommended that all its readers see "La Rosa del Rancho, a Love Story of Early San José," a drama set in "sleepy San Juan in the days of July, 1846" in which Juanita, the "daughter of a Spanish mother and American father," was forced to choose between two suitors, Captain Stephen Kearney of the invading U.S. Army and "a darkly handsome and romantic Spaniard, Don Luis de la Torre." Amid the publication of a spate of articles warning about the arrival of dark Mexican peons, a 1930 fiesta play, "The Madonna of Monterey," produced just five months after anti-Filipino rioting and no doubt prompted by concerns about miscegenation, dealt with similar themes of interracial romance. That drama's heroine learned to distinguish between the positive and negative qualities of Spanish and Mexican Indian men, and a local reviewer noted that unlike mixed-race Mexicans, "white men" such as the Spanish priests could "be kind."[42]

During this period when ethnic Mexicans congregated in East San José and had little choice but to take low-wage employment in local fields, these myths about the region's white Spanish past buttressed ongoing racial segregation and the position of Mexican immigrants at the bottom of the local economic ladder. County business and labor leaders cemented these structures in the mid-1920s with their plan for an annual fiesta that would encourage whites to identify with the Californio elites of the early nineteenth century. Started in 1926, the Fiestas de las Rosas became an attraction comparable to Pasadena's Rose Parade, attracting as many as half a million onlookers, including the governor and mayors of other California cities who joined in cheers for the annual "Fiesta Queen" and the dozens of floats that passed along San José's streets. Employees of the San José post office and other local businesses contributed to the excited atmosphere of the Fiestas as they wore sombreros and "Spanish" costumes for weeks leading up to each annual event. Local newspapers advertised new films depicting the conquistadores and Spanish *doñas*, while prominent businessmen built "Spanish homes" in the nearby foothills and attended balls dressed as "dashing cavaliers." Other boosters entered the act. AFL officials helped advertise the area's Spanish "flavor" in order to promote the arrival of new industries, while promotional pamphlets informed visitors how the Valley "'Twas in the Days of the Dons."[43]

Fiesta celebrations and similar events encouraged San Joseans to recognize the long tradition of white residency in the Valley and to appreciate the dangers associated with the arrival of nonwhites. Fiesta organizers favored the construction of floats sponsored by a variety of county organizations, including San José's Italian immigrant community, suburban improvement associations in neighborhoods such as Willow Glen, and local labor unions, service clubs, school marching bands, and veterans' organizations. These diverse groups easily performed the roles of "Spaniards" and emphasized their deep roots in the Valley. Residents affirmed that Northern California ought to grow by natural increase rather than through further immigration. In 1929 parade spectators witnessed proud mothers marching with their young children, a scene that prompted a local reporter to note that, despite concerns about Mexican immigrants' high birth rates and the growing population of nonwhites worldwide, in fact "the future of the commonwealth was secure." Boosters reaffirmed visions consistent with Bayard Taylor's "dreams" about the area, dreams in which permanent Mexican residents threatened neither the present nor the future of San José. Flashpoints for anti-immigrant sentiment among working-class residents, Fiesta weeks prompted unionists to urge locals to block the permanent settlement of Mexican *peons.* After entering a float entitled "Union Labor" in the 1927 parade, AFL leaders cheered that they had been "able once again to demonstrate to San José that labor organizations are organized not alone for their own benefit, but also for the good of the community in which they live."[44]

Politics and popular culture in 1920s San José can only be understood in light of the massive disruptions wrought by contemporary Mexican immigration to the state. In this context, Fiesta week emphasized racial distinctions between long-dead Californios, played by white San Joseans, and contemporary peons, entirely absent from the public sphere. The celebrations made clear that the region's early dons and doñas had been racially pure rather than mixed-blooded mestizos, and migrant Mexican peons found no forebears in these representations of the region's early "civilizers." Floats and skits avoided reference to living Mexican residents of the region. While descendants of Californio families such as Charlotte Bernal were occasionally included in the pageantry, organizers more commonly chose to recruit white residents like the Lindeman sisters, who had spent "years of residence in Mexico," to dress as "señoritas of Old Madrid" in Fiesta ceremonies. During years of surging anti-Mexican sentiment throughout the Southwest, white Valley residents affirmed their common interests and firm hold on local politics. Civilization in the region had developed progressively from Indian to Spanish to American, according to their origin myths, and local white inhabitants would rightly remain at the top of the regional hierarchy. Mexicans had no voice in public political discussions during the 1920s, forcing their community's continued look outward to Mexico.[45]

Although the Fiesta pageants ended in 1933, by which time government and business coffers had been drained by the economic depression, the Valley's romance with its Spanish past persisted and continued to inspire journalists and government officials to reassert the boundaries of what was native and what was "alien" to the region. Most important for immigrants who arrived during the 1920s and 1930s, the Spanish myth deflected critical attention from the racial ideologies that shaped residency and labor relations. At times it also helped to deny nonwhites access to political power. Reflecting on hegemonic explanations of Mexican marginality, Ray Salazar recalled that "all the Italians, Portuguese, whites were interested in the Spanish history," and María Soto noted that "this city loved the Spanish but hated the Mexican." Indeed, few white politicians or journalists showed any concern about the plight of Salazar, Soto, and their compatriots or sought to understand their ties to other homes. Local government officials either ignored or complained about the presence of poor immigrant neighborhoods, and in 1937 the County Board of Supervisors announced that it would "let nature take its course" rather than disburse funds to uplift local barrios.[46]

The shroud of the Spanish fantasy heritage would not cloak the region in those racial myths for long. Ethnic Mexicans still endured little recognized but harsh patterns of racial discrimination, but the Depression decade stretched the social fabric upon which those earlier historical legends had been sewn. Growing numbers swelled East Side barrios and began struggling to redress the Valley's persistent inequalities, pushing their way into the public sphere in new ways. The political energies of the Mexican Revolution found voice in Northern California. From homes in Sal Si Puedes and neighboring communities, members of left-wing labor unions pressed for civil rights and capitalized on the East Side's transnational orientation. As economic hard times fell on the region, Mexicans and Mexican Americans began to forge creative political responses to Northern California inequalities.

Chapter 5

Striking Identities

Those were brutal but exciting times.
—Eulalio Gutiérrez (1995)

The Great Depression of the 1930s fell hard on the 1.9 million ethnic Mexicans in the United States, and those living in East San José witnessed a startling show of violence on November 26, 1933. On that evening, a mob of local residents descended on the city's downtown jail, forced their way inside with a battering ram and crowbars, and dragged two men to a city park nearby. The accused had kidnapped and murdered Brooke Hart, the twenty-two-year-old son of a prominent Jewish department store owner. As thousands gathered in anger about the crime, the vigilantes threw ropes around the necks of their two prisoners, suspended the lines from two gallow trees, and pulled the men to their deaths. Many of those assembled had spent the early part of the evening at local speakeasies, but the crowd of men, women, and children likely also included respected members of the county grand jury and other prominent citizens, spectators who gathered souvenir pieces of the tree and took photos of the naked victims suspended in clear view of the park's statue of President McKinley. Following the grisly lynching, an onlooker set fire to one of the hanging bodies.

Those brutal events became front-page news around the country and prompted many prominent politicians to respond. California governor James Rolph announced that San Joseans had done the right thing, that the spectacle would "show the country that the State is not going to tolerate kidnapping," and that he would pardon any citizen arrested for the crime. Herbert Hoover and Franklin Delano Roosevelt decried the evening's events. Like them, Mexicans in East San José found much to worry about in the mob's actions, and no extant evidence suggests their support for the lynching.

Many knew that similar violence had long defined their forebears' place in the United States; some had recently felt the sting of vigilantism in California's Central Valley and other regions of the state. While residents of Sal Si Puedes and nearby barrios rarely patronized Hart's Department Store on West Santa Clara and Market streets and had little personal contact with Brooke Hart, Eastsiders did come to a clear understanding about the meaning of that violence. In later years some recalled this 1933 episode as a formative moment in which whites once again put Mexicans in their place. Typical was the reminiscence of Cecilia Romero that "when they hung those two men in the park we all got scared. We all felt vulnerable here." Joaquín Andrade identified with the lynched victims because "we on the East Side had seen this kind of thing before." For many, the St. James Park lynching stands as a dominant memory of the period, an episode that frames broader understandings of the decade.[1]

Ethnic Mexican accounts downplayed one essential truth about the November 26 violence. The lynched men, Thomas Harold Thurmond and John Holmes, were white and not Mexican. Though this fact was clear in every contemporary newspaper account, ethnic Mexican perspectives over time elided it. Remarkably, those who recall the November 1933 events retain excellent command of most of the other salient details, just not the victim's ethnicity. It is a telling oversight, for as has been noted, discrepancies between fact and memory actually underscore the poignant value of oral sources to historical research. In ethnic Mexican memories we see the Devil doing his work, with these recast reminiscences speaking to the forceful power of ongoing racial conflicts. From the standpoint of the East Side, the specter of angry whites bringing accused criminals to justice echoed other moments in which white hegemony had made itself forcefully clear, and even when directed at non-Mexicans, vigilantism reminded many of the subtle and not-so-subtle methods that had long buttressed the political order in rural California.[2]

This chapter argues that ethnic Mexicans defined their own interests under the weight of violent spectacles and economic poverty during the Depression decade. Relying on their immigrant institutions and new labor organizations, they attempted to drive a stake through the racism endemic to this Valley of Heart's Delight. Speaking truth to power, they threw their efforts behind nascent community organizations committed to changing the fate of agricultural workers and East Side communities. Their established ties to Mexico provided critical support in struggles against local inequalities, but Depression conditions proved a tough match for resilient Eastsiders. Spiraling racial tensions engulfed workplaces, Mexicanos and Mexican Americans encountered new problems in locating secure employment, and armed guards rousted potential strikers from California fields and canneries. Thurmond and Holmes met their death in a Northern California powderkeg of

racism and rural poverty, and the Depression decade marked a critical fulcrum in the ongoing development of the ethnic Mexican community.

MEXICAN INSTITUTIONS

As hard times dominated the Valley after 1929, residents of the East Side
gathered in homes, cantinas, and small grocery stores scattered throughout
their neighborhoods. Poor health, struggles to feed hungry children, and the
sight of compatriots dying young from various unnatural causes concerned
everyone. Men and women discussed their situation and the future of the
San José region, and some found special comfort in Baptist, Pentecostal, and
Catholic churches that reached out to residents over the course of the decade. Desperate Eastsiders worried when President Hoover and other national politicians blamed ethnic Mexicans for the growing economic depression, and many expressed concern that white residents of the South Bay were
attempting to drive Chinese Americans and other nonwhites from the region. Unemployed white citizens increasingly demanded the orchard and
field jobs considered Mexican work during the previous decade. The sight of
arriving "Okies" and other white migrants seemed a real threat to ethnic
Mexican prospects. When unemployed, Joaquin Andrade shot the rats gathered at one San José cannery and offered them to his hungry family members. Others worked longer hours and pushed their children to do the same.
Still more left the area to undertake crippling work with short-handled hoes
in the agricultural fields of California and other parts of the American West,
and the sight of returning children with spines permanently bent from such
labor remained all too common throughout the decade. Growing tensions
sparked fights between Mexicans on San José relief lines, domestic disputes
between wives and husbands, and painful hopes that labor contractors might
offer more permanent work. As they confronted deepening poverty in the
early 1930s, residents struggled to hold onto the very bottom rungs of the
regional economic ladder.[3]

While optimistic rumors abounded on the East Side about better jobs to
come, many agreed that tough times called for new strategies of self-protection. Latinos in the 1850s had at times resorted to banditry and outright
violence, but barrio residents now relied on the tradition of self-help long
nursed by working-class Mexican communities on both sides of the U.S.-
Mexico border. An ethic of mutualism guided many Mexicanos in California.
During the late nineteenth century New Almadén miners had been among
the first in the Valley to form a mutual-aid society—an organization of
members committed to helping one another through hard times—and many
other immigrants throughout the Southwest would later do the same. Mutual aid organizations peaked in importance during the 1930s as members

provided one another insurance benefits and other forms of financial security for a nominal monthly fee. Those organizations affirmed residents' reciprocal ties. Ana Ortega described it this way: "The Mexicans here in California knew that we had to take care of one another. Plenty of people went
their own way, but in the end we had to do things together to make ends
meet. If you had food, you shared it if you could. If someone's child needed
something that you could give or lend, you did that. . . . Our clubs and
societies began with this in mind." From South Texas to central Colorado to
Northern California, an ethic of Mexican mutualism proved "crucial to
workers' survival" during the early twentieth century. The fact that many
government agencies during the 1930s discriminated against noncitizens in
dispensing welfare relief further solidified the importance of such self-help
associations. Mutualism called ethnic Mexicans to remain loyal to their families and subsume individual desires to group needs.[4]

Their societies became the very cultural and political foundation of many
southwestern barrios prior to World War II, and by the late 1920s arriving
migrants had established several such groups in and around San José. The
immigrant Rodolfo Montalvo recalls that between three and four hundred
had joined San José's Mexican Benevolent Society during the early years of
the Depression, and organizations such as the Sociedad Benito Juárez, the
Logia Progresista, and the Club Tapatío also experienced considerable
growth. Pillars of the Depression-era East Side, these lodges and clubs
adopted secret handshakes, passwords, and greetings to distinguish them
from other mutual-aid organizations, and each became a unique forum for
socializing, soliciting relief, and defining Mexican culture in Northern California. Organizations drew strength from immigrants' common ties to other
locales, the widespread need for financial insurance, and members' desires to
gather together after hard days at work. Life insurance, death benefits, and a
small lending fund provided some measure of security; evening social events
prompted Eastsiders to dance, sing, and forget some of their daytime struggles; and association meetings, held in Spanish, became festive occasions,
events in which members urged group solidarity against long odds.[5]

Residents also adopted other strategies of self-protection that gave them a
sense of optimism and a measure of security in the area. San Joseans continued to take strength from their attachments to villages and towns left behind,
and immigrants continued to speak openly about their home country. Many
recalled with nostalgia places they had left years before. Eulalio Gutiérrez's
fathers and aunts "stressed that we were Jaliscenses [from Jalisco] and most
importantly from Tepatitlán. It was important to them that all the kids remember the town, the songs people sang, the food, everything. When they
would meet someone in California from Tepa they'd spend hours talking to
them about the people they knew together, recent news, that sort of thing."[6]
Such commitments shaped social groups in the Santa Clara Valley when

ethnic Mexican men began to establish town clubs that brought residents together to remember their home regions on a regular basis. These organizations often emerged from *mutualista* social circles. In the late 1920s, for example, Manuel Ramírez helped create the "Club Chihuahua de San José" from one established society, giving immigrants from that northern Mexican state the opportunity once or twice a month to "get together and tell stories, drink beer, talk about how and when we would get back there."[7]

Remembering their roots in Mexican *patrias chicas*, immigrants from the states of Jalisco and Guanajuato also created town clubs, and the San Francisco newspaper *Hispano-America* recorded that immigrants in Sunnyvale had established a "Jalisco Youth Hall" by November 1933. *Tejanos* stuck together in Northern California, and Mexican Americans from Los Angeles at times gathered in groups to read Southern California newspapers as a way of keeping abreast of events elsewhere in the state. Organizing their social lives around ties to other locales, the parents of Harry Ramírez met with ethnic Mexicans from Laredo, Texas, each week to chat about common friends, and Ray Salazar remembered that on his days off work, he "used to go down to the barber and all the men there, they would be talking Mexican politics, about the new law for this or that, what some governor had done."[8]

Town clubs elected officers and held social activities in city parks and private homes to raise funds for their organizations. Like mutual-aid societies, their fraternal twin, these groups often provided members financial assistance, although their ostensible focus remained social. *Tamaladas*, gatherings in which Mexican women made a traditional dish of meat and corn, became one source of income. Mexicans also gathered to celebrate national holidays and mark saint days important to their specific home region. Rent parties accumulated money for desperate individuals, and Adela Santana and her aunts shared housework, cooked, and watched after children with other women from their hometown in Michoacán. Some also used town club connections to secure agricultural work in Northern California. Manuel Ramírez thought of the Club Chihuahua as a sort of employment agency; important members of that organization earned money by acting as labor contractors and finding jobs for other immigrants.[9]

As translocal ties and economic hardship shaped ethnic Mexican activities during the early 1930s, mutual-aid organizations and hometown clubs grew, helped many to remain in the San José area, and fostered both nationalist attachments to Mexico and a sense of local identity. They did so as Depression conditions put the brakes on circular migration to and from that country; it became impossible for most throughout the Southwest to afford temporary trips to Mexico as they had in the 1920s, and the heightened restrictions on border crossings contributed to fewer and fewer back-and-forth travels. Many of those who stayed in Northern California felt increasingly removed from kin in Mexico. Instead of temporary visits to the *patria*, greater numbers of Eastsiders found inspiration to repatriate permanently to their home country. The Mexican consulate had urged just that since the early 1920s, and the lure of a better life in Mexico tempted many struggling Northern Californians. As in other parts of the state, foreign officials based in San Francisco worked with San José mutual-aid societies, sponsored local celebrations of the *fiestas patrias*, and exhorted Valley migrants to continue seeing themselves as part of the Mexican body politic. Mexican government officials extolled the virtues of repatriation, and María Santana and Federico Garza remembered that town clubs encouraged the trip. Remittances from San José to Mexican hometowns likely declined because of Depression-era economic pressures, and some who thought of their East Side barrios as a *Mexico de afuera* took their property and left for their home country. Lydia Ramírez recalled that Eastsiders who departed still "felt very Mexican," while Cecilia Romero recalled that "There was just not enough work for them and there were only certain jobs we could do." Return migrants would be, the newspaper *Hispano-America* hoped, the new driving force in that country's economic modernization.[10]

All this was a local chapter of a much larger story. Perhaps as many as five hundred thousand of the nearly two million ethnic Mexicans in the United States did return to Mexico during the 1930s, eager to make a better life for themselves, and driven by formal and informal repatriation drives throughout the country. Long-time residents recall that perhaps as many as a third of the nearly four thousand Mexicans in the San José region also chose that course. Their subsequent lives in Mexico are difficult to trace, but the memories of Federico Garza suggest something about what they sought to find there. In the late 1920s, at age fifteen already concerned about the scarcity of permanent employment and the escalation of anti-Mexican racism, he first began to discuss a move to Baja California with his brothers. San Francisco journalist Nestor G. Arce captured his attention with stories about that region's agricultural potential, good schools, and "beautiful girls." With hopes of acquiring land and forging a stronger Mexican nation, this broke and unemployed Eastsider eventually took advantage of the financial help provided by the Mexican consulate to leave San José. "Mexico needed people like me and my brothers," he recalled.[11]

While no one forced Garza to leave San José at gunpoint, neither he nor most other repatriating ethnic Mexicans made free and unfettered choices about their futures. Immigrants who gathered at the city's downtown rail station to board trains for Mexico responded to three important Depression-era dynamics in Northern California. First, as Garza and others knew, the dual power of white racism and economic hardship dominated East Side concerns. Denied welfare assistance as noncitizens, Mexicanos often found it impossible to sustain their residency. "Many people decided it was best to return, that things would not be harder in Mexico since the fighting there

was over, and that they could live with their families," according to Luz
Rendón. Second, immigrant nationalism prompted many to take this opportunity to reconnect with their Mexican *patria*. Some, like Garza, no doubt
idealized what lay ahead of them in places like Baja California, and they did
so by comparing the poverty they knew in the Santa Clara Valley with the
greater abundance and increased security they believed awaited them in
Mexico. Finally, repatriates depended upon their immigrant institutions and
the Mexican government to make the trip. Eastsiders had few resources of
their own for surviving the Depression, and their mutual aid and town clubs
remained unsteady rocks during stormy times, more successful in reinforcing
Mexicanidad than in providing a long-term financial base.[12]

While ethnic Mexican neighbors, club members, and kin who left the
region expressed hopes that they would find the bright future seemingly
denied them in the Santa Clara Valley, those who stayed continued in many
ways their established patterns of life. They participated in club events, frat-
ernized with family and friends, and worked hard when jobs became available. Many no doubt began increasingly to see themselves rooted in Northern California, as well. Given the opportunity to leave for Mexico, they had
chosen to remain, and those affirmations of residency brought new commitments to improving the local area and paved the way for their subsequent
involvement in other Valley institutions. Rodolfo Montalvo remembers that
"I guess we did want to stay and decided we'd make the best of it. Children
would grow up here." Adela Santana similarly "began to look at the Italians
and Portuguese in my [Catholic] parish a little different. We were not the
same, but we were all neighbors in a way. They were not going through what
we were going through, but I began to see them as neighbors. . . . I figured
we would be here for a long time." In Los Angeles and other locales, as well,
repatriation drives left behind groups of residents who would begin to consider themselves "Mexican Americans" over the course of the decade, a
"change in political direction . . . from a community dominated by the Mexican-born to one which centered around the American-born," in the words
of historian George Sánchez.[13]

But East San Joseans who remained did not assimilate in conventional
ways into Valley society. Unlike their Los Angeles counterparts, few bought
houses or experienced upward mobility into the middle class. The mainstream labor movement gave little thought to organizing them, and San José
was not large enough to boast the urban mass culture that helped assimilate
Mexican immigrants in Chicago, Los Angeles, and other cities. While many
European immigrants in San José made their way into mainstream politics,
most East Side residents avoided becoming U.S. citizens and clung to Mexican cultural practices, committed throughout the decade to their mutual ties
to one another. No extant records survive of new organizations dedicated to
promoting a "Mexican American" identity, and town clubs and mutualistas

instead kept a sense of Mexicanidad alive. Ongoing discussions about Mexico encouraged a sense of attachment to the *patria*, and Spanish remained the dominant language heard on East Side streets and in local homes, barber shops, Protestant churches, and grocery stores. Most children still learned the language of their immigrant parents, and families downplayed distinctions between U.S. and Mexican citizens, as Valley barrios included residents born on both sides of the international border, and as Mexican Americans married Mexican immigrants in roughly half of the county's ceremonies during the 1930s. All told, East San José remained a Mexican immigrant community in many ways; residents held firm to their Mexican cultural and political practices during the era of the Depression and New Deal.[14]

While critics then and since wondered about this apparent refusal to assimilate into mainstream California society, affirmations of Mexican identity made good cultural and political sense during these years. Naturalization offered Mexicans few tangible rewards. Throughout the United States, Mexicanos showed less inclination to become U.S. citizens than other eligible immigrants, precisely because race trumped citizenship in defining social positions. White residents of the Valley had long discriminated against ethnic Mexicans regardless of nativity, and many Mexicanos knew that becoming Mexican American would make little difference in their search for permanent work, decent housing, and higher wages. Class position also shaped East Side reactions to naturalization: farm workers who became citizens still enjoyed few federal protections under the New Deal labor provisions of the 1930s. For all these reasons, only 117 Mexicanos filed intentions to naturalize in the county between 1900 and 1945, and in 1936 Rayo Gutiérrez Chávez, a widowed cannery worker born in Chihuahua, became the county's first Mexican woman to do so in the twentieth century. Working in local fields and construction jobs, Ray Salazar recalled asking himself "why would I have wanted to be a U.S. citizen? It was not going to help me any." Ana Ortega concurs that "The work was the same whether you were one or not, and the government did nothing for the people who worked in the fields in those days." While a politics of U.S. citizenship became more important in some

TABLE 8

Naturalization Cases Involving Mexican Immigrants, Santa Clara County

	Mexican Men	Mexican Women	Women as Percentage of Mexicans Filing Petitions
1900–1936	48	1	2.0
1937–1940	28	9	24.3
1941–1945	41	28	40.5

Source: Santa Clara County Petitions for Naturalization 1900–1945.

other locales during the Depression, including San Antonio and Los Angeles, it still meant little in this semirural community defined by agricultural work and residential instability.[15]

NEW UNIONS

Mutualism, family ties, and connections to home towns retained their paramount importance during the 1920s and 1930s, but local barrios also changed significantly under the stresses of the Depression decade. Mexicanidad and ethnic Mexican organizations gave shape to vibrant political responses to Depression conditions, responses that would make the decade the county's most politically charged since the New Almadén strikes of the 1860s. First and foremost, many ethnic Mexicans made new allies with other marginalized residents, particularly the region's Filipino and Japanese denizens. A common threat of racial violence helped unite those diverse groups, and one man remembered that many feared that farm owners and labor contractors "might . . . shoot first [and] later ask questions" of local troublemakers. "Who," he wondered, would "care if I or a Filipino gets killed?" According to local resident Eulalio Gutiérrez, Mexicans and Asians often worked together in agriculture without complaint, and an agent of the California Immigration and Housing Commission noted in a previous decade that "the Japanese and Mexicans mingle and fraternize perfectly, and neither have any particular love or respect for the white laborers." White racism prompted some to acknowledge their similar positions in area workplaces. In another context, the Mexican American Sofia Mendoza recalled how she "mostly socialized and associated with Japanese students and not so much with the Anglo students" while growing up in the town of Campbell.[16]

Ethnic Mexicans also found some new friends among white San Joseans, particularly those involved in Depression-era labor organizations. The rumbles of agricultural unionism grew to a crescendo throughout the West during the 1930s as working people came to question the structures of American capitalism, and San José soon became a startling hotbed of white and Mexican coalitional politics. Mexican immigrants often led the activist charge, and the Communist party set a new standard throughout the United States for civil rights work. Buoyed by fresh interest in left-wing causes, a young woman named Dorothy Healey worked with other Party members to develop the Cannery and Agricultural Workers Industrial Union (CAWIU) in San José in 1931, an independent labor organization with ties to Southern California's Mexican mutual-aid societies. Fresh from labor strikes in the Imperial Valley, she and others sought to refashion the Valley of Heart's Delight by reaching out to Mexican workers. Healey and other white leftists' sincere interest in Eastsiders' well-being marked a sea change in local politics.

For the first time in the twentieth century, at least a few white San Joseans began to criticize the racism bedeviling local Mexicans. Trumpeting an anti-racist platform that would integrate workers of all backgrounds under their banner, those organizers lambasted existing AFL unions that "discriminate against colored workers and refuse to allow them to join its ranks."[17]

The CAWIU entered an East Side political landscape shaped by notions of mutualism and small acts of workplace resistance, and the union adapted well to that political culture. In previous years, the anti-Mexican politics of California unions and the more transient nature of the Valley's Mexicano population had assured that most ethnic Mexican labor activities would remain sporadic and short-lived. Although the 1920s had seen Mexican immigrant labor unions forming elsewhere in California, residents of the Santa Clara Valley had managed only episodic responses to labor exploitation. Orchardists valued Mexicans as a quiet and deferential bunch, a stereotype that failed to recognize small acts of immigrant resistance on local job sites. For example, Rudy Calles once urinated on a local grower's fruit. "That's for the rich people who eat good and we don't," he and his brother laughed. Ray Salazar recalled that Mexican workers in Valley fields at times slowed their pace of work when they became engaged in a wage dispute, and Ana Ortega remembered that Mexican women confronted foremen in the fields to complain about working conditions. Others broke the boss's tools, fought with the son of a local foreman, or showed their frustration in other ways.[18]

Supported by mutual-aid organizations and Communist Party organizers, residents departed from their seeming deference to make greater noise on the San José stage after 1931. CAWIU members contacted barrio *mutualistas* and town clubs in East San José, exhorted Mexicanos to continue their political commitments under the union banner, and urged community leaders to become CAWIU officers. Wildcat strikes—brief walkouts from the workplace—remained the central union tactic. When Mexican workers left jobs to protest inadequate wages or working conditions, unionists shared their flyers and broadsides with disgruntled residents. Mary Contreras recollected that white organizers "used to come around to the meetings of the Mexican lodges" in attempts to encourage more residents to become members, and those visits inspired others to engage in walkouts from local fields. Novelist José Villarreal remembered a pear pickers' strike in the Valley in 1931 sparked by the union, while others learned about the CAWIU from new radical newspapers. The establishment of *Lucha Obrera* in 1934, a Spanish-language edition of the Communist Party organ *The Western Worker*, touched many. "I remember reading a newspaper from the Communists to my compadres at a bar on Second Street," recalled one resident. Many responded to editorials about farm workers and race relations, and writers enthusiastically repeated in 1934, for example, that "The solidarity of the Mexican, Filipino, American, Negro, and Puerto Rican workers is marvelous."[19]

As the CAWIU and other Communist organizers preached working-class solidarity, some Eastsiders believed that this union would at last protect their rights of residency and labor. But the center of CAWIU activities remained elsewhere, and in 1933 the organization prompted the most extensive strikes in the state's history in Central Valley cotton fields. Still, those distant campaigns emboldened Eastsiders, many San Joseans became more involved, and María Velásquez recalled that local Mexicans in the 1934 Salinas lettuce strike "just wanted a decent living and not to get fired for joining a union." The county's *Union Gazette* reported that 2,500 Filipinos, 500 "Mexicans," and 3,000 "Americans" participated, and East Side town clubs and *mutualistas* raised money to support those picketers. To the dismay of many, efforts to develop similar strikes within Santa Clara County met the outright hostility of local officials. The county's agricultural commissioner L. R. Cody complained, for example, that the area was "swarming with 'Red' and communistic agitators from San Francisco and southern California" who were "attempting to dissuade workers from entering the fields." Business and government officials cracked down against radical organizing in the county, and the Valley's proximity to San Francisco increased fears that the spirit of that city's 1934 waterfront strikes would spread south. The San José chief of police sent his officers to help subdue marching unionists in Salinas, towns such as Sunnyvale passed antipicketing ordinances, and new vigilance committees formed in 1934 and 1936 prepared to fight labor unionists. Growers and prominent citizens stood as armed guards at the Richmond-Chase cannery and other local job sites to fight off the "bunch of Reds [who] are trying to get the Cannery Workers out for more pay," and many Eastsiders shied away from the sight of deputized white citizens carrying firearms.[20]

As in the nineteenth century, white vigilantism limited ethnic Mexican prospects. Those who continued to work with the CAWIU put themselves at real risk of severe injury, formal arrest, or deportation. Government officials supported the violence. When the 1934 strikes mobilized thousands in Northern California, the San José district attorney called local Filipino leaders into his office. In a barely concealed threat, the chief of police and the county sheriff announced "that both the police department and the sheriff's office will be powerless if a mass mob attack is made on the Filipinos." Nonwhite residents could only wonder about their own fates at the hands of a San José mob so shortly after the lynchings of Thurmond and Holmes. Other events made it equally clear that local law enforcement stood against farm worker interests. Deputized sheriffs incarcerated Pedro Gasco, Joseph Frausto, and "several score [of other] suspected Communists" in 1933 who attempted to organize local pea field workers, for instance. Captured when "squads" of Santa Clara County deputy sheriffs "went through the camps of pea and spinach workers" and "rounded up loiterers refusing to work in the fields," Gasco and Frausto were turned over to federal immigration inspectors and taken to San Francisco in order to arrange for their deportation.[21]

As thousands throughout the state challenged California elites, these conservative crackdowns against labor organizing threatened the welfare of all ethnic Mexicans in the state. Local CAWIU members, as well as more conservative Northern Californians, registered their anger, and, when workers in northern Santa Clara County struck briefly in June 1933, even a Spanish-language newspaper correspondent for San Francisco's *Hispano-America* warned readers about the ridiculous redbaiting of local immigrants. "These fine workers are neither reds nor communists," he wrote, "but rather are honorable fathers and sons of families demanding something just and reasonable." Many working-class Eastsiders struggled to remain involved in the CAWIU as strong centrifugal forces propelled their departure from the Santa Clara Valley. From Pescadero to the northwest to Salinas in the south, CAWIU-inspired strikes appeared at critical harvest times, and San José residents recruited to work outside California helped launch such protests in Colorado and points farther north and east. Lydia Ramírez recalled traveling to Idaho, discovering that "things were terrible there, the beds, the food, everything," and joining other workers who refused to cut sugar cane for "almost a week." Influenced by CAWIU organizers, several hundred Santa Clara Valley men became involved in unionization activities as far away as Alaska where they had begun to work in the salmon canneries, and "headstones bearing the names of Garcia, Ramirez, etc." marked their place.[22] During the enormous wave of strikes launched by farmworkers throughout California in 1933, Eulalio Gutiérrez was working in the fields of San Mateo County to the north of San José when he and others "heard about what was going on" elsewhere. He set about organizing a committee of Mexican and Filipino pickers to negotiate a wage increase on the farm where he worked. CAWIU organizers and "a journalist from San Francisco" helped his committee, and a two-week walkout won them a small wage increase.[23]

From 1931 into the summer of 1934, the CAWIU successfully urged tens of thousands of ethnic Mexicans in Northern California to turn their attention to unionization and labor strikes in local fields. Building on the region's vital mutual-aid organizations and town clubs, Communist Party organizers redirected some barrio residents' longstanding political energies. Appealing to their ethic of mutualism, unionists shaped an agricultural movement attentive to the powers of racial discrimination. All this marked a startling rupture in local race relations, but it was a union that would not last. Repression from conservative interests in California in the end combined with new Communist Party priorities to betray the interests of activist Eastsiders. First came the force of growers, politicians, and law enforcement, who, under the banner of a group called the Associated Farmers, descended on CAWIU headquarters in Sacramento, arrested key leaders on criminal syndicalism charges, and saw most sent to prison. Union activists in San José recall the chilling effects of that repression on their own efforts. Soon thereafter the Comintern of the Soviet Union announced that because of the threat of fascism worldwide, their party operatives in the United States would take a less confrontational stance toward liberals, no longer support independent trade unions, and "bore from within" established labor organizations. This spelled an end to the party's commitment to the CAWIU and signaled the coup de grace that eliminated that organization from the San José scene.[24]

SECOND CHANCES

Tragic as it seemed to many at the time, the CAWIU's sudden collapse did not topple ethnic Mexican commitments to mutual aid and political change in the Santa Clara Valley. The mid-1930s became desperate times for many, but existing organizations continued to provide services, financial resources, and social diversions to those struggling to find permanent work and make ends meet. Families migrated to fields in other parts of the West, children labored alongside parents, and small and occasional acts of resistance punctuated each harvest season. Ethnic Mexicans forged new reciprocal connections. For example, East Side town clubs organized a baseball league from 1934 to 1936 that pitted Mexicanos from different states against one another in friendly competition. Meeting on an unplanted local field near Sal Si Puedes, they tested their athletic skills and affirmed their loyalties to teammates. Thrown back on their own devices when formal resistance to Depression conditions became impossible, some found strength and succor in these moments of leisure.[25]

But baseball games and town clubs did not alone define ethnic Mexican reactions to the CAWIU's decline. A new political force eventually emerged on the national scene that would capture the attention of Eastsiders and other ethnic Mexicans in California. Elsewhere in the United States, John Lewis and his fellow dissident members of the American Federation of Labor established a Committee for Industrial Organization (CIO) in 1936 to organize new sectors of the national workforce and launch sit-down strikes and other hard-hitting tactics. It would take time for them and others on the Left to invest any energy in California's agricultural workers, but in 1938 the CIO finally announced the formation of an organization that would exceed the CAWIU in importance and influence. It had been several long years since the CAWIU had provided shape to ethnic Mexican resistance, but by the end of the decade the East Side would again feel the effects of a labor organization devoted to agricultural workers, to antiracist organizing around civil rights, and to the equal treatment of women and men.

Created by former AFL official Donald Henderson, the United Cannery, Agricultural, Packinghouse, and Allied Workers of America (UCAPAWA) became the CIO's seventh-largest affiliate by 1939. Like other progressive labor organizations of the late 1930s, this union devoted itself to "organizing the unorganized," to involving diverse groups of workers, and to pressing for a broad array of political changes. Until its demise in the late 1940s, that union and its successor, the Food and Tobacco Association (FTA), found success in the Santa Clara Valley by urging women workers to take leadership positions and by organizing civil rights efforts in Spanish-speaking communities. Their efforts marked the second flashpoint in Depression-era politics for local ethnic Mexicans. Mickey Shevlin, a Salinas resident and leader of the Fruit and Vegetable Workers Local 18211, and East San José's Manuel Ramírez together lobbied for the establishment of UCAPAWA locals, and the Club Chihuahua de San José hosted organizing meetings to urge its members to press for that new CIO affiliate. In 1938 these and other calls for union support brought the Salinas-based fruit workers a charter as Local 78 of UCAPAWA and made some San José cannery workers members of Local 11.[26]

Within and beyond the Valley's boundaries, farm workers and cannery workers found in UCAPAWA a Popular Front organization even more committed to civil rights activism than the now-defunct CAWIU. The union claimed by 1939 that "at least one-sixth" of its members were "Mexicans and Spanish Americans," and labor officials passed a resolution at the national level that expressed "opposition to the vicious exploitation and discrimination directed against the Mexican workers and workers of Mexican descent, and welcomes them into the ranks of organized labor in the United States for the improvement of their conditions."[27] The West Coast chapter developed a strong following among fruit canners, Alaskan salmon packers, fruit and vegetable pickers, and established Mexican and Filipino organizations. Throughout California, UCAPAWA also attracted a representative cross-section of the state's multi-ethnic population. Dedicated to promoting equality regardless of the race or national origin of workers, union organizers helped to build an institutional bridge between many ethnic Mexicans and whites in the San José area. Adela Santana recalls that "the Italians respected us because we were members of that organization with them. We didn't know many of them before that time." By 1939, former organizers Leo Vargas and Manuel Ramírez recall, Local 11 often attracted up to three hundred Mexican workers at its meetings in East San José, and that support led UCAPAWA to its first union contract with a Mountain View cannery in 1939.[28]

The CIO affiliate became the heartbeat of late 1930s' union organizing in Northern and Southern California, as the historian Vicki Ruiz has shown, and East San Joseans supported UCAPAWA for several reasons. First, many Mexicanos and Mexican Americans had recently taken jobs in Valley canneries. The worst years of the Depression had come to an end in the Valley, and large numbers of local Italian and Portuguese residents left their long-held positions in food processing for better employment opportunities. Many ethnic Mexicans first stepped into the cannery workforce around the time of UCAPAWA's formation. Second, Valley canneries became tense and exciting centers of late-1930s' union organizing. Several organizations tried to woo those employees and win the right to represent them in collective bargaining agreements. But while AFL and Teamsters officials attracted some ethnic Mexicans, organizers for UCAPAWA Local 11 best understood ethnic Mexican political culture. Clubs, living room, and canneries became sites for UCAPAWA organizing on the East Side, and their rhetoric emphasized that members would be a "family" with strong reciprocal obligations. Eulalio Gutiérrez supported UCAPAWA because that organization stressed "that we needed to take care of one another. . . . They talked about us as brothers and sisters, people who could do something to change things and help each other out."[29]

Moreover, while UCAPAWA attempted to organize all cannery workers, many unionists also put ethnic Mexican interests front and center in their thinking about labor relations in the Valley. Above all, the organization showed unparalleled concern for Eastside women workers and a strong interest in promoting Mexicanas to positions of leadership. Organizing in workplaces and homes, CIO activists addressed their concerns about speed-ups, the lack of bathroom facilities in local canneries, frequent sexual harassment by foremen, and similar issues. María Velásquez's mother, for example, became involved in the UCAPAWA campaign in Sunnyvale "because they wanted to help the women in particular and they were the ones who could talk to the Mexicans in Spanish." While AFL officials declared that they only wanted to organize field workers because their "low living standards" provided "a drain on the standards of all wage earners," and while Teamster unionists hoped to control "every phase of the fruit and vegetable industry" in order to increase the bargaining power of their existing members, UCAPAWA struggled to make real connections with Eastsiders. Manuel Ramírez canvassed local town clubs and mutual-aid societies to find out more about those residents' concerns; his 1939 survey gave him a sense of that neighborhood's priorities and indicated the union's interest in taking its cues from local residents.[30]

Finally, CIO activists understood better than AFL officials that successful political organizing on the East Side required strategies to involve both U.S. and Mexican citizens. While local Teamsters demanded that their immigrant members become naturalized, the CIO union refused to denigrate the foreign-born or demand their assimilation in this way. Meetings were conducted in Spanish and English. Rather than emphasizing preferential treatment for United States citizens, UCAPAWA organizers stressed that both Mexicanos and Mexican Americans should participate on equal terms in their multi-national labor movement. María Santana and Leo Vargas were but two immigrant members who did not become citizens until many years later. Manuel Ramírez stated that "there was absolutely no pressure to be a U.S. citizen. Besides, we all had family from Mexico, at least." Demanding more rights and benefits for both U.S. and Mexican-born workers, these local unionists joined their national organization in 1940 to support efforts to include farm workers under the nation's social security system. Pushing an expansion of New Deal protections that would include noncitizens, a committee of local ethnic Mexicans began in 1939 to write letters to Congress and to travel to the state capital in Sacramento to press for the passage of a Fair Employment Practices Committee responsive to their needs.[31]

Above all, CIO activists earned the respect and interest of many on the East Side because they understood that ethnic Mexicans faced troubles beyond the orchard field or cannery line. As Eastsiders struggled to establish their position as equal residents of the area, the Santa Clara Valley local focused attention on the often violent and dehumanizing nature of life in surrounding neighborhoods. In the late 1930s UCAPAWA became the county's earliest civil rights organization to lobby local government agencies to address the poor living conditions in Sal Si Puedes and other parts of the East Side. In visits with members of the County Board of Supervisors, Leo Vargas and other union organizers attempted to persuade local officials to pave the neighborhood's roads, build a local park, and provide more fire and police protection in the area. Many had become more convinced that their futures lay in Northern California and not in Mexico, and the union showed a remarkable willingness to go beyond bread-and-butter workplace issues in its outreach efforts. Meetings of the San José local at times addressed the issues of police harassment and brutality, and Governor Culbert Olson appointed three UCAPAWA members in Southern California in 1939 to investigate "the shooting in the back of Faustino Sánchez, 17, by a state highway patrolman and the alleged suicide of Benjamin Moreno, 13, at Whittier Reformatory." When local whites attacked San José ethnic Mexicans who wore zoot suits in 1943, moreover, members of Local 11 visited detained Mexican American youth in the local jail and then corralled the city manager to urge "the people to quit beating up on the Mexicans."[32]

Vargas, Ramírez, and others active in the CIO built UCAPAWA on the political foundation that already existed in East San José. Members worked with mutual-aid organizations and other associations, following the CAWIU example by capitalizing on Northern California's strong self-help tradition. By 1940 San José's branch of the Alianza Hispano-Americana, the largest mutual-aid organization in the Southwest with many chapters around the region, had provided assistance to the union, and chapters of other mutual-aid societies such as the Logia Progresista soon did the same. Perhaps most importantly, those who understood the Mexican community knew the power of their patriotic sentiments and celebrations, and organizers employed a strategy that relied on the persistence of Mexican nationalism. When town clubs and mutualistas celebrated Mexican national holidays on the East Side, CIO members urged them to do more than simply remember their Mexican *patria* in glowing speeches and small parades. In unionists' view, such patriotism needed to bolster unionization. Celebrations on May 5 and the September 16 could suggest connections between Mexico's past struggles for freedom and the contemporary challenges facing Eastsiders, and Local 11 cooperated with San José organizers of the Cinco de Mayo and 16 de Septiembre celebrations who announced that Mexicanos would best "honor Mexico" by fighting for better employment and improved Valley neighborhoods. They found some success. Manuel Ramírez believed that the *fiestas patrias* "were some of our best events. We handed out union flyers on the streets and parks and got a very positive response. People were up in arms about many things, very excitable, thinking about politics already."[33]

But unionists knew that appeals to Mexican nationalism remained a tricky business. Patriotism could serve far more conservative purposes, and journalists, foremen, labor contractors, and employers at times expressed hostility toward UCAPAWA and other organizations on the grounds that true Mexicanos ought to keep out of trouble and fix their sights on returning to Mexico.[34] In the name of Mexican patriotism, the Mexican consul openly discouraged some Northern and Southern Californians from joining the CIO, and those officials rarely if ever intervened on local Mexicans' behalf in complaints about living or working conditions. Frustrated with Mexican government officials, Vargas and other activist ethnic Mexicans likened the consul's "sentimental" patriotism to support for the Associated Farmers and other California employers. One journalist offered the story of Elias Pérez, a worker at Rancho Scaglioni in Santa Clara County, as an example of the perils of such affections for the *patria*. "He is a Mexican by birth and like all enemies of other workers, he is a patriot to the bone," the journalist explained. While celebrating Mexico's *fiestas patrias*, he watched his wages and those of other workers fall, and he did his best to assure that no unemployed worker replaced him on the job. This was a patriotism damaging to Mexicano interests. "If, as he says," the author concluded, "Mexico is the greatest country in the world, why does he not go there?"[35]

Despite these pitfalls, UCAPAWA utilized expressions of Mexican nationalism to bring cannery and field workers under the union banner, a form of working-class Americanism that sought both to affirm ethnic pride and to urge their alliance with other groups. Unionists opposed ongoing repatriation calls issued by the Mexican consulate, members of town clubs, and others on the grounds that Mexicano workers needed to focus on staying in the West and building a new labor movement. Above all, UCAPAWA members hated to see elderly Northern Californians leave to retire in Mexico after years of work in the state. Eduardo Quevedo, the Los Angeles–based president of a civil rights organization supported by UCAPAWA members, made this sentiment most clear in 1940 when he demanded state relief for retired noncitizens on the grounds that they have given the best years of their life to building up the wealth of this great State which originally belonged to their ancestors; and now that they have attained the age where they can no longer be of use to the exploiters, instead of doing the fair and honorable thing by providing them with a measure of security in their old age we offer them repatriation. Repatriation indeed. To repatriate one means to restore him to his own country. Mexico is no longer their country.[36]

Along with urging Eastsiders and others to recognize the United States as "their country," Local 11 organizers demanded that the Mexican and United States governments address the exploitation of immigrant and U.S.-born Mexicans. Others, such as Octavio Cano, chair of the Discrimination Committee for UCAPAWA's West Coast region, blamed officials' timidity on the "Good Neighbor Policy." Rather than rhetoric about hemispheric unity, Cano called for a "real effective Good Neighbor policy of 'deeds,' and stressed that 'the just and friendly treatment by our country' of the Mexican people right in California will be one good place to start being more 'neighborly.'"[37]

THE SECOND GOLD RUSH

Sharp challenges to Valley politics and creative appeals to working-class Americanism excited passions in the late 1930s and early 1940s, but the coming of World War II sounded the death knell for San José's UCAPAWA and Depression-era Left. Some have called this period the "second Gold Rush" to suggest its profound demographic and economic consequences on the state, and those years did prove nearly as transformative for ethnic Mexicans as had the 1840s. World War II has rightly been called the most important turning point in the twentieth-century history of the American West, a sharp transition marked by a massive influx of federal spending. As in other parts of the region, the arrival of war brought an end to economic hardship for most white San Joseans. "The lean years are over," the *San Jose Mercury* announced in 1941, and once destitute Valley residents now laughed and joked about what to do with their "mad money." Government military contracts to local businesses brought millions of new dollars to the Valley, and wages skyrocketed. While manufacturing industries had paid workers only $15,329,000 in 1940, by 1945 their annual salaries totaled $54,590,000. The AFL's Central Labor Council claimed "no unemployed members" in Valley locals shortly after Pearl Harbor, and it seemed clear that many had already begun to put greater stock than ever in maintaining regional peace and prosperity.[38]

The Second World War pulled San José out of the Depression but brought few major improvements to ethnic Mexican barrios. Shut out from California's booming wartime economy, most local ethnic Mexicans remained poor and tied to agriculture in this Valley transformed by rapid urbanization and industrialization. White residents who abandoned orchard and cannery jobs for more profitable and less physically demanding employment left Mexicans the region's low-wage, seasonal, and most dangerous work. Racial restrictions on new county jobs proved further isolating. Federal officials discovered that employers such as the Navy's Ship Service Laundry made it a practice not to hire "Mexicans or Negroes," that the Eckhart Seed Company in nearby Salinas requested that the U.S. Employment Service not send "colored or Mexicans," and that Kaiser Permanente and other county employers turned Mexicanos away because of their citizenship status. At least one cannery owner pledged that he would never hire Mexican-origin residents for managerial positions in his fruit-packing plant, and by 1947 only nine of the Valley's roughly one thousand county employees were Mexicans.[39]

These all seemed good reasons to expect that UCAPAWA might find new followers on the East Side, but political pressures instead quieted organizing efforts to a whisper, particularly those based in any way on Mexican nationalism. Amidst calls for national and hemispheric unity, San Joseans looked askance on radical unions, and local canneries seemed too important a wartime industry to risk labor stoppages. Allegiance to the Allied cause limited the range of union activities. Many employees of local fruit-packing companies devoted a portion of their wages to buying war bonds, "enthused over their patriotic movement," and one AFL member affirmed that "All of us must realize that food comes first with our fighting men; let us see to it that they get all they need and that none goes to waste for lack of help." UCAPAWA had little choice but to follow many other labor organizations and agree to a no-strike pledge. As wildcat strikes halted, political conservatism found new allies under the fire of war, and many unionists with experience in earlier Northern California strike activities left for the armed services. A plaque with the names of four hundred members gone to war hung in one San José union hall by May 1943, and at least a quarter of those departed from the Sutter Packing Company had Spanish surnames.[40]

In addition to out-migration of this sort, other wartime changes challenged UCAPAWA's work after 1941. Ethnic Mexicans arrived in San José and other parts of California in massive numbers, and when growers called for additional Mexican workers to fill vacant work crews, the federal governments of the United States and Mexico rushed to help. The Emergency Farm Labor Agreement, signed by officials from both countries, sent thousands of contracted *braceros* (men who work with their arms) across the international border, low-wage recruits whom Mexican officials congratulated for agreeing "to substitute in the fields for the soldiers who left to defend their country." Mexicanos arrived during this second Gold Rush under intensive government

Four of the tens of thousands of braceros given a medical inspection for work in the United States during the early 1950s. Photograph by Ernesto Galarza, in the Ernesto Galarza Papers, box 65, folder 3, Department of Special Collections, Stanford University.

supervision and careful isolation in agricultural employment. Those laborers proved a delightful boon to local growers, a "Godsend," according to one Valley farm manager, and county growers shared a pool of 4,033 contracted Mexicans in 1943 and 1944, prompting the local supervisor of the War Food Administration Office to announce that braceros "will be shifted from one section to another as rapidly as the apricot, pear, prune, and vegetable crops are ready to harvest." While guaranteeing that crops would be picked on time, the Bracero Program encouraged greater cooperation among growers, leading to the establishment of the Santa Clara Cherry Growers Association in 1944 and similar pacts designed to rationalize the use of agricultural labor in the county. This, indeed, was a time of new strength for anti-union forces.[41]

Contacting braceros and other field workers became no easy task for the union after 1941. UCAPAWA members had few resources for locating migrant labor camps squirreled away on farms throughout the region, and Mexican consular officials warned those workers not to become involved in Valley unions. The U.S. government likewise discouraged braceros from thinking of themselves as anything more than temporary workers, and the local supervisor of the War Food Administration proudly reported only scattered problems with American agitators urging braceros "to slow down in their work and to demand more pay." Many contracted laborers wanted above all to make quick dollars and return to their *patrias chicas*, and members of this "reserve labor army" accordingly became the migrant darlings of white San Joseans. "I have not found a surly one among them," one grower declared in 1943, "and they all have a sense of humor." Boosters praised Mexicanos for helping the Valley recover from economic Depression, and the San José press portrayed the racial characteristics of imported workers such as "Benito Luz Tupataro, whose gentle touch removes the fruit from the tree without a bruise." Clear racial differences separated most braceros from white Americans, the newspaper argued in 1944, as arrivals "represent every conceivable type found south of the border. Some of them could have stepped straight from the pages of National Geographic magazine, with their closed Indian faces, their shoulders lumpily enshrouded in blankets and their hats made of straw which never saw the inside of a factory and looked as if they might have been handed down from father to son for several generations." Many San Joseans wanted to meet those seemingly exotic visitors for themselves. Gawking onlookers met bracero trains in the hope of purchasing their genuine peasant clothing, and, with a typical flourish, the *San José Mercury News* announced in August 1944 that these "birds of fancy plumage . . . wore serapes with their heads poked through the hole in the center, sombreros, carried guitars and luggage in baskets of Indian weave."[42]

Such spectacular descriptions missed a major transformation underway in California. Local ethnic Mexican and imported braceros became ever more dominant in state agriculture, but fewer white residents expressed concern about farmworkers. While many had actually paid attention to rural poverty during the heady union drives of the 1930s, World War II directed San José energies into the national fight against fascism and the county's role in that struggle. Urban prosperity dulled interest in the surrounding fields. Few noted the difficult and dangerous labor performed by low-paid contract workers, and, in the view of some U.S. officials, the program's greatest administrative hurdle was providing "the kind of food [braceros] were accustomed to in Mexico." As the following chapter makes clear, braceros in fact encountered far greater difficulties securing adequate wages and working conditions. Other ethnic Mexicans also struggled during the war. Cannery laborers worked longer and harder to meet production quotas, and their unions did little more than settle individual wage and promotion disputes. Cherry pickers in the Valley complained in May 1944 when government employees of the War Food Administration reduced harvest wages from $1.50 to $1.00 per hour to combat inflation, and "considerable unrest" among them prompted rumors, quickly squashed, of strike activity. Injuries remained commonplace in those agricultural industries and others, and job accidents led to the death of at least three county braceros during a one-month period in the summer of 1944 alone.[43]

As the early 1940s reshaped the Valley economy and political atmosphere, activist Eastsiders could do little more than act as a token lobbying group. Formal union strikes disappeared in the county, UCAPAWA members rarely met or spoke with contracted immigrants during the war years, and CIO members instead pushed government officials to monitor local working and living conditions in the name of hemispheric unity. It took courage enough for San José's Local 11 to write "letters to the governor [of California] and to the president asking them to help the braceros out, to boost the wages they made so that everyone would do better," a task they undertook as national UCAPAWA officials took brave stands on behalf of Filipinos' rights to naturalize, for the desegregation of the armed services, and for a permanent Fair Employment Practices Commission. Most AFL unionists in San José showed far less enthusiasm about such matters, choosing either to ignore the region's nonwhite workers or to affirm that those residents rightfully remained outside the labor movement. It was the rare AFL cannery union that threatened to expel any member twice "found guilty of discriminating against another member because of race, color, or religious or personal beliefs." In fact, the Valley's labor press cited only one example of an antidiscrimination clause in a union constitution during the war years. Few labor organizations invited the participation of nonwhites, and no ethnic Mexicans seem to have been members of the Retail Clerks Union, the Painters, the Culinary Workers, the Carpenters, or many other important AFL unions in the area. The national struggle against the Axis powers did little to drive the Devil from the Santa Clara Valley. Racist minstrel shows depicting stock African American characters remained a common form of entertainment for white war workers, and Eastsiders relied again on their own devices to survive the hostile political climate.[44]

Ethnic Mexicans neighborhoods in San José and other parts of the state changed dramatically during the war. New migrations led to the even greater crowding of segregated East Side barrios as job opportunities in Valley canneries prompted Texans and Southern Californians to settle permanently, as undocumented immigrants arrived from Mexico, and as untold numbers of braceros broke their contracts and put down fast roots in Northern California. By the early 1950s the Santa Clara Valley hosted one of the largest ethnic Mexican populations in the state, but few local policymakers gave any sustained thought to that community, so close to downtown but so far from booster's concerns. The area's disparity from most other county neighborhoods was startling. Most ethnic Mexicans remained confined to the region's least remunerative jobs, Mexican women dominated cannery work, a position they would retain until the industry's decline in the 1970s, and other immigrant and U.S.-born residents of Mexican descent found themselves stuck in equally unrewarding employment. Residents of Sal Si Puedes and adjacent barrios would also suffer life with few streetlights or paved roads into the mid-1950s, and county officials showed little concern for Eastsiders' health and welfare. A drive to test ethnic Mexicans for tuberculosis, for instance, came only in August 1945 at the insistence of San José resident José Alvarado, president of the newly formed Latin American Association.[45]

World War II altered and enriched San José's ethnic Mexican culture. By July 1945 popular Mexican films and musicians arrived in this burgeoning city to entertain Valley residents, and San Joseans flocked to live performances by the likes of Pedro Infante and Miguelito Valdez, and to films such as *La Virgen Morena* and *Los Miserables*. Town clubs and other associations at times met in local movie theaters throughout the 1940s, although scattered evidence suggests that the in-and-out movements of wartime proved extremely disruptive for local mutual-aid societies. New barrio organizations reflected recent demographic transformations. Tejanos formed an Eagle Pass Club and a Del Rio Club during World War II, organizations that would survive into the 1990s, and ethnic Mexicans from Central California created a San Joaquin Valley Club to organize men's Saturday football and baseball competitions. A researcher after the war discovered that "families from Texas or Colorado or Coahuila or Michoacán may form a clique within a single neighborhood and establish close relationships primarily with members of that clique." Regional loyalties led to some intraneighborhood conflicts, and one Eastsider from South Texas found that her New Mexican neighbor "always talks about people from Texas, and says that all Texans are no good. I tell her that Texans are as good as anybody from New Mexico—maybe better. She has her own friends, and she can stick with them; I don't ever invite her to my house any more."[46]

These newly arrived San Joseans and others expressed loyalties to distant home barrios and colonias, and memories of those places shaped youth associations, clubs, and "gangs" during the early 1940s. Many transplanted Southern Californians wore long coats and baggy pants, the so-called zoot suits of the day, and a small percentage of those teenagers fought one another downtown on summer weekends, continuing disputes over territory and social boundaries first developed on the streets of Los Angeles, Riverside, Santa Barbara, and other cities. Anti-Mexican violence did not disappear during World War II, and zoot suiters became the most recent target of vigilante depredations. After white military men attacked ethnic Mexican youth in Los Angeles County in 1943, a riot blamed immediately on the Mexican American victims rather than the soldier aggressors, San José officials began in the name of county peace to crack down on those youth who sported ducktail haircuts, small tattoos on the backs of their hands, or long coat jackets. Conflicts spread north into the Bay Area and other parts of the state. Sailors "intent on starting their own 'zoot suit' war on North Market Street" hunted for Mexican American San Joseans that summer, and Superior Judge William James warned "that we certainly don't want to see anything happen here like it is in Los Angeles." Under his watch, zoot suiters arrested for petty crimes in the summer of 1943 were given probation on the condition that they join the army. Angry Marines drove other Latinos from a nearby Santa Cruz beach, and five Mexican Americans, despite being juveniles, were held in the city jail by San José police "because of their large sizes." A year later, twenty-five zoot suiters were rounded up for "frequenting streets and public places at late hours of the night," and law enforcement arranged for the deportation of three of the "city's bad boys," as the *San José Mercury* called them. A month later, police in the Valley town of Gilroy rounded up thirty others for violating curfew laws.[47]

Entrenched stereotypes about Mexican criminality shaped wartime San José. Suspecting that "Los Angeles Mexicans" imported marijuana into the Valley, local law enforcement officers questioned farmworkers who visited the city in the evenings, and such harassment nearly caused a riot when police officers arrested two Mexicans in St. James Park. A fight had broken out between the two on one August night in 1943, and officers Joséph Pinkston and Douglas Daly soon appeared at the scene. Pinkston and Daly gave chase, and the suspects ran toward the corner of San Antonio and Market streets, where a large group of ethnic Mexicans was just emerging from a dance club. Fellow police officer Keith Kelly apprehended the two in front of the crowd of 150 onlookers, and Pinkston "took charge" of one of the suspects, eighteen-year-old Joe Riveria, "using a hammer-lock as the Mexican became abusive." Daly moved the other suspect toward the police station several blocks away, but as the officers and suspects approached the station, "the Mexicans closed in," according to news reports, and concerned zoot suiters and cannery workers began "demanding the release of the prisoner." Pinkston forced Riveria to cross the street to escape the crowd, but the latter "fell to the ground, claiming he had been struck and moaning loudly." The men and women observing the scene ran forward in protest, but military police and twelve other police officers rushed ahead and dispersed the onlookers. Riveria was ushered into the station, but the confusion allowed several Mexicans to free the other suspect from Officer Daly. News reports assured *San José Mercury* readers that justice had prevailed: Doctors at County Hospital announced that Riveria was "faking" injuries caused, he said, by Officer Pinkston, and the courts incarcerated Riveria for disorderly conduct.[48]

St. James Park, the site of the hanging of Thurmond and Holmes, also witnessed a dramatic clash between several zoot suiters and sailors toward the end of the war. This, more than any other spot in the Valley, was a place haunted by recent violence, and ethnic Mexicans who had also witnessed the 1933 lynchings must have felt more than a little wary about their own safety. Not surprisingly, the young ethnic Mexicans arrested that evening were charged with disturbing the peace while the sailors were released. Here again, racism worked its black magic, affirming that Mexican American youth deserved imprisonment rather than equal treatment before the law, and seeing that white vigilantism against nonwhites went unpunished. New iterations of much older racial conflicts taunted San Joseans eager to exorcise Depression-era demons of poverty and powerlessness, but East Side residents did not abandon civil rights work. Despite the overt violence displayed in St. James Park and its more subtle forms—seasonal unemployment, child labor, rat-infested housing, and unsafe barrio streets, to name a few—ethnic Mexicans entered the late 1940s with greater residential stability and deeper roots on the East Side. They were more sure of their place in the Valley than their predecessors of the 1920s or the 1850s, and local activists from Sal Si Puedes and other neighborhoods would follow UCAPAWA's example in forging new civil rights organizations dedicated to tackling postwar inequalities.[49]

Chapter 6

Braceros and Business Machines

Enthusiastic publicizers of San Jose are six attractive
young ladies who arrived in town Sunday morning with a
group of men and women who came out from Endicott,
New York, to work in IBM's new plant here.

Features of the city that natives take for granted are
drawing huge exclamations of wonder and surprise from
these girls, all of whom are employed as operators of the
Carrol card press.

"I've never seen such huge flowers—the roses are
magnificent."

"Is the weather always this cool in summer? Doesn't it
ever rain?"

These are a few of the questions with which they ply
longtime residents.

—*San José Mercury-Herald*, August 25, 1943

Like so many California cities, San José witnessed remarkable demographic
growth during and immediately after World War II. Economic, cultural, and
political transformations were cause and consequence of this population explosion, developments that began to make the modern Valley a site of high-
technology production. Attracted by the presence of Stanford University in
the northern part of the county, a Cold War "windfall of contracts for military research, development, and production" supported the production of
cutting-edge electronic devices, particularly radio equipment. Boosters believed year-round industrial employment far more promising than seasonal
cannery labor; state-funded adult education classes provided white San Joseans training in accounting, office machines, and shorthand; and prominent

companies such as Hewlett-Packard, Lockheed, Sylvania, Varian Associates, General Electric, and IBM made the area ground zero for the new economic development that would eventually spread throughout the Southwest. World War II prompted most Valley unionists to seek more cooperative relationships with their employers. Corporations trusted that Valley labor activists would be politically moderate, committed to regional growth, and "all part of the community," unlike, presumably, radical CIO unions of the 1930s. Innovators like Frederick Terman, who turned Stanford into a major research university during these years, and David Packard, whose work in electronics made him an almost mythical figure in the region's high-technology community, have long received accolades for guiding the Valley into the industrial era.[1]

As the county's population exploded in size and the area became increasingly well known as a suburban mecca, few unionists or civic leaders during the 1950s attended to the Valley's racial inequalities. World War II was followed by an obsession with economic growth. Some members of the armed services who had passed through the San Francisco Bay Area decided to settle and work for newly arrived companies, while other white migrants learned about the Valley in national magazines. Middle-class neighborhoods built on former farm lands encouraged corporate relocations, and these changes made the region a new mecca for the white middle class. One booster promised that "There is elbow room for outdoor living where a man may even operate a family-sized farm on the side if he so desires." College-educated employees could often see rows of fruit trees from the windows of their high-tech firms "sandwiched among the prune, apricot and pear orchards, among vegetable farms and in the outskirts of towns." A worker at IBM who resided in the nearby town of Saratoga gushed that "we have a garden and the acre of ground around our house is generously shaded with fruit trees. Around us are the foothills. Though tennis and other outdoor sports are within easy reach, we prefer swimming or trips to the theatre in San Francisco." By 1950 San José had one of the lowest percentages of "nonwhite" residents of any major California city.[2]

While most contemporaries celebrated Valley growth, local ethnic Mexicans continued to raise different and often damning questions about the costs and consequences of San José's development. Californians faced new threats to their civil rights. Racial ideologies continued to shape the Santa Clara Valley, but white racism did not necessarily mean the renewal of open expressions of anti-Mexican sentiment. Government officials instead tended to ignore the presence of the East Side and urbanizing farmworkers. Political parties devoted little energy to registering Mexican American voters. Legislators passed laws disastrous for rural and urban Latinos, and few political lobbyists attempted to counter such trends. As a new civil rights movement developed in California neighborhoods and workplaces, ethnic Mexican organizations began to tackle the region's longstanding problems of poverty and racial discrimination. Relying on approaches to political organizing developed before World War II, their struggles within labor unions and other organizations were slow and often frustrating, but this generation of activists laid the foundation for greater Latino political success in subsequent decades.

POSTWAR COMMUNITIES

The wartime economic boom failed to save many ethnic Mexicans from a life of real economic hardship. A critical if unrecognized foundation to the Valley economy, thousands remained agricultural laborers forgotten in the rush to the high-tech era. While the 1930s had seen few new immigrants and significant emigration back to Mexico, regional economic prosperity, farm mechanization, and the international sponsorship of contracted braceros reversed those trends. Many who once toiled in Idaho, South Texas, and the Imperial Valley settled in Northern California, while others arrived after stints in the armed services, an experience that left more than one veteran "haunted" by the racism of white officers. Thousands of undocumented migrants came from the U.S.-Mexico border region, shepherded by private labor contractors based in Redwood City, San José, Gilroy, and other local municipalities. The San José area's permanent ethnic Mexican population boomed to around eight thousand by 1950 and some twenty-five thousand by 1960, and Santa Clara County soon boasted the third largest ethnic Mexican population in the state.[3]

For the first time in the twentieth century, large numbers of these urbanizing Valley residents scattered outside of East San José. As subdivisions appeared to support the new industries headquartered in the area, the racial covenants that had restricted nonwhite settlement there and in other neighborhoods were declared illegal by the U.S. Supreme Court in 1948. Some Mexican Americans called those middle-class suburbs their home, but the area's largest barrio remained the affordable, and the historically Mexican, East Side, where migrants still settled near friends, family members, and the local canneries. The work of the neighborhood's 4,500 residents bore little resemblance to that of Valley engineers and scientists. Many "lack[ed] adequate food, clothing, and shelter," and nearly every wage-earning resident of Sal Si Puedes, women and men, labored in unskilled jobs into the mid-1950s. The majority did seasonal work for low wages, barrio children commonly remained out of school until the end of the September harvest, and some women began household cooking at four o'clock prior to heading to work. Hoping to abandon this life and move up the economic ladder, women and men complained about their low rates of pay, seasonal unemployment, and lack of seniority rights. Those men able to move from agricultural industries commonly found that the available construction jobs left them, like others in their neighborhood, unemployed when work crews ceased working from November to March, and most residents, including the elderly and disabled, continued to pick crops or can produce for at least part of each year.[4]

Some combination of applicants' frequent lack of a high school education, their often limited English skills, and the continuing racial discrimination in Valley employment assured that few ethnic Mexicans would join the workforces at IBM, General Electric, and similar companies. Job advertisements in the local newspaper at times specified that applicants "must be white," and an activist during the late 1960s would charge that "The federal government . . . is as guilty as private industry in its discriminatory hiring practices involving the Spanish-speaking community in the Bay Area." Other obstacles also made economic advancement difficult. Property remained hard for many to obtain. Many ethnic Mexicans who discussed the purchase of a home encountered suspicious creditors who "investigate[d] Mexican loan prospects a little more thoroughly than someone else . . . because so many are transients" and considered barrios such as Sal Si Puedes "special risks." Ethnic Mexican kids encountered discriminatory treatment from teachers and white students in Valley schools, but many East Side adults emphasized to their children the importance of finishing their high school educations. One mother explained that

> My main worry is keeping the children in school, especially my fifteen-year-old son—he wants to quit and get a job. I've made him go on because I know you can't get a decent job without a high school education. My husband feels the same way I do—he only went through grade school; his family wanted to send him on to high school, but he wouldn't go. Now he is always saying that just because he isn't educated he's spent the best years of his life as a slave. That's why we want our kids to get an education.[5]

Such commitments to advancing beyond agricultural work were common among California Latinos, and they assured that a small number of East Side ethnic Mexicans would profit during the postwar boom. Rather than employees of national companies, these more privileged ethnic Mexicans tended to be the storeowners, radio disc jockeys, barbers, hair stylists, automobile mechanics, and pharmacists who served the Spanish-speaking community. The Mexican American real estate agent Jesús Eduardo García offered special help to barrio clients frustrated by the way white agents treated them, and others like him began to form the region's first Mexican American middle class, a development in which San José lagged far behind Los Angeles County. Known at times as *Mexicanos de alta sociedad*, or high-society Mexicans, some of these self-employed residents left the city altogether, following

the white middle class into surrounding suburbs like Cupertino and Saratoga. Others ceased speaking Spanish at home, and, in an unwitting bow to
earlier San Joseans who had labeled themselves "Californios," began to insist
that as "Spanish Americans" they remained above the region's Mexican rab-
ble. One successful businessman made his derision for the East Side's poor
clear in 1955, declaring that "There are a lot of us who are trying to get
ahead and make a decent life for our children, but most of the people just
don't seem to care. Most of the people in Mayfair are pretty low class; they
are lazy and don't care how they live. That place is really a slum, and the
Mexican people ought to be ashamed of it."[6]

But whether working class or self-employed, only a small minority of
Mexican Americans made such open pronouncements, as places like the East
Side retained a fragile sense of community forged from common experiences
of migration, labor, and settlement in the Mayfair district. The dominant
political current was one of simmering discontent and frustration with the
lingering poverty of the East Side. Now intent to remain permanent residents
of the area and to abandon migrant labor, barrio inhabitants worked extremely long days, particularly during the busy summer months, called
themselves Mexicans, Mexican Americans, Mexicanos, Americans, Tejanos,
and a variety of other names, and remained, in general, "uneasy" about
white neighbors. Strong memories of earlier waves of anti-Mexican violence,
particularly the police maltreatment of zoot suiters, caused some to "fear
that [violence] may come back again," and most preferred to shop for goods
and services in businesses run by other ethnic Mexicans. Stores established
along Alum Rock and Santa Clara avenues offered tortillas, tripe, and other
products common in Mexican kitchens, and many Eastsiders attended
churches built during the 1940s and 1950s to serve local Spanish-speakers,
including Our Lady of Guadalupe Chapel, the region's first Catholic mission
in the twentieth century devoted to the ethnic Mexican population.[7]

Influenced by new businesses and churches catering to the East Side, ethnic Mexican communities became more elaborate and diverse as San José
urbanized. Spanish remained the dominant idiom of local neighborhoods,
"generally preferred for situations of friendship and intimacy," but "a surprising number of teen-agers . . . perhaps half, chatter[ed] together in an
Americanized Spanish argot." Protestant churches sprang up throughout San
José, and by 1958 the area housed more than a dozen Spanish-speaking
congregations, including Baptists, Assemblies of God, Methodists, Seventh
Day Adventists, Pentecostals, and Jehovah's Witnesses. While some Protestants aimed to assimilate like the region's Italian and Portuguese, many
others focused on what they could do to help migrants adapt to the barrio. A
commitment to working-class mutualism prevailed that proved indispensable
to those facing hard times, and mutual-aid organizations, a dominant East
Side institution prior to World War II, continued to prosper in San José.

Women and men in associations like the Logia Alma Mexicana paid dues by the 1950s to assure coverage of their funeral expenses after their deaths, those with year-round jobs encouraged bosses to hire East Side friends and kin, and some wired one another money to make it through difficult periods. One Eastsider admitted that "I don't know how we'd get by if it wasn't for my married daughter in Los Angeles. In the winter when my husband can't find work, she always sends a little money every time she gets a paycheck."[8]

As ethnic Mexicans became more settled in the area, booming economic times also made transnational cultural practices all the more intense. Residents visited makeshift community centers such as the De La Rosa Grocery Store, which advertised itself as "a miniature Mexico," East San Joseans affirmed their Mexicanidad in proud terms, and one woman recalled that "My mother never stopped telling us about the old days in Mexico. She never tired of telling us stories of her native village in Guanajuato; she never let us children forget the things that her village was noted for . . . the old traditions, the happy people, and the dances and weddings and fiestas. From the time I was a small child I always wanted to go back to Mexico and see the village where my mother was born."[9] Affirming distinctive allegiances, residents maintained strong attachments to Mexican hometowns, continued to join established organizations such as the Club Tapatío, and gave new businesses names like Hotel Jalisco. The small middle class developing in the 1940s and 1950s helped immigrants define themselves vis-à-vis their Mexican patria. Mexico's proximity shaped numerous other aspects of barrio life, as when one Sonoran woman popularized her village's version of the *pastorela*, a traditional Mexican Christmas pageant. Communicating by mail in 1954 with her hometown schoolteacher, she transcribed local oral tradition and presented other churchgoers with a Christmas Eve program replete with "shepherds, angels, an old hermit, a devil, and . . . an Indian who insisted on going to Bethlehem to offer the Christ Child a plate of enchiladas." In similarly transnational ways, other Eastsiders venerated the Virgin of San Juan de los Lagos, a popular figure in the Mexican state of Jalisco, or traveled to Mexico City to pray at the shrine of Our Lady of Guadalupe.[10]

Such activities indicated not only the importance of Mexican culture but also the vibrancy of ties to distant *patrias chicas* on both sides of the U.S.-Mexico border. Many urbanizing San Joseans sought out other Valley residents who hailed from their state or county, and new businesses—including the Tiajuana [*sic*] Café, the Arizona Café, the Tampico Restaurant, the Tampico grocery, the Morelia Café, and the Del Rio Café—attempted to capitalize on regionalist affections. Protestant churchgoers often hailed from New Mexico and Texas, states that had experienced intense missionary activity since the 1920s, and these congregations drew strength from that common regional background. "Where are you from?" remained a standard question that helped urbanizing Eastsiders make sense of one another. While the majority of local ethnic Mexican teenagers had been born in other areas of California, and while many others hailed from Arizona and Colorado, a non-Mexican researcher in 1950s' *Sal Si Puedes* reported hearing "comments of this sort: 'Whenever my car breaks down, I take it to Manuel's garage; I can trust him, because he's from Jalisco, like me.'" In part because attachments to Mexican hometowns and states remained so important, few immigrants became naturalized U.S. citizens in the immediate postwar period, and the more elderly of barrio residents almost always remained Mexican nationals.[11]

Regardless of residents' citizenship or home region, many found leisure and meaning in the circulation of Mexican popular culture, a tie to the patria that became much tighter after World War II. Eager to watch recently released Spanish-language films, San Joseans turned out in droves to the Teatro Liberty and other local movie houses, enjoying cinematic productions that became hallmarks of Mexican cultural nationalism during the 1940s and 1950s. Stars such as Tito Guizar, Cantinflas, Pedro Infante, and Dolores del Río stood as ready symbols of Mexicanidad, and visits by Fernando Fernández and other celebrities excited crowds of local fans. Mexican musicians who performed in the region developed a similar following, and the San José entrepreneur Frank Dávilla hosted weekly dances that often concluded with shouts of "Viva México!" Three local radio stations also kept Spanish-language residents abreast of musical developments and breaking news on both sides of the international border, and the area's five Latino announcers became popular intellectuals of a sort, thanks both to their willingness to speak forcefully about important political issues and to the high rates of illiteracy among working-class Spanish speakers. Most disc jockeys, including Carlos Aganza Graham, who had recently worked in Mexico City radio, and Jesús Reyes Valenzuela, a former band leader from the state of Chihuahua, were immigrants, and José J. Alvarado, a Mexican citizen and member of the city's *fiestas patrias* committee, was considered by some residents the "only man who ha[d] helped" the East Side.[12]

Alvarado's work echoed the concerns of Spanish-language newspapers in California, another foundation of postwar ethnic Mexican culture, and an institution that harkened back to New Almadén miners' attachment to the San Francisco press during the 1860s. Grocery stores that served ethnic Mexican clients sold Los Angeles's *La Opinión* and San José's *El Excéntrico* during the 1940s and 1950s, and copies of the former disappeared "soon after the papers are put on sale each day." Like local disc jockeys, the handful of ethnic Mexican journalists working for the Valley's three Spanish-language newspapers spoke out on behalf of barrio residents, worked closely with San Francisco's Mexican consulate, and reminded readers that "it is the duty of every good Mexican to remember from time to time our beloved Mexican soil." The bilingual press became a vehicle for expressions of postwar Mexican and Mexican American identities, as *El Excéntrico* ran photos and stories about the "most popular newcomers" in local barrios, and as coverage of the nightclub scene encouraged young farmworkers, cannery employees, and others to enjoy performers such as Bobby Zamora, "the king of the sax," who played traditional Mexican corridos as well as the latest mambos and be-bop numbers. Announcing those events and others, *El Excéntrico* popularized dance competitions that awarded winners hundred-pound sacks of pinto beans, a staple of Mexican households, offered advice on how to dance the rumba, and included columns written by Valley high school students.[13]

In the process, *El Excéntrico* both witnessed and shaped cultural practices in postwar San José. Above all, journalists urged participation in the *fiestas patrias* celebrations, and the booming size of local barrios made Cinco de Mayo and 16 de Septiembre spectacular community events, far grander than anything Valley residents had imagined in the 1920s or 1860s. Dances, speeches about the French occupation of the *patria*, performances of the Mexican national anthem, and long parades from St. James Park found the support of San José's Comisión Honorífica Mexicana as well as the Mexican consulate. For weeks prior to each holiday, the East Side buzzed in anticipation, and San Joseans rented traditional *charro* and *china poblana* outfits from neighborhood grocery stores. These were not just immigrant occasions, and more than eight thousand residents from different areas of Mexico and the United States flocked to the May 1951 fiesta. The crowds increased in future years as the press helped to make San José a regional center for celebrating the Mexican holidays. Taking their cues from other organizations throughout the Southwest, disc jockeys and journalists promoted a "fiesta queen" competition among young women in Northern California, and contestants from as far south as Monterey County entered the pageants, circulated glamorous photos of themselves, gained the endorsement of Mexican merchants and clubs, and urged friends to cast their ballots at popular Mexican nightclubs in the city.[14]

As they attended church services and musical performances, read local papers, and attended biannual fiestas, ethnic Mexicans experienced a cultural atmosphere that took many cues from contemporary Latin America. But like other Californians, they also developed hobbies, clubs, and passions that reflected their residency in the Santa Clara Valley. San José and nearby San Francisco offered an exciting blend of cultural offerings. Young Mexican Americans declared their love for rock and roll and discussed the latest records of Elvis Presley, for example, even as they sang along to the tunes of Trio Los Panchos and other Spanish-language stars. Residents formed social clubs in local high schools with non-Mexican students, expressed a fondness for Cuban and Puerto Rican dance steps, and became sporting enthusiasts, taking to the football field, the bowling alley, and even the golf course to compete with one another before heading downtown to the Spanish-language movies or the Mexican dances.[15]

FARM LABOR UNION

This was the cultural terrain that gave life to postwar ethnic Mexican politics, and one of the nation's most creative civil rights organizers made good use of these Santa Clara Valley developments. Ernesto Galarza was oracle and visionary in the eyes of many of his contemporaries, a critic of agricultural labor relations and a Mexicano whose perspective on Northern California differed wildly from that of the area's civic boosters. An immigrant himself, Galarza appealed to his co-ethnics' transnational sensibilities and to their involvement in community organizations, becoming, in the process, an activist of national and international prominence. Although he lived in suburban Willow Glen, he understood that farmworker neighborhoods were not sharply defined by the geographic parameters of the East Side, that a unique cultural geography in fact rooted these places to many other locales, and that booster rhetoric about regional growth obscured ethnic Mexican struggles to make ends meet.[16]

Galarza's biography both paralleled and diverged from that of most of his immigrant contemporaries. Born in Mexico in 1905, he moved to California as a boy, labored in agricultural fields, and went on to attend Occidental College and Columbia University. A government employee charged with monitoring hemispheric labor relations during World War II, he grew particularly concerned about anti-Mexican violence, and he publicly called the 1943 retributions against Los Angeles zoot suiters "open race warfare." Long worried about "economic, social and racial discrimination in the Southwest," Galarza saw little to celebrate in the county's pockets of ethnic Mexican poverty, and he met hundreds of former field workers similarly disenchanted with their work and residency in Northern California. He settled in San José in March 1948 to help organize ethnic Mexicans into the National Farm Labor Union, a group recently arrived in the state that had made a name for itself in the South and Midwest during the 1930s as the Southern Tenant Farmers Union (STFU). He remained, until his death in 1984, more interested in the Valley's working poor than in its technology rich.[17]

Galarza understood that World War II had transformed ethnic Mexican communities in California. He noted that an indigenous activism in the state's barrios and colonias had survived the decline of UCAPAWA and other Depression-era organizations, and he learned that Eastsiders were particularly concerned about poverty and the lack of urban services in their neighborhoods. Some church leaders showed interest in changing rural labor relations, and agricultural communities throughout the state boasted "much more young [farmworker] leadership than is generally recognized."[18] Interest ran high in renewing the union drives seen throughout the state during the 1930s, and one San Josean declared that

> If general improvement in standard of living among our people is to come, it will have to come through reform in agricultural labor. Emphasizing industrial problems is foolish, since Santa Clara County is an agricultural area and will probably continue to be so for years. There isn't really enough industrial development here to furnish jobs for the Mexican people. . . . You can't help the Mexican people right now by assuming that they will all go into industry and ignoring the problems of the migratory workers.[19]

Because San José barrios retained intimate ties to agriculture, many stressed that low wages and harsh working conditions in rural California were the cause of local hardship in this urban area. Elsewhere, too, city residents would complain that "There are many of us poor people who are watching our precious children suffer for having to go to school dressed in tattered clothing and shoes and sometimes poorly fed because their parents have been denied work." Pointing to growing concerns about police brutality, the housing crisis for urban and rural workers, and racial segregation in public schools, Galarza believed that they and others were ready to move "on several fronts at once—economic organization, political education, civil liberties and the like."[20]

In this era that witnessed the rise of an African American civil rights movement in the South, Galarza believed that ethnic Mexicans needed to forge ties with California labor unions to advance their demands. He faced daunting odds. The 1940s had seen eliminated the unionists who stood the best chance to help the East Side; UCAPAWA had labored hard on behalf of local Mexicans' civil rights into the beginning of the decade, but red-baiting and open intimidation in 1946 finally squashed that organization, now known as the Food and Tobacco Association (FTA), and cannery union contracts had gone to conservative Teamster officials. The newly powerful AFL unions in the county showed little interest in ethnic Mexican workers. Mexicanas registered alienation with the union's male leadership, and Ray Salazar found that his Hod-Carriers local was "made up of a bunch of Portuguese and Italian guys that never cared about the Mexicans." Other Eastsiders like Charlie Galindo and Gilbert Perez appeared at their union meetings during the 1950s only if "fined for not attending," and Galarza would warn over the next decade that traditional unionists' dismissal of ethnic Mexican concerns risked alienating Mexicans and Mexican Americans for years to come.[21]

An ardent anti-Communist long suspicious of "red" CIO activists like Donald Henderson, Galarza believed the AFL and its newly reorganized

A Mexican bracero cutting sugar beets in California. Farm Service Administration Papers, box 7, folder 327, Bancroft Library.

National Farm Labor Union (NFLU) could far surpass the previous successes of UCAPAWA. The NFLU had already launched a major strike against the DiGiorgio Corporation, one of the state's most powerful growers and a political force in the San Joaquin Valley, and San Joseans tied to rural California heard news of that conflict immediately. The AFL union had not yet reached out to ethnic Mexicans, and some white unionists believed Mexican immigrants a threat to their movement and to the U.S. standard of living. Intent to protect rights to residency and fair wages, Galarza disagreed. The impoverishment of farm workers seemed a transnational problem, and he told government officials that "we of the National Farm Labor Union do not propose to forget . . . that in both Mexico and the United States farm workers are dying in poverty and starvation. We do not propose to forget that thousands of farm families *in both countries* are living in shacks and even under trees." In the context of the DiGiorgio strike, he met with AFL officials in San José and around the country to begin a unionization drive targeting Mexican workers, stressing that developments since the early 1940s had made life difficult for most rural ethnic Mexicans in California. Urging California unionists to imagine their common cause with ethnic Mexicans "as workers and citizens of the America," Galarza would continue his union work until 1960.[22]

Galarza argued throughout the 1950s that the Mexican and U.S. governments were most responsible for California's rural poverty, and, from his San José residence, he attacked the reputation of Mexican government officials. The 1940 election of Miguel Alemán to the Mexican presidency had marked the beginnings of a new conservatism among ruling policymakers in that country, and some Mexicanos both within and outside the nation's borders expressed growing concerns about the ruling state's apparent retreat from a revolutionary social agenda. Beginning in the late 1940s, Galarza echoed those contemporary complaints and earlier ones expressed by San Joseans worried about the consulate's retreat from lobbying on their behalf. He argued that U.S. and Mexican officials could not simply visit the bracero labor camps to deliver "patriotic speeches" about the common destiny of the two countries, as many consul officials continued to do in an apparent deflection of serious engagement with workers' material complaints. Galarza spoke out against more conservative appeals to the Good Neighbor Policy, noting, as CIO organizers had before him, that such rhetoric buttressed the racial division of labor in the region. Calling attention to rural poverty, he debunked racist myths about the laziness of Mexican farmworkers, noting for instance that "Mexican children in the West . . . do not spend all their time dozing. Thus, ten-year-olds will do a ten-hour stretch hoeing or weeding or thinning. At twelve the boys wrestle with eighty-pound lugs or sacks or crates. At half that age both boys and girls are allowed to go into the hop fields and pull down the hot, sticky vines which their elders will pick."[23]

In addition to appeals to the conscience of postwar liberalism, Galarza launched unionization drives dependent to a large extent on references to ethnic Mexican cultural practices. The transnational orientation of East San José and similar neighborhoods throughout California defined the NFLU. Laboring to develop closer ties between Mexicanos and Mexican Americans, on the one hand, and between existing organizations and NFLU Mexican committees, on the other, Galarza followed UCAPAWA's example by linking Mexicanidad and unionization. Meeting Hurtado and other farm workers already "involved in mutualistas," Galarza made visits to San José lodges and associations a basis for his union drives. Those organizations spread news about the union, and NFLU members who lived in East San José began to participate in, and in some cases to organize, *fiestas patrias* celebrations. San José's Lupe Castro distributed fliers at San José's Mexican holidays to publicize the NFLU's presence from 1949 until 1955, and Galarza displayed the Mexican flag to rally Mexicanos and Mexican Americans at his meetings, printed posters that bore Mexico's eagle and serpent, and informed potential strikebreakers that crossing picket lines constituted a betrayal of the raza Mexicana. Cultural nationalism, a conservative tool of the Mexican state during these years, served different purposes in the NFLU. As San José resident and one-time NFLU member Luis Manríquez remembered, "Galarza's union allowed the Mexican people to be very Mexican [and] gave everybody a sense that we could be Mexicanos and also demand our rights as residents of California." Manríquez and other San Joseans set an example of nationalist labor organizing followed in places like nearby Tracy, where Juan Oviedo, the president of the local Comisión Honorífica Mexicana, helped the NFLU and believed unionization "a matter of importance to all of us."[24]

In the fast-changing environment of postwar California, the NFLU relied on the cultural practices of migrants to build support for the union movement in rural California. Galarza urged ethnic Mexicans to carry union flyers on their travels in search of work, and he took advantage of supporters such as "a young Mexican minister by the name of Reyes who works for the Methodist missions up and down the valley." Union organizers attended community dances and Mexican movie houses in San José and smaller towns and invited farmworkers enjoying those outings to NFLU meetings. Galarza also made union appeals in local bars, "the beer joints where the Mexicans seem to do most of their politicking" after work. Pitching a masculinist idiom of national pride, he contended that good fathers and providers needed to join the union to protect their rights. Seeking those who "demand a wage adequate to meet your needs as a man and as the father of a family," unionists circulated handbills summoning "MEN FILLED WITH THE SPIRIT OF MEXICO, DEFEND YOUR RIGHTS AND YOUR COMMON CAUSE . . . FOR YOUR OWN GOOD TODAY AND TOMORROW." Other strategies also reflected ethnic Mexican migrant practices. Noting that workers from the Imperial Valley often carved their names in bunkhouses and signed the walls of company tents to leave their marks in northern California, Galarza copied their graffiti, accumulating addresses in order to make personal contacts before beginning a unionization drive elsewhere.[25]

Translocal ties to other hometowns also influenced the development of the NFLU. After 1950 San José and other California cities witnessed the arrival of hundreds of ethnic Mexican farmworkers from the Imperial Valley, residents forced to move north because of rural poverty and the arrival of new immigrants who took available work in the area. Galarza met with urbanizing Mexicanos and Mexican Americans from El Centro and other small California towns who felt, as one San Josean explained, "That we didn't really want to come here [to San José] in the first place. We were pushed here. And we were mad when we arrived. El Centro and the Imperial Valley were hot and tough places, but they had been home to us. We should have been able to stay there, work there. I wanted to go back." In part because no hometown club developed among former residents of the Imperial Valley who had moved to San José, Galarza attempted to channel those workers' frustration about their displacement into the union movement. One-time residents of El Centro like Manuel Hurtado and Luis Manríquez became the core of the NFLU's membership in the Santa Clara Valley. Informal discussions of life in Calexico and other border towns could be heard before the beginning of many NFLU meetings.[26]

In these ways and others, Galarza moved well beyond traditional U.S. strategies of labor organizing. Support from mutualistas, *fiestas patrias* organizers, and former Imperial Valley residents seemed critical in the late 1940s and early 1950s because of widespread bitterness toward white union organizers in many ethnic Mexican communities. These hard feelings dated from World War II as well as earlier decades. Barrio residents had few positive feelings about the labor movement, and Galarza knew that Mexicanos and Mexican Americans were as concerned about their neighborhoods as they were about their wages, the narrow and often exclusive focus of most AFL leaders. Many Eastsiders remembered anti-immigrant or racist white unionists of the past, and other ethnic Mexicans must have scoffed that even the most enlightened, including CAWIU and UCAPAWA members, had abandoned their barrio outreach work within a few years. Galarza hoped that, along with the establishment of partnerships between unions and existing neighborhood groups, appeals to Mexican cultural nationalism would reassure local ethnic Mexicans that the AFL's "historic race policy" had changed for the better.[27]

As a way to combat ethnic Mexican concerns about the AFL, Galarza decided in 1949 to establish what he called "Mexican committees," groups that would be loosely associated with each NFLU chapter. Modeled on union auxiliaries, these groups held separate meetings in Spanish, fostered pride in the raza Mexicana, and promised that ethnic Mexican issues would not be forgotten by white unionists. In approaching communities of farmworkers throughout the state, Galarza often called "a general public meeting to explain the general aims of the Union," and he then created a smaller "Mexican organizing committee" to discuss issues of special concern to Mexicans and Mexican Americans. One or two organizing committee members joined the local NFLU's Executive Board, but the organizing committee meetings at times became sustained forums for postwar civil rights talk. San José and other locales saw "young people, community leaders, store keepers, cafe owners, and other types" joining those NFLU conversations about rural wages and working conditions, and Luis Manríquez remembers that topics like substandard housing, police brutality, and the need for educational reforms prompted heated exchanges among those gathered in Galarza's living room or a local Mexican restaurant.[28] Driven by the Mexican committees, the hundreds of ethnic Mexicans involved throughout the state—including an estimated 2,400 in the Imperial Valley by 1952—considered pressing matters of residency and work, and one NFLU organizing pamphlet called farmworkers to address:

Living conditions—slums burnt by poverty
Health—dust, trash, and cronic illness
Youth—forgotten, errant, without purpose
Politics—property of these landowners
Culture—schools which discriminate by race

Meeting of Ernesto Galarza's National Farm Labor Union in the early 1950s
somewhere in rural California. Notice the prominent Mexican flag to the right
along with the symbol of the Mexican eagle on the union banner. Ernesto Galarza
Papers, box 65, folder 3.

By the early 1950s, several dozen "Mexican committees" existed around the
state, and East Side NFLU meetings drew between forty and two hundred
members.[29] Aside from several churches, few contemporary organizations in
East San José boasted so many members.

As committees rallied both Mexicans and Mexican Americans under the
union banner, the group went so far as to target braceros as potential members, a task that many in UCAPAWA had deemed impossible. Because many
resident agricultural laborers were incensed at the presence of low-wage braceros working throughout the region, union meetings often bogged down
when it came to discussing this issue. Former Imperial Valley residents in
particular blamed the braceros who had come to dominate that region's
rural agricultural employment for stealing the jobs of longtime El Centro
residents. Despite hostility to the presence of those imported workers, the
NFLU stressed that the Bracero Program and not its participants deserved
the animus of unionists. Galarza argued with some success that resident
ethnic Mexicans needed to enlist bracero support in their struggle against
conservative growers and government officials, as the program systematically

denied braceros' contractual rights in ways that threatened all farmworkers. Ray Salazar and many other residents came to agree that "we thought the thing to do was to make all the braceros part of unions here."[30] A 1952 strike song from the Imperial Valley illustrated the NFLU's sense of common cause with those members of the transnational working class:

No me tomen por rival	Do not take me for the rival
Del bracero contratado	Of the contracted bracero
Pero también me hace mal	Although it hits me hard
Que me dejen desplazado.	That they leave me displaced.
Donde hay trabajo para uno	Where there is only work for one
Les gusta poner de a tres	They want to send three
Así no come ninguno	So that no one will eat
Y se mueren de una vez.	And they will all soon pass away.
Y como el gallo en su casa	And as the rooster in his house
Sacude su roja cresta	Shakes his red crest
Yo le contaré a mi raza	I will tell my people
Las glorias de nuestra gesta.[31]	The glories of our effort.[31]

Despite such union calls, many longtime resident farmworkers continued to look down on braceros—fistfights between individual braceros and resident farmworkers were not uncommon in California fields—and most contracted workers expressed little interest in joining the NFLU. Focused on work routines and their impending return to the *patria*, those migrants remained closely connected to home communities through the pages of *La Opinión* and other Spanish-language newspapers. Many registered fear about becoming involved in California politics, and few ever saw a union organizer, in part because rural labor camps were often located far from main roads and other settlements, and in part because growers and government officials deported suspected radicals. Those laborers sympathetic to the NFLU worried that others—including the "contractor, cook, camp caretaker, field foreman, storekeeper, usual apple shiners, [and the] relatives of [the] contractor"—would report them to agribusiness officials, a well-founded paranoia given longstanding grower commitments to keeping unions out of California agriculture. Still, Galarza knew that those contracted workers did express their dissatisfaction with the program:

The conversations in the camps, the work stoppages in the fields, the desertions, the violations which were obvious even to casual observers, the private legal actions by a few braceros, the quantity of mail addressed to their consuls, the pilgrimages of men from their camps to nearby towns in search of advice from anyone who would listen to them—all were symptoms of a distress which was not officially recorded.[32]

Believing that undercurrent of resentment might be channeled into the union movement, he snuck into bracero camps and approached immigrant workers in California fields to spread news of the NFLU. It was, for Galarza, a frustrating exercise, but he scored minor victories in 1951 in successfully encouraging dozens of braceros to join the NFLU in the Salinas and Imperial valleys.[33]

Galarza came to realize that official Mexican labor unions, in the pocket of Mexico's ruling party, would be weak allies at best, as national labor leaders like Lombardo Toledano showed little interest in NFLU efforts. Hoping to assist braceros and bring order to the chaotic California labor market, Galarza set out instead to affiliate with independent Mexican labor unions, noting optimistically that "In the long run, we may have something that we could not find even in the [traditional] labor movement." His best hope lay with the Alianza de Braceros Nacionales de México, a small Mexico City organization that had attempted intermittently since World War II to unionize certified contract laborers before their departures north. The small number of braceros who joined either the NFLU or the Alianza automatically became members of both, but Galarza remained frustrated with this arrangement, aware that the Alianza did not wield much influence in Mexico, and annoyed that the small union frequently took months to respond to his letters.[34]

NFLU efforts to unionize braceros and work closely with Mexican labor unions illustrated the latest and perhaps most creative turn in ethnic Mexican efforts to think transnationally about pressing political matters. In addition to organizing with community groups, individual braceros, and an independent Mexican union, NFLU members expressed their opposition to the Bracero Program directly to Mexican government officials. Farmworkers hoped that the Mexican government would cease to renew the farm labor program, and, in part to garner the attention of the Mexico City press, Mexicanos and Mexican Americans in California picketed Mexico's San Francisco and Bakersfield consulates in the early 1950s. Lupe Castro and more than a dozen other East Side residents frequently traveled to one of those offices to stress that the Bracero Program violated Mexican constitutional guarantees about union organizing. In his correspondence and conversations with both government officials and farmworkers, Galarza emphasized that Mexican citizens retained the right to unionize "in Mexico and no international agreement should abrogate it."[35]

Noting the apparent violation of this grand achievement of the Mexican Revolution, San José NFLU member Mario Espinosa recalled that "all the farmworkers were really pissed at the consulate in those years," and other California unionists circulated handbills that explained that the Mexican government received ten dollars for each bracero who worked in U.S. fields. "This is not labor contracting," their fliers announced in Spanish, "It is a *sale of cattle at ten dollars per head,*" further evidence of the Mexican government's postwar "business in brown flesh." Emphasizing pride in the raza Mexicana, Galarza made appeals to a single ethnic Mexican working class when he argued that the bracero agreement put imported Mexicano workers "in competition with sons of the same *patria.*" According to Galarza's formulation, the Mexican government had sacrificed the interests of its citizens and "sons" both in Mexico and *en el extranjero* in forcing contracted workers "to share in the misery of their counterparts on this side of the Rio Bravo," and he urged NFLU locals to establish pickets and letter-writing campaigns that might pay "off big in terms of public opinion and press contacts in Mexico." Galarza also met with journalists from California newspapers like *El Excéntrico* and *La Opinión,* and he reported with satisfaction in 1952 that "the small Mexican papers in the state [of California] are giving the consuls hell."[36]

DEPORTEES

Like CAWIU and UCAPAWA activists before them, Galarza and members of NFLU gained few wage increases or work contracts in the Santa Clara Valley or other areas of the state over the course of the 1950s, but their struggles illustrated something of the extent to which transnational currents shaped postwar ethnic Mexican politics. Thousands of rural Mexicanos and Mexican Americans arriving in places like East San José came into contact with the National Farm Labor Union, including later luminaries like César Chávez, who would go on to found a new farm labor union in the 1960s. But few national leaders in the United States or Mexico showed interest in Galarza's vision. The disinterest of the American Federation of Labor and Mexico's CTM threatened rural unionization from the start, and Galarza likened their lack of commitment to a violent "abuse" of the state's rural poor. Galarza insisted that farmworkers remained critical to the California economy. He knew that many Eastsiders remained tied to agriculture and had recently arrived in the area angry at growers and braceros elsewhere in the state, and he stressed that San José's growth depended on the reorganization of California agriculture, a regional development that left many urbanizing ethnic Mexicans poor and unprotected.[37]

Unable to forge a union movement with the Alianza de Braceros in Mexico City, frustrated by AFL and CTM disinterest, and foiled in their attempts to involve large numbers of imported contract workers in NFLU locals, the NFLU began to demand a new type of state intervention to defend the residency and jobs of local farm laborers. Even as they articulated the need for transnational solutions to farmworker poverty, unionists demanded greater regulation of the farm labor pool, and San Joseans involved in the NFLU joined other chapters in calling for at least a temporary end to immigration from Mexico. They found willing listeners among policymakers in Washington, D.C. Concerned in part that Communist "fifth columnists" might be hiding amidst the "wetback hordes," the U.S. government was already deporting Mexicanos in large numbers, a campaign that INS Commissioner Joseph Swing called "Operation Wetback." Rounded up on job sites, in local parks, and in their places of residence, thousands of undocumented immigrants (and untold numbers of U.S. citizens) from East San José and from virtually every other major Mexican community in the United States were returned to Mexico against their will, making that deportation drive far greater in scope than its predecessor of the 1930s.

Mexican American San Joseans who had lost rural jobs to new immigrants often supported the deportation of local "wetbacks," and NFLU members made strong arguments to support those government efforts. Scarred by losing his job in the Imperial Valley to recent immigrants, Manuel Hurtado was happy to see government agents stopping trucks to question East Side farmworkers going to work in surrounding fields and orchards, and he and others went so far as to call Immigration agents when they suspected that a particular Northern California grower had hired large numbers of undocumented workers. Two hundred ethnic Mexicans in the San Joaquin Valley community of Delano sent a petition to the INS in December 1951 requesting the removal of undocumented Mexicanos from their area, and in Southern California the farmworker Sal Ortega wrote Galarza to demand "for god's sake please prevent this situation by sending these wets and contract nationals to their own country to get out of our way so that's the best way to prevent bad situations, then wages will be put up some, treatments will be better to all."[38] Galarza noted with interest that "in California it is the local, resident Mexican farm worker who has taken the lead in opposing the 'wetback,'" an opposition based on residents' fears that all local jobs would be lost to those immigrants. He subsequently distributed a form letter to make it easier for union locals to summon the Immigration Service:

> Dear Sir:
> Members of this Local have reported to the Executive Board that persons who entered this country illegally are working, living or generally being harbored on the premises indicated below.
> It is our understanding that the Alien Registration Act of 1940, as amended by the National Internal Security Act of 1950, required the registration and fingerprinting of these persons.
> Since we have reason to believe that these requirements have not been met in the present case; and further since it appears that the presence of these unregistered aliens suggests fraudulent arrangements to violate Federal laws, we request that the Department of Justice investigate these prem-

ises without delay to the end that the Alien Registration Act and the National Internal Security Act be complied with.

Sincerely yours,

President

AFL cannery union officials in San José followed the NFLU's lead to express concerns that "wetbacks" might "infiltrate" local fruit-processing jobs, and the INS roundups of the early and mid-1950s left a large group of ethnic Mexican wives and daughters alone in the area, isolated from husbands and fathers captured at work. That violent separation of family members was a bitter denouement to Galarza's otherwise enlightened efforts to forge a transnational response to rural poverty.[39]

The NFLU tried in these and other ways to grapple with rural poverty amid postwar California's demographic and political turmoil. Many ethnic Mexicans who established homes in East San José sought to join this and other Valley political organizations, and residents' growing dissatisfaction with rural and urban discrimination defined their neighborhood political culture. Rather than being simply accomodationist in outlook, as some historians have suggested about this generation, ethnic Mexicans fashioned creative responses to difficult circumstances. Transnational connections with Mexico enlivened Northern California, but few local political organizations seemed attentive to Latino interests. Union officials avoided organizing cannery and agricultural workers, rallied members around the tenets of U.S. citizenship, and expressed considerable suspicion of nonwhites. The AFL's decision to leave Latino workers unprotected in low-wage industries had enormous consequences on the East Side and in other barrios statewide. Most young people—"Chicanos," as they began to call themselves—would claim few positive experiences with the union movement by the 1960s. Some had heard vague reports about the more enlightened organizers who once directed UCAPAWA, but most maintained at best a rhetorical connection to contemporary labor leaders. Not until the 1980s and 1990s would white unionists in San José and other California cities make a concerted effort to organize ethnic Mexicans, and these campaigns had stunning effects on local politics. In the interim, as the following chapter suggests, the disinterest of most union leaders allowed a vibrant new neighborhood group to take the civil rights stage away from the NFLU, and that organization would become the standard-bearer for California's postwar civil rights movement.[40]

Chapter 7

Political Power

The L.A. Policeman is my protector
I shall not want.
    to protest false arrest
    or false treatment
For I'll wish I hadn't.
He leadeth me behind closed doors
And strippeth me to the waist
And proceedeth to administer JUSTICE
Till my head and my bloody nose runneth over.
And if I don't get bailed
I shall dwell in the Lincoln Heights Jail
For Ever, and Ever, and Ever.
Amen.
—Fabian Elorriaga, "Anent Brutality" (1952)

While Ernesto Galarza and other members of the National Farm Labor Union struggled to organize and deport farmworkers in nearby agriculture, other Santa Clara Valley Latinos had more urban concerns. The size of San Jose's ethnic Mexican community grew from perhaps 8,500 in 1950 to more than 25,000 by 1960, and young residents increasingly gathered at places like the Flamingo Ballroom to enjoy musical performances and to meet friends who lived in other parts of the growing city. The social scene found ethnic Mexican teenagers and young adults forming social clubs with other friends from their high schools, neighborhoods, or hometowns; dozens of small groups popped up in San José by the mid-1950s, sporting names like Club Diamante, Los Lobos, Genie, Volantes, Cuahtémoc, Riviera, Venus, Zanzaree, Mexico-America, Estrella, and Gardenia.[1]

As they made the Santa Clara Valley a festive place of Latino music, Mexican film, and weekly *tardeadas*, club members and other residents began to change local ethnic Mexican culture and politics. Many struggled to escape field and cannery work in favor of other types of more remunerative employment, and new organizations of working- and middle-class ethnic Mexicans began to confront the poverty of East Side neighborhoods. One such group was the Latin American Men's Club, founded in 1950, an organization that worked to "obtain political representation, do away with all signs of discrimination, take part in civic activities, work and fight for all the Spanish-speaking to the level of the Anglo-Saxon, because that is how it should be. In this way we will better our community and contribute as an integral part of this entire country."[2] Older groups also confronted urban problems. By 1950 Mexican immigrants from the state of Jalisco and their U.S.-born children who belonged to the Club Tapatío donated clothes and other items for the large number of migrant farmworkers "in need who for various reasons are not eligible to obtain assistance from the Welfare Department." As the booming home of the largest group of ethnic Mexicans in the Valley, these Eastsiders and others responded to problems of residency and labor.[3]

A new club called the Community Service Organization (CSO) clearly emerged as the state's leading Mexican American political group in the decade after World War II, rallying county residents to combat racial discrimination and to mobilize political power along ethnic lines. Stressing neighborhood issues and developing in the political vacuum left by the decline of Depression-era organizations such as UCAPAWA, the CSO was just one of dozens of clubs to appear in San José during the early 1950s, but it had an influence unparalleled among East Side organizations. Its history provides a critical link between earlier community groups and those that would develop in the 1960s, as the CSO relied on Mexican immigrant institutions as well as new Mexican American concerns. Unlike the National Farm Labor Union's Mexican committees, the Community Service Organization downplayed the importance of ethnic Mexican ties to other locales, choosing instead to stress their common residency in the Valley. They demanded a greater role in determining California's future. These San Joseans contested the county's uneven economic development and pushed for new political power, and ethnic Mexicans elsewhere established thirty-three chapters in California and ten in Arizona, making the CSO the most important civil rights organization of its kind in the West.[4]

INTEGRATION

Like many East Side organizations, San José's CSO traced its roots to another part of the state. No single individual contributed more to its development than the community organizer Fred Ross, who helped to establish the first chapter of the CSO in East Los Angeles in 1947, and who, even more than white labor organizers of years past, brought to his work a deep empathy for ethnic Mexicans. When, in early 1952, his boss, Saul Alinsky, decided to move him from the Los Angeles chapter to organize a similar group outside of California, Ross began searching frantically for an alternative location that would keep him working with ethnic Mexican people. Responding to a lecture request from Claude Settles, a sociology professor at San José State College and member of the American Friends Service Committee, Ross visited the county and spoke to a class on race relations. He toured the city's East Side and learned that the county was home to one of California's largest ethnic Mexican communities; while only a few Mexican Americans attended the college in the early 1950s, at least three local residents—Herman Gallegos, Leonard Ramírez, and Alicia Hernández—attended Ross's presentation. Excited by what they heard about community organizing, these three young residents approached the visitor, spoke with him at greater length, and immediately elected Alicia Hernández the temporary chair of a new CSO organizing effort in Santa Clara County. The American Friends Service Committee and the Federation for Civic Unity agreed to finance Ross's stay in the area for several months, hoping that he would help establish a Mexican American community organization "similar to the NAACP and the Japanese American Citizens League."[5]

The key to CSO organizing in Los Angeles had been the establishment of house meetings with potential recruits, and Ross taught Hernández, Gallegos, and Ramírez how to make similar contacts with San José's ethnic Mexicans. In "long leisurely conversations in dimly lit kitchens, noon-hour chats in the fields between rows of cabbages," and other encounters with Valley residents, the group spread the word about the extensive civil rights activities of the CSO in Southern California. Visiting families in their homes, Alicia Hernández, a public health nurse, talked up the CSO over coffee tables and above the sounds of crying children. Working as an attendant at an East Side gasoline station, Gallegos also began to discuss the organization with his customers, while Ramírez and other early members mimeographed CSO fliers and handbills and circulated leaflets in local canneries and bars. These charter members found that some San Joseans, keen to racial violence, already knew that the Los Angeles chapter had addressed the recent "Bloody Christmas" case in which Los Angeles police officers brutally assaulted several Southern California CSO members. Valley residents seemed eager to confront the local poverty, police brutality, and workplace discrimination that shaped their lives in San José.[6]

The day after his first encounter with the three young Mexican Americans at San José State College, Fred Ross met with Father Donald McDonnell, a local priest who earlier in 1952 had founded Our Lady of Guadalupe parish,

Three children playing in a South 33rd Street ditch. Many other parts of East San José's Mayfair district also lacked basic urban services into the late 1950s, and the sight of children playing around open sewage was not uncommon. Fred Ross Papers, box 32, folder 3, Department of Special Collections, Stanford University.

the city's first Catholic church to serve Mexicans and Mexican Americans living on the East Side. McDonnell had also shown interest in Galarza's union, and the priest quickly became the CSO's most important religious ally in the San José area. Urging his congregation to become active in politics, he stressed "educating our Mexican American community in civic responsibility and in taking the initiative in the solution of their problems," and he invoked Catholic social teachings to push ethnic Mexicans to fight racial discrimination, improve local living conditions, and advocate for higher agricultural wages. McDonnell instructed residents about agricultural labor law and the Bracero Program, attended the organization's meetings regularly, allowed the group to convene in the hall of Our Lady of Guadalupe Church, and installed newly elected officers of the local chapter throughout the 1950s. Perhaps most importantly, his support and the help of other religious leaders forestalled red-baiting of the CSO. The Church had taken a hard line against radical FTA unionists several years before. Reflecting on the cold war political atmosphere, Herman Gallegos acknowledged that "The presence of a few Roman collars helped immensely."[7]

After dozens of house meetings with local residents and many consultations with Father McDonnell, over 130 ethnic Mexicans gathered at the Mayfair School in June 1952 to establish California's second chapter of the CSO. The occasion set into motion developments that would reshape the Santa Clara Valley. Herman Gallegos, who became the first elected president of the local chapter, remembered that the organization attracted a diverse cross-section of the East Side, in part thanks to Church support. César Chávez would become the most famous, but he was then an unemployed lumberyard worker; others in attendance labored in agricultural, cannery, and construction jobs, and all agreed to "develop ourselves and our neighborhoods; to prevent violation of human rights; to achieve full participation in civic affairs." Members prioritized neighborhood improvement, and one woman spoke her frustration about "how . . . it makes our kids feel to always have to play where they aren't wanted, in the street, someone else's yard, the cow pasture." The large crowd hoped that Mexican Americans would soon become a political force in state politics. Los Angeles CSO president Tony Ríos and Los Angeles City Councilman Edward Roybal penned letters to the new members urging them to build a strong organization, and by 1954 the San José chapter claimed 439 dues-paying members.[8]

Eastsiders sparked a CSO wildfire that spread throughout California. Other chapters formed elsewhere, thanks in part to the fact that urbanizing San Joseans maintained ties to other parts of the state, and in part to San José's Spanish-language radio announcements heard as far away as New Mexico. Less than two years after the establishment of the San José chapter, delegates from distant California and Arizona communities gathered in the Pacific Coast community of Asilomar to federate as a single, regional organization, hoping to increase their political power at the state and national levels. Members recognized at that March 1954 meeting that "some of our most serious problems . . . can never be solved by the individual action of each CSO," and members elected a national board to guide the organization. While Los Angeles members claimed the top two spots on the board, the San José contingent made the strongest showing. Delegate Andy Esparza led members in a discussion of the CSO's "Major Legislative Goals," while Oscar Anslie translated speeches from English for Spanish-speaking members. Herman Gallegos won the position of first vice-president of the organization, Alicia Hernández became the group's first treasurer, and Hector Moreno, who served as the first national secretary, subsequently wrote the first constitution for the national CSO.[9]

The CSO movement departed from the rhetoric of Mexican cultural nationalism that had shaped the NFLU and many earlier Latino political groups in Northern California. Like other contemporary Mexican American organizations during the 1950s—particularly the League of United Latin American Citizens (LULAC), the dominant Mexican American political organization in postwar Texas—local chapters and national leaders successfully represented themselves as politically moderate and dedicated to mainstream activities. On the surface, San José members stressed political assimilation, stating that they only wanted to participate in "New England town hall democracy" and to "integrate the Spanish-speaking people into our overall community life." The rise of Cold War anticommunism led the CSO carefully to avoid any taint of radicalism, the by-laws of their constitution prohibiting Communists from joining the group. "Integration" seemed radical enough, and members claimed that their interests departed completely from earlier Mexican immigrant political efforts in the state, and from contemporary left-wing groups like ANMA. Gallegos and others distinguished the CSO from "old time organizations such as funeral insurance groups, patriotic societies and nationalistic movements" that did not have the "sophistication" to deal with social and political problems affecting the community, and many CSO members accordingly approached community organizing with an ardent and almost religious zeal, hoping to overcome ethnic Mexican residents' seemingly defeatist approach to their circumstances in the United States.[10]

This was, in part, the enthusiasm of youth, as Gallegos and many other CSO activists in their early twenties declared themselves ready to take over the local political scene. Organizers sensed little connection between their own efforts and those of ethnic Mexicans who had been active before World War II. Many young San Joseans expressed disappointment that older family members and neighbors had seemed to approach politics in a spirit of deference rather than demand. One future chapter president joined the organization to "break that cycle where reticence in our culture, where the respect you have in the family structure towards the elders . . . is bred right into you," and others distinguished their cohort from older generations who had "resigned themselves to being second class citizens" and remained "bitter and frustrated" with their lives in the United States.[11] The CSO made it clear that an optimistic new Mexican American generation was articulating its interests in the Valley, but membership was not restricted to the young. While no extant records state the nativity of San José members, Alameda County's adjacent CSO chapter boasted in 1954 that "fifty percent of their membership is elder[ly] Mexican people," and established patterns of ethnic Mexican politics retained a strong influence.[12]

Unlike Galarza and members of the NFLU, Eastsiders involved in the CSO did not see themselves integrating the American labor movement. Santa Clara Valley labor unionists remained inattentive and even hostile to ethnic Mexican interests during the 1950s, and the organization stepped into "the general political vacuum" that Galarza believed the union movement "should have filled." While support from Los Angeles unions built chapters in Southern California, San José Teamsters officials, the dominant union in the area due to the large number of cannery employees, never provided financial assistance. Few East Side members had positive experiences with the American labor movement, and even César Chávez, the century's most famous Mexican American farmworker activist, had joined his first union only several months before entering the CSO. The organization invited the participation of all ethnic Mexicans regardless of class status or occupation, and local farm labor contractors sat beside farmworkers at chapter meetings. Tellingly, leaders of the San José chapter believed they would have more luck securing financial support from the local Ford Motor Company than the Valley's United Auto Workers Union.[13]

CSO efforts at integration also reflected the new upward mobility of some Eastsiders after World War II, a process evident in Ross's encounter with Mexican Americans at San José State College in May 1952. Although residents such as María Vallejas, a thirty-year-old widow and mother of three who picked strawberries "at 50 cents a crate," formed the organization's local membership base, most CSO leaders enjoyed regular, year-round employment in nonagricultural industries. They were young and energetic, and these aspiring middle-class residents provided the organizational stability that seasonal, low-wage laborers could not. Office holding required long hours and significant resources to drive county streets for committee events and house visits, and cannery employees who worked evenings during peak packing seasons struggled just to make general membership meetings. The CSO took pains to involve those residents. César Chávez noted in March 1956 that "so many people [in the CSO] are unemployed" and that "those who would like to pay their dues are not working." He and other officers struggled to build up membership from this unstable foundation. They did so attentive to the rigors of cannery labor. When the local chapter decided to hold a carnival to raise money for the organization, officials scheduled the event in August "because of the high employment during this period," hoping that Eastsiders would spend some of their hard-earned cash at the event.[14]

Dozens of local businesses catered to the growing Spanish-speaking population during the 1950s, and the San José chapter found critical support from Mexican American storeowners, lawyers, and other professionals. Some of the most active CSO members had experienced significant upward mobility since World War II. Herman Gallegos soon left his job at an East Side gas station for a position in the city's Department of Youth Services; Luis Juárez worked as an employee in the city's Health Department; officers Natalie Cruz and Viola Cadena worked together at Crescent Pharmacy; Hector Moreno earned his degree from the University of Santa Clara and became a practicing attorney; Edith Salcido worked for another immigration lawyer downtown; and Juan Marcoida was an employee of General Electric. A similar group took charge in other California barrios. As the Decoto chapter a few miles to the north and east of San José was forming in 1953, one organizer reported that "[I] sure have met a lot of rich [Mexicans]. Didn't know we had so many professional men. Crazy. And they seemed very interested and want to help."[15]

The ethnic Mexican mutualist tradition so clear in the 1920s and 1930s drove many of these upwardly mobile residents into the CSO. More privileged members expressed a strong interest in serving neighbors and family members who had not attained middle-class status. They struggled to change local municipalities in which ethnic Mexicans lagged far behind white residents in economic status and political representation. The real estate agent Alberto Piñon, for example, remembered that he entered the CSO because he simply wanted "to help people," and he and others provided important assistance to urbanizing Eastsiders like Jesús Grimaldo who had been denied assistance by local Welfare Department officials. In Grimaldo's case and others, CSO members took advantage of a new interest among some white San Joseans in "assimilating" Mexicans into the San José community. With a son in County Hospital diagnosed with leukemia, Grimaldo had quickly lost his job and exhausted his savings. CSO members appealed for community help through the local Spanish- and English-language media, and dozens of offers of assistance arrived from local individuals and businesses. A mortuary promised free burial service for Grimaldo's son, IBM and other companies invited Grimaldo to work for them, and pledges of financial support kept CSO phones ringing until midnight.[16]

Such cooperation with local business and government officials marked a sea change in an ethnic Mexican political culture driven by labor concerns since the 1860s. Other new aspects also appeared. Unlike East Side political efforts of the past, this organization claimed no regional ties to specific hometowns or *patrias chicas,* stressing instead residents' common home in the Valley. Mexicanos and Mexican Americans still remained tied to other towns and cities, however, much to the regret of local leaders. CSO organizers encountered Mexicanas like Mrs. Hernández, a Mayfair district homeowner who expressed no interest in joining the organization and hoped, instead, to save money to "go buy a piece of land in Mexico." Chapter organizers attempted to overturn these residents' longstanding suspicion of white San Joseans. One of the CSO's first public appearances also found Herman Gallegos, Vice-President Mike Aguilar, Treasurer Lena Manríquez, and active member Alicia Hernández speaking to county social workers "to build good will for the Mex[ican] American," and members wrote annual letters of commendation to the white San Joseans who had "done the most to better inter-racial relations in this county." CSO leaders expressed faith in many government agencies. The San José chapter received strong support from the city's Adult Education Department, intent since World War II on providing citizenship and naturalization classes for Valley immigrants, and some other government officials seemed just as receptive. Welfare Department officials referred ethnic Mexicans to the group, a local school principal paid for the CSO's telephone service in 1954, and a member of the San José Board of Supervisors celebrated that the CSO was "one of the most outstanding civic organizations in Santa Clara County." By the end of the decade, the California Senate would commend the CSO's "constructive civic action [which] has promoted the harmonious integration of the Spanish-speaking people into all areas of community life."[17]

As it received lavish praise for its new integrationist approach, the San José chapter also showed clear debts to earlier East Side political efforts. For one thing, the organization grappled with longstanding questions about the role non-Mexicans should play in ethnic Mexican politics. Despite their integrationist rhetoric, many members, like their neighbors involved in the NFLU, remained uneasy about white involvement in their affairs. Some had expressed hostility to Fred Ross in 1952 when he had begun knocking on neighborhood doors to hold house meetings, thinking him just another white student "coming down from Berkeley [or] Stanford to write [his] thesis about the barrio." And while the vast majority came to love Ross, members still insisted that their organization be ethnic Mexican–led and concerned primarily with issues that affected their community directly. In forming an advisory committee of white Valley residents, Herman Gallegos hoped those non-Mexicans might concentrate their efforts on CSO fundraising. From the Salinas Valley chapter came the warning that apparently sympathetic non-Mexicans in fact often hoped "to counteract the advance of our crusade," and that chapter's correspondence secretary opined that "every obstacle we encounter is placed in our path by the prejudiced elements of the majorities who are beginning to see the handwriting on the wall."[18]

There were other continuities with the past. Wartime conflicts had defined Latino politics in California since the mid-nineteenth century, and demands for postwar integration drew rhetorical strength from Mexican American participation in World War II and the Korean War. As with African American activists elsewhere, those military contributions provided a powerful argument against racial discrimination on the home front, and Los Angeles member Edward Roybal reminded members immediately after the Korean conflict that "We have shed our blood in every battlefield. It is our country because our men have distinguished themselves on those battlefields and given a good account of their bravery and integrity. . . . an indication that we are fighting for the country we love so much. . . . The war is over. Those who fought in the battlefields of the European and Korean conflicts are back, ready to assume their responsibilities in the community and do their civic part." The Mexican War and the French occupation had reshaped politics for earlier generations of Valley residents, and these mid-twentieth-century military ventures proved nearly as formative. Chapter leaders like

César Chávez, Luis Zárate, Albert Piñon, and Hector Moreno had spent time in the Armed Services, and one San José organizer reminded a white audience that the blood of Mexican American patriots had been lost in the European and Pacific theaters, and that nearly one in four of the "missing or dead [in] WWII were Spanish-speaking." There was widespread local support for veterans, and thirty-five Mexicano and Mexican American business owners supported a Mexican American Armistice Day parade in November 1949 "to carry forward the work [of making others recognize] the brotherhood, the rights, and the respectability of our race."[19]

While pronouncements about Mexican American military service carried a powerful sway with the American public, CSO members commonly also emphasized that it was their residency and labor that demanded an end to discriminatory treatment. Calls for respect as working people at the bottom of the economic ladder infused organizational rhetoric. The Community Service Organization did not distinguish between the rights of veterans and those of other ethnic Mexican residents. "This was never a veterans' group," attorney Hector Moreno recalled. Claims that "They've got no right to treat me like dirt, I was born here," and "I pay taxes too" made no reference to military service, and members stressed above all that Mexicans and Mexican Americans had long performed the nation's punishing, low-wage work in agricultural fields, canneries, and other industries. As Gallegos and César Chávez expressed it in 1956, "for many years, a large section of the Spanish-speaking residents of the area, while giving a disproportionate share of bodily strength to the development of the region, have been in the lowest income bracket, socially disadvantaged and civically weak."[20]

Gender politics shaped the Community Service Organization as postwar transformations raised new questions about women's places in political movements. The prevailing attitude among most East Side men was that women ought at best to take secondary positions. Dance promoter and San José resident Ted Dávilla likely summarized the opinion of many when he wrote in 1952 that Mexican women's fundamental role was to be a wife and mother: "Intelligence, beauty, education, sociability, loyalty, valor, tolerance, and understanding, these are the most beautiful qualities that a woman can show, making her a model wife." Most CSO chapter leaders clearly affirmed that men would direct the integration of San José's Eastsiders into the Valley, an assumption shared by local patriotic societies such as the Comisión Honorífica Mexicana and the Consul de Coordinación Cívica. When officers knocked on neighborhood doors to begin house meetings, they typically asked to speak with "the head of the house," and many male activists resented wives who spent long evening hours working for the organization. Men defined the structure and content of CSO politics, and in 1959 chapter leaders announced that CSO lawyers would not help a woman who complained of domestic abuse by her husband. Only rarely did female members persuade men in the organization to take on issues of particular concern to women, as in 1956 when the chapter began "to gather information available regarding day care child centers" for mothers who worked in local canneries and agricultural fields.[21]

But despite these obstacles, the CSO became a movement dominated by women, in part because Mexicanas found that postwar cannery unions no long welcomed their leadership. The NFLU and other groups showed far less interest in their participation, and many women followed Alicia Hernández's lead to demand involvement in CSO programs. As women undertook many of the daily tasks critical to each chapter's survival, the organization came to depend on female organizers. Edith Moreno and others did most of the work of going from house to house to encourage East Side residents to join the CSO, made phone calls to remind members of upcoming meetings, cooked and sold tamales to raise money for the organization, and operated a CSO-owned second-hand store. Those with professional skills made other contributions, and Rita Medina, Jessie de la O., and Alicia Hernández helped Mexicanos process their immigration documents for naturalization cases. The only available membership list for the San José CSO chapter enumerates 274 members in 1956, of whom 189 were women.[22]

Dozens of women also held office in San José and other chapters over the course of the 1950s, and the CSO outdid UCAPAWA in nurturing women's leadership in the county. In the aftermath of that union's decline, Lena Manríquez became the chapter's first treasurer in 1952, and in 1956 six of the seventeen candidates for office in San José were women, including individuals running for second vice-president, treasurer, recording and correspondence secretaries, and sergeant-at-arms. Viola Cadena, Angie Ramírez, and Nettie Ruíz won offices in that election, and Ramona González later served as president of the local chapter. In Bakersfield, too, five of eight charter officers in 1955 were women, and several women rose to top posts in the national organization. Alicia Hernández won the position of treasurer of the national CSO at the organization's first national convention in 1954. In the following year Arizona's Carmen García became the organization's second vice-president.[23]

MEXICANOS

As it reflected the new influence of Mexican American veterans and the growing activism of local women, the CSO also depended on recently arrived Mexicanos for its success. The group welcomed immigrants as members and leaders, and while CSO rhetoric suggested that the organization devoted itself to leaving "old-style" politics behind, members who worked and lived in

During the Cold War 1950s, chapters of the Community Service Organization
throughout California and Arizona organized citizenship classes to encourage the
naturalization of young and old Mexican immigrants. Fred Ross Papers, box 32,
folder 3.

Valley neighborhoods still depended on Mexicano institutions. Officers and
members focused attention on the social costs of deportation campaigns
directed at local immigrants. Mexican immigrants and U.S.-born Mexican
Americans joined the chapter, and CSO meetings were conducted in both
Spanish and English. The group offered immigrants English classes, not because they stressed that Mexicanos needed to abandon ties to Mexican culture, but rather because they believed that "the more you use your English in
your meetings, the more effectively you will be able to deal with the Anglo
groups." Local immigrants were considered permanent neighbors rather
than future repatriates, and while Andy García and others questioned
whether noncitizens should be allowed to hold group office, San José's general membership twice rejected proposals to limit that privilege to Mexican
Americans. Mexican citizens held high posts alongside U.S.-born members of
the San José chapter, at least one Mexicano in the area served as chapter
president, and members could be surprised to learn that fellow officers
whom they had known for forty years had never become naturalized U.S.
citizens.[24]

Vestiges of earlier Mexican immigrant political culture shaped CSO politics. Like prewar labor organizations, CSO members cooperated with leaders
of local mutual aid and patriotic societies, including many immigrants who
advised the Mexican consulate on political issues affecting Northern California

residents. The CSO relied on the support of San José disc jockeys José J. Alvarado and Lalo Caballero, as well as assistance from Humberto García, editor and publisher of *El Excéntrico*, San José's leading Spanish-language newspaper. In conversations with these Mexicanos and others, CSO organizers emphasized that their demands for postwar integration embraced the spirit of Mexican cultural nationalism. Urging Eastsiders to develop local programs to address community needs, Lucio Bernabé worked closely with the Mexican consulate to promote the *fiestas patrias.* Leonard Ramírez, a founding member and second chapter president, briefly resigned from the CSO in 1956 because his responsibilities with the local Comisión Honorífica Mexicana occupied all his attention. Because the *fiestas patrias* remained central community celebrations, the CSO, like the NFLU, hoped to capitalize on those gatherings. In 1956 a CSO fundraiser on September 16 sought "to cash in on the fact that many Spanish Speaking people come to San José on the 15th and 16th for the celebration of the Mexican Independence."[25]

In other ways, too, CSO members attempted to use Mexican cultural practices to advance their organization's demands for integration. Members relied on the support of Protestant churches that remained as much "Mexican organizations" as American institutions, and organizers persuaded local Baptists, Pentecostals, Methodists, and others that the CSO was not "a Catholic plot," as some feared. CSO activists also helped organize dances with popular Latin American musical bands to attract new members, and officers contacted potential recruits in Mexican movie theaters, grocery stores, and barbershops. While Fred Ross believed that Mexican patriotic societies were "generally speaking, uninfluential, purely social and impotent," the CSO began in 1957 to sponsor their own beauty contests during the *fiestas patrias,* an effort to redirect an already popular practice for a different end. These became membership drives, competitions for the loyalty of Eastsiders involved in many clubs and associations, and contests to win ethnic Mexicans more favorable publicity among white observers. They sent a strong message to suspicious Mexicanos that the CSO was legitimately Mexican in orientation. By inviting local politicians and law enforcement officers to judge the contestants, the organization again promoted itself as the inheritor of Mexican cultural practices even as it advertised its "American" pageantry to other San Joseans.[26]

The CSO's dependence on older Mexicano institutions became clear in other ways. San Joseans enlisted the support of the Sociedad Progresista Mexicana and similar groups that promoted "Education, Culture, and Respect for Rights," and some local residents joined the chapter because the CSO seemed to echo the concerns of the *comisiones honoríficas* and mutualistas that had long tried to help residents of the Southwest. Canvassing mutualistas for new recruits, Rita Medina spent one night at "an insurance society social" and sold thirty-five CSO membership cards. Consuelo Granados became a CSO activist while maintaining her membership in "a number of lodges in the Mexican American community." Nellie Guardado, a fifty-nine year-old mother of ten, known for her tremendous skills in recruiting new members to the organization, belonged to three mutual-aid organizations in San José, and in 1956 she successfully encouraged San José's Sociedad Progresista chairman Frank Espinoza to take an active role in the CSO's Membership Committee. Members such as Oxnard's Antonio Del Buono, the one-time second vice-president of the National CSO, had first become politically active in the farm labor unions during the 1920s and had since remained involved in Mexican mutualistas and patriotic organizations. At their urging, the Community Service Organization eventually admitted that its work in fact echoed the efforts of the "traditional" groups it purported to replace. National CSO officials decided in 1962 to offer members funeral insurance and other "mutual-aid programs" as a way of "eliminating . . . the turnover and instability of CSO's membership."[27]

But the CSO offered services and political arguments that went far beyond the traditional program of Valley mutualistas, a fact that organizers like Lenny Chávez spun to encourage teenagers to turn their backs on groups who "aren't doing anything for the 'Raza.'" Above all, the Community Service Organization confronted other ethnic Mexicans who seemed to take advantage of local Mexicanos. San Joseans in the CSO worried about their city's self-described "immigration experts" who charged exorbitant fees to process naturalization papers, and in this era when INS agents rounded up thousands in the name of Operation Wetback, the fraud of those Mexican American "coyotes" became "one of the biggest gripes of the older folks." In response, the organization's officers began to provide free immigration services to residents such as "Mrs. Simon" whose husband had been "deported back to Mexico," "Mr. Cruz" who wanted to help his wife in Mexico immigrate to the United States, and others worried about their immigration status. Capitalizing on postwar Spanish-language media in the Valley, Hector Moreno developed a weekly radio show that lambasted opportunistic coyotes, recognized the transnational nature of many local families, and publicized the CSO's no-cost naturalization services. When César Chávez went to organize a CSO chapter in Bakersfield in 1954, members of a local Mexican patriotic society there were interested above all in his promise to provide "immigration services, 'gratis.'"[28]

Immigrant rights at times became the primary focus of the San José CSO. Members defended immigrant residency, particularly when deportation drives threatened to break apart local ethnic Mexican families. The chapter heard many such cases, and those traumatic stories of loss guided Mexican American politics during the 1950s. Scheduled for deportation in less than a month, Josephine Santana approached the CSO to request help because she hoped "to come back—she has three girls (and two are American citizens)

. . . they have to go to Mexico too." Margaret Espinoza had lived in the United States since 1942, and in 1956 she hoped that the group might help arrange for the return of her deported husband. An angry Socorro Artiaga struggled to feed her three children when the INS sent her husband to Mexico. Local welfare officials told Artiaga that in order to receive any assistance she had to sign a complaint against her husband for desertion and "failure to provide," a ridiculous demand that the CSO in San José protested with no success.[29]

The Community Service Organization took advantage of a loophole in U.S. immigration law to help these Mexicanos and others become U.S. citizens and remain with their kin. The McCarran-Walter Act of 1952, designed to limit immigrant radicalism and the growing "world Communist movement," amended the Nationality Act of 1940 that had required prospective citizens to demonstrate their ability to "read, write, and speak" English. While the legislation's anti-immigrant provisions prompted great anger among CSO members, the new law paradoxically allowed immigrants over the age of sixty to take citizenship exams in their native language, a clause that César Chávez called "about the only favorable feature in the McCarran act." Working under the pressing conditions of "Operation Wetback," organizers exploited the loophole, reassuring elderly Spanish-speakers that they were not abandoning their ties to the *patria* in choosing U.S. citizenship. The local barber Johnny Torres developed new Spanish-language course materials to prepare immigrants for citizenship exams, and long-time Mexican residents of the area such as "Mr. and Mrs. Reyes Fuentes," who had lived in Sal Si Puedes since 1926, and "Mrs. Vargas," the mother of four children born in the United States, enrolled in those classes. Other CSO chapters around the state adopted Torres' handbook, and by 1955 members had enrolled hundreds of Mexican immigrants in citizenship classes, including 125 in Madera, 150 in Fresno, 175 in Kern County, 650 in San Bernardino County, 235 in Imperial County, and 200 in Monterey County. In the following year, the San José chapter alone claimed 500 students.[30]

Many recognized the importance of these efforts and pushed a broader political agenda, in part because immigrants and the U.S.-born continued to experience significant obstacles to their "integration." Martín Haro and others contended that "the CSO should not be afraid to fight and that we should not put up with anything that smells of discrimination," and the organization seemed, at times, ready to address every issue affecting East Side residents. Members formed committees to provide others help with income taxes, immigration, court translation, and similar concerns, and these groups pushed government officials to be more receptive to Mexicano and Mexican American residents. Helen Valenzuela and other Education Committee members responded to complaints of anti-Mexican discrimination in local schools, and other leaders demanded that principals hire "more qualified teachers [who] can deal objectively with the problems of the Mex[ican] American child." After the U.S. Supreme Court ruled on the *Brown vs. the Board of Education* case in 1954, other chapters' Education Committees pushed local government officials to integrate segregated school districts. Mexicans in the CSO Health Committee promoted greater awareness about the high tuberculosis rates among Eastsiders. Driver's License Committees in the San José and San Benito CSO chapters protested proposed legislation in 1957 and 1959 that required California residents to take driving examinations in English. CSO members in San José formed a Health and Welfare Committee "to write to all agencies in the County" and to pressure government officials to adopt government programs specifically designed "to help the Mexican American."[31]

The CSO's political agenda outlined the staggering array of problems that faced ethnic Mexicans in postwar California. Theirs was an exhausting program, and the organization also threw its energies into lobbying government agencies to improve East Side neighborhoods. UCAPAWA had started to do the same in the late 1930s, and when the CSO first investigated conditions in the Mayfair district in 1952, members learned that local residents of a two-block section of the area had recently reported 125 cases of amebic dysentery. Hernández, Gallegos, Primo Chavarría, and others involved in the chapter's Neighborhood Improvement Committee demanded sewage systems and paved roads, arguing that Sal Si Puedes and adjacent neighborhoods had not reaped the benefits of the region's economic growth since World War II. Combating the devil of racial discrimination, "everywhere in evidence . . . expressed as official neglect in the curbless, lightless roads and dirt sidewalks, and the absence of adequate facilities for medical care, housing and recreation," the CSO followed the lead of "Mrs. Peña," who in 1953 rallied her neighbors to urge city officials to lay pavement and provide sidewalks on Parmer Street. By 1955 CSO members had persuaded city officials to install twenty-five street lights in recently incorporated sections of the Mayfair district, which until that time "were totally dark." Members established neighborhood improvement committees on South 33rd Street, South 31st Street, San Antonio Court, Sunset Avenue, and other roads that had been the home of ethnic Mexicans for decades. Reverend Hidalgo of the Apostolic Church of God joined the organization's efforts in 1956 because "it's very hard to get his congregation to the church due to all the water and mud on the street." Others expressed outrage to county supervisors that "we pay taxes as well as everybody else, why aren't our neighborhoods improved[?]"[32]

As they tackled the problems evident in many California barrios, CSO members issued strong reminders that ethnic Mexicans had lived in the state for generations. Young Mexican Americans demanded greater respect for their parents and grandparents, and the organization struggled on behalf of elderly Mexican immigrants who had lived and worked in California since the Mexican Revolution. Representatives from the San José chapter spent a great deal of time in the state capital from 1953 to 1961 arguing that those Mexicanos deserved old-age pensions because they had helped build the region's economy. UCAPAWA organizers had first initiated the fight to extend welfare entitlements to aged noncitizens, and in 1953 CSO delegations from San José, Los Angeles, and Decoto began to do the same. The San José chapter mailed more than thirty-five thousand letters to state legislators urging them to pass "*pensiones para los ancianos*" (pensions for the elderly) over the course of the decade. The national president announced in 1957 that "We will . . . fight to gain for our elderly noncitizens the rights and privileges to which they are entitled as tax-payers and long-time residents of California."[33]

Women organized letter-writing campaigns, Mexican patriotic organizations assisted this CSO effort, and the *pensiones* campaign found overwhelming support from Mexican or Mexican American organizations in the Valley. The disc jockey José Alvarado became a more active member of the chapter in order to help with the pension effort, and other mutual-aid organizations joined hands with the CSO in Mexican colonias and barrios throughout the state. Bakersfield, Delano, Stockton, and San José residents made mutualistas and *juntas patrióticas* the foundation of this CSO agenda; Hanford's voter registration was led by the chairman of the local Comisión Honorífica, and Bakersfield's Juárez Club became the foundation of the Kern County CSO when that group expressed interest in pushing policymakers to support the pensions bill. Because of such continuing pressure, the governor of California finally signed the welfare provisions in 1961.[34]

In addition to promoting the rights of elderly immigrants, local CSO members fought police harassment of young Mexican Americans. That violence had plagued ethnic Mexicans in California for decades, and when San José teenagers formed "jacket clubs," groups often linked to other hometowns in the Southwest, law enforcement officers reacted with predictable suspicion. Dozens of Mexican Americans who wore stylish leather coats with embroidered names such as "Club Diamante" or "Los Lobos" were arrested en masse in 1954 and 1955, at times when they began fistfights with one another, and police hysteria about ethnic Mexican criminality prompted greater scrutiny of the East Side. Longtime barrio residents must have feared a renewal of the sort of anti-Mexican violence seen during World War II, and Bernie Frausto and other officers of the chapter began to visit youth clubhouses, "suggesting that the groups could be serving some useful purpose in the county." Just as CSO members hoped to turn mutualistas to work on behalf of the pension campaign and other projects, local leaders sought to redirect jacket club energies. But they also stressed that youth delinquency stemmed from the Valley's longstanding economic and political realities. There was "a reciprocal process at work between the youthful offender and the community at large," CSO officers argued, and fights between Mexican American youth showed yet again the damning effects of "deteriorating" East Side conditions and persistent racial "discrimination." Gathering together members of twenty-two teen clubs, the CSO helped those groups to elect delegates to a new Youth Committee. This fragile arrangement did not last for more than a year, but many teenagers became involved in CSO voter registration, fundraising for the Cancer Society, and similar projects, making that committee the first organized political effort of Mexican American youth in Santa Clara County, a brief precursor to more sustained activities that developed after 1965.[35]

In the aftermath of the Youth Committee's decline, the CSO still worked to protect Mexican teenagers from local police and government harassment. While the details of the differential police treatment of ethnic Mexicans can be difficult to uncover, the available evidence suggests that the police did torment Latinos over the course of the 1950s. By 1957, for instance, nearly 30 percent of the Juvenile Probation Department's new cases involved the "Mexican race," despite the fact that ethnic Mexicans comprised less than 15 percent of the local population. Members of the CSO rallied to support East Side teens when police officers or the local press represented them as a "criminal element," and, when a local newspaper reported in 1957 that "a gang" of Mexican prisoners ran the county jail, "a delegation from CSO including John Torres, Attorney Hector Moreno, and César Chávez" gathered to confront the columnist just "two hours after the paper hit the stands," asking for evidence of the journalist's allegations. Spurned by the reporter, the CSO delegation investigated the jail and formally protested the story, eventually eliciting an apology from the newspaper. Chapter leaders also demanded that government officials hold law enforcement officers accountable in cases of police brutality. Members protested, for example, when Watsonville police officers beat Frank Pérez and ruptured his intestines, when San Leandro officers broke Tony Garule's nose, when a San José officer knocked a local twenty-year-old Mexican unconscious, and when Patrolman B. J. Collins shot and killed the San Josean Frank Victor Alvarez.[36]

ELECTORAL POWER

As postwar residents began to beat back the devil of discrimination, the electoral system seemed an effective way to exorcise county inequalities. The CSO was a critical player in efforts nationwide to democratize the ballot box. Voter registration drives became an obsession of members convinced that local policymakers would more quickly heed their demands if Mexican Americans became an active electorate. Only 1,600 of the roughly 21,000 eligible Mexican American voters in the area had registered in 1952. Moreover,

CSO members established voter registration booths like this one to encourage
Mexican American voters to develop a civil rights movement in postwar California.
Fred Ross Papers, box 32, folder 2.

some arriving Tejanos believed that California, like their home state, required residents to pay a poll tax. When they first organized in the Valley,
Fred Ross and the charter members of the San José chapter had demanded
the appointment of Spanish-speaking voter registrars for the first time in the
area's history, but government officials "said 'if we give registrars to the Mexicans we'll have to give the Blacks their own registrars, the Japanese their
own, and every other group will want their own, as well.'" Gallegos remembered that "we said, 'That sounds good to us,'" and CSO members subse-

quently urged the local "Council for Civic Unity, the AFL, State Senators, Women's League of Voters, newspapers and other influential groups" to pressure the county on this issue.[37]

The CSO won the fight for six Spanish-speaking registrars in time for the November ballot, and members began to enroll voters by going from house to house on the East Side. Announcements aired on Spanish-language radio, and Eastsiders shouted through bullhorns to urge San Joseans to "vote, vote, everybody get out to vote." Deputy registrars set up information tables at Sunday masses, downtown department stores, and neighborhood theaters and groceries, and Father McDonnell often "devoted his sermon to the importance of voting and urged the people to register to vote after mass." San Joseans who registered Mexican Americans in other parts of the county relied on local priests at Gilroy's Saint Mary's Church, where Father Casgrove "announced that we were outside and all people who were not registered [ought] to do so." The growing number of Mexican business owners also pushed this campaign, and the barber Johnny Torres joked that he only gave haircuts to customers who intended to cast their ballots. For the first time in the history of the Santa Clara Valley, CSO members began to create a Mexican American electorate, and in 1952 alone, the San José chapter registered four thousand local residents "of Mexican extraction," many of whom voted for the first time.[38]

Election day 1952 confirmed that their struggle to integrate Valley voting booths had only begun. Racial intimidation still threatened to limit ethnic Mexican political rights. At one site on the East Side, poll-watchers from Republican Party Headquarters demanded that four Mexican Americans prove that they could in fact "read and write English," a state requirement for voting. Those singled out were nervous first-time voters who "froze up and just couldn't do it" when asked to read from the Constitution. César Chávez, the chairman of the "Get-Out-the-Vote Committee," protested that because Republicans only asked "citizens of Mexican extraction" to prove their literacy, they had assured "the injection of a racial issue into the election." The Community Service Organization immediately dispatched its own monitors to East Side polls, and while all four of the challenged voters returned to pass the literacy exam, news of that intimidation discouraged many others from casting ballots.[39]

Mexican American voters later encountered other apparent opposition to their voter registration efforts. After eight Mexican American deputy registrars registered 1,200 local residents in 1956, Republican poll-watchers vowed again to monitor voting booths in Mexican neighborhoods for signs of electoral fraud. Anticipating trouble, the local CSO wrote U.S. Attorney General William P. Rogers and California Attorney General Pat Brown to warn that California was witnessing civil rights violations comparable to those seen in the Southern United States. Requesting a federal and state investigation of

"Dixiecrat tactics in East San José"—a phrase that suggested fears that voter registration might turn violent—members urged national leaders to protect Mexican Americans as they had the African American electorate. Chapter president Ernest Abeytia, owner of an East Side grocery store, reminded government officials of earlier Republican efforts at intimidation, and he expressed hope "that any move to intimidate such voters on the basis of race, color, or creed from exercising their rights of franchise are summarily dealt with." Although the federal and state governments apparently did not investigate accusations that Republicans planned to harass Mexican American voters, there seem to have been few complaints in the 1958 election, the first time in the region's history that large numbers of ethnic Mexicans cast their ballots.[40]

CSO members believed that voter registration would force political candidates to pay attention to ethnic Mexican concerns, and many East Side residents hoped throughout the decade to follow the Los Angeles chapter and elect a Mexican American to public office. Such dreams were a hallmark of postwar Mexican American politics throughout the Southwest. The prize in many local eyes remained a city council seat, and new visions of Mexican American representation had appeared in 1950 when two San Joseans vied as the first Latino candidates in the city since the nineteenth century. The grocery store owner Charles Esparza spoke out against "job and educational discrimination," while attorney Manny Gómez, born in Chihuahua, Mexico, and once a star running back on the University of Santa Clara football team, promoted a similar platform. Both candidates lost badly in the 1950 Democratic primary, however, left "gritting their teeth," and many observers concluded that if Mexican Americans had cast their votes for just one candidate, the city might have elected its first Mexican American councilman in the twentieth century.[41]

Hopes of political power sprang anew thanks to the CSO presence, and a local organizer noted when he visited a dance for Mexican American teenagers in 1956 that some participants said "it's about time a Mexican-American is elected to public office." Many stressed that the organization needed to stay out of the game of endorsing candidates. Chapter officers had decided in 1952 and 1953 to stress a nonpartisan approach, a policy later written into the CSO national constitution. Instead of creating a solid ethnic voting bloc, the CSO sponsored "Meet Your Candidates Nights," in which hundreds of Mexican Americans grilled candidates for the Board of Supervisors, the California Legislature, and the 10th Congressional District about housing, police harassment, "the McCarran-Walter Immigration law, the importation of foreign labor [braceros] to toil in the fields of California, along with social security coverage, like the unemployment compensation." Officers urged members to reject candidates who had broken earlier campaign promises or had not shown interest in assisting East Side residents. They feared that

Residents of East San Antonio Street and other parts of San José's East Side pushed city and county officials to pave local streets, build sidewalks, and install outdoor lights during the 1950s. Fred Ross Papers, box 32, folder 3.

formal endorsements would make the CSO the newest tool of the Democratic party, a cog in the Valley's creaking political machine rather than an independent force.[42]

Ethnic Mexican political culture had long been driven by strong ideological stands on race, immigration, and labor, and many postwar Mexican Americans expressed frustration with the CSO's new vision of nonpartisan activism. Some wanted to use those group meetings as a forum to make political speeches of their own, and officers in the Fresno chapter felt compelled to demand that onlookers ask questions of candidates and avoid long-winded pronouncements. Many ethnic Mexican San Joseans expressed hope that one of their own would run again for local political office, and by 1956 the chair of the San José *pensiones* committee decided to do just that. Leo Sánchez's bid for City Council ran into the brick wall of CSO nonpartisanship, however, and other, less-experienced Mexican Americans in the area led his political campaign, including Mexican American teenagers concerned about police brutality who had formed a "Youth for Sánchez" organization and held dances to raise money for that effort. Mexican American women such as Kay Méndez walked house-to-house to encourage East Side support for Sánchez, but the CSO did nothing more than send poll-watchers, and Sánchez came in a disappointing ninth place in the primary.[43]

His loss weighed heavily on Eastsiders who had hoped that "a Sánchez on the ballot" would encourage widespread Mexican American turnout, and Hector Moreno and other CSO membersbegan to prioritize Mexican American political solidarity over open debate, representation in local government over the long-term cultivation of an informed electorate.[44] The desperate circumstances facing ethnic Mexicans seemed to demand a quicker approach to political power. More interested in seeking an elected government position than in providing service after service to Eastsiders, Leo Sánchez left the CSO to emphasize his "political commitments," and others would soon do the same. Many influential leaders abandoned the group and shaped the broader Chicano civil rights movement developing nationwide in the 1960s. César Chávez, the founder of the United Farm Workers Union, is perhaps the best remembered individual to emerge from the San José CSO chapter, but others made important marks on political history, as well. Herman Gallegos, for instance, helped to establish the National Council of La Raza and the Mexican American Legal Defense and Education Fund, and San José attorney Hector Moreno became a charter member of the Mexican American Political Association and served as John F. Kennedy's campaign liaison in Northern California Mexican communities. Despite these departures, the chapter still remained strong for a time. The statewide organization registered 137,096 Mexican American voters in California in 1960, but growing demands for political representation made nonpartisanship seem less relevant to many.[45]

New community groups began urging Mexican Americans to vote as an ethnic bloc to achieve greater political influence in Northern California. Following on CSO voter registration success, a small group of San Joseans, many of them businessmen, worked after 1960 to groom one of their own for elected office. These local residents stressed their fundamental Americanism, and the newly hired policeman Bob Rodríguez urged Mexican Americans in 1962 to drop their "hyphenated identity," to "be Americans and integrate fully within our society," even as he declared that "we shall vote for a Mexican that can represent us with intelligence as well as representing all of the people of San Jose, with dignity and maturity. We have a wonderful city and we must give to it for what we receive."[46]

Those who made such pronouncements in the early 1960s were often members of the county's modest Mexican American business and professional class. Small business owners and civil servants such as the policeman Danny Campos led the way, and veterans began to dominate middle-class organizations like the American G.I. Forum, groups that proved less accommodating to women and immigrants than the system developed by the CSO in the previous decade. The number of Mexican American professionals in the city remained minute, confined to roughly five lawyers, twenty teachers, and six social workers according to one estimate in 1964, but they exerted a political influence beyond their numbers. The life of San Jose–born Henry Coca, Jr., illustrated that some had moved far from the region's working-class barrios and colonias. Born in 1932, Coca attended Jackson Grammar School, worked for a time in local agricultural work, and eventually became a salesman and then a manager at Great Western Furniture. In 1962 *El Excéntrico* carried photos of Hank at home in the "quite serene" foothills nearby, a postwar Mexican American success who loved lounging in his "heated swimming pool."[47]

A wide gap continued to exist in the Valley between Coca and the majority of local ethnic Mexicans, and the decline of the CSO left poor and working-class residents without a political organization to articulate their interests. CSO ideas about community service and political power survived, but the rush to elect a Mexican American city councilman proved complicated, and it was not until 1972, nearly twenty-five years after the Los Angeles CSO had helped elect Roybal to a similar post, that San José's Al Garza won a council seat. In the meantime, the Valley's economy continued to leave most ethnic Mexicans in the dust of agricultural industries. Some tried to bridge the technology gap. Aware that IBM and similar companies were hiring thousands of white residents of the Valley, one man established the Aztec Electronic Production Institute in the early 1960s to offer Spanish-speakers twelve-week classes in electronics, hoping that he might integrate them into the high-tech county economy. But the Mayfair district and other ethnic Mexican neighborhoods remained poor, often painfully so. Just as New Almadén's Latino residents had suffered bodily harm in the mid-nineteenth-century industrial boom, the twentieth century's working poor remained similarly vulnerable. To take but one example, nearly 90 percent of the county's pregnant farmworkers in 1958 received no prenatal care, and one researcher reported that "prematurity, toxemias of pregnancy and congenital abnormalities are fairly high in this group."[48]

The early 1960s were a low point in ethnic Mexicans' postwar efforts to fashion a democratic civil rights movement, but the coming of the Vietnam War and other developments would again transform their political culture in a few years. New organizations stepped into the breach created by CSO's decline, as the following chapter makes clear, and important elements of post-1965 Chicano politics were inspired by the Community Service Organization's example. One particularly influential group was United People Arriba (UPA), an East Side association that traced its origins to 1967 protests at Roosevelt Junior High School, where white students and teachers called African American and Mexican American students *changos*, or apes. Following the lead of the CSO, Sofia Mendoza encouraged that group in 1968 "to broaden their action beyond school problems, to seek improvements in health conditions, to protect the rights of welfare recipients, to resolve differ-

TABLE 9
Median Household Income, 1959 and 1965

	1959	1965
County	$7,417	$8,662
City	6,949	N/A
Mayfair District	5,720	5,432

Source: City of San Jose, "Application to the Department of Housing and Urban Development for a Grant to Plan a Comprehensive City Demonstration Program," May 1, 1967.

ences with the police, to find jobs, and [to] get better housing." Subcommittees of UPA responded to crises of police brutality, and members helped urbanizing farmworker families to find housing in local neighborhoods. In just the first year of the group's existence, Mendoza and other participants lobbied for new stoplights, picketed a store that discriminated against Mexican Americans in its hiring practices, distributed wallet-sized cards "outlining Constitutional rights in case of arrest," pushed officials to name a newly constructed school either Benito Juárez or Crispus Attucks, and demanded other changes. These Eastsiders claimed no backyard swimming pools or suburban estates. Paying clear tribute to the CSO, this "Chicano" organization and others demanded full equality for working-class ethnic Mexicans. "We are not fancy people," they declared. "We don't live in rich homes or drive expensive cars, but we think we have the same rights as anybody."[49]

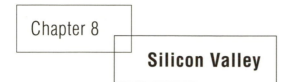

Chapter 8

Silicon Valley

What are the big corporations, banks, and hospitals doing
for poor people? Nothing!
—San José's *El Boletín* (September 1969)

Urban economic growth and booster efforts to attract new businesses transformed the rural Santa Clara Valley during and after World War II, and local
government and business officials worked ever harder during the 1960s and
1970s to change the San José area into a high-tech "Silicon Valley." That
name for the region first emerged in 1971, soon "evoked images of a variety
of entrepreneurs producing what appeared to be a liberating technology,"
and elicited its chorus of celebratory journalists. Boosting has been a Santa
Clara Valley pastime since before the Gold Rush, and a great deal of ink has
been spilled in accompaniment to the region's high-tech wonders and woes.
Far less has been said about the lives of its working-class residents, or about
the new political visions that San Joseans brought into greater focus during
and after the Vietnam War era. Rushes to celebrate the Silicon Valley oblite-
rated memories of mercury mines and fruit orchards, and they too often
ignored the present circumstances of local nonwhites. As in the 1940s, few
ethnic Mexicans enjoyed runaway economic success in the Gold Rush atmosphere of the late-twentieth-century information age. The Latino community
boomed in size after 1960 and came to comprise more than 25 percent of
the city by 1990, but its recent history only highlighted the Valley's greatest constant, the power of race for structuring local political and cultural
developments.[1]

From a Latino standpoint two episodes illustrate the continuities between
the recent past and earlier eras. The first developed from an effort to revive
an old vision of local history. In early 1969, civic boosters announced that

the city would sponsor a Fiesta de las Rosas similar to the one popular during the 1920s. Organizers invited the television star Lorne Greene to serve as master of ceremonies, and the parade in June featured a host of costumed Spanish conquistadors, nearly all of them whites dressed like Iberian warriors, accompanied by a Mexican "peon" and his burro. As in early twentieth-century celebrations, fiesta organizers celebrated the Valley's picturesque "white" Spanish past rather than its longtime Mexican and Indian residents, even as they called for new business investors to join IBM and Hewlett Packard in the county. Seventy-five thousand onlookers witnessed the day's events, but hopes of civic unity quickly shattered. Many Mexican Americans had boycotted the festivities out of a sense that the Valley was having "a party at our expense," but some five hundred local Chicanos, offended enough to protest the spectacle, turned the day into what later would be called the "fiasco de las rosas." In loud tones, they shouted "traitor" and other epithets at the handful of Mexican Americans involved in the celebration, and they insisted that the fiesta had been nothing more than a pro-business celebration of Spanish colonialism. A much-publicized fight with the San José police followed. Protestors were arrested and charged with disturbing the peace, and those jailed alleged police brutality. Dozens of Mexican Americans gathered to cheer the release of the jailed protesters several days later, and the resulting controversy catalyzed local ethnic Mexican politics and brought a quick end to booster hopes of renewing the once popular fiesta.[2]

Several months after the aborted "fiasco de las rosas," another incident illustrated the persistence of more openly virulent forms of anti-Mexican racism in the area, notions of white racial superiority fostered by the local justice system since the mid-nineteenth century. In September 1969, San José received nationwide attention when Superior Court Justice Gerald S. Chargin launched a tirade of racist slurs. Upon hearing a case of a young Mexican American boy accused of committing incest with his fifteen-year-old sister, Chargin predicted that the sexually active young girl "probably . . . will have a half a dozen children and three or four marriages before she is 18" and suggested that the boy was not unlike the criminal Mexican "greasers" so hated in the nineteenth century. As so often in the past, race drew fateful meanings from references to Latino sexuality and violence. "You will probably end up in State's Prison before you are 25," he warned the boy and other observers in his courtroom, "and that's where you belong, anyhow." Threatening deportation, Chargin told the accused youth that

> we ought to send you out of the country—send you back to Mexico. You belong in prison for the rest of your life for doing things of this kind. You ought to commit suicide. That's what I think of people of this kind. You are lower than animals and haven't the right to live in organized society—just miserable, lousy, rotten people.

There is nothing we can do with you. You expect the County to take care of you. Maybe Hitler was right. The animals in our society probably ought to be destroyed because they have no right to live among human beings.[3]

Images of violence, the presumed criminality of Mexicans, memories of World War II, and allusions to California's nineteenth-century past all shaped Chargin's thinking, and ethnic Mexican residents screamed their objections. As in the fiesta episode, crowds in San José and other parts of the Southwest rallied to protest Chargin's statements—often in St. James Park, the site of the Thurmond and Holmes lynchings more than thirty years before—and those gathered drew energy from the burgeoning Chicano movement nationwide. Given the long local history of judicial discrimination and police harassment against ethnic Mexicans, it was no surprise that the Western Center on Law and Poverty discovered that Mexican Americans interviewed in San José and other California cities "*all* believed that discrimination existed in the legal system toward Mexican Americans."[4]

These events of 1969 may have been extreme examples of entrenched anti-Mexican racism, but they point to ongoing truths that gave shape to Silicon Valley as it became home to the information age. Ideologies of race still clouded the visions of elected officials, and local Mexicans and Mexican Americans continued to develop new political movements, often in ways more emphatic than those of their predecessors in the CSO or UCAPAWA. Thousands of Latinos had established firm roots in the Valley, large numbers of teenagers born to Tejano or Mexican immigrant parents now considered Northern California their primary home, and many expressed new interest in San José's future. The concerns of these local "Chicanos," as many now called themselves, would rock the Valley and challenge the area's institutions in ways never before seen in Northern California.

Ethnic Mexicans also tangled with one another. Concerned about local inequalities, some directed their anger at seemingly more moderate Mexican Americans, including parents and grandparents who had been involved in the Community Service Organization or the National Farm Labor Union. Others mocked self-aggrandizing Hispanics who seemed driven to capitalize on the region's economic boom. Only a few Mexican American organizations found ways to reach out to the newly arrived immigrants who performed the low-wage jobs enabling Silicon Valley's development. Most white San Joseans paid even less attention to those Latino workers. An enthusiasm for dot-coms and microprocessors overtook government officials and local journalists, obscuring the effects of Silicon Valley's development the ways in which Mexicans and Mexican Americans electrified and reshaped the San José area. All this signaled a new chapter in Valley history. The following pages trace some of the broader political changes that electrified residents of many stripes, the local economic developments that affected different groups, and the new patterns of Mexican immigration and residency that continued to shape regional politics and culture after 1965.

SILICON INEQUALITIES

Like earlier economies based on mining, wheat, and fruit processing, the Silicon Valley has owed a great deal to its large ethnic Mexican population. Here large numbers of Latinos clustered in service and assembly work from the 1970s forward, the sorts of jobs that would come to define ethnic Mexican experiences throughout the United States by the mid-1990s. As in the nineteenth century, economic developments in the San José area foreshadowed those in many other places. Immigrant workers arrived in large numbers after the end of the Bracero Program in 1964, and the sizable growth of the Latino population more than kept pace with the overall demographic expansion of the region as a whole. Tens of thousands of immigrant and U.S.-born Mexican Americans moved to the Valley over the next thirty years, entering a variety of local jobs. Latinos had provided low-wage labor that drove Valley agricultural production in decades past, and it seems less than surprising that most continued to occupy the bottom rungs of the regional economic ladder. The racial stereotypes so evident in 1969 played a powerful role in defining employment opportunities, and Latinos and African Americans remained more likely than white San Joseans to be members of the Valley's working poor. The 1960 census reported that 11 percent of Mexican immigrant men and 39 percent of Mexicana women in the local workforce were unemployed; by 1970, Latino households were twice as likely as white San Joseans to live in poverty, and the per capita median income of Spanish-speakers remained only $2,372 compared with $4,023 for white residents. Nearly a third of the Spanish-speaking women in the county still worked as blue-collar "operatives," particularly in local canneries and in emerging high-tech industries, and Valley poverty plagued ethnic Mexican women more than men. East San José continued to serve as the home for many newly arrived, working-class, ethnic Mexicans during the 1970s and 1980s, and economic poverty assured that the city's ethnic Mexican neighborhoods would continue to look more than a little like the impoverished California towns—Hanford, Corcoran, El Centro, King City, Salinas, and others—from which many San Joseans had migrated since World War II.[5]

Local institutions helped keep Latinos out of the corporate board room. A study of patterns of educational attainment in the area found that in 1963 a whopping 78 percent of local Spanish-surnamed youth had dropped out of high school before completing their degrees. Thus continued the de facto educational discrimination evident in the Valley and other parts of the Southwest since the nineteenth century. San José public schools often channeled resident Latinos into low-wage employment sectors. Frances Palacios was one San Josean who remembers having been discouraged by high school guidance counselors from going to college, and thousands like her simply moved into low-wage electronics assembly jobs in the new Silicon Valley from the 1970s through the 1990s. Women were the primary wage-earners in many ethnic Mexican homes, making the East Side a "female ghetto" in the eyes of some observers, and by the mid-1970s Latinos as a group made up nearly 50 percent of the participants in federal poverty programs such as the Comprehensive Employment and Training Act (CETA). The economic marginality of many ethnic Mexicans was further assured by the decline of the local fruit-processing industry, an employment sector that since the 1940s had provided jobs to many women and men. By 1977 nearly all of the canneries had closed, and this agricultural de-industrialization threw many out of work, a development that hit women hard.[6]

These processes seem only to have increased the Valley's gap between rich and poor. From the mid-1960s into the late 1990s, Silicon's racial logic aped that of mercury, as low-wage Latinos again created a booming economy that capitalized on the presence of underemployed Mexicana and Mexican American women, in particular. Recently arrived Asian immigrants often labored in low-wage sectors alongside Valley Latinos, just as earlier groups of Filipinos and Mexicans had encountered one another in local orchards and fields. By the late 1980s local microelectronics industries employed more than fifty thousand workers in low-paid operatives jobs, and most of those employed in the unskilled positions were women of color. Mexicanos also typically worked for subcontractors as janitors, landscapers, construction workers, and dishwashers, service occupations that boomed in the region, thanks to the demands of the region's middle and upper classes. Often invisible to a white middle class that designed software in Valley cubicles, these Mexican men and women worked at night to clean the offices of international corporations such as Apple Computers in nearby Cupertino. Their labor remained tough, low-paid, and often dangerous. Janitors like Jose Celis were instructed "to clean bathrooms with a solvent that dissolved his gloves," and employees like Leonarda Pineda was fired when she "rebuffed her foreman's sexual propositions." Patterns of racial segmentation in the workforce established in previous decades shaped the modern Silicon Valley. As the United States Commission on Civil Rights concluded in 1982, the workforce in the San José area "is sharply divided along ethnic, sexual [sic], and educational lines. In general, white males hold the positions with the highest incomes and greatest power. Non-white men (including Hispanics) and white women fall in the middle of the high tech hierarchy. And minority women stand at the bottom of the occupational structure."[7]

Some ethnic Mexicans enjoyed more economic success than did area janitors and assembly workers. Subcontractors and foremen in charge of those crews were one example, and they frequently hired kin from their own hometown. Some Mexican Americans educated in the Valley experienced upward mobility, and while their graduation rates at city high schools remained low, the number of Mexican Americans who completed four years in the East Side Union High School District jumped from 12.3 percent to 29.6 percent between 1956 and 1971. Government programs targeting ethnic Mexican students diversified colleges and universities throughout the state, and these helped guide some into the professional ranks. Often attracted by San Jose State's educational outreach programs that recruited in farmworker communities, hundreds of local Mexican-origin residents took advantage of educational opportunities in local colleges and universities available to working-class Mexicans for the first time in the late 1960s. Latinos entered colleges in much higher numbers than they had in the past; only 34 percent of ethnic Mexican graduates had done so in 1956, but that number increased to 54 percent in 1966 and 71 percent in 1971. The result was a population of college students much larger than the area had seen during the 1950s, and the number of middle-class Mexican Americans in the area increased steadily during the 1960s and 1970s.[8]

POLITICS

As resident ethnic Mexicans became more active in local educational institutions, Mexicanos and Mexican Americans found in local colleges the public forum for their opinions that had often eluded the CSO and the NFLU a decade before. Students throughout the United States became a new political force in the 1960s, and Mexican American veterans of the armed services who enrolled in college on the G.I. Bill became particularly important in the era of the Vietnam War. The murmurs of a Chicano student movement could be heard by 1965 when many Tejanos who lived in the South Bay began to influence local ethnic Mexican political affairs. Students like Humberto Garza, Jesus Reyna, Eduardo Flores, and Tino Esparza started "meeting each other, [and] talking about . . . what's happening here." They decided by the spring of 1966 to institute a tutoring program to assist younger Mexican American college students at San José State. In the meantime, other Mexican American veterans joined a small group of Guatemalans, Peruvians, and Salvadorans at San José City College to form "Los Amigos," the first pan-Latino student organization in the area.[9]

Valley students during the 1950s had worked with the CSO to provide social services, to protest police brutality, and to contribute to the City Council campaign of Leo Sánchez, but activists of the 1960s were cast from a different mold. They felt growing hostility toward many government institutions. Young Mexican Americans also began to name anti-Mexican racism as a primary cause of local and national patterns of inequality. Their political rhetoric developed in part from contact with national civil rights leaders who emphasized that Mexican Americans had long been constrained by discrimination against them. The FEPC Commissioner Louis García spoke to an audience of San José ethnic Mexicans in June 1964, for example, and urged them to compare the racial discrimination accorded to African Americans and Mexican Americans in the United States in order to "impress upon you what many of us will not accept: We *are* a minority group." The former Colorado resident Lino López reminded San José activists upon his arrival a year later that "most discriminations are thought of as only towards the Negro but there is this large Spanish American minority which is growing because of immigration." African American activists influenced the Latino students who joined Los Amigos and other groups after 1965, and four hundred residents signed a petition in 1967 to urge the Board of Education to name a local school either Crispus Attucks or Benito Juárez. At San José State, the African American sociology professor Harry Edwards was a prominent if controversial voice, and the newly formed Mexican American Student Confederation (MASC) parroted the language of Black power in their 1968 announcement that they would adopt "whatever means necessary in order to establish a society in which justice is truly possible."[10]

While often sharing a critique of Valley racism, Latinos and African Americans also came into conflict with one another. What some later considered the founding episode of the student movement at San José State illustrated Chicano students' demand that "Brown Power" be taken seriously in the Santa Clara Valley, more seriously even that "Black Power." Responding to charges of racism at the college, in early November 1967 the San José State faculty sponsored the filming of the documentary *A Day of Concern*, a project that relied on interviews with eleven African American students and four Mexican Americans but which focused more heavily on "the plight of the Black student at the college." Angered that the film had not given them equal attention, Mexican American students demanded that it not be screened, met with members of the college administration, and reminded the press that while African Americans accounted for only 2 percent of San José's population, Mexican Americans by contrast made up 20 percent of the city. Stressing that Chicanos were "the largest minority, and, in fact, the most deprived," the students succeeded in having the film changed to include a broader representation of local race relations, but these proponents of Chicano power angered many African Americans in the process.[11]

The reaction to *A Day of Concern* and the development of more organized Mexican American student protests in the Valley marked important changes in regional politics by the late 1960s. In the San José area, many increasingly defined themselves as "Chicanos," a term of self-designation among working-class Mexican Americans that had circulated (and drawn much criticism) in East San José since the early 1950s. It took off at the same time among Latino high school and college students in San Francisco, Los Angeles, and other parts of the Southwest. By the late 1960s many throughout the United States believed that term best expressed the fact that they were Mexican Americans who "did not have an Anglo view of themselves," and the Fiesta de las Rosas protest and other events saw these young residents defining identities in opposition to Valley racism, speaking out about the United States "colonization" of the Southwest, stressing their community's long-standing oppression at the hands of white Americans, and urging ethnic Mexican control of barrio institutions.[12] Their pronouncements seemed a far cry from CSO struggles to obtain voter registrars or Ernesto Galarza's efforts to organize immigrant braceros.

Many now placed a new emphasis on changing educational institutions rather than labor unions, the dominant concern of many earlier activists in the region. The efforts of student organizations in San José echoed those by Mexican Americans in other parts of the West during these years, and local institutions such as Gavilan College in Gilroy witnessed students and recently hired faculty like John Paul Ornelaz, a one-time migrant field worker, arguing for more Mexican American faculty appointments in the name of democratizing that institution. As colleges and universities became new arenas of political struggle, San José State's Richard Olivas drew poetic attention to the way his faculty at that college continued to teach as if the student body had not changed since the 1940s:

> I'm sitting in my history class,
> The instructor commences rapping,
> I'm in my U.S. History class,
> On the verge of napping.
> . . .
>
> What did he say?
> Dare I ask him to reiterate?
> Oh why bother.
> It sounded like he said,
> George Washington's my father.
>
> I'm reluctant to believe it.
> I suddenly raise my mano.
> If George Washington's my father,
> Why wasn't he Chicano?[13]

Chicano students and faculty stressed that changing institutions of hiring learning would have strong ripple effects on Valley barrios, on local policy-makers, and on law enforcement officials. Likening the educational system at San José State to a form of "bondage," one participant complained that the college only produced "incompetent teachers, social workers, policemen, counselors, sociologists, political scientists, historians, journalists, and other such products who are contributing to the destruction of the Chicano in this nation." Moved by similar frustrations, José R. Villarreal and eleven other students at San José State walked out of the college's commencement exercises in the spring of 1968, creating a separate annual "Chicano commencement" that has continued into the twenty-first century, an effort to make ethnic Mexican students comfortable in an institution that often seemed at best indifferent to their presence.[14]

Chicano students became intent on understanding the Santa Clara Valley's Latino history, recognizing the presence of Yóscolo as well as contemporary Indians in the region, and discussing the ways in which Manifest Destiny and the Treaty of Guadalupe Hidalgo had shaped the fate of earlier generations of ethnic Mexicans. Residents of the Valley often celebrated the vibrancy of Mexican American culture, following the lead of Colorado resident Corky González, whose Plan Espiritual de Aztlán sought to unite ethnic Mexicans across lines of class, gender, and region. Claiming that "many Mexican-Americans don't know enough about the Mexican culture," one group in 1968 created a summer cultural program that taught junior high school students visual art, music, "dances such as El Jarabe Tapatío and La Bamba," and "cooking as well as . . . sewing." San Joseans openly celebrated the history of Mexican Americans in the United States, and several in early 1968 proposed the creation of a "Mexican American Culture Center" that would emphasize that community's positive role in the Valley, a place "where we are going to have a Spanish language library, a museum, an art gallery, a depository of records dealing with the contributions people of Mexican descent have made to the growth of this nation, and a small theater." Recovering local history would forge greater solidarity between ethnic Mexicans, provide a more accurate education not available in Valley high schools and colleges, and emphasize that ethnic Mexicans were not just yesterday's immigrants, but long-time Valley inhabitants whose residency preceded that of white Americans. These sentiments found eventual expression in the 1999 completion of the $36 million Mexican Heritage Plaza on the East Side.[15]

Chicano cultural politics remade the area from below during the early Silicon Valley era, although the slang heard on East Side streets, the lowrider cars that cruised local barrios, and the clothes worn by young Chicanos also drew heavily from styles developed by zoot suiters in the 1940s. The one-time San Josean José Montoya penned an elegy to the pachuco generation that proved influential to the burgeoning Chicano arts movement, and many young residents, emboldened by new celebrations of Chicano culture, affirmed that *carnalismo* (brotherhood) would build "Brown Power." Just as the Spanish-language media had played a central role in earlier political movements, new bilingual publications like *La Palabra de MASC*, *El Machete*,

Chicanas hang out in a south San José park in 1972. The woman standing by the car wears a "Chicano Power" patch near her ankle. Photo courtesy of Jesús M. Garza.

and *Liberación* paid enormous attention to articulating what it meant to be truly "Chicano." Replacing Mexicanidad as the dominant political idiom on the ethnic Mexican left, at least for a time, Chicano cultural nationalism captured the imaginations of many Eastsiders by the early 1970s. Young Mexican Americans celebrated their *mestizaje*, drew attention to their indigenous roots, and lay claim to a "bronze culture" of longstanding resistance to white oppression. Some former farmworkers in the area identified strongly with the United Farm Workers movement established by César Chávez. But at its most extreme, cultural nationalism elided distinctions of class and gender among ethnic Mexicans and emphasized that Chicanos shared a common essence derived from their blood or their common experiences with racial segregation and economic poverty. As one San Josean expressed it,

The influential Chicano poet and activist Colorado's Corky González visited San José and promoted his vision of Brown Power at El Centro Cultural de la Gente in downtown San José. Photo courtesy of Jesús M. Garza.

"This is the belief that all Chicanos have a common identity through their ethnic likeness, regardless of socio-economic background. Also the Bato (the guy) in the Barrio, the suburban factory worker, and the Tio Taco (Uncle Tom) who has 'made it' are our brothers by race."[16]

The broader political atmosphere shaped by the Vietnam War proved critical to new expressions of identity that placed in the foreground the power of racism in defining Valley society. As in the past, wartime reshaped ethnic Mexican politics. Ernesto Galarza, always close to the front in pressing political matters, warned a Bay Area audience that the military escalation threatened the success of the Mexican American civil rights movement, particularly in the area of educational reform. "As long as the priority in our nation is on war and killing," he told members of the League of United Latin American Citizens—a group that traced its origins to the post–World War II arrival of Tejanos in Northern California—"Mexican Americans and all other children will suffer." As the death tolls of Mexican American soldiers mounted, more and more local residents angrily decried the use of nonwhites as *carne de cañón* (cannon fodder) and circulated Spanish-language fliers announcing that "As human beings we feel that the war is immoral and unjust and ought to be ended immediately. As Chicanos and Latinos we are more profoundly opposed to the war since it is a direct attack on us." Those critiques of U.S. foreign policy did not find immediate consent in all Mexican American quarters, but they fed growing suspicions that the national government discriminated against people of color. The more politically conservative, including veterans in the American G.I. Forum, initially insisted on supporting the war, but even that group changed its position when the organization's Women's Auxiliary protested the Forum's stance in 1971.[17]

Opposition to the Vietnam War propelled many young Mexican Americans to express a more defiant approach to white institutions. Their predecessors in the 1930s and 1950s were often concerned about joining organizations dominated by non-Mexicans, but young Chicanos in the 1960s and 1970s went further. Some likened their own circumstances to those of the Viet Cong, "our Third World brothers" who faced "the same system that oppressors and exploits us in the United States." Emphasizing the racism of dominant society, Mexican-origin residents of San José, like those in Los Angeles and other California cities, asserted that "rather than a reliance on gabacho-controlled news media, we must develop our own channels and networks of communication," and some challenged anti-Mexican discrimination by creating separate educational institutions. Similar calls for Chicano "self-determination" echoed in Denver and other Southwestern cities. For a short time, Eastsiders in 1971 maintained their own "Colegio de La Raza" that worked "for the liberation of the Barrio," but committed activists had to admit that most Chicanos who went to college continued to matriculate at San José City, San José State, or the University of Santa Clara.[18]

By 1971 opposition to the Vietnam War was nearly universal among ethnic Mexicans, but despite the new passionate attempts to rally locals around Chicano Power, no single organization took the lead in ethnic Mexican politics. The CSO had been more successful in speaking for the broad ethnic Mexican community—understandably enough, given that the county boasted more than two hundred thousand ethnic Mexicans by 1970—and many ethnic Mexicans openly resented the fiery rhetoric and apparent exclusivity of the new young turks. Some older San Joseans saw Chicano cultural nationalism as fraudulent invention and expressed frustration that youth did not either remain culturally Mexican or become mainstream Americans. Nationally prominent Mexican Americans such as Texas Congressman Henry B. González issued similar complaints. Noting that youth mixed Spanish and English words and spoke caló, a working-class patois developing throughout the Southwest since the early twentieth century, one San José magazine provided the confused a "short course in contemporary Chicano" with colloquial expressions popular in local barrios:

Trucha!	Watch Out!
Vato	Cat, Dude, Guy
Calcos	Shoes
Chueco	Fink
Lucas	Marijuana
Grifa	Marijuana
Chante	House
Wisa	Girlfriend, Broad . . .[19]

Above all, the cultural nationalist vision of *carnalismo* seemed anathema to those called "wisa" or "broad," ethnic Mexican women who often continued to lead local neighborhood-based organizing efforts, much as they had since the 1930s. While many Chicanas threw their support behind cultural nationalism, others issued trenchant critiques of that emerging rhetoric. Sofia Mendoza, Graciela Olivárez, and others challenged movement rhetoric that celebrated masculine political resistance and defined proper Mexican women as nurturing mothers and faithful wives. They pressed instead for recognition that both Valley employers and local Chicanos were guilty of gender-based discrimination. New groups such as Mujeres de Aztlán and Women Who Care emerged by the early 1970s, often to counter the discriminatory treatment that Chicanas faced at the hands of ethnic Mexican men. Pushing local governments to hire more Chicana employees, some declared that their applications faced the "fiercest opposition . . . from the [male] Chicano" who, in the name of Brown Power, often opposed the promotion of women beyond the clerical ranks. This context prompted ethnic Mexican women in Northern California and throughout the United States to develop new political responses. Many appealed to Chicanismo for their own purposes and wrote poetry and plays "on the emerging dignity of the Chicana."[20]

As with contemporary calls for "Black Power," celebrations of *carnalismo* never united the diverse ethnic Mexican population throughout the Southwest. Despite appeals to brotherhood and sisterhood, cultural nationalism did not keep ethnic Mexicans from attacking one another's credibility. Returning Vietnam veterans often felt shunned by Chicanos who viewed them as traitors to the cause, murderers of women and children in Southeast Asia. Others felt the stinging criticism of Chicano artists in El Teatro Urbano, a group established in the spring of 1968 that satirized those who seemed complacent and apolitical, including "students who received financial aid but did little or nothing for the Chicano community" and the other so-called *vendidos* (sellouts) who seemed to stand in the way of La Causa. Young and old argued above all about the use of the term Chicano, a word associated with lower-class people during past decades, and a moniker that to some now suggested a penchant for violence. When the Mexican American Student Confederation (MASC) adopted that term, at least a few members

Inspired in part by the San José playwright Luis Valdez, new theater troupes dedicated to exploring Chicano politics emerged throughout the Southwest during the Vietnam War era. Here members of San José's Teatro de la Gente perform a farm worker skit in the early 1970s. Photo courtesy of Jesús M. Garza.

walked away, declaring "I'm not Chicano, I'm Mexican American." A new group called Students for the Advancement of Mexican Americans (SAMA) claimed to "represen[t] the majority opinion of Mexican American students at San Jose State," noting that "Our group does not want to be violent. We believe things can be accomplished through due process, and that our complaints will be heard through our legal system. We're not trying to topple militant leadership at San Jose State. . . . we feel the majority want moderation."[21] As in so many past moments in the Valley's long history, violence emerged yet again to shape ethnic Mexican politics.

DEBTS TO THE PAST

These social and political divisions—rarely acknowledged by Chicano historians who have slouched toward hagiography in representing the heady politics of the 1960s—were not inconsequential in San José and other cities, nor did the activists of that era break with political traditions begun by earlier Californians. Chicano cultural nationalism had real weaknesses when it came to addressing local needs, as affirmations of *carnalismo* alienated many if not most San Joseans, including residents who had one non-Mexican parent, those considered *vendidos* to the cause of Brown Power, older immigrant residents, and many women. Voices of dissent called for a new vision of politics. The editors of an early 1980s' youth magazine called *Teen Angels* recognized that "we have people who are [ethnically] half this and half that," and that "it's good that the Raza want to unite. But why stop there? Let's *all* of us unite!" In the midst of bitter internecine struggles, the model of unified political organizing laid down by the CSO seemed attractive, and many young activists in the 1970s and 1980s believed that before its demise the organization had been "on the right track" in its efforts to lobby and work within established city and county channels.[22]

A few college students had long pushed to build political coalitions with white residents instead of basing their efforts on bronze *carnalismo*. When those at San José State and San José City College formed the group Student Initiative (Sí) in 1965 as one of the first Chicano student organizations in the country, the former CSO organizer Armando Valdez took the helm and directed members toward assisting farmworkers. White supporters were allowed membership at the outset, and the students' slogan—"Sí! The accent is on initiative!"—illustrated the strength of their predecessors' legacy of self-help. Intent on establishing a student center for Mexican-origin college students and on encouraging teenagers attending local high schools to continue in school, members of Sí were also guided by the faculty member Y. Arturo Cabrera—also a former CSO activist—and by the advice of established local *políticos* like Ernesto Galarza, Herman Gallegos, and César Chávez.[23]

Some organizations devoted to community service avoided the nasty political backstabbing endemic to cultural nationalist affiliations. A prominent new group known as the Mexican American Community Service Agency (MACSA) further illustrated the local legacy of self-help, coalition building, and neighborhood organizing that traced its roots to the CSO and earlier groups. Directed for a number of years by former CSO President Al Piñón, it sought to develop a broad community base and "fost[er] a more self-assertive effort on the part of the Mexican-American." MACSA remains today a critically important political and service organization on the East Side. Sponsoring "forums, discussion groups, lectures, and workshops," the director Lino López and other charter members hoped from the mid-1960s forward to create an agency that would function "as a go-between for the Anglo and Mexican cultures" and a way for Mexican Americans to "achie[ve] proper proportionate representation." In a statement that might have been taken from a CSO pamphlet written a decade earlier, López declared his concern in 1968 for

placing more Mexican-Americans in key positions in our society. Proper representation doesn't begin, of course, until the responsibility of decision is shared by all the groups that make up the total society. To bring this about we act as interpreter for those with a language difficulty. We bring to the attention of the Mexican-American community any career opportunities that are open to them and advise the job seeker on a myriad of related problems. . . . It is our belief that active participation and commitment will better serve the Mexican-American than waiting for the slow drift of social change to catch up to the special problems of the minority peoples.[24]

Under the direction of José Villa, a resident born in Clovis, New Mexico, MACSA attempted during the mid-1970s to take the lead in building political coalitions among local ethnic Mexicans. The organization's vision was not unlike that of other contemporary community groups in Los Angeles or San Antonio that focused on providing services to barrio residents. Confronting police brutality and developing youth programs on the East Side, that center became "a very influential power base" from which Mexican Americans in San José appealed to city government.[25]

Following the lead of the CSO, Chicano activists often defended immigrant rights to residency from the 1960s into the 1990s, a continuation of a longstanding concern of local community groups. Many Latinos throughout the Southwest registered growing concern about INS human rights abuses, and new immigration sweeps by federal agents prompted MACSA to pay greater attention to immigration policy and immigrant rights; other groups also followed the CSO example and provided low-cost immigration services.[26] Many residents asserted that Mexican Americans and Mexican immigrants needed to struggle together to forestall those deportation drives. In 1989 Michael Alvarado wrote the *San José Mercury-News* and government officials to stress that "the callous insensitivity of the Immigration and Naturalization Service must not be tolerated" and to argue that "the abuse and racist tactics they inflict on the South Bay's Hispanic community must stop now." The Confederación de la Raza Unida's newspaper included a description of several INS agents who scouted for undocumented San Joseans in 1976, and the resident Marisa de los Andes addressed a 1973 poem to those who

golpea mi dignidad,	hammer away at my dignity,
insulta a la raza mía	insult my race
y mi nacionalidad atacan en	and my nationality is attacked by
su jauria	your hunting packs
por la discriminación que avanza	because of the discrimination
día tras día	advanced from day to day
en la U.S. inmigración.[27]	in the U.S. immigration [service].[27]

While MACSA and former CSO activists frequently criticized the INS, others attacked entrenched patterns of local poverty by participating in the federal Model Cities program. Established in 1969 as an extension of Lyndon Johnson's vision of a Great Society, the program enlisted young college graduates such as José Villa, Humberto Garza, Frances Martínez, and Henry López to "carry out comprehensive physical, social and economic programs which will significantly 'improve the quality of life.'" At once a significant governmental commitment to local barrios and a training program for young activists, this seemed a CSO dream come true. Thanks in part to Chicano lobbying efforts, the Gardner, Olinder, Mayfair, and Tropicana neighborhoods of San José received federal designation for special attention under Model Cities. These barrios boasted a collective population of forty-three thousand residents, 43 percent of whom were ethnic Mexican and 8 percent of whom were African American. During its first year, Mexican Americans and other neighborhood residents working under the program's auspices attacked problems of longstanding local concern. With significant federal financial support, they developed a Youth and Education Task Force that trained some thirty local people to serve as credentialed teachers in area schools; organized a Health Task Force that remodeled local health clinics and provided many residents with basic dental care; established a Comprehensive Child Care Project that provided day-care services to some 230 local children; and formed a Law and Police Task Force that founded a Halfway House and a Narcotic Residential Treatment Center for the treatment of various drug and alcohol addictions. Perhaps most importantly, Mexican Americans and others involved in these programs also attempted to address the high unemployment of recently urbanized, former agricultural workers badly in need of job training programs. All told, these marked major efforts to undo the historical patterns of inequality that had shaped the Valley for generations.[28]

But institutional politics were tricky, and Model Cities never lived up to the expectations of many participants. Much of the blame for the ongoing poverty and political powerlessness of ethnic Mexicans can be laid at the door of federal government officials who failed to follow through on promises of a Great Society. Programs targeting racial discrimination and economic inequality also created new conflicts between Mexican Americans organizations that competed for federal grants. Some accused others of being "poverty pimps" eager only to earn high salaries at the expense of the region's poor, even as the federal government began to cut back its commitment to the antipoverty effort. Ernesto Galarza tried to counter such charges by urging San José organizations to cooperate in order not to "cripple distribution of shrinking federal funds to community self-help projects," and he counseled local Mexican American activists on how to deal with state agencies like the Equal Opportunities Commission. This aging veteran of Latino political struggles continued to exert considerable authority into the late 1970s. One young participant in the Chicano movement remembered that

"We used to go to [Galarza's] house and he used to kind of advise us. That's why we were very involved in this thing, he used to give us good advice, do it this way, channel this flow through this channel so you can get the results. We followed a lot of his advice on this." Still, even the most experienced, including Lino López, the chair of MACSA, went so far as to announce in July 1971 that "the American G.I. Forum in San Jose has worked against the best interests of the poor."[29]

Ethnic Mexicans did agree on a distinctly anticorporate, antibooster vision of the Santa Clara Valley during these years. Activists involved in Model Cities often pushed local governments to hire Latinos and thereby share the Valley's new wealth. In 1968 nearly two thousand residents protested when building contractors working for the city employed no Mexicano or Mexican American construction workers on the job site of San José's new Center for Performing Arts, and the area would witness similar fights in later decades. Other local residents attempted after 1960 to influence urban development by resorting to different tactics. The Confederación de la Raza Unida, a local coalition of sixty-seven Chicano organizations formed to protest the Fiesta de las Rosas in 1969, took the lead in pushing government officials on redevelopment and gentrification issues. Members secured additional low- and moderate-income housing for East San José and demanded that Valley businesses pay greater attention to the needs of ethnic Mexican residents. Jack Ybarra called the two hundred thousand ethnic Mexicans in the county "refugees in their own valley"—a phrase that pointed yet again to the historical centrality of migration and violence—and he accused local public officials of "refus[ing] to address themselves to our problems." With this in mind, the Confederación organized its coalition—whose members ranged from the Association of Mexican American Educators, to the Comisión Honorífica Mexicana, to United People Arriba—to press for Mexican American representation on city and county agencies, a project that met with considerable success over the course of the 1970s.[30]

Others, buoyed by the encouragement of older activists as well as current exigencies, stuck instead to plans to democratize Valley educational institutions. In a development with parallels in Southern California, Valley students walked out of Roosevelt High in 1967 and 1968 to draw attention to institutional racism there. Others later followed their lead. Students continued to make similar protests throughout the late twentieth century, and events at the University of Santa Clara and on other local campuses tore open the political envelope of the conservative 1980s. Angry that university administrators seemed unwilling to establish closer ties with working-class Mexican American communities in the area, Chicano students protested in 1981 that "the long awaited report of the [University of Santa Clara's] Committee on Services to Ethnic Minorities . . . was filled with misleading quotes, inaccuracies, false information, and above all, ignorance of what the real problems of third world people at Santa Clara U. are, i.e. minorities experience a culture shock coming from 'SEGREGATED communities to an INTEGRATED university.'" Confronting similar issues, MEChA at San José State instituted "Raza College Information Day" in the early 1980s to introduce and encourage East Side high school students to attend the college, a strategy reminiscent of educational outreach programs operated by local Mexican Americans during the late 1960s and early 1970s.[31]

IMMIGRANTS

While they remained engaged in different forms of politics, just as they had for decades, many Mexican-born residents of San José showed little interest in the particular brand of Chicano politics developing in California from the 1960s forward. Chicano cultural nationalism held little meaning for those transplanted en masse from places like Aguililla, Michoacán, to Valley municipalities like Redwood City, particularly since most remained in close contact with home *patrias chicas*. Mexican culture and politics found vibrant expression in immigrant households and places of leisure. Mexicanos made themselves comfortable in churches, bars, parks, and other places throughout California, but an average of only 196 Mexicans naturalized annually in San José between 1978 and 1991, and assimilation into Chicano political culture more often fell to the U.S.-born. New technologies helped immigrants maintain their pulsing ties to home regions of Mexico, connections that followed a long regional history of transnational connections with that *patria*. Residents with no access to the Internet communicated with distant kin via short-wave radios, and musicians-for-hire played local versions of popular Mexican *corridos* in hundreds of bars and restaurants throughout the Valley. Continuing trends begun during the 1940s, Spanish-language radio stations and touring *rock en español* bands kept residents abreast of the latest musical developments in Tijuana and Mexico City, and local residents developed artistic styles that influenced listeners on both sides of the U.S.-Mexico border.[32]

Most prominent was the San José–based Los Tigres del Norte, one of the most popular *norteño* bands in Latin America and the United States during the 1980s and 1990s, and a group widely known for pointed political critiques. Beginning with their first album in 1972 and extending into the twenty-first century, Los Tigres extolled the benefits of immigration on the California economy, criticized anti-Mexican racism, made heroes of immigrants who evaded INS capture, and voiced nostalgic connections to distant family and friends in Mexico. Los Tigres in some ways represented the culmination of transnational cultural activities begun in the Valley during the 1860s. Hailing from the northern state of Sinaloa, band members arrived in

San José in 1968 to perform for the September 16 fiestas. They soon began to play small concerts in local parks where immigrants congregated, and small business owners began to hire them to perform at the openings of furniture stores and other shops. Their first album found heavy rotation on local Spanish-language radio, prompting Los Tigres to turn their attentions to exploring the difficult lives of Mexicanos living *en el extranjero*. Songs like "Vivan Los Mojados" (Long Live the Wetbacks) celebrate the economic contributions of undocumented immigrants, and their most famous recording "La Jaula de Oro" (The Gold Cage) describes a Mexicano's struggle to understand his U.S.-born children while living in constant fear of INS deportation.[33]

Los Tigres have openly criticized government politics damaging to ethnic Mexicans on both sides of the political border. Like those musicians, other San Joseans also stressed the bankruptcy of the postwar Mexican state from the 1960s forward. Immigrants lambasted Mexico's Partido Revolucionario Institucional, the singularly powerful political party in that country, for monopolizing control of the federal government and for officials' supposed involvement in drug trafficking. Local residents also condemned Adolfo G. Domingues, the consul general of Mexico, who told a San José audience in 1964 that California could expect a larger number of undocumented "wetbacks" after the Bracero Program ended later that year, an unfortunate development because while Japanese and other farmworkers in California had the "mental resources and education to take care of himself . . . the Mexican bracero is helpless without supervision." Shocked at the affront to Mexican citizens, San José's *El Paladín* asked readers "how it seems to you, what a representative we have." Students during the Vietnam War era made similar complaints. Young Chicanos criticized the Mexican government when "Teatro groups [from Mexico] put on skits and let us know what the government in Mexico was doing" during the late 1960s, and immigrant San Joseans flocked to hear the left-wing critic Cuahtémoc Cárdenas, on the campaign trail for the Mexican presidency, when he arrived to speak locally about his reform efforts in the early 1990s.[34]

These ethnic Mexicans and others retained political visions that looked well beyond the geographical boundaries of the county and transcended the rhetoric of Chicano Power. While transnational developments kept many concerned about events in Mexico, other San Joseans threw their energies into local labor movements designed to challenge the Valley's widening economic inequalities. Since the mid-1960s, political organizing around employment issues has enlivened many neighborhoods and workplaces. Mexicans and Mexican Americans during the Vietnam War era were the first to successfully challenge the Valley's traditional unions. Women led the charge. Taking a dramatic swipe at the conservative Teamsters who had defeated the FTA union more than twenty years before, Mary San Miguel and hundreds of other female cannery workers established democratic committees within

Silicon Valley landscaping workers marching through downtown San José, pushing lawnmowers and demanding that contractors respect their right to form a union. Photo courtesy of David Bacon.

those organizations. After laboring for nearly forty years in that industry following her arrival in San José in 1949, she became the first female business agent in her Teamster local. Others by the 1980s focused attention on organizing workers in the Silicon Valley's new high-tech economy, a sector in which the vast majority of Latinos remained low-wage employees, most often assembly workers and after-hours custodians. Inspired by the example of César Chávez, Mexican American labor leaders like Mike García took the organizing mantle once held by Ernesto Galarza, and white unionists like Amy Dean reshaped the Central Labor Council to be more attentive to lower-working-class Mexicanos for the first time in the Valley's history. By the mid-1980s the Service Employees Industrial Union (SEIU) Local 1877 had begun to organize immigrant janitors at Apple Computers and other Valley industries. That union later led struggles to combat statewide anti-immigrant efforts such as California's Proposition 187, a measure that promised to deny undocumented immigrants access to public schools, hospitals, and other facilities.[35]

Ernesto Galarza died in 1984, too early to witness the flowering of this new immigrant activism, but late twentieth-century union organizing in many ways represented a continuation of his transnational work. It also clearly reflected the influence of César Chávez and others who had struggled to develop a Mexican American civil rights movement in 1950s' California.

Like earlier Valley activists successful in ethnic Mexican communities, a new generation of unionists began to address local workplace grievances, problems associated with valley neighborhoods, and vital cultural connections to Mexico. The dramatic rise of Silicon Valley cannot be understood without reference to their political movements. Appealing to immigrant residents' familiarity with Mexican popular music, the local SEIU organizer Rosalino Pedres encouraged unionization in the late 1980s by changing the lyrics of the popular tune "Caminos de Michoacán" to address conditions in Northern California. His "Caminos de Cupertino" blasted the home community of Apple Computers, stressed the transnational orientation of that place's low-wage workforce, and urged workers to see

Ya cinco pesos no alcanzan	Five dollars is not enough
ni para comprar tortillas,	even to buy tortillas,
menos pa' pagar la renta	not to mention paying the rent
o echarse unas cuantas frías,	or throwing back some cold beers,
tampoco si quieres algo	nor if you want to have anything
pa' mandarle a la familia.	to send to your family.
Caminos de Cupertino	Roads of Cupertino
y pueblos que voy pasando	and you people whom I pass by
tú sabes cuánto los miro,	you know how much I watch you,
tú sabes cuánto los ando,	and how much I walk by you,
¡Echale un grito paisano,	Shout it out my *paisano*,
vámonos organizando!	let's get organized![36]

In no small part because Mexicanidad remained an effective political tool for encouraging local activism, the culture of unionization changed drastically in the Valley as software start-ups and dot-coms tightened their grips on the Valley economy. But while new in many ways, these late twentieth-century labor movements clearly followed a local tradition that stretches back before UCAPAWA in the 1930s to the New Almadén miners of the 1860s.

Other ethnic Mexicans, part of the power structure in the Valley, expressed concerns quite different from those of SEIU members. Longtime Chicano activists remained involved in struggles over police brutality, the incarceration of immigrants, and other pressing agendas, but booming economic times and a more conservative political climate also fostered the growth of a new Latino elite. That group announced its arrival in 1990 with the publication of the first Hispanic Business Directory, a text that profiled Latinos' involvement in area commerce, described more than seven hundred Valley companies, and summarized the history of local Hispanic businesses since 1777 to encourage new entrepreneurs. History, in their formulation, celebrated the ethnic Mexican businessperson. Many of those who found such success in the Valley belonged to the American G.I. Forum, a powerful political force during the 1990s led by the South Texan Victor Garza and others who had served in World War II, Korea, or Vietnam. That organization had long held its meetings in English and declared that its members were preeminently American, but by the 1980s the forum became the chief sponsor of San José's Cinco de Mayo and 16 de Septiembre *fiestas patrias*. Using those opportunities to teach young Mexican Americans about their "cultural heritage," the forum organized massive parades that drew some one hundred thousand onlookers by 1990. By 1994 the group would endorse favored political candidates by inviting them to ride in fiesta floats. While most ethnic Mexicans likely considered these events far superior to the 1969 Fiesta de las Rosas, the forum had many detractors. Local immigrants, especially, accused these veterans of using the *fiestas patrias* for their own purposes, throwing a Mexican party but inviting few Mexicanos to help plan the event, all the while earning great profits for their organization.[37]

Some of those who prospered during the 1980s and 1990s cannibalized the rhetoric of earlier Chicano activists, building on older concepts of ethnic "self-determination" to urge Mexican Americans to abandon their culture of poverty, for example. To its credit, the G.I. Forum labored hard in CSO fashion to assist drug addicts and alcoholics in East San José, but others focused solely on positioning themselves as leaders of a new Latino push into the Valley's high-tech world. The development since 1981 of San José's National Hispanic University, one of only two accredited universities in the country designed to serve Latino students, reflected the emergence of that white-collar elite. Only moderately successful for many years, the university's President Roberto Cruz by 1997 claimed, with self-serving hyperbole, that his school would confront the local "apartheid" and "adobe ceiling" that kept Latinos in low-wage jobs and subjected them to ongoing racial discrimination. He forecast that "without a college education and leadership development, we will have our own 'latino South Africa' in the United States—a few will control the majority Hispano population." Offering degrees and certificates in business, computer science, liberal studies, and translation/interpretation studies, school administrators tweaked the self-help rhetoric of the CSO in promising to "open doors of opportunity and WAKE UP OUR RAZA." While he identified the existence of real structural barriers that denied opportunities to many Californians, Cruz also suggested that somnolent ethnic Mexicans would need to overcome their own self-defeating tendencies, the adobe ceilings that they had built for themselves, in order to appreciate the riches of the Silicon Valley. Mexican Americans who had made it in California were, presumably, less encumbered by that cultural baggage.[38]

As signs emerged during the 1990s that the computer industry might go the way of mercury and orchards, other Latinos criticized the easy embrace of the high-tech scene by social climbers like Cruz. Resting their hopes on mobilizing both immigrant and U.S.-born residents, many unionists re-

Female immigrants have dominated low-wage jobs in Silicon Valley's electronics industry since the 1970s. Photo courtesy of David Bacon.

mained skeptical about the Valley's ongoing boom mentality and predicted that dot-com would quickly go dot-bomb. Some Mexican American youth also registered suspicion of high-tech Latino business types. The poet Marc David Piñate contended in 1997 that too many local Chicanos had become upwardly mobile "yuppies" who cloaked themselves in a mantle of 1960s radicalism. Mocking the sort who defended the NHU in the name of Chicano nationalism and self-determination, Piñate playfully urged local Mexican Americans to

> Wake up and smell the
> Coffee
> Beans that Colombian peasants
> Picked
> At 10 cents an hour so that
> You can sit at Starbucks
> With your Anglo friends
> Talking about
> Cool
> Internet sites and stock options,
> Slurping down frapachinos [*sic*]
> And mocha grandes.
>
> Enjoy that shit my brother
> Cause when the REVOLUTION comes . . .
> Ain't gonna be no cappuccinos with it!"[39]

There would be no political "revolution" in the late twentieth century, Piñate knew, only the ongoing demographic transformations associated with the surging migrations from Latin America that had shaped the region's development for decades.

Silicon Valley experienced growing economic disparities in the early twenty-first century, a problem known firsthand by many ethnic Mexicans and other

Latinos. Some predicted that dramatic political change was on the horizon in 1998 when a Mexican American candidate was finally elected San José mayor. That achievement was long in coming, and Ron Gonzales owed clear debts to past organizers who had devoted themselves to electoral politics and voter registration since the 1950s. Perhaps Mexican American officeholders and other activists may yet redeem the Silicon Valley, addressing entrenched inequalities and moving beyond booster rhetoric. But at the dawn of the twenty-first century, Mexican immigrants still labor for low pay, young students still drop out of high school in high numbers, Valley celebrants still promote the region as a suburban wonderland, and the Devil still makes trouble for Latino janitors. These are echoes of an old story, a long history, the troubled place of Latinos in the Santa Clara Valley.

Epilogue

Devil's Future

The set sun gives out and comes away all painted
mercury.
—Lorna Dee Cervantes, "On the Fear of Going Down"

Since I first set out to write this history in the early 1990s, the Silicon Valley
has seemed to become both a more promising and a more threatening place
for Mexicans and Mexican Americans. Despite the surging interest in Latino
culture, few sensitive scholars have written about the San José area, and
Mexican American history has received only scant attention. It's a scandalous
fact that no one else has attempted an extended historical study of Latinos in
Silicon Valley, a population of undeniable importance and a place roundly
celebrated and reviled. Dozens of books have been written about Mexican
Americans in Los Angeles and dozens more about the Silicon Valley's high-
tech community.

The late twentieth century was a propitious moment for me to capture
memories of San José's last surviving Mexican immigrants who had arrived
more than fifty years before. Those residents seemed intent to reflect on the
history of the region in part because many faced new challenges. Despite the
booming economy, the political air was strangely poisonous, bitter thanks to
the ongoing social problems many observers associated with Mexican immigration. Draconian public policies at the state level threatened to limit immigrants' access to publicly funded hospitals, schools, and welfare services.
Crackdowns against bilingual education, spearheaded by the Valley businessman Ron Unz, combined with widespread opposition to affirmative action,
new changes to federal welfare laws, and growing economic disparities between
rich and poor, all of which seemed to threaten the livelihoods of the Valley's
low-wage workers. New national initiatives to police the U.S.-Mexico border

further threatened the safety of undocumented Mexican immigrants, even as the passage of the North American Free Trade Agreement (NAFTA) in 1994 accelerated transnational processes already underway. And the so-called information superhighway built by Valley software firms seemed to bypass the East Side and other working-class neighborhoods throughout the state.[1]

The late twentieth century was a time of startling change, but it also witnessed manifestations of old patterns of race relations in the American West. Archival digging and in-depth interviews made clear to me that the Santa Clara Valley has been a site of contentious and at times internecine rivalries for well more than a century. It has also played host to central developments in Mexican American history, including the rise of corporate agriculture, changing patterns of urbanization, and the development of a Latino civil rights movement. Many aspects of San José's hidden past had national and transnational implications, but few in California have yet fully to acknowledge just how deeply connected Latinos have been to the region. Local boosters deserve much of the blame, first helping to displace ethnic Mexicans from their lands in the 1850s, then robbing local peoples of their rightful histories. Low-wage labor, physical hardship, and vibrant political activism nonetheless defined this valley of gold, of fruit, of mercury, of silicon, but primarily of people, for decades.

The history of Latinos in Silicon Valley explodes local myths about the area's universal prosperity and social peace. Knowledge of the past ought certainly to put to rest the now-tired celebrations of high-tech entrepreneurs, and we ought to stress instead that the twin forces of nineteenth-century conquest and ongoing immigration from Latin America have been far more central to local dynamics. Wave after wave of Mexicanos have settled in San José for more than 150 years. Conquest and migration elicited unsavory responses from many San Joseans, and Californians ought to be held accountable for their often violent treatment of Mexican Americans from the 1850s forward. Those who continue to struggle on behalf of disenfranchised populations might take heart in the ways that politically active Latinos have defied the logic of local xenophobes, for generations hounding boosters and pressing for new political rights. The vibrant labor, electoral, and transnational movements underway in the twenty-first-century United States are in fact an extension and elaboration of past efforts by miners, exiles, and farmworkers in Santa Clara County, forgotten Northern California forebears of a dynamic oppositional politics.

Matters of history and memory have taken on new importance as growing numbers of Latinos throughout the United States argue for their political and economic rights. Visions of history guide progressive movements for change. Although none today can claim to remember the early strikes at New Almadén, those whom I interviewed in Valley homes, on rooftops, in bowling alleys, and in cafés did express considerable frustration about the high-tech robber barons so beloved by most of the local press. Many who shared with me their memories had grown angry that popular accounts of the region's high-tech growth routinely failed to include any mention of Mexicans or Mexican Americans. Their frustration had been building for years, and local Latinos expressed particular outrage in 1990 when Mayor Tom McEnery proposed a statue commemorating Thomas Fallon, a seldom-remembered "pioneer" credited with raising the first American flag in the Valley during the Mexican War. Local white elites, by contrast, considered Fallon an inspiring symbol for the developing Silicon Valley economy. Corporate executives rallied to support the building of this memorial to the city's Manifest Destiny, and politicians spoke of San José, Sunnyvale, Palo Alto, Cupertino, and other municipalities as the new business frontier, places free from the constraints of old-style business models, locales where young men and women would find the always elusive California dream.

This was pure romance, a historical cover-up that hid a much uglier past. Many local Latinos continued to criticize journalists who appeared too sanguine about the Valley's future, too ready to promote the Valley as a place of entrepreneurial freedom, ["the Wild Wild West of private enterprise," and seemingly too intent to forget the longtime Mexican American presence in the area.[2]/Like dominated groups elsewhere in the world, ethnic Mexicans have clung for generations to their own counternarratives that explained their place in local society. In drawing attention to past farm labor and cannery work, some continue to contest official narratives of Silicon Valley's development. Residents who had been activists in the Chicano movement of the 1960s and 1970s have recently led the charge in urging the city to pay greater care to Latino history. Such efforts have developed hand-in-hand with the movement of greater numbers of Mexican Americans into local government. Investigations of the past, these activists have argued, must be a more democratic enterprise, an effort to understand, for example, the "political subordination" of local Latinos begun "in the nineteenth century and continued in the twentieth." Many have demanded that the Valley celebrate a more multicultural cast of local heroes. After a coalition of Mexican Americans defeated plans to construct the Fallon monument, they managed to see the completion of two new statues located downtown, a memorial to Ernesto Galarza and a statue of the Aztec serpent god Quetzalcoatl.[3]

My sense of Silicon Valley emerged in conversations with those local residents interested in promoting a rebellious but more accurate version of the region's past. I wrote with an eye to growing concerns throughout the Southwest about immigrant civil liberties, and I carried out my research in the immodest hope that it might make some difference for the region's future. What I discovered was a counterhistory that tells a story of broad importance, capturing the conflicts around race seen in many areas of the country. I took some of my cues from Latino artists, particularly the 1981 "Poema

Para Los Californios Muertos," written by the one-time San Josean Lorna Dee Cervantes, a poem that underscores the vital importance of Latino histories throughout the American West.

Cervantes's observations serve as a fitting coda to any meditation on the California past. Like other Mexican Americans, she excoriated the Santa Clara Valley's longstanding penchant for obscuring the formative importance of race relations. She began her verse by citing a simple plaque found at a Los Altos restaurant that reminded visitors that the place was "Once a refuge for Mexican Californios." Chilled by the way such romantic language cloaked the state's vivid history of violence, Cervantes evoked the processes that made "Californios moan like husbands of the raped / husbands de la tierra [of the earth], tierra de la madre [earth of the mother]." In language that must have shocked any Valley booster still interested in reviving the once popular Fiesta de las Rosas, she rejected facile Spanish myths about local history, described the San José area as "a bastard child, this city / lost in the soft / llorando de las madres [crying of the mothers]," and remembered nineteenth-century Mexican Americans as "los antepasados muertos" (her dead forebears). Insisting on a more accurate rendering of the booming Silicon Valley, the "Poema Para Los Californios Muertos" asked

> What refuge did you find here,
> ancient Californios?
> Now at this restaurant nothing remains
> but this old oak and an ill-placed plaque.
> Is it true that you still live here
> in the shadows of these white, high-class houses?
> Soy la hija pobrecita
> pero puedo maldecir estas fantasmas blancas.
> Las fantasmas tuyas deben aquí quedarse,
> sola las tuyas.
> [I am your poor daughter
> but I can curse these white ghosts.
> Only your ghosts should remain here,
> only yours.][4]

Like many other San Joseans, Cervantes continued to lambast self-satisfied visions of the Santa Clara Valley as a pastoral place, insisting instead that past episodes of violence still haunt the region. As many Latinos have known first-hand, Silicon Valley has long been a place of great hardship for those deemed nonwhite, but ethnic Mexicans and others have also challenged the damning inequalities of life "in the shadows of these white, high-class houses." It falls to historians to help throw light into those shadows if scholars, poets, and others are to continue beating back the stubborn Devil who continues to haunt the United States.

Prologue
The Devil Defined

1. U.S. Bureau of the Census, "Census 2000 Redistricting Data (Public Law 94-171)," Summary File, matrices PL1 and PL2.

2. For a discussion of new western cities, see Robert B. Fairbanks and Kathleen Underwood, eds., *Essays on Sunbelt Cities and Recent Urban America* (College Station: Texas A & M Press, 1990); John M. Findlay, *Magic Lands: Western Cityscapes and American Culture after 1940* (Berkeley: University of California Press, 1992).

Chapter 1
Devil's Destiny

1. See Ramón A. Gutiérrez and Richard J. Orsi, eds., *Contested Eden: California before the Gold Rush* (Berkeley: University of California Press, 1998).

2. Joseph and Kerry Chartkoff conclude that native people settled in the Santa Clara Valley between six and eight thousand years ago. Joseph L. Chartkoff and Kerry Kona Chartkoff, *The Archaeology of California* (Stanford: Stanford University Press, 1984), 128. See also David W. Mayfield, "Ecology of the Pre-Spanish San Francisco Bay Area," (Master's thesis, San Francisco State University, 1978), and Alan K. Brown, "The European Contact of 1772 and Some Later Documentation," in *The Ohlone Past and Present: Native Americans of the San Francisco Bay Region*, ed. Lowell John Bean (Menlo Park, CA: Ballena Press, 1994), 28–29.

3. William Mason, *The Census of 1790: A Demographic History of Colonial California* (Menlo Park: Ballena Press, 1998), 98–100; Gregorio Mora Torres, "Los Mexicanos de San José, California: Life in a Mexican Pueblo, 1777–1846," paper presented at the Pacific Coast Branch of the American Historical Association, August 11, 1994, 4; Robert H. Jackson, "Introduction," in *The New Latin American Mission History*, ed. Erick Langer and Robert H. Jackson (Lincoln: University of Nebraska Press, 1995), vii. The establishment of Spanish settlements and Catholic missions on land

previously occupied by Indian villages or sacred space was not uncommon in what is today the U.S. Southwest and Mexico. See Lisbeth Haas, *Conquests and Historical Identities in California, 1769–1936* (Berkeley: University of California Press, 1995), 13.

4. Quoted in Daniel J. Garr, "A Frontier Agrarian Settlement: San José de Guadelupe [*sic*], 1777–1850," *San José Studies* 2:3 (November 1976), 94.

5. "Interrogatorio," reproduced and translated in Francis Florence McCarthy, *The History of Mission San José, California, 1797–1835* (Fresno: Academy Library Guild, 1958), 275; A. L. Kroeber, *Handbook of the Indians of California* (Berkeley: California Book Co., 1953), 466. On the Ohlone, see David J. Weber, *The Spanish Frontier in North America* (New Haven: Yale University Press, 1992), 306; Richard Levy, "Costanoan," in *Handbook of North American Indians*, ed. Robert F. Heizer, vol. B (Washington, D.C.: Smithsonian Institution, 1978), 485–495; and Malcolm Margolin, *The Ohlone Way* (Berkeley: Heyday Books, 1978). San José's annual rate of growth of 3.7 percent exceeded that of the Los Angeles pueblo, developing at a rate of 3.68 percent between 1828 and 1846. David J. Weber, *The Mexican Frontier, 1821–1846: The American Southwest under Mexico* (Albuquerque: University of New Mexico Press, 1982), 227.

6. Sherburne F. Cook and Woodrow Borah, "Mission Registers as Sources of Vital Statistics: Eight Missions of Northern California," in *Essays in Population History* (Berkeley: University of California Press, 1971–1979), 263–264; Jack D. Forbes, "Hispano-Mexican Pioneers of the San Francisco Bay Region: An Analysis of Racial Origins," *Aztlán* 14:1 (Spring 1983), 175–189.

7. Quoted in Randall Milliken, *A Time of Little Choice: The Disintegration of Tribal Culture in the San Francisco Bay Area, 1769–1820* (Menlo Park: Ballena Press, 1995), 125.

8. Robert H. Jackson and Edward Castillo, *Indians, Franciscans, and Spanish Colonization* (Albuquerque: University of New Mexico Press, 1995), 104; Clyde Arbuckle, *History of San José* (San José: Smith and McKay, 1985), 21; Weber, *The Spanish Frontier*, 307; Milliken, *A Time of Little Choice*, 69; Robert H. Jackson, "Population and the Economic Dimension of Colonization in Alta California: Four Mission Communities," *Journal of the Southwest* 33:3 (Autumn 1991), 402. See also Frederic Hall, *The History of San José and Surroundings* (San Francisco: A. L. Bancroft, 1871), 40–42. At the same time, however, friars continually argued that Indians were not ready to make this transition to full equality, and that neophytes were as yet "unfit and unready to take their place in Hispanic society." Weber, *The Mexican Frontier*, 46. Intent on converting local people to Roman Catholicism, for example, Father Francisco Palóu in 1774 praised the more familiar qualities of the local Ohlone as "well formed and tall, many of them bearded like a Spaniard, with long hair hanging like a mantle from their shoulders to their waists." Quoted in John Francis Bannon, *The Spanish Frontier Borderlands Frontier, 1513–1821* (New York: Holt, Rinehart and Winston, 1970), 223.

9. Between 1802 and 1833 the friars at Santa Clara baptized 7,324 and presided at Christian wedding ceremonies for 2,056 others. By 1824 missions San José and Santa Clara were home to 1,806 and 1,450 residents, respectively. Eugene Duflot de Mofras, *Duflot de Mofras' Travels on the Pacific Coast*, 2 vols., trans. and ed. Marguerite Wilbur (Santa Ana: The Fine Arts Press, 1937), 2:188; Robert H. Jackson, *Indian Population Decline* (Albuquerque: University of New Mexico Press, 1994), 104–106.

10. "Manuscript Written in 1883 in Spanish by Nasario Galindo and Translated by the Great-Grand Daughter of Ygnacio Alviso, Cristina Alviso Chapman," Bancroft Library, MSS C-D 5159, 8; letter from Moraga to José Arguello, October 30, 1794,

trans. and reprinted in Milliken, *A Time of Little Choice*, 281; Francis Guest, O.F.M., "An Inquiry into the Role of Discipline in Mission Life," *Southern California Quarterly* 61 (1979), 3.

11. Religious leaders in other cases trusted the Ohlone more than the mixed-race colonists of San José pueblo, who often seemed to demonstrate imperfect morals and slothful habits, according to Franciscans. Father Barcenilla, for example, worried that the soldiers attached to the mission were in fact providing a bad example for the neophytes and complained to the governor in 1797 that "The most savage Indian is more willing to lend a helping hand than the lazy soldiers." In 1798 the same *padre* would add that "the work of a mission without the cooperation of its employees is enough to kill a priest." Quoted in McCarthy, *The History of Mission San José*, 82.

12. The archaeologist Paul Farnsworth has concluded that at least at Mission Nuestra Señora de la Soledad, south of San José, neophytes also retained much of their traditional material culture. Paul Farnsworth, "The Economics of Acculturation in the Spanish Missions of Alta California," *Research in Economic Anthropology* 2 (1989), 247.

13. Milliken, *A Time of Little Choice*, 13–23.

14. Jackson, "Population," 399–400, 404. See also, Daniel Reff, *Disease, Depopulation, and Culture Change in Northwestern New Spain, 1518–1764* (Salt Lake City: University of Utah Press, 1991), 277–278; "Interrogatorio" and letter from Padre Tapis to Arrillaga, March 16, 1806, in McCarthy, *The History of Mission San José*, 112, 272; H. S. Foote, *Pen Pictures from the Garden of the World* (Chicago: Lewis Publishing Company, 1888), 36. According to Francis McCarthy, twenty-three Indians died at San José Mission on two successive days in April 1805. McCarthy, *The History of Mission San José*, 114. On the population and death rates of Indians at the missions, see Jackson and Castillo, *Indians, Franciscans, and Spanish Colonization.*

15. Similarly, the friars of Mission San José noted in 1812 that "no other races are recognized but the 'gente de razón' and the Indians. The former are all considered to be Spaniards, although it may be that there is among them the same variety as in other parts of America. But in this peninsula, ever since the conquest, no other distinction has been made." Frederic W. Beechey, *Narrative of a Voyage to the Pacific and Bering's Strait* (London: Henry, Colburn, and Richard Bentley, 1831), 2:47; "El Interrogatorio del Año de 1812," reproduced and translated in McCarthy, *The History of Mission San José*, 268; Weber, *The Spanish Frontier*, 327; Douglas Monroy, *Thrown among Strangers: The Making of Mexican Culture in Frontier California* (Berkeley: University of California Press, 1990), 22; Rosaura Sánchez, *Telling Identities: The Californio Testimonies* (Minneapolis: University of Minnesota Press, 1995), 57.

16. The map is reprinted in McCarthy, *The History of Mission San José*, interleaf; Moraga is quoted in Milliken, *A Time of Little Choice*, 75.

17. McCarthy, *The History of Mission San José*, 169; Yvonne Jacobson, *Passing Farms, Enduring Values: California's Santa Clara Valley* (Los Altos: William Kaufmann, 1984), 26. See also Robert L. Hoover, "Notes and Documents: The Death of Yóscolo," *Pacific Historical Review* 51:3 (August 1982), 312–314; William Heath Davis, *Sixty Years in California* (San Francisco: A. J. Leary, 1889), 340.

18. Milliken, *A Time of Little Choice*, 82–83; Jackson, "Population," 391; "Interrogatorio," in McCarthy, *The History of Mission San José*, 269, 274–275.

19. Nasario Galindo, "Manuscript Written in 1883 in Spanish by Nasario Galindo and Translated by the Great-Grand Daughter of Ygnacio Alviso, Cristina Alviso

Chapman," Bancroft Library, MSS C-D 5159, 2. Hubert Howe Bancroft, *California Pastoral* (San Francisco: The History Company, 1888), 292.

20. Weber, *The Spanish Frontier*, 306; Farnsworth, "The Economics of Acculturation," 230; Galindo, "Manuscript," 2. As Tomás Almaguer notes, "The principal difference between the precapitalist economy of the Mexican period (1821–1848) and that which European Americans introduced after the United States–Mexico War was the predominance of a formal free-wage labor system: the coercive and paternalistic class relations of the Mexican period were quickly replaced by the instrumental and impersonal class relations of capitalism and its apparatus of legal enforcement." Tomás Almaguer, *Racial Fault Lines: The Historical Origins of White Supremacy in California* (Berkeley: University of California Press, 1994), 30.

21. Jackson, "Population," 391; Carlos N. Híjar, "California in 1834" (recollections, 1877), Bancroft Library, MSS C-D trans, 55; Galindo, "Manuscript," 11–12; Auguste DuHaut-Cilly, *Voyage Autour du Monde* (Paris: Arthus Bertrand, 1835), 291. According to Gregorio Mora Torres, the Spaniard Antonio Suñol alone "reportedly employed fifty to 150 Indian servants in his household." Mora Torres, "Los Mexicanos de San José, California," 26.

22. Albert L. Hurtado, *Indian Survival on the California Frontier* (New Haven: Yale University Press, 1988), 49, 99.

23. George H. Von Langsdorff, *Voyages and Travels in Various Parts of the World* (Ridgewood, NJ: Gregg Press, 1968), 2:175–176; Weber, *The Mexican Frontier*, 137–139; Arbuckle, *History of San José*, 144; Davis, *Sixty Years in California*, 304; Farnsworth, "The Economics of Acculturation," 218. See also Robert Archibald, *The Economic Aspects of the Alta California Missions* (Washington, D.C.: Academy of American Franciscan History, 1978).

24. Edwin Beilharz, *San José: California's First City* (Tulsa: Continental Heritage Press, 1980), 52; Josiah Belden, *1841 California Overland Pioneer: His Memoir and Early Letters*, ed. Doyce B. Nunis, Jr. (Georgetown, CA: Talisman Press, 1962), 47; Doyce B. Nunis, Jr., *The California Diary of Faxon Dean Atherton, 1836–1839* (San Francisco: California Historical Society, 1964), 36; Hurtado, *Indian Survival*, 59; C. Alan Hutchinson, *Frontier Settlement in Mexican California: The Híjar-Padrés Colony, and Its Origins, 1769–1835* (New Haven: Yale University Press, 1969), 61; Milliken, *A Time of Little Choice*, 76–77; letter from Narciso Durán to Pío Pico, December 26, 1845, quoted in Zephyrin Englehardt, *The Missions and Missionaries of California* (San Francisco: James H. Barry, 1915), 4:452.

25. Ann Laura Stoler and Frederick Cooper, "Between Metropole and Colony: Rethinking a Research Agenda," in *Tensions of Empire: Colonial Cultures in a Bourgeois World*, ed. Frederick Cooper and Ann Laura Stoler (Berkeley: University of California, 1997), 3; Hutchinson, *Frontier Settlement in Mexican California*, 82. In the context of political debates about the Republic of Mexico, many Alta California residents during the 1820s and 1830s showed little respect for the Spanish priests who still claimed considerable authority in the region. Non-Mexicans arriving in the region in these years at times noted the disdain with which local Californios regarded the clergy, in part because these friars seemed an antinational embodiment of Spanish tradition and authority. One American, for instance, was certain that "a more irreligious civilized people is not to be found on the globe than the Californianos. . . . Catholicism in this country is not what it is in the United States. When people are about to die priests are sent for to confess them, etc., but when in good health

scarcely anyone thinks of religious observances. On feast days they pretend to observe the forms of the Catholic Church, but it is all form, there is no evidence of sentiment or feeling." Letter from Henry Smith Turner to "My Own Dear One," April 8, 1847, in *The Original Journals of Henry Smith Turner*, ed. Dwight L. Clarke (Norman: University of Oklahoma Press, 1966), 163–165.

26. José Maria de Echeandía, "Copia fiel de un decreto publicado en el Puerto de Monterey de la Alta California el dia 6 de Enero del año 1831, con comentario o notas al fin puestas por numeros," Bancroft Library, C-C 203.

27. Hutchinson, *Frontier Settlement in Mexican California*, 107, 134; Jackson, "Population," 403; George Harwood Phillips, *Indians and Indian Agents: The Origins of the Reservation System in California, 1849–1852* (Norman: University of Oklahoma Press, 1997), 28; Robert H. Jackson and Edward Castillo, *Indians, Franciscans, and Spanish Colonization*, 96; Guest, "An Inquiry into the Role of Discipline in Mission Life," 10; Antonio María Osio, *The History of Alta California: A Memoir of Mexican California*, trans. and ed. Rose Marie Beebe and Robert M. Senkewicz (Madison: University of Wisconsin Press, 1996), 86. Between 1810 and 1815 the number of horses at Mission San José declined from 1150 to 280, most likely as a result of Indian raids. Robert H. Jackson, "The Development of San José Mission, 1797–1840," in *The Ohlone Past and Present*, 236. For earlier accounts of the stealing of cattle in the area, see Milliken, *A Time of Little Choice*, 123.

28. Douglas Monroy, *Thrown among Strangers: The Making of Mexican Culture in Frontier California* (Berkeley: University of California Press, 1990), 139; Angela Moyano Pahissa, *La Resistencia de Las Californias a la Invasión Norteamericana (1846– 1848)* (Mexico: Consejo Nacional Para la Cultura y las Artes, 1992), 38. See also Timothy E. Anna, *Forging Mexico, 1821–1835* (Lincoln: University of Nebraska Press, 1998).

29. Pahissa, *La Resistencia de Las Californias*, 38; "Manifestacion del Comandante de Monterey a los habitantes del Pueblo de San José Guadalupe," Santa Clara County Records, Bancroft Library, CA 329; Hutchinson, *Frontier Settlement in Mexican California*, 42, 96. These grants comprised a relatively small proportion of the more than 1,400 grants bestowed in the region between 1822 and 1846, some of which were located in California's Central Valley. Weber, *The Mexican Frontier*, 196. Although a few residents who were neither Indian, Spanish, nor Mexican, such as the Scot John Gilroy, had settled in the area during the last years of the Spanish colonial period, the government's hostility to foreigners meant that "it was not until the Mexican era that San José became a veritable mecca" for European and American immigrants. Some of these Santa Clara Valley settlers arrived on ships that had stopped in nearby Monterey; others traveled across the plains with the Bidwell-Bartleson party, the first westward overland immigrants to California, and with other overland parties after 1841. Winther, *The Story of San José*, 10, 13–16.

30. The local resident Thomas Doak, for instance, who had been the first U.S. citizen to settle permanently in California in 1816, was known in the Santa Clara Valley for many years as Felipe Santiago. Mora, "Los Mexicanos de San José, California," 28; see also Harlan Hague and David J. Langum, *Thomas O. Larkin: A Life of Patriotism and Profit in Old California* (Norman: University of Oklahoma Press, 1990). There were exceptions to this trend. See, for instance, Faxon Atherton, *California Diary, 1836–1839*, ed. Doyce B. Nunis, Jr. (San Francisco: California Historical Society, 1964), 36.

31. Roberta Marguerite Cháver, "Intimate Alliances: Intermarriage between Mexicans and Anglos in Nineteenth-Century San Jose; 1820–1880," paper presented at the Pacific Coast Branch of the American Historical Association, August 7, 1995.

32. Galindo, "Manuscript," 13; "Henry Jubilee Bee's Recollections of History of California," handwritten transcript of Thomas Savage, June 1877. Bancroft Library, MSS C-D 41, 21. Despite having taken an oath of allegiance to the Mexican government in 1835, for example, the settler Henry Bee later recalled that many American immigrants sought "to aid the Californians in liberating their country from Mexican domination" during the years before 1845, and that they told local residents "that they ought not to allow the Mexican officers and others to come and rule over them and rob the country of its substance, that they thought the native-born Californians were fully able to govern themselves." "Henry Jubilee Bee's Recollections"; David Montejano, *Anglos and Mexicans in the Making of Texas, 1836–1986* (Austin: University of Texas Press, 1987), 31–41.

33. "Judge R. J. Peckham, An Eventful Life," *San José Pioneer,* June 9, 1877; Hubert Howe Bancroft, *History of California* (San Francisco: The History Company, 1888), 6:75–76; Davis, *Sixty Years in California,* 335; Winther, *The Story of San José,* 20; Phillips, *Indians and Indian Agents,* 32, 35–36. See also Weber, *The Mexican Frontier,* 93–94; Cook and Borah, "Mission Registers as Sources of Vital Statistics," 268–269. The entrance of Anglo and European men into local Mexican society through intermarriage suggests not only the adaptation of non-Mexicans to Mexican culture prior to the U.S. takeover, but also the gendered nature of Anglo-Mexican social relations during this period. Anglo men frequently celebrated the sexuality of Spanish-Mexican women in California, and visitors to San José made it clear that American men would find suitable, and perhaps grateful, companions in these *Californianas.*

34. Nunis, *The California Diary of Faxon Dean Atherton,* 9–10.

35. Juan Bojorques, "Recuerdos Sobre la Historia de California" (interview transcript, Santa Clara, June 1, 1877), Bancroft Library, C-D 46.

36. Osio, *The History of Alta California,* 92–93.

37. Alexander Forbes, *California: A History of Upper and Lower California* (San Francisco: John Hay Nash, 1937; reprinted 1972), 131.

38. C. Alan Hutchinson, *Frontier Settlement in Mexican California: The Híjar-Padrés Colony, and Its Origins, 1769–1835* (New Haven: Yale University Press, 1969), 96–106.

39. Thomas Jefferson Farnham, *Travels in California* (Oakland: Biobooks, 1947), 148, 161. The historian Antonia I. Castañeda has persuasively argued that, by the mid-1840s, "the [gendered] stereotypes of Mexicanos" in these and other narratives "functioned as instruments of conquest, and thus served the political and economic interests of an expanding United States." Antonia I. Castañeda, "The Political Economy of Nineteenth Century Stereotypes of Californianas," in *Between Borders: Essays on Mexicana/Chicana History,* ed. Adelaida R. Del Castillo (Encino, CA: Floricanto Press, 1990), 220.

40. Almaguer, *Racial Fault Lines,* 33.

41. Quoted in Weber, *The Mexican Frontier,* 122. For a useful survey of the importance of cartography in the "political order of the Anglo-American frontier," see Gregory H. Nobles, "Straight Lines and Stability: Mapping the Political Order of the Anglo-American Frontier," *Journal of American History* 80:1 (June 1993), 9–35.

42. David J. Weber, *The Californios vs. Jedediah Smith, 1826–1827: A New Cache of Documents* (Spokane: Arthur H. Clark, 1990), 58–63.

43. Charles Franklin Carter, "Duhaut-Cilly's Account of California in the Years 1827–1828," *California Historical Society Quarterly* 8:3 (September 1929), 227; *U.S. vs. Castillero* 4, 2678; John C. Frémont, *Memories of My Life* (Chicago: Belford and Clarke, 1887), 451. See also A. Brook Caruso, *The Mexican Spy Company: United States Covert Operations in Mexico, 1845–1848* (London: McFarland, 1991), 115–116. Even as Benton and Buchanan conspired on behalf of the United States, the French consul urged its minister of foreign affairs to take advantage of the political turmoil in the late 1840s' California to acquire the mine, hoping in the process to establish a stronger French presence along the entire Pacific Coast. See Abraham P. Nasatir, "The French Consulate in California, 1843–1856," *The Quarterly of the California Historical Society* 12:1 (March 1933), 35.

44. Belden, *1841 California Overland Pioneer*, 47. Because horses grazed in open pastures throughout the territory, one observer later recalled that "all that a poor man living in the countryside had to do if he wished to obtain fine horses was to tame them. He could ask permission of the owners or simply take them from among the strays." Osio, *The History of Alta California*, 69. Later historians such as Edwin Beilharz happily concurred that arriving Americans, unlike settled Mexicans and Indians, "believed in hard work, valued the rewards it could bring and regarded sloth and idleness with distaste." Beilharz, *San José*, 63; Charles Sellers, *The Market Revolution: Jacksonian America, 1815–1846* (New York: Oxford University Press, 1991), 396–427; Eric Foner, *Free Soil, Free Labor, Free Men: The Ideology of the Republican Party before the Civil War* (New York: Oxford University Press, 1970); Almaguer, *Racial Fault Lines*, 45–74.

45. Nunis, *The California Diary of Faxon Dean Atherton*, 79–80; "Judge R. J. Peckham, An Eventful Life," *San José Pioneer*, June 9, 1877; "Recollections of Mary A. Jones, 1825–1918" (ms.), Bancroft Library.

46. During the 1830s and 1840s, the stealing of Mexicans' horses became a widespread problem in California, and stallions and mares were sent as far as Oregon, New Mexico, and Missouri. Narrating his life story in 1877, Robles remembered that troops under Captain Sánchez's direction "se habían levantado contra los americanos en vista de los robos escandalosos de propiedades que estos estaban haciendo." "Relación de Secundino Robles," Bancroft Library. Charles White, *Letter from San José, California, March 18, 1848* (Los Angeles: Glen Dawson, 1955); Weber, *The Mexican Frontier*, 101–102; Weber, "American Westward Expansion and the Breakdown of Relations between *Pobladores* and '*Indios Bárbaros*' on Mexico's Far Northern Frontier, 1821–1846," in David Weber, *Myth and the History of the Hispanic Southwest* (Albuquerque: University of New Mexico Press, 1988), 129.

47. Andrés Reséndez, "Guerra e Identidad Nacional," *Historia Mexicana* 47:2 (1997), 422–423.

Chapter 2
The Golden State

1. Bayard Taylor, *Pictures of California*, quoted in J. P. Munro-Fraser, *History of Santa Clara County, California* (San Francisco: Alley, Bowen, 1881), 31; Almaguer, *Racial Fault Lines*, 1–16; *Alta California*, December 20, 1858; Bailey Millard, *History of the San Francisco Bay Region* (San Francisco: American Historical Society, 1924),

56. On Taylor, see Richmond Croom Beatty, *Bayard Taylor, Laureate of the Gilded Age* (Norman: University of Oklahoma Press, 1936). See also John Richie Schultz, *The Unpublished Letters of Bayard Taylor in the Huntington Library* (San Marino: Huntington Library, 1937).

2. Albert L. Hurtado, "Sex, Gender, Culture, and a Great Event: The California Gold Rush," *Pacific Historical Review* 68:1 (February 1999), 3.

3. *The Californian*, May 3, 1848; T. B. Goffoy, "Reminiscenses," in Bancroft Library MSS C-Y 295. Cox is quoted in Owen Cochran Coy, *The Great Trek* (San Francisco: Powell Publishing Company, 1931), 262.

4. Hall, *The History of San José and Surroundings*, 442–443; East San Jose Homestead Association, "Good News for the Homeless!" (pamphlet, 1869), in Bancroft Library; Camarillo, *Chicanos in a Changing Society* (Cambridge: Harvard University Press, 1979), 33–52; Richard Griswold del Castillo, *The Los Angeles Barrio, 1850–1890* (Berkeley: University of California Press, 1979), 30–61.

5. Hall, *The History of San José*, 243; *Santa Clara Register*, June 2, 1853; Tawni Hileman, ed., *"I Am So Sick": The Diary of a Nineteenth Century Housewife* (San José: Sourisseau Academy for State and Local History, 1983), 34; Daniel D. Hruby, *Mines to Medicine* (San José: O'Connor Hospital, 1965). Most white residents of the Valley during the 1850s supported political candidates who opposed the extension of slavery into the region, and a man who identified himself only as "Settler" wrote the *San José Telegraph* to oppose a Know Nothing candidate for sheriff on the grounds that the office seeker "was formerly a Negro-trader in Missouri." *San José Telegraph*, August 14, 1855. For a useful secondary account, see David R. Roediger, *The Wages of Whiteness: Race and the Making of the American Working Class* (New York: Verso Press, 1992), 49.

6. *Santa Clara Register*, June 13, 1853 and September 23, 1853; "Jones' Pantoscope of California" [1852], reprinted in *California Historical Society* 6:3 (September 1927), 250; Suzanne Oboler, *Ethnic Labels, Latino Lives: Identity and the Politics of (Re)Presentation in the United States* (Minneapolis: University of Minnesota, 1995), 35.

7. Munro-Fraser, *History of Santa Clara County*, 162; *Alta California* (San Francisco), August 19, 1860.

8. *The Californian* (San Francisco), March 15, 1848, quoted in Almaguer, *Racial Fault Lines*, 34–35.

9. Chester Smith Lyman, *Around the Horn to the Sandwich Islands and California* (New Haven: Yale University Press, 1924), 217, 230–231. The French journalist Etienne Derbec, by contrast, wrote that it was San José's "good fortune" that the town boasted so many residents of Mexican descent. See the letter of May 16, 1850, in A. P. Nasatir, ed. *A French Journalist in the California Gold Rush: The Letters of Etienne Derbec* (Georgetown, CA: The Talisman Press, 1964), 93–94.

10. Francis P. Farquhar, ed., *Up and Down California in 1860–1864: The Journal of William H. Brewer* (Berkeley: University of California Press, 1966), 181; Rockwell D. Hunt, "Houses That Came Around the Horn for the 'Alameda Gardens,'" *Overland Monthly* 49:3 (March 1907), 69; Jacobson, *Passing Farms, Enduring Values*, 65–66, 72. On the rise of Bay Area agriculture, see Steven Stoll, *The Fruits of Natural Advantage: Making the Industrial Countryside in California* (Berkeley: University of California Press, 1998), 27; Eugene Taylor Sawyer, *The History of Santa Clara County, California* (Los Angeles: Historic Record Company, 1922), 55; Bayard Taylor, *El Dorado, or Ad-*

venture in the Path of Empire (New York: G. P. Putnam, 1859), 95; Afred Doten, The Journals of Alfred Doten, 1849–1903, ed. Walter Van Tilburg Clark (Reno: University of Nevada Press, 1973), 1:597; and Munro-Fraser, History of Santa Clara County, 542. Wheat farming would become a major industry as rural California developed its "bonanza agriculture" by the 1870s, although large-scale farming of the sort practiced in the Central Valley did not develop until the mid-twentieth century in the area around San José. On the emergence of corporate agriculture and wheat farming, see Sawyer, History of Santa Clara County, 55; Cletus Daniel, Bitter Harvest: A History of California Farmworkers, 1870–1941 (Ithaca: Cornell University Press, 1981); Frank Adams, "The Historical Background of California Agriculture," in California Agriculture, ed. Claude B. Hutchison (Berkeley: University of California Press, 1946), 41–42; Paul S. Taylor and Tom Vasey, "Historical Background of California Farm Labor," Rural Sociology 1 (September 1936), 401–419; Richard Steven Street, "Tattered Shirts and Ragged Pants: Accommodation, Protest, and the Coarse Culture of California Wheat Harvesters and Threshers, 1866–1900," Pacific Historical Review 67:4 (1998), 573–600.

11. Alta California, October 17, 1850; Nasatir, "The French Consulate," 270. Los Angeles resident Antonio Coronel, who passed through the town in August 1848 in order to learn about the best "gold-bearing regions" from Californios in San José, subsequently arrived at Stanislaus Camp to find "several other parties of Spanish people who came from San José and other nearby points." Antonio Coronel, "Cosas de California," trans. Richard Morefield, The Mexican Adaptation in American California, 1846–1875 (San Francisco: R and E Research Associates, 1971), 76. The Alta California reported in 1850 that "foreigners continue to pour into Tuolumne County from San José and from Southern California." Alta California, September 2, 1850. Many local Californios returned temporarily to San José for traditional feast-days and other religious celebrations several times during their stints in the Sierras, and they left the foothills for longer periods of time to spend the rainy season in San José. Nasatir, "The French Consulate in California," 270. See the letter of Moerenhout to the Minister of Foreign Affairs, August 17, 1848, in George Ezra Dane, "The French Consulate in California, 1843–56 (The Moerenhout Documents)," California Historical Society Quarterly 13:2 (June 1934), 66.

12. Santa Clara Register, September 1, 1853; E. A. Van Court, "Reminiscences of Mrs. E. A. Van Court" (ms., March 26, 1914), in Beinecke Library, Yale University, WA MSS S-1655. Embracing the same view of natural selection, other settlers in the area would continue to favor American territorial expansion to other parts of the hemisphere in the 1850s, believing that "it is written in the log-book of 'Manifest Destiny'" that the United States needed to take over other regions. Santa Clara Register, July 7, 1853. San José attorney Frederic Hall wrote that American technology had eclipsed the premodern Mexican villagers living in the area. When telegraph poles were erected in October 1853, Hall joked, Californios had found them to be "a novelty, and quite an event in the history of the place. The natives could not comprehend it. One old Mexican waited nearly all one day to see the mail pass on the wires." Hall, The History of San José, iii, 257–258. As white residents and travelers trumpeted the natural beauty of their valley, they also commonly represented conquered inhabitants as a throwback to the less democratic society that had preceded the Americans. Don Mitchell, The Lie of the Land: Migrant Workers and the California Landscape (Minneapolis: University of Minnesota Press, 1996), 6.

13. While the white rancher and merchant Charles Weber successfully upheld his claim in a hearing with alcalde John Burton, Californios such as Antonio Pico lost their bids. Hall, *The History of San José*, 277–279; testimony of William J. Lewis, August 19, 1856, in *U.S. vs. Guadalupe Mining Company* (published transcript, 1856), 47–86, in New Almadén Papers, Green Library, Stanford University, box 82, folder 15; W. Turrentine Jackson, "Mazatlán to the Estanislao: The Narrative of Lewis Richard Price's Journey to California in 1849," *California Historical Society Quarterly* 39:1 (March 1960), 42; Leonard Pitt, *The Decline of the Californios* (Berkeley: University of California Press, 1966), 83–103; William W. Morrow, *Spanish and Mexican Private Land Grant Cases* (San Francisco: Bancroft-Whitney, 1923), 1–7; Treaty of Guadalupe-Hidalgo, Art. 8, *U.S. Government Documents, House Executive Documents*, 30th Congress, 1st Session, vol. 8, Executive Doc. no. 69. Between 1851 and 1856, 813 land claims were presented to the commission, and 604 were eventually confirmed. Of these, only 330 were confirmed as belonging to Californios, however. See Pitt, *The Decline of the Californios*, 83–103.

14. California Attorney General J. S. Black similarly complained that there was "not an island or place for a fort, customhouse, hospital, or post office, but must be purchased" from one of the Californios. J. S. Black to the Chairman of the Senate Judiciary Committee, May 22, 1860, in James F. Shunk, "Report of the Attorney General of the United States upon Surveys in California and Other Matters Pertaining to Mexican Land Grants" (ms., Washington, D.C., May 15, 1861), 3, 18, in Stanford Law Library, DJ AUP AAr.

15. See *United States vs. Manuel Alviso* (1856), *United States vs. Antonio Suñol* (1855), *United States vs. Agustín Bernal* (1856), *United States vs. Juana Briones* (1855), in Ogden Hoffman, *Reports of Land Cases Determined in the United States District Court for the Northern District of California, June Term, 1853 to June Term, 1858, Inclusive* (San Francisco: Numa Hubert, 1862).

16. *San Francisco Bulletin*, July 1, 1876; *San Francisco Chronicle*, March 26, 1876; Mariano Castro, statement conferring power of attorney, December 6, 1850, in Murphy Family Papers, folder 11; J. P. Davison to Murphy, May 20, 1857, in Murphy Papers, folder 23; William Wood to Murphy, August 31, 1851, in Murphy Papers, folder 21. In April 1850, in the city's first legal case heard in district court, a local merchant successfully sued four Californios who had failed to pay back $5,000 that he had lent them at a monthly interest rate of 8 percent. The creditor obtained the mortgages to several land claims in the area, and cash-poor Californios would become embroiled in hundreds of similar cases throughout the state during the 1850s and 1860s. Hall, *The History of San José*, 227. On contracts in Mexican California, see David J. Langum, *Law and Community on the Mexican California Frontier: Anglo-American Expatriates and the Clash of Legal Traditions, 1821–1846* (Norman: University of Oklahoma Press, 1987), 163–86.

17. In 1870 James Murphy claimed property holdings valued at $375,000 and a personal estate estimated at $125,000. Federal Manuscript Census, 1860 and 1870, "San José"; Doten, *The Journals of Alfred Doten*, 1:385; Foote, *Pen Pictures*, 94. A report in the *San José Mercury* in 1868, for instance, declared that only 12 of the 172 county residents with an income over $2,800 in that year were "Mexicans." *San José Mercury*, June 18, 1868.

18. Federal Manuscript Census, 1860, "San José"; *Santa Clara Register*, July 21,

1853; Susan Lee Johnson, "'Domestic' Life in the Diggings: The Southern Mines in the California Gold Rush," in *Over the Edge: Remapping the American West*, ed. Valerie J. Matsumoto and Blake Allmendinger (Berkeley: University of California Press, 1999), 119; Sawyer, *The History of Santa Clara County*, 22; *Alumni of the San José High School* (pamphlet, n.d.), in Bancroft Library, "Pamphlets, San José (misc.)." Between 1876 and 1894 only 2 of the 372 graduates of San José High School were Mexicans. On changing occupations after the Mexican War, see Juan Gómez-Quiñones, *Mexican American Labor, 1790–1990* (Albuquerque: University of New Mexico Press, 1994), 47–48. On saddle makers in California, see also Arnold Rojas, *The Vaquero* (Charlotte: McNally and Loftin, 1964).

19. Isidoro Coubet's reminiscences are translated and reprinted in Edwin A. Beilharz and Carlos U. López, *We Were 49ers: Chilean Accounts of the California Gold Rush* (Pasadena: Ward Ritchie Press, 1976), 162; Camarillo, *Chicanos in a Changing Society*, 116. In 1850 Mexicans were the largest group of foreign-born residents in the state. California was home to 6,454 foreign-born Mexicans in 1850 and 9,150 in 1860. Doris Marion Wright, "The Making of Cosmopolitan California: An Analysis of Immigration, 1848–1870," part 1, *California Historical Society Quarterly* 19:4 (December 1940), 340.

20. Munro-Fraser, *History of Santa Clara County*, 346. Colton proposed that the nation's proper and natural division of labor should include nonwhite workers, stressing that "if you want to perform this drudgery yourself, drive out the Sonorians, and upset that cherished system of political economy founded in a spirit of wisdom and national justice." Walter Colton, *Three Years in California* (New York: A. S. Barnes, 1851), 368.

21. Doten, *The Journals of Alfred Doten*, 1:107.

22. "Judge R. J. Peckham, An Eventful Life," *San José Pioneer*, June 9, 1877; *Santa Clara Register*, June 16, 1853; *San José Telegraph*, July 22, 1854.

23. Antonio Berreyesa, "Relacion," May 25, 1877, and June 1877, Bancroft Library, C-D 44.

24. *San José Telegraph*, October 9 and November 13, 1855; Munro-Fraser, *History of Santa Clara County*, 220–240. In 1853 a general fear that white travelers would be attacked by "a murderous band . . . now prowling about seeking the destruction of all not of Spanish origin" swept through Santa Clara County, and the newspaper reported that "no American is safe, who may happen to meet an overpowering number of the Spanish race." *Santa Clara Register*, reprinted in *Alta California*, October 2, 1853.

25. Munro-Fraser, *History of Santa Clara County*, 346; William H. Ellison, "The Federal Indian Policy in California, 1846–1860," *Mississippi Valley Historical Review* 9:1 (June 1922), 42–43; Hall, *The History of San José*, 243; *San José Telegraph*, October 2, 1855; Doten, *The Journals of Alfred Doten* 1:328, 410. When a San José jail keeper, caught up by the excitement of the Gold Rush, led the ten Indian prisoners in his custody to the mines and forced them to work for him in the diggings, he came under attack in the Santa Clara Valley for perpetuating the apparent "slavery" of the Mexican era. Owen Cochran Coy, *Gold Days* (San Francisco: Powell Publishing Company, 1929), 62. In part because of extensive anti-Indian violence throughout the state, between 1848 and 1870 California's Indian population declined from approximately 100,000 to 58,000. Robert F. Heizer and Alan F. Almquist, *The Other Califor-*

nians (Berkeley: University of California Press, 1971), 21–22. Because of the historic ties between Northern California Indians and Mission Santa Clara, the largest number of Native American residents continued to reside in the town of Santa Clara, which nevertheless boasted only 79 Indian residents by 1860. Federal Manuscript Census, 1860, "Santa Clara."

26. Hall, *The History of San José*, 245–375; Munro-Fraser, *History of Santa Clara County*, 336–342; *Santa Clara Register*, June 16, 1853; Bancroft, *History of California*, 6:752. When he saw Pedro traveling on a public road that passed through his property, Dietzman immediately "thought the Spaniard was stealing a horse," fired his revolver in warning, and told Pedro to stop. Pedro turned, "threw up his hands [and] offered no resistance," but Dietzman fired again, this time wounding Pedro. When Pedro attempted to leave his horse and climb through Dietzman's fence to safety, Dietzman followed and "fired the remaining charge of his revolver" at point-blank range. While a Mexican who had killed a white settler in this way would undoubtedly have either been lynched by vigilantes or sentenced to formal execution by the courts, two days after the killing of Pedro a local judge sentenced Dietzman to only ten years in jail for second-degree murder. Munro-Fraser, *History of Santa Clara County*, 227. In part because local residents feared a social environment in which Mexican criminality seemed to threaten them on all sides, settlers in San José were the first in California to demand, on December 11, 1848, a constitutional convention "to organize a civil government for California." Coy, *Gold Days*, 62.

27. Country Club, *History of Washington Township, Alameda County, California* (Washington Township, CA: Women's Club of Washington Township, 1904), 49, 68–69, 102; Thomas McEnery, ed. *California Cavalier: The Journal of Captain Thomas Fallon* (San José: Inishfallen Enterprises, 1978), 88.

28. *Santa Clara Register*, reprinted in *Alta California*, October 2, 1853.

29. The corrido and translation can be found in María Herrera-Sobek, *Northward Bound: The Mexican Immigrant Experience in Ballad and Song* (Bloomington: University of Indiana Press, 1993), 16–18; Luis Leal, "*El Corrido de Joaquín Murrieta*: Origen y difusión," *Mexican Studies/Estudios Mexicanos* 11:1 (Winter 1995), 1–23.

30. Beilharz and López, *We Were 49ers*, 163. As the Catholic Church became dominated by non-Mexican clergy in the 1850s and 1860s, changes in religious life similarly "disrupted a 'way of life' in Mexican communities" in San José and elsewhere. Albert L. Pulido, "Mexican American Catholicism in the Southwest: The Transformation of a Popular Religion," *Perspectives in Mexican American Studies* 4 (1993), 94–95.

31. Pablo de la Guerra is quoted in Almaguer, *Racial Fault Lines*, 55–56. Vásquez explained his banditry in an interview published in the *Los Angeles Star* on May 16, 1874, quoted here from Robert G. Cleland, *The Cattle on a Thousand Hills* (San Marino, CA: Huntington Library, 1951), 274. On the establishment of Mexican American identity during this period, see Camarillo, *Chicanos in a Changing Society*, 46–71; Griswold del Castillo, *Los Angeles Barrio*, 41–61. See also Martha Menchaca, *The Mexican Outsiders* (Austin: University of Texas Press, 1995), 1–30; Patricia Nelson Limerick, *The Legacy of Conquest: The Unbroken Past of the American West* (New York: W.W. Norton, 1987), 27.

32. While Peralta de Castro struggled to maintain her properties, the Irish immigrant and Valley empresario Martin Murphy Jr. persuaded the San Francisco–San

Jose Railroad to establish a depot on his Mountain View property by selling the railroad a right-of-way for one dollar. John Dirks, "The de Castro Family and the San Francisco and San Jose Railroad," *Local History Studies* (Fall 1968, De Anza College), 33–41; Deed of July 27, 1861, in Murphy Family Papers, folder 5, Santa Clara University Archives, 995-032.

33. The sheriff, in fact, likely had made this effort not out of a selfless regard for the property rights of Californios, but because his family had already become established as the largest property holders in the county, dependent on the legitimacy of Californio titles to defend their own titles against squatters. Hall, *The History of San José*, 285.

34. Letter from Ben Bolt to "Rock," May 21, 1861, in Doten, *The Journals of Alfred Doten*, 1:603; Hall, *The History of San José*, 285.

35. Jan Otto Marius Broek, *The Santa Clara Valley, California: A Study in Landscape Changes* (Utrecht: Uitgevers, 1932), 61, 64; Timothy J. Lukes and Gary Y. Okihiro, *Japanese Legacy: Farming and Community Life in California's Santa Clara Valley* (Cupertino: California History Center, De Anza College, 1985), 5; *San José Mercury*, June 18, 1868.

36. Juan Gómez-Quiñones, *Roots of Chicano Politics, 1600–1940* (Albuquerque: University of New Mexico Press, 1994), 193.

37. Almaguer, *Racial Fault Lines*, 72; David G. Gutiérrez, *Walls and Mirrors: Mexican Americans, Mexican Immigrants, and the Politics of Ethnicity* (Berkeley: University of California Press, 1995), 14.

38. Born at Mission San José in 1844, Guadalupe de Jesús Vallejo echoed those sentiments. The daughter of the church's administrator Don José de Jesús Vallejo, she penned a poem describing her "thousand fond memories" of her family's old home. Critical of the supposed progress brought by American settlers during the 1840s and 1850s, her verse spoke romantically about the mission as a benevolent institution with no counterpart after 1848. In the 1870s the aging San Josean Nasario Galindo similarly described the 1830s as halcyon decades in which *gente de razón* had held political sway. Reminding others about the past supremacy of local Californios, Galindo noted their managerial skills and work before the arrival of U.S. troops during the Mexican War. Country Club, *History of Washington Township*, 121; Galindo, "Manuscript," 10.

Chapter 3
Transnational Industries

1. *El Nuevo Mundo* (San Francisco), January 18, 1865. Histories of the mine's economic development include Milton Lanyon and Laurence Bulmore, *Cinnabar Hills: The Quicksilver Days of New Almadén* (Los Gatos, CA: Village Printers, 1967), and Jimmie Schneider, *Quicksilver: The Complete History of Santa Clara County's New Almadén Mine* (San José: Zella Schneider, 1992).

2. *U.S. vs. Castillero*, 4:2485, 2639; Joseph W. Revere, *A Tour of Duty in California* (New York, C. S. Francis, 1849), 56; *Hutchings Magazine* (April 1856), 59.

3. *U.S. vs. Castillero*, 1:541; Valencia, "New Almadén and the Mexican" (M.A. thesis, San José State University, 1977) 22–23; *A Contested Election in California*,

Testimony of the Qualified Electors and Legal Voters of New Almadén (San José: Daily Mercury, 1887), 24–25, 39, 62, in New Almadén Papers, box 112, file 13. Richard Lingenfelter and other historians have argued that California's and Nevada's capital-intensive mining in the early 1860s helped shape the industrial labor movement in the American West, although most Californios and Mexican immigrants had been driven out of California's gold country before workers' associations formed in Sierra Nevada counties in the 1860s. "The mining labor movement in the West began," according to Lingenfelter, "with the industrialization of deep mining on the Comstock Lode of Nevada in the early-1860s." Richard Lingenfelter, *The Hardrock Miners: A History of the Mining Labor Movement in the American West, 1863–1893* (Berkeley: University of California Press, 1974), 5–6, 31–34. See also Rodman Paul, *Mining Frontiers of the American West, 1848–1880* (New York: Holt, Rinehart, and Winston, 1963); Mary Wyman, *Hard Rock Epic: Western Miners and the Industrial Revolution, 1860–1910* (Berkeley: University of California Press, 1979); Ralph Mann, *After the Gold Rush: Society in Grass Valley and Nevada City, California, 1849–1870* (Stanford: Stanford University Press, 1982). For an excellent account of the West's industrial miners outside of California, see David M. Emmons, *The Butte Irish: Class and Ethnicity in an American Mining Town, 1873–1925* (Urbana: University of Illinois Press, 1989).

4. *San José Mercury Herald*, December 30, 1935. Newspaper articles published in San José about the mine were rare, and no local government investigations seem to have been conducted. Visitors' accounts at most celebrated the Mexican workers' skills and said little about Spanishtown society. The labor movement in the county and the state paid no attention to these workers in the 1850s and 1860s, preferring instead to focus organizing efforts on the carpenters, printers, and other urban trades based in San Francisco, Stockton, and Sacramento. Published histories of San José and its surroundings have done little more than mention the presence of Mexican and Chilean mine workers, concentrating instead on celebrating the development of new business methods and technologies that made the site the world's second leading producer of mercury during the late nineteenth century. See, for example, Hall, *The History of San José*; Winther, *The Story of San José*; Lanyon and Bulmore, *Cinnabar Hills*; Schneider, *Quicksilver*.

5. Richard Morefield, *The Mexican Adaptation in American California, 1846–1875* (San Francisco: R. and E. Research Associates, 1971), 14; J. R. Bartlett, *Personal Narrative of Explorations and Incidents in Texas, New Mexico, and California* (New York: Appleton, 1854), 63. Mary Halleck Foote noted that "the trying part of the underground work is that it requires this absolute steadiness of eye, hand, head and nerves under the greatest physical discomforts—hot, bad air, or keen draughts, sometimes up to his knees in water—sometimes obliged to keep a stooping position for hours at a time." Letter from Foote, October 21, 1876, in Mary Halleck Foote Papers, Special Collections, Green Library, Stanford University, box 1, folder 22. Schneider, *Quicksilver*, 19–26. A visitor to the area in 1865 noted that "the Sonorians [*sic*] and native Californians are generally expert miners. As prospectors they are unsurpassed. They possess a great natural sagacity, know every indication by instinct, are willing to run any amount of risk, and seem imbued by an adventurous spirit which fits them peculiarly for the business of mining." J. R. Browne, "Down in the Cinnabar Mines," *Harper's* 31 (October 1865), 553.

6. S. A. Downer, "The Quicksilver Mines of New Almadén," *California Monthly* 2 (October 1854).

7. Ibid., 44; letter from Mary Halleck Foote to Helea de Kay Galena, December 22, 1876, in Mary Halleck Foote Papers, box 1, folder 23; "Testimony of Superintendent Jennings," *A Contested Election in California*, 15.

8. Rodman W. Paul, ed., *A Victorian Gentlewoman in the Far West: The Reminiscences of Mary Hallock Foote* (San Marino, CA: Huntington Library, 1972), 125; "Romance of Indian 'War Paint,'" *San José Mercury Herald*, September 2, 1923.

9. Mary Halleck Foote, "A California Mining Camp," *Scribner's Magazine* 15:4 (February 1878), 480–484.

10. Ibid.; Downer, "The Quicksilver Mines of New Almadén," 258. Of the 170 Mexican women residing near the New Almadén mine on Mine Hill who were counted by the census in 1860, the enumerators recorded that nearly all of them were either "keeping house" or "at home." Only two of those residents were listed as "working"—in both cases as "washerwomen"—making it likely that most women's economic activities went unrecorded by census officials. Federal Manuscript Census, 1860, "Almadén Township."

11. Fernando Bernaldez and Ramón Rua Figueroa, "Table 20: General Statement Showing the Infirmities of 7748 Sick Miners Treated at the Hospital of Almadén from 1841 to 1855 Showing Class of Malady and Respective Mortality," in "Memoirs of the Mines of Almadén and Almadéneos" (unpublished booklet, 1861), New Almadén Papers, OS Book 67; "Miscellaneous Papers," New Almadén Papers, box 80, folder 12; "Physician's Reports," New Almadén Papers, box 94, folder 19; David T. Day, *Report on Mineral Industries in the United States at the 11th Census* (Washington, D.C.: Government Printing Office, 1892). The dangers of blasting powder and open flames continued into the twentieth century to threaten the small group of Mexican workers who worked underground at New Almadén. Coroners' records and insurance reports filed with the California Industrial Accidents Commission register the deaths of the Chilean-born Daniel Díaz in 1909 and the Mexican-born Félix Cazares in 1925, the former by "accidental suffocation" and the latter by an explosion caused by wet fuses. California Industrial Accident Commission Insurance Report, April 18, 1925, in New Almadén Papers, box 94, folder 6; Coroner's Jury Report, June 10, 1909, in New Almadén Papers, box 94 folder 2.

12. "Jones' Pantoscope of California," 250.

13. Bernaldez and Figueroa, "Table 20."

14. Federal Manuscript Census, 1880, Almadén Township; "Physician's Monthly Reports, January–December 1891," in New Almadén Papers, box 94, folder 19.

15. "Salivation" was one of the most common and deadly symptoms of mercury poisoning in which the afflicted suffered from an excessive flow of saliva. *A Contested Election in California*, 39.

16. *Clamor Público*, May 31 and July 19, 1856; Monroy, *Thrown among Strangers*, 220. On the Gadsden Purchase, see *La Crónica* (San Francisco), November 19, 1856; For articles critical of William Walker, see, for example, *El Bejareño* (San Antonio), May 12 and November 19, 1855; *Clamor Público* (Los Angeles), May 17 and June 28, 1856. On ties between Peruvians and Mexicans around foreign policy issues, see, for example, *Eco del Pacífico* (San Francisco), April 9, 1857. In Los Angeles the Chilean Juan Silva in 1865 likened William Walker to Hernán Cortés in an anti-imperialist

speech given on September 16, Mexico's Day of Independence. In 1878 *La Reforma* in Los Angeles translated and serialized Colonel Horace Bell's published memoirs describing his activities in Nicaragua. El Paso's *El Defensor* echoed the comparison between Walker and Cortés in 1894. *La Reforma*, May 16, 1878; *Nuevo Mundo*, October 2, 1865; *El Defensor*, October 15, 1894. As Richard Griswold del Castillo has suggested, the discourse of la Raza stressed the ties between residents of "Spanish descent" and a "cultural tradition that was separate from the . . . 'norteamericanos.'" Griswold del Castillo, *The Los Angeles Barrio*, 133–134. Studies that discuss the Mexican immigrant workforce in other parts of the Southwest during the nineteenth century include Andrea Yvette Huginnie, "'Strikitos': Race, Class, and Work in the Arizona Copper Industry, 1870–1920," (Ph.D. dissertation, Yale University, 1991); David Montejano, *Anglos and Mexicans*; Neil Foley, "The New South in the Southwest: Anglos, Blacks, and Mexicans in Central Texas, 1880–1930," (Ph.D. dissertation, University of Michigan, 1990); Mario García, *Desert Immigrants* (New Haven: Yale University Press, 1982). Beilharz and López, *We Were 49ers*, 81–82. On conquest and the imagination of a broader Mexican community in the Southwest, see in particular *El Defensor* (El Paso), October 15, 1894.

17. Bartlett, *Personal Narrative of Explorations*, 63; Federal Manuscript Census, 1860, New Almadén Township; Federal Manuscript Census, 1870, New Almadén Township; *A Contested Election in California*, 45. On citizenship, see *Clamor Público*, July 31, 1855. The Chilean Roberto Hernández Correjo noted in 1849 that "no one can be a property owner [in San Francisco] unless he is a citizen, so I have to make purchases under the name of someone else; but I have made up my mind to remain a citizen of Chile." Beilharz and López, *We Were 49ers*, 213.

18. *Alta California* (March 11, 1863), quoted in Prezelski, "Lives of the California Lancers," 31, 33.

19. Mexican women in other Northern California communities were apparently at least able to join patriotic and other community organizations as members of women's auxiliaries during this period. *Nuevo Mundo*, April 26, 1865.

20. Latinos were effectively cut off from visiting San José on a daily basis since the trip to town from the top of Mine Hill for many years required a mile walk to catch the stagecoach, then a day's wages to travel to and from the city, and finally a long climb of a mile uphill to return to Spanishtown.

21. *El Nuevo Mundo*, September 28, 1864, and August 16, 1865; "Judge R. J. Peckham, an Eventful Life," *San José Pioneer*, June 9, 1877. Mutual-aid organizations became the foundation for labor struggles here and in other parts of the U.S. West and Mexico. See John M. Hart, *Anarchism and the Mexican Working Class, 1860–1931* (Austin: University of Texas Press, 1987), 14–17; Gómez-Quiñones, *Chicano Politics: Reality and Promise, 1940–1990* (Albuquerque: University of New Mexico Press, 1990), 52; José Amaro Hernández, *Mutual Aid for Survival* (Malabar, FL: Robert Krieger Publishers, 1983); García, *Desert Immigrants*, 223–228; Ricardo Romo, *East Los Angeles: History of a Barrio* (Austin: University of Texas Press, 1983), 150–155; George J. Sánchez, *Becoming Mexican American* (Berkeley: University of California Press, 1993), 231.

22. Pedro Ruíz Aldea's description can be found in Beilharz and López, *We Were 49ers*, 225. For Islas's comments, see *Clamor Público* (Los Angeles), October 23, 1855. On the colonization movement, see *Clamor Público*, August 17, September 11, and

October 23, 1855; April 26, May 10 and 17, 1856. Pitt, *Decline of the Californios*, 210; Griswold del Castillo, *Los Angeles Barrio*, 119–124. Of the only fourteen Chilean residents enumerated by the census at New Almaden, six had married by 1860. Four of these partners had been born in Mexico, while two were Spanish-surnamed residents born in California. Federal Manuscript Census, Almadén Township, 1860. Some elite Chileans and Mexicans in California lamented the growing ties between the two groups. Contemporaries such as the liberal academic and former Chilean Minister of the Interior José Victorino Lastarria discouraged his fellow citizens from associating with the "lazy" Mexicans who could be found in California, and the pioneering Mexican immigrant journalist Francisco Ramírez, always attuned to improving his community's reputation in the eyes of white residents of the state, urged Mexicanos to avoid contact with Chileans, who, he believed, were inclined as a group to senseless acts of violence. *Clamor Público* (Los Angeles), September 25, 1855.

23. Schneider, *Quicksilver*, 39–55; Valencia, "New Almadén and the Mexican," 33–37. These changes developed, as the testimony of mine officials in the 1880s would later suggest, in part from a distrust of Mexican "criminal elements" residing on Mine Hill. The new owners set out to institute changes to control or drive out Spanishtown residents. *A Contested Election in California*, 73–90.

24. *Nuevo Mundo*, September 25, 1864, and January 23, 1865.

25. Ibid., January 18, 20, and 23, 1865. Angry at the company's efforts to isolate them farther from the nearby town, Mexicanos in Spanishtown complained to the San Francisco press that "no one is allowed to bring in anything for their home or it might be confiscated. No box or trunk can be brought in without having it first examined, and if they find that it contains any prohibited items, they take it without listening to our protests or begging." Ibid., January 18, 1865.

26. *Nuevo Mundo*, January 20, 1865. On drinking and working-class Mexican culture at the mine, see ibid., July 24, 1864; Mary Halleck Foote to Helena de Kay Gilder, December 22, 1876, in Foote Papers, box 1, folder 23. See also Roy Rosenzweig, *Eight Hours for What We Will: Workers and Leisure in an Industrial City, 1870–1920* (New York: Cambridge University Press, 1983); David Brody, "Time and Work during Early American Industrialism," *Labor History* 30 (Winter 1989), 5–46.

27. *Nuevo Mundo*, January 20 and 23, 1865.

28. Ibid., January 23, 1865; *A Contested Election in California*, 39; San José *Patriot*, reprinted in *Nuevo Mundo*, April 13, 1866.

29. *Nuevo Mundo*, November 18, 1864, and January 18, 1865.

30. Ibid., January 18 and 20, 1865.

31. Ibid., November 4, 1864, and January 20, 1865; Mary Halleck Foote to Helea de Kay Galena, December 22, 1876, in Mary Halleck Foote Papers, box 1, folder 23.

32. *Nuevo Mundo*, January 20 and February 8, 1865; *A Contested Election in California*, 98. Of the Spanish-surnamed residents enumerated at the mine in the 1860 census, only 121 had been born in California while 277 had arrived from Mexico, 15 from Chile, and 4 from Peru. See also *Nuevo Mundo*, July 6, 9, and 12, August 5, and September 25, 1864. For Spanish-language theater in the Southwest during this period and its role in community formations, see Arthur L. Campa, *Spanish Religious Folktheatre in the Southwest* (Albuquerque: University of New Mexico Press, 1934); Nicolás Kanellos, *A History of Hispanic Theatre in the United States: Origins to 1940* (Austin: University of Texas Press, 1990); Haas, *Conquest and Historical Identities in*

California, 145–148. On politics in the Mexican gold and silver mines, see Doris M. Ladd, *The Making of a Strike: Mexican Silver Workers' Struggles in Real del Monte, 1766–1775* (Lincoln: University of Nebraska Press, 1988); Elinore M. Barrett, *The Mexican Colonial Copper Industry* (Albuquerque: University of New Mexico Press, 1987); Anne Staples, *Bonanzas y Borrascas Mineras: El Estado de Mexico, 1821–1876* (Zinancantepec: El Colegio Mexiquense, 1994); Margarita García Luna Ortega, *Huelgas de Mineros en el Oro de México, 1911–1920* (Toluca: Secretaria del Trabajo del Estado de Mexico, 1993); Eduardo Flores Clair, *Conflictos de Trabajo de una Empresa Minera: Real del Monte y Pachuca, 1872–1877* (Mexico: Instituto Nacional de Antropología e Historia, 1991). On Mexican Americans and the press, see Roberto Treviño, "*Prensa y Patria*: The Spanish-Language Press and the Biculturation of the Tejano Middle Class, 1920–1940," *Western Historical Quarterly* 22 (November 1991), 451–472; Carlos Cortés, "The Mexican-American Press," in *The Ethnic Press in the United States*, ed. Sally M. Miller (New York: Greenwood Press, 1987), 247–260; Anabelle M. Oczon, "Bilingual and Spanish-Language Newspapers in Territorial New Mexico," *New Mexico Historical Review* 54:1 (1979), 45–52; George J. Sánchez, *Becoming Mexican American*, 108–125.

33. *Nuevo Mundo*, October 2, 1864.

34. Ibid., September 20 and 25, October 2, 1864; March 8, April 17, July 7 and 12, September 4, October 18, 23, and 25, and November 1, 3, and 22, 1865. On segregation and the development of community politics, see also Camarillo, *Chicanos in a Changing Society*, 53–78; Arnoldo de Leon, *The Tejano Community, 1836–1900* (Albuquerque: University of New Mexico Press, 1982), 87–112.

35. *Nuevo Mundo*, October 2, 1864; March 8, and September 4, 1865. Of 420 residents enumerated, census officials counted 156 women in 1860. Federal Manuscript Census, New Almadén Township, 1860.

36. *Nuevo Mundo*, January 20 and March 8, 1865.

37. Ibid., January 23, 1863; November 18, 1864; September 27, January 20 and 23, October 2, and November 22, 1865.

38. Ibid., July 24 and November 18, 1864; January 18, 20, and 23, and February 8, 1865. After a non-Mexican worker fell and suffered serious injuries in the mine shaft in late January 1865, for example, a Spanishtown resident reported to *Nuevo Mundo* that "something shameful happened in the mine." In his words, "as a Frenchman named Jean Jencibe was unwrapping a cord from a pole, the platform on which he stood wobbled and he fell from a height of 35 or 40 feet and suffered various injuries, particularly on his feet which had been dislocated. Immediately, Dr. Caraza (an esteemed Italian) was called by the Superintendent. The patient is in his care, and although gravely beaten up, he will recover. I believe this is the first philanthropic act shown by the superintendent; when accident after accident has befallen our countrymen, he doesn't even notice. Now you see, this worker is French and they are the privileged ones here." Ibid., January 20, 1865.

39. Ibid., October 9 and December 22, 1864; January 10, 18, 20, and 23, 1865.

40. Juan Gómez-Quiñones dates the origins of significant Mexican union activism to the formation of the Knights of Labor in 1886. Emilio Zamora has found that among the earliest acts of resistance was an 1883 strike by three hundred West Texas vaqueros led by the cowboy Juan Gómez. Juan Gómez-Quiñones, *Development of the Mexican Working Class North of the Rio Bravo: Work and Culture among Laborers,*

1600–1900 (Los Angeles: University of California, Los Angeles, Chicano Studies Research Center Publications, 1982), 45; Emilio Zamora, *The World of the Mexican Worker in Texas* (College Station: Texas A & M Press, 1993), 53.

41. Ibid., November 4 and 18, 1864; February 8 and 24, 1865, and April 20, 1866. The best source on Cornish workers in the Comstock is Arthur Cecil Todd, *The Cornish Miner in America* (Glendale: Arthur H. Clark Company, 1967), 50–113.

42. *Nuevo Mundo*, January 23, 1865.

43. Ibid., January 27, 1865; *San José Mercury*, February 2, 1865. Women in Spanishtown were not allowed to join these activities, and one observer instead described the "strength" he received from the mere sight of local Mexicanas watching miners talk with New Almadén officials from the surrounding hillside. It was a "beautiful picture," he wrote. The overhanging rocks were "adorned with the presence of our beautiful mexicanas all about, and choosing the highest points they encircled their fathers, husbands, brothers, and sons, it being one of those afternoons in which nature enjoys decorating everything with the brilliant rays of a pleasant sun." *Nuevo Mundo*, January 23, 1865. They suggested that the Quicksilver Company had instituted reforms making it impossible for workers to maintain their roles as protectors of local women. A local Mexicano protested, for instance, that the location of the new company store so far from Spanishtown often made it impossible for husbands to join their wives on the errand, and that unaccompanied women "are treated by the store owners as if they were nothing more than animals." His demand for either the store's relocation or a continuation of the services of door-to-door peddlers characteristically affirmed Mexicana subservience, a common feature of many masculinist political movements during this period. *Nuevo Mundo*, November 18, 1864.

44. Ibid., January 26, February 2 and 15, 1865.

45. Ibid., March 7, April 3, 11, and 25, September 13, October 4 and 6, November 10, and December 6, 1865; January 22 and April 2, 1866.

46. Ibid., April 11, 1866.

47. The author of one letter to *Nuevo Mundo* referred to this latest action not as a *huelga*, but as a *sublevación*. Ibid., April 1 and 11, 1866; Valencia, "New Almadén and the Mexican," 37–38.

48. *San José Evening Bulletin*, quoted in *Nuevo Mundo* April 11, 1866.

49. *Nuevo Mundo*, April 20, 1866.

50. *A Contested Election in California*, 13, 21, 24, 29, and 38.

51. Paul, ed., *A Victorian Gentlewoman in the Far West*, 126.

52. *A Contested Election in California*, 73, 98. See Pitt, *The Decline of the Californios*; Monroy, *Thrown among Strangers*, 220. The best study of Mexican immigrants in mid-nineteenth-century California remains Sister Mary Colette Standart, "The Sonoran Migration to California, 1848–1856: A Study in Prejudice," originally published in *Southern California Quarterly* 57 (Fall 1976), 333–357; reprinted in *Between Two Worlds: Mexican Immigrants in the United States*, ed. David Gutiérrez (Wilmington: Scholarly Resources, 1996), 3–21. The focus of most work in the 1960s and 1970s on Californios was a notable departure from earlier scholarly studies of Mexicans in the state, however. See Paul S. Taylor, *Mexican Labor in the United States*, 7 vols. (Berkeley: University of California Press, 1928–1932); Emory S. Bogardus, *The Mexican in the United States* (Los Angeles: University of Southern California Press, 1934); Manuel Gamio, *Mexican Immigration to the United States* (Chicago: University

of Chicago Press, 1939); Carey McWilliams, *North from Mexico* (New York: J. B. Lippincott, 1949). For an analysis of early studies of Mexican immigration, see David G. Gutiérrez, "Significant to Whom?: Mexican Americans and the History of the American West," *Western Historical Quarterly* 24:4 (November 1993), 519–539.

53. *A Contested Election in California*, 62; Foote, "A California Mining Camp," 480–484.

Chapter 4
Residence in Revolution

1. Langdon Winner, "Silicon Valley Mystery House," in *Variations on a Theme Park: The New American City and the End of Public Space*, ed. Michael Sorkin (New York: Hill and Wang, 1992), 31–32.

2. Kevin Starr, *Endangered Dreams: The Great Depression in California* (New York: Oxford University Press, 1994), 64.

3. Schneider, *Quicksilver*, 121–142; Department of Commerce, *United States Census of Agriculture, 1925. Report for States, Part III, Western States* (Washington, D.C.: Government Printing Office, 1927), 460.

4. Most Valley farmers planted orchards during the years between the world wars, and, by 1925, 5,031 growers in the valley were harvesting over six million prune trees. Jaclyn Greenbert, "Industry in the Garden: A Social History of the Canning Industry and Canning Workers in the Santa Clara Valley, California, 1870–1920" (Ph.D. dissertation, University of California, Los Angeles, 1985), 111; Department of Commerce, *United States Census of Agriculture, 1925*, 460; William F. James and George H. McMurry, *History of San Jose, California* (San José: Smith Printing Company, 1933), 132. See also "The Famous Santa Clara Valley" (advertisement), *Sunset Magazine* 19:4 (August 1907), 4. Valley residents had experimented with other crops, including opium, raised locally by T. Appleby and the Mexican War veteran Captain Aram in 1871. "Notes of Travel in Santa Clara County," *Pacific Rural Press*, December 2, 1871. See also "Notes of Travel in Monterey and Santa Clara Counties," *Pacific Rural Press*, November 4, 1871, and "Notes of Travel in Santa Clara County," *Pacific Rural Press*, November 25, 1871.

5. Interview with María Soto, Sunnyvale, California, May 11, 1996; Rodolfo Montalvo, "Memoir" (ms., 1938[?]), 3, in possession of Adela Montalvo, San José.

6. Charles C. Derby, "Diaries" (entry of August 10, 1923), in Derby Papers, box 1, folder 2, Bancroft Library, Mss 95/14 c. George L. Henderson, *California and the Fictions of Capital* (New York: Oxford University Press, 1999), 83. While Texas cotton workers earned approximately $1.75 per day and Arizona farmworkers made $2.75 a day, for example, residents of the San José area earned daily wages of between $2.50 and $4.00. Mario Barrera, *Race and Class in the Southwest* (Notre Dame: University of Notre Dame Press, 1979) 58–103; Montejano, *Anglos and Mexicans*, 169–174; Sánchez, *Becoming Mexican American*, 66; Camarillo, *Chicanos in a Changing Society*, 168–169. It is impossible to determine with accuracy the number of migrant Mexican Americans who passed through the Valley before World War II or to know from which states they arrived. However, naturalization records record the birthplaces of 251 local children born to Mexican immigrants during the years 1911 to 1945 and

suggest that most migrants passed through either a Southern California city, such as Los Angeles or Santa Barbara, or one of the agricultural counties in the state before arriving in the San José area. Los Angeles was the birthplace of 8 percent of the Mexican American children recorded in naturalization records, while Santa Barbara had been home to 5 percent. Nearly 34 percent had been born in Brawley, Bakersfield, Oxnard, or a similar agricultural *colonia* within the state, while 17 percent had been born in San José. Santa Clara County Petitions for Naturalization 1900–1945, 47 vols., Santa Clara Courthouse. Still, this portrait may be misleading in at least one sense. Like many local records, the available data only capture individuals in a moment of statis, documenting an immigrant community seemingly still and rooted in place. If anything, the available records documenting these migrations likely underestimated the extent of ethnic Mexicans' travels prior to their arrival in San José since those who began citizenship proceedings seem not to have been among the most transient members of working class communities.

7. *San José Mercury*, March 6, 1928; Federal Manuscript Census, 1920, Santa Clara County; interview with Ray Salazar, San José, October 22, 1995; Division of Labor Statistics and Research, *Work Injuries in Agriculture, 1950* (San Francisco: Government Printing Office, 1951), 12; Division of Labor Statistics and Research, *Work Injuries in Agriculture, 1951* (San Francisco: Government Printing Office, 1952), 5; Division of Labor Statistics and Research, *Work Injuries in Agriculture, 1957* (San Francisco: Government Printing Office, 1958), 34; Division of Labor Statistics and Research, *Work Injuries in Agriculture, 1959* (San Francisco: Government Printing Office, 1960), 32. Health records provide another indicator of the punishing nature of Latino labor. Mexicans accounted for nearly 4 percent of the patients admitted in the county hospital during the 1920s, which was more than double the percentage of Mexican residents in the entire county. George B. Margold, *Building a Better San Jose*, 105–106, 177. See the *Union Gazette*, April 3, 1938. On "common laborers," see David Montgomery, *The Fall of the House of Labor: The Workplace, the State, and American Labor Activism, 1865–1925* (New York: Cambridge University Press, 1987), 58. Mexicans inherited unskilled positions that had first been occupied by the Chinese workers who helped build San José's railroad to San Francisco in 1864. Of eight Mexican workers who applied for jobs at the New Almadén mine between 1940 and 1942, for example, only two had mining experience, while the remaining six had arrived after working elsewhere as truckers, packers, general laborers, and wood cutters. "Applications for Employment, May 30, 1940–June 19, 1942," in New Almaden Mines Collection, box 102 folder 5. See Lukes and Okihiro, *Japanese Legacy*, 12; Sucheng Chan, *This Bittersweet Soil: The Chinese in California Agriculture, 1860–1910* (Berkeley: University of California Press, 1986), 316–317. See also William S. Hallagan, "Labor Contracting in Turn-of-the-Century California Agriculture," *Journal of Economic History* 40:4 (December 1980), 757–776.

8. James and McMurry, *History of San Jose*, 132; *San Jose Letter*, May 9, 1896. Caroline M. Churchill had claimed in 1886, for instance, that "There is no country in the world where people can endure poverty as well as in this," precisely because the fruits of the land seemed always ready to be harvested. Caroline M. Churchill, *Over the Purple Hills* (Denver: Mrs. C. M. Churchill, 1884), 15. The State Department of Education found in 1928 that local schools near Mission San Jose had recently been overrun with new students due "to an influx of Portuguese and Mexican families who

work in the orchards and ranches surround[ing] Decoto." Report of the State Depart-
ment of Education, in Andrew Hill Papers, series II, box 1, folder 2: Centreville-
Washington UHS, 1933, UOP. For a useful account of European immigration to the
United States during this period, see John Higham, *Send These to Me: Immigrants in
Urban America* (Baltimore: Johns Hopkins University Press, 1984).

9. *San José Letter*, May 30, 1896. For a detailed treatment of racial thinking during
the late nineteenth and early twentieth centuries, see George Fredrickson, *The Black
Image in the White Mind* (New York: Harper & Row, 1971), 228–319. Anti-immigrant nativism receives its classic treatment in John Higham, *Strangers in the Land:
Patterns of American Nativism, 1860–1925* (New Brunswick: Rutgers University Press,
1955).

10. *San José Letter*, July 29, 1927. There are numerous examples of such racism in
the Santa Clara Valley during the late nineteenth and early twentieth centuries. The
journalist Henry Dimond remembered that the arrival of a minstrel troupe sparked
one of the city's greatest celebrations in 1889, as a brass band led the company
through the town while white residents watched with excitement. More than forty
years later, the P.T.A. of Hester School sponsored its own minstrel show to raise
money, and workers at the Kaiser Permanente factory during World War II apparently staged similar theater for their own amusement. During World War II, jobs ads
for cooks and similar positions around the Valley frequently specified "must be
white." While many did not want African Americans in their neighborhoods or
workplaces, San José residents flocked to the "Allstar Colored Floor Shows" arranged
by the Club Casablanca, which boasted performers "straight from Harlem." *San José
Magazine*, August 29, 1912; *San José Mercury*, February 27, 1930; September 23, 1936;
July 14, 1945.

11. *San José Evening News*, November 2, 1904; *Union Gazette*, July 27, 1928; Kim
Anzalone, "'From Chisler to War Work to Excess Labor?': Women's Work in the
Santa Clara Valley in the 1930s and 1940s" (M.A. thesis, San José State University,
1991), 46; Matthews, "California Middletown," 61. Lukes notes that "in demeaning
the Chinese laborers, the [old guard] were able to gain working class alliances that
defied economic rationality." Lukes, 377, 385. See also *The Comet* for white labor's
perspective on Chinese laundries in the 1880s, in particular the issues of March 13,
March 27, July 24, December 11, and December 25, 1886. On Progressivism in the
Valley, see Greenberg, "Industry in the Valley," 195–196; Valerie Ellsworth and Andrew J. Barbely, "Centralization and Efficiency: The Reformers Shape Modern San
José Government, 1910–1916," in *Businessmen and Municipal Reform: A Study in
Ideals and Practice in San Jose and Santa Cruz, 1896–1914*, ed. David W. Eakins (San
José: Sourisseau Academy for California State and Legal History, San José State Uni-
versity, 1976), 10–24. Micaela di Leonardo explores racial thinking among Italian
Americans in Northern California in *The Varieties of Ethnic Experience: Kinship, Class,
and Gender among California Italian-Americans* (Ithaca: Cornell University Press,
1984), 168–177. The classic sociological and historical literature on racialization and
"whiteness" includes David Roediger, *The Wages of Whiteness*; Michael Omi and
Howard Winant, *Racial Formation in the United States: From the 1960s to the 1980s*
(New York: Routledge Press, 1986).

12. Starr, *Endangered Dreams*, 62–63; Greenberg, "Industry in the Garden," 199.
See the annual reports of the Associated Charities of San Jose (1908, 1910–1915,

1918), in the Bancroft Library, F869 S33A6. On Filipinos and local charities, see *Union Gazette*, March 6, 1931. The participation of more than four hundred Italian fruit workers in a local agricultural union in 1917 likely paved the way for Italian participation in the labor movement. See Greenberg, "Industry in the Garden," 203. The Native Sons of the Golden West in the county fought the Italian political machine in the early twentieth century, but as the *San José Letter* had noted in the 1890s, hostility toward European immigrants was somewhat muted because many of the region's "old settlers" surviving into that period were also Roman Catholics. See *San José Letter*, January 25, 1896; Glenna Matthews, "The Community Study: Ethnicity and Success in San José," *Journal of Interdisciplinary History* 7:2 (Summer 1976), 318. By the early twentieth century, the presence of European immigrants became a selling point for Valley boosters. See James A. Clayton, *San Jose and Santa Clara County, California* (San Jose: James Clayton, n.d.), in Bancroft Library; Pioneers Sons and Daughters, *California: The Empire Beautiful, Her Great Bays, Harbors, Mines, Orchards and Vineyards, Olive, Lemon and Orange Groves, Her Men and Women, A Prophecy of the Coming Race* (San Francisco: Pacific Press Publishing, 1899), 8.

    13. *Union Journal of Santa Clara County*, September 18, 1925; *San José Mercury*, March 19, 1930; March 23, 1930. See also Mark Reisler, "Always the Laborer, Never the Citizen: Anglo Perceptions of the Mexican Immigrant during the 1920s," *Pacific Historical Review* 45:2 (May 1976), 231–254; Mark Reisler, *By the Sweat of Their Brow: Mexican Immigrant Labor in the United States, 1900–1940*; Taylor, *Mexican Labor in the United States*; Barrera, *Race and Class in the Southwest*, 76–91; David Montejano, *Anglos and Mexicans*, 101–178. Local growers who favored the arrival of Mexican workers warned county residents that, if Congress restricted immigration from Latin America, "twenty thousand negroes from the southern states" would soon arrive to fill the jobs currently being taken by Mexicans. *San José Mercury*, February 16, 1928, and February 2, 1930. The pioneering journalist Carey McWilliams of course coined the term "factories in the field." See Carey McWilliams, *Factories in the Field: The Story of Migratory Farm Labor in California* (Boston: Little, Brown, 1939). The formation of Mexican communities in Orange County agribusiness is described in Gilbert G. González, *Labor and Community: Mexican Citrus Worker Villages in a Southern California County, 1900–1950* (Urbana: University of Illinois Press, 1994).

    14. *San José Mercury*, April 29, June 10, August 27, and October 14, 1927; April 28, July 2 and 17, 1928. Other wealthy residents of the Valley shared this concern, and when Bernice Downing of Santa Clara returned from a trip to Latin America with stories of Mexico's poverty, she announced to the Pen Women's meeting that "the peons must be made to value time if the country is to progress." Ibid., February 2, 1930.

    15. *Union Gazette*, December 18, 1925; October 22, 1926; August 22, 1930; *San José Mercury*, May 28, 1927. San José labor officials worried openly about employers developing an "American Plan" like the one already in place in Los Angeles. The *Union Gazette* in 1926 characteristically accused employers of using Mexican peons to create "China conditions" in San José, an effort that contradicted the AFL's longstanding desire to work cooperatively with local growers and other employers. Local workers clearly felt that they were in danger of being overrun by nonwhites from around the world. In 1931 a labor journalist wrote that "as to [the term] 'American Plan,' the word 'American' can be applied to any people or place on the American

continent be it Esquimo [sic], Mexican, or semi-skilled patagonian." See *Union Ga-*
zette, December 31 and February 13, 1931. On the efforts of the AFL to discourage
strikes and work cooperatively with local business leaders, see ibid., February 28,
1930 and March 18, 1932; Matthews, "A California Middletown," 209–210. On the
"American Plan" in San José, see Matthews, "A California Middletown," 22; Irving
Bernstein, *The Lean Years: A History of the American Worker, 1920–1933* (Boston:
Houghton Mifflin, 1960). While such anger at the arrival of Mexicans seems to have
been the typical response of San José residents in the late 1920s, others in the city did
accept the presence of Mexicans in the city and hoped to "Americanize" them. Native-born women taught "American cooking methods" to Mexican women in the
evenings at Longfellow School in February 1928, for instance. *San José Mercury*, February 6, 1928. In the view of the *Mercury News*, the shocking infant mortality rates in
Southern California barrios and *colonias* provided yet another reason to hope that
Mexican workers would not introduce social problems related to "ignorance, lack of
cleanliness, care and proper feeding" of their children into the Santa Clara Valley. See
the comments of Walter M. Dickle, head of California's Department of Public Health,
in the *San José Mercury*, January 27 and June 22, 1928; November 14, 1929; March
15, 1930. General studies of immigration during this period include George C. Kiser,
"Mexican American Labor before World War II," *The Journal of Mexican American
History* 2 (Spring 1972), 122–142; Lawrence A. Cardoso, *Mexican Emigration to the
United States, 1897–1931* (Tucson: University of Arizona Press, 1980), 38–54.

16. *Union Gazette*, August 29 and October 31, 1930; Dewey Anderson, *Always to
Start Anew* (New York: Vantage Press, 1970), 25. During one organizing drive later in
the decade, AFL organizers would complain of "coolie wages" in local agriculture.
Union Gazette, August 19, 1938. Others, such as San José Central Labor Council
official F. M. Vermillion, blamed the presence of Asians in California on the expul-
sion of the Chinese from Mexico, thereby arguing that an unmonitored U.S.-Mexico
border presented residents with both illegal Mexicans and Chinese "aliens." Ibid.,
May 9 and August 15, 1930; February 28, 1934; January 4, 18, and 25, 1935; February
1 and 22, 1935; May 1, 1936; August 17, 1937; and January 26, 1940. San José residents followed the lead of California State Attorney General Ulysses Webb, who in
1930 announced that "It is well known that the greater part of the population of
Mexico are Indians and when such Indians emigrate [sic] to the United States they are
subject to the laws applicable generally to other Indians." Ibid., January 25, 1930.
These ideas can also be traced throughout the 1930s. See ibid., February 28 and
March 21, 1930; October 26, 1934; and November 2, 9, and 23, 1934. George J.
Sánchez has noted that early concerns about an open U.S.-Mexico border often fo-
cused on the ease with which Chinese immigrants might be able to cross into the
United States. Sánchez, *Becoming Mexican American*, 50–51.

17. *Union Gazette*, May 6 and 20, 1931; *Hispano-America* (San Francisco), August
2, 1932. The canning industry developed after 1900 thanks to the Italian and other
European immigrant women willing to cut and pack local produce on a seasonal
basis. The canneries employed, for instance, 46 percent of San José's entire workforce
during 1905. Donald Anthony found that workers from Italy and Portugal constituted 71 percent of the cannery workforce by 1928. Greenberg, "Industry in the
Garden," 110, 126; Department of Commerce, *Population: 1920, Occupations* (Washington, D.C.: Department of Commerce, 1923), 313; Department of Commerce,

Census of Manufactures, 1905: California, Oregon, and Washington, Bulletin 49 (Washington, D.C.: Government Printing Office, 1906), 32; Department of Commerce, Table 8, "Wage Earners, By Months," *United States Census of Agriculture, 1925. Report for States, Part III, Western States* (Washington, D.C.: Government Printing Office, 1927), 87; Donald Anthony, "Labor Conditions in the Canning Industry in the Santa Clara Valley of the State of California" (Ph.D. dissertation, Stanford University, 1928), 18; Governor C. C. Young's Fact-Finding Committee, *Mexicans in California* (San Francisco: R and E Research Associates, 1970). The industry boomed and in 1945 Santa Clara County workers canned nearly 45,000 tons of bartlett pears, more than a third of the entire volume produced in California during that year. *California Canning Bartlett Pear Statistics, 1938–1947 Inclusive* (Sacramento: California State Department of Agriculture, 1947), 4. Men and women's work inside the canneries remained strictly segregated, as historians Vicki Ruíz and Kim Anzalone have shown. By early 1942, only 60 percent of union contracts in local canneries guaranteed that men and women received comparable pay. See Vickie L. Ruiz, *Cannery Women, Cannery Lives: Mexican Women, Unionization, and the California Food Processing Industry, 1930–1950* (Albuquerque: University of New Mexico Press, 1987); Anzalone, "'From Chisler to War Work to Excess Labor,'" 37–39, 42; *San José Mercury*, February 2, 1942. For a description of the different jobs assigned men and women in peach processing, see *San José Mercury*, May 1, 1919; July 19, 1945. In 1930, again, the courts in Santa Clara County discouraged ethnic Mexican residency. Judge Percy O'Connor gave the arrested "vagrants" F. Coronel, Frank Perez, and Joe Casas suspended sentences of 180 days "with the provision they leave San José." *San José Mercury*, February 25, 1930. In 1924 the grand jury had recommended deportation of immigrants who twice violated the Volstead Act and other antiliquor laws. *San José Mercury*, December 19, 1924. On efforts to discourage the migration of "transients" to the Santa Clara Valley, see George B. Margold, *Building a Better San Jose* (pamphlet, Board of Supervisors and Community Chest, 1930), 40–41.

18. Anderson, *Always to Start Anew*, 25; *San José Mercury*, January 21 and March 4, 1928; *Union Gazette*, August 29, 1930. The AFL in San José frequently worried about left-wing radicalism as well. In 1927 a local official counseled union leaders to monitor "Bolsheys . . . wild men who whine for free speech as an excuse to bore from within." *Union Gazette*, February 11, 1930. See also ibid., February 6, 1931.

19. "The Spread of San Francisco," *Sunset* (September 1907), 440, 446; "Racial Prejudices in San José, California, as observed by a College Class in Race Relations," (ms., San José State University, 1948), in Stanford University Library.

20. Federal Manuscript Census, 1910, Santa Clara County; José Antonio Villarreal, *Pocho* (New York: Doubleday Press, 1959), 42; *Fresno Republican*, July 13, 1920.

21. Interview with Joaquin Andrade, San José, November 5, 1995.

22. These San Francisco organizations included the Pacific Woodcutters' Association, the Peruvian Mutual Auxiliary, and groups such as the Alliance of Mutual Auxiliaries and the Chapultepec Mexican Mutualista (mutual aid organization). Five additional Latin American clubs had become active in San Francisco by 1933 as well, including the Club Azteca de Señoras, the Alianza Hispano-Americana, and the Cruz Azul Mexicana, while Oakland's Mexican residents participated in their own Club Ignacio Zaragoza and in a branch of the Alianza Hispano-Americana. San Francisco and Oakland organizations received assistance from the Mexican Consulate in San

Francisco, an established group of Mexican businessmen who wanted to promote trade between the United States and Latin America, and from Mexican workers' associations that had developed at industrial job sites. See, for example, the list of local organizations in *Hispano-America*, April 15, 1933, and the patriotic activities of Victoria Mugarrieta de Shadburn, the daughter of the former consul in San Francisco, in *Hispano-America*, February 4, 1933. Some also settled in the Gardner district, home of immigrants seeking cannery work since the early twentieth century. Matthews, "A California Middletown," 58–60.

23. Armand J. Sánchez and Ronald M. Wagner, "Continuity and Change in the Mayfair Barrios of East San José," *San José Studies* 5:2 (May 1979), 9.

24. *San José Mercury*, January 4, 1981; interview with Nellie Hurtado, San José, April 11, 1996; Jacques E. Levy, *César Chávez: Autobiography of La Causa* (New York, W.W. Norton, 1975), 50. For a vivid illustration of the East Side's ongoing rural character, see the map in Santa Clara County Planning Department, *Eastside Interim General Plan* (Santa Clara County Planning Department pamphlet, 1956), in the "East Side" file, California Room, Martin Luther King, Jr. Public Library, San José.

25. *San José Mercury*, May 16, 1940; Camarillo, *Chicanos in a Changing Society*, 53–78; Menchaca, *The Mexican Outsiders*, 26. As a result of these early patterns of racial discrimination in housing, the largest number of Mexicans would live on the East Side after World War II, although new migrants in the 1940s and 1950s also settled in other areas of the city. By the mid-1960s nine other cities in the state were more segregated than San José, according to UCLA researchers. U.S. Commission on Civil Rights, "The Spanish-American Community of the San Francisco Bay Area" (unpublished staff report to the commissioners, April 28, 1967), 19, in Ernesto Galarza Papers, box 15, folder 9, Special Collections, Green Library, Stanford University; Nancy LaNelle Geilhufe, "Ethnic Relations in San José: A Study of Police-Chicano Interaction" (Ph.D. dissertation, Stanford University, 1972), 42.

26. Sánchez and Wagner, "Continuity and Change," 12–13. Many Eastsiders did park their vehicles on Jackson, the best street in the area, and walked to their homes in the hope that they would be able to drive away again when the next rains hit. César Chávez remembers that when they first arrived in the area, workers were returning to their homes after shifts at the Mayfair Packing Company, and "my mother asked the ladies where there was a house or a place or a room where we could stay the night. Our two cars, loaded with mattresses, baggage, and kids, told everyone a familiar story. But the answer was always the same. They were too crowded. There was no room." Levy, *César Chávez*, 51; interview with Herman Gallegos, Stanford, May 3, 1996; Hurtado interview, April 11, 1996; *San José Mercury*, April 30, 1993. José Villarreal remembers that the practice of pitching tents in residents' backyards was common during this period among the small group of Mexicans living in the adjacent town of Santa Clara as well. See José Antonio Villarreal, *Pocho* (Garden City: Doubleday, 1959), 43.

27. Hurtado interview, April 11, 1996.

28. Interview with Dolores Andrade, San José, October 17, 1996. The cases of 563 Mexican immigrants and their families are recorded in local naturalization proceedings before World War II. "Santa Clara County Petitions for Naturalization 1900–

1945," 47 vols., Santa Clara Courthouse. For a similar account of Mexican intrana-
tional migrations before crossing the border into the United States, see Sánchez, *Becoming Mexican American*, 17–29.

29. Sánchez, *Becoming Mexican American*, 49–62.

30. Herrera-Sobek, *Northward Bound*, 102.

31. Interview with Lorena Castillo, Santa Clara, October 2, 1996; Rudy Calles,
Champion Prune Pickers: Migrant Worker's Dilemma (Los Alamitos, CA: Hwong Publishing Company, 1979); interviews with Eulalio Gutiérrez, San José, March 12, 1995;
María Santana, Santa Clara, May 8, 1995; José Aldama, San José, October 5, 1996. See
also Father Donald McDonnell, "Report on 1950," in Donald McDonnell Papers, box
2, "Reports: Missionary Apostalate," Chancery Archives, Archdiocese of San Francisco, Menlo Park California. In his pioneering studies of Mexican migration during
the 1920s, Manuel Gamio noted that immigrants sent wages earned in distant parts of
the United States back to Mexican towns and home communities. See Gamio, *Mexican Immigration*, 13–28. A few other studies examine the migrations of South Texas
Mexicans to other regions of the United States, an important development in Mexican American history after 1920. See, for instance, Zaragosa Vargas, *Proletarians of the
North: A History of Mexican Industrial Workers in Detroit and the Midwest, 1917–1933*
(Berkeley: University of California Press, 1993); Dennis Noldin Valdés, *Al Norte: Agri-
cultural Workers in the Great Lakes Region, 1917–1970* (Austin: University of Texas
Press, 1991); Niles M. Hansen and William C. Gruben, "The Influence of Relative
Wages and Assisted Migration on Locational Preferences: Mexican Americans in
South Texas," *Social Science Quarterly* 52:1 (June 1971), 103–114.

32. Santa Clara County Petitions for Naturalization 1900–1945.

33. Ibid.

34. Andrade interview, October 17, 1996.

35. Santa Clara County Petitions for Naturalization 1900–1945.

36. Interview with Ray Salazar, San José, October 22, 1995. Anthony Soto, "History of Our Lady of Guadalupe Parish" (ms., n.d.), in Anthony Soto Papers (un-
processed papers), Special Collections, Green Library, Stanford University, box 2.
Mexican-born Pedro Vandanos arrived in San José with his family in July 1928 from
Tulare in California's Central Valley. Living in tents, Vandanos and Osuna built the
Mexican Pentecostal Church in June with adobe bricks. *San José Mercury*, June 20 and
22, 1929. Some migrants of that area felt well treated by other Catholic immigrants.
Rudy Calles remembers that Portuguese Catholics at Holy Family Church treated his
family well when they arrived from Southern California to work in local orchards
each summer during the late 1920s. "The Portuguese families we met there were kind
and friendly," he later recalled. Calles, *Champion Prune Pickers*, 45.

37. Interviews with Ray Salazar, October 22, 1995; Estela Ramírez, San José, November 3, 1995; Lydia Ramírez, May 9, 1995; Dolores Andrade, San José, October 17,
1996.

38. Interviews with Andrade, October 17, 1996; José Aldama, San José, October 5,
1996. Gamio is quoted in Sánchez, *Becoming Mexican American*, 85.

39. Groups such as the Pioneers' Society and the Native Sons and Native Daughters of the Golden West had emphasized California's romantic history for decades. At
the Panama-Pacific celebration in October 1915, thirty-three San José residents had

helped organize a "Pioneer Day," which residents of the state who had arrived in the years immediately following the Mexican War were invited to attend. Valley residents such as E. M. McCracken, "the first American woman married in San José," and Charles C. Reed, "the first American child born in San José," stood before a large crowd at the San Francisco exhibition to inform the audience about the early years of California statehood. Mrs. George J. Bucknall, president of the Women's Auxiliary of the Pioneers' Society and the self-proclaimed "first child born of Anglo-Saxon parentage in San Francisco," announced at the San Francisco celebration that "the story of the Santa Clara Valley reads like some romance of a world far beyond the seas; yet that life was lived, and not so long ago but that here and there a faint trace of it remains." *A Souvenir of Pioneer and Old Settlers' Day, Panama Pacific Exposition* (pamphlet, n.d.), 49–50, 75–80. Local unionists also celebrated the history of California's nineteenth-century pioneers during the 1920s, and AFL member wrote confidently in the midst of the San Francisco General Strike that "the blood of Daniel Boone, Abraham Lincoln, Buffalo Bill still races through the veins of many Americans." *Union Gazette*, February 24, 1933; July 20, 1934. On Bayard Taylor, see James and McMurry, "History of San José," 132, as well as the comments by San José Chamber of Commerce President A. M. Mortensen in the *San José Mercury*, May 18, 1930.

40. *San Francisco Bulletin*, June 9, 1901; *San Jose Mercury*, April 5, 1932; July 17, 1939; and September 15, 1940. See also Peter T. Conmy, "Historical Development of San José, The Native Sons' 1938 Parlor City," *The Grizzly Bear* (May 1938), 6. Other parts of the state had celebrated their Spanish roots since the publication of Helen Hunt Jackson's *Ramona* in 1881, and many cities and railroads had called upon romantic descriptions of "California before the gringos" to promote tourism. Unlike other California missions, which had been abandoned, torn down, vandalized, or neglected in the years after 1848, Mission Santa Clara had remained in nearly constant use on the campus of Santa Clara College, founded by the Jesuit Order in 1851. McWilliams, *North from Mexico*, 35–47; Starr, *Americans and the California Dream*.

41. The pageant also included "faithful Indians" who recited hymns and prayers in Latin, and the festivities portrayed the peaceful conversion of local native people by performing the "miracle" of bringing rain to local crops. As the mission bell rang, the first act concluded with neophytes "rais[ing] their arms in thanksgiving and praise" and falling to the ground while the curtain fell. *San Francisco Chronicle*, April 20, 1915.

42. *San José Mercury*, May 6, 1927; *Union Gazette*, May 12 and May 19, 1927.

43. The Chamber of Commerce and local labor unions also intended the Fiesta celebrations to attract tourism and new industries to the Valley. *Souvenir of the First Annual Santa Clara Valley Fiesta de las Rosas* (San José: Hillis-Murgotten, 1926), 2–3, in the California Room, Martin Luther King Public Library, San José; *Souvenir of the Santa Clara County Fourth Annual Fiesta de las Rosas, 1929* (San José: Hillis-Murgotten, 1929), in the California Room, Martin Luther King Public Library, San José; *Union Gazette*, May 24, 1930. On the beauty contests, see *San José Mercury*, May 16, 1928; January 8, 1929; January 19 and May 4 and 18, 1930. Concerning film, the *Union Gazette* praised *Senior Americano*, for example, because it "depict[ed] a festival of the colorful type peculiar to California in the days of the Spanish occupation."

Union Gazette, January 5, 1930. See also *Union Gazette,* May 13,1927; May 4, 1928; May 24, 1929.

44. *Union Gazette,* May 13, 1927; May 19, 1928; May 17, 1929.

45. *Souvenir of the Santa Clara County Fourth Annual Fiesta de las Rosas, 1929; In the Valley of Heart's Delight, San Jose/Santa Clara County, California* [Souvenir Program of the Fiesta de las Rosas, 1931] (San José: Hillis-Murgotten, 1931), 8; *Seventh Annual Fiesta de las Rosas of Santa Clara County, San Jose, California, May 21, 1932* (San José: Hillis-Murgotten, 1932), 1; *San José Mercury,* May 19, 1929. Thanks to a boost from the Good Neighbor Policy, the Lindemann sisters went on to perform frequently at local graduation exercises and other community events during the 1940s. *San José Mercury,* June 6, 1943. Boosters also stressed that European immigrants could find a usable past in local history before California's statehood. San José Chamber of Commerce in 1938 thus reminded residents that "although Spaniards had been in control of the community until 1848, men of other nationalities had settled in the Santa Clara Valley many years before that time." San José Chamber of Commerce, "History of San José" (mimeographed promotional pamphlet, 1938). Although most of the men and women who envisioned and planned the Fiestas were native San Joseans descended from some of the more established families in the area, Italian Americans such as Harry Canelo, A. Forni, F. G. Canelo, and Louis Cavala were involved in organizing the celebration in 1926. *Souvenir of the First Annual Santa Clara Valley Fiesta de las Rosas, 1926,* 3.

46. *Union Gazette,* August 20, 1937; interviews with Ray Salazar, October 22, 1995; María Soto, May 11, 1995. Workers at the Kaiser Permanente plant in Los Altos held a Fiesta de Permanente in 1944 to maintain high morale among workers and raise money for the U.S.O. during the war. Mrs. Fremont Older, who helped create the Fiesta de las Rosas in 1925, continued to sponsor "California Fiestas" at her Woodhills Estate home during the war, inviting guests to arrive in the costumes of "old California." Diverse groups of Italian, Portuguese, and native-born women gathered in local women's clubs during the war for "Spanish teas," which sought to replicate the "enchanting atmosphere of Spain," and the city's Pioneer Society organized to erect plaques memorializing the homes of the area's first "white" residents. During the 1940s the county recorder, local historian Clyde Arbuckle, and others promoted greater awareness of the region's Spanish past as a way of forging national solidarity around the war effort, and "old settlers picnics" continued to draw crowds and the attention of the local press. *San José Mercury,* July 13, 23, and 30, 1944; August 2, 1945; August 4 and 5, 1946; January 5, 1947. City and county officials even made references to the Spanish fantasy during World War II to alert white residents about the dangers of Japanese submarines thought to be patrolling in San Francisco Bay and of Japanese Americans who seemed to constitute a national security threat. Reporting about "rangers in our county defense organization," the *San José Mercury* in 1942 drew parallels to distant Spanish military efforts to capture the Indian rebel Estanislao in the early nineteenth century. *San José Mercury,* March 22, 1942. City officials attempted in 1955 to revive the Fiesta de las Rosas celebrations that had been so popular during the late 1920s and early 1930s, but the new Fiesta de San José, "based on our Pioneer Spanish History," survived for only one year. *Santa Clara County Employee* 7:5 (May 1955), 8.

Chapter 5
Striking Identities

1. *New York Times,* November 28, 1933; *San José Mercury Herald,* November 28, 1933; *San Francisco Chronicle,* November 27, 1933; interviews with Cecilia Romero, Santa Clara, June 11, 1996; Joaquín Andrade, San José, November 5, 1995; Brian McGinty, "Shadows in St. James Park," *California Historical Society Quarterly* 57:4 (1978–1979), 290–307.

2. Alessandro Portelli, *The Death of Luigi Trastulli and Other Stories* (Albany: State University of New York, 1991), 26.

3. Interviews with Romero, June 11, 1996; Ana Ortega, San José, December 2, 1996.

4. Ortega interview, December 2, 1996; Devra Weber, *Dark Sweat, White Gold: California Farm Workers, Cotton, and the New Deal* (Berkeley: University of California Press, 1993), 10; Hernández, *Mutual Aid for Survival;* Gutiérrez, *Walls and Mirrors,* 95–99; Zamora, *The World of the Mexican Worker,* 86–109.

5. Rodolfo Montalvo, "Memoir," 7; Eulalio Gutiérrez interview, March 12, 1995.

6. Gutiérrez interview, March 12, 1995. The importance of Mexican immigrants' regional identities are noted in Sánchez, *Becoming Mexican American,* 108–125; and Gamio, *Mexican Immigration to the United States,* 13–29.

7. Interview with Manuel Ramírez, San José, June 9, 1996.

8. Interviews with María Santana, Santa Clara, May 8, 1995; Federico Garza, San José, June 28, 1995; Frances Maldonado, San José, September 3, 1995; Manuel Ramírez, San José, June 9, 1996; Harry Ramírez, San José, February 3, 1995; Salazar, October 22, 1995; *Hispano-America,* November 4, 1933.

9. Interviews with Maldonado, September 3, 1995; Santana, September 8, 1995; Manuel Ramírez, June 9, 1996.

10. Interviews with Santana, May 8, 1995; Garza, June 28, 1995; Anzalone, "'From Chisler to War Work to Excess Labor,'" 81; *Hispano-America,* March 7 and April 11, 1931.

11. Interviews with Lydia Ramírez, San José, May 9, 1995; Garza, June 26, 1995; Luz Rendón, San José, April 1, 1996; Federico Garza, Santa Clara, June 26, 1995; *Hispano-America,* August 10, 1931. For an account of these departures in the East Bay, see *The Martinez Gazette,* October 13, 1931. On repatriation and deportation in Southern California, see Abraham Hoffman, *Unwanted Mexican Americans in the Great Depression: Repatriation Pressures, 1929–1939* (Tucson: University of Arizona Press, 1974); Sánchez, *Becoming Mexican American,* 209–226.

12. Interviews with Lydia Ramírez, San José, May 9, 1995; Rendón, April 1, 1996. The San José resident Salvador Gascon remembered that his father, a U.S. citizen, had been deported in the 1930s but returned to the United States with his family in the 1950s. Interview with Salvador Gascon, March 29, 1989, in Chicano Studies Resource Library, SJSU.

13. Sánchez, *Becoming Mexican American,* 228; Rodolfo Montalvo, "Memoir," 8; María Santana interview, May 8, 1995.

14. Of the sixty-eight Mexican families described in county naturalization records during the 1930s, almost a third included children born on both sides of the interna-

tional border. The 1920 manuscript census recorded that 81 percent of the U.S.-born Mexican Americans in the county had at least one parent born in Mexico. Federal Manuscript Census, 1920, Santa Clara County. Of the 428 marriages of Mexicans in the county in 1930, 1935, and 1941, respectively, 46 percent (or 201) involved a U.S. and a Mexican citizen. Santa Clara County Marriage Records, 1930, 1935, and 1940, in the Office of the Santa Clara County Recorder, San José, California. Interview with Luz Rendón, San José, April 1, 1996. The assumption that the 1930s witnessed the emergence of a "Mexican American generation" intent on achieving their rights as American citizens dominates studies such as Mario García, *Mexican Americans* (New Haven: Yale University Press, 1989); Richard García, "The Making of the Mexican American Mind," in *History, Culture and Society: Chicano Studies in the 1980s* (Ypsilanti, MI: Bilingual Press, 1983), 67–93; Sánchez, *Becoming Mexican American.*

15. Santa Clara County Petitions for Naturalization 1900–1945, 47 vols., Santa Clara Courthouse; interviews with Salazar, October 22, 1995; Ortega, December 2, 1996. A 1927 study found that Mexicans had the lowest percentage of any "white" foreign-born group in the United States. See Niles Carpenter, *Immigrants and Their Children, 1920* (Washington, D.C.: Government Printing Office, 1927), 263. On the New Deal and farm workers, see the excellent discussion in Weber, *Dark Sweat, White Gold*, 112–136; and the essays in Steven Fraser and Gary Gerstle, *The Rise and Fall of the New Deal Order, 1930–1980* (Princeton: Princeton University Press, 1989).

16. Interviews with Eulalio Gutiérrez, March 12, 1995; Sofia Mendoza, March 2, 1988, 3, transcript in Chicano Studies Library, San José State University; *Fresno Morning Republican*, February 12, 1917.

17. *The Agricultural Worker* (Official Organ of the CAWIU, San José), December 20, 1933. CAWIU organizers struggled against a climate of AFL hostility. In 1935 Paul Scharrenberg of the California State American Federation of Labor made clear his organization's disinterest in field workers by asserting that "only fanatics" attempted to organize those laborers. *New York Times*, January 20, 1935. Dorothy Healey and Maurice Isserman, *Dorothy Healey Remembers a Life in the American Communist Party* (New York: Oxford University Press, 1990); Daniel, *Bitter Harvest*, 105–140.

18. Calles, *Champion Prune Pickers*, 22–23; interviews with Salazar, October 22, 1995; Ortega, December 2, 1996; Santana, May 8, 1995.

19. James C. Scott, *Weapons of the Weak: Everyday Forms of Peasant* Resistance (New Haven: Yale University Press, 1985); interview with Ray Morelos, Santa Clara, August 2, 1996. Mary Contreras adds that "I'll tell you who were saying the most things for the Mexican people working on the farms back then. It was the Communists. I never wanted to join and didn't really know many who did, but they made a lot of sense to my family." Interview with Mary Contreras, San José, May 8, 1995; Villarreal, *Pocho*, 55–56; Manuel Ramírez interview, November 3, 1995; *Lucha Obrera* (San Francisco), March 1934. See also James Gray, "The American Civil Liberties Union of Southern California and Imperial Valley and Agricultural Labor Disturbances, 1930–1934" (Ph.D. dissertation, University of California, Los Angeles, 1966).

20. *Union Gazette*, March 23, May 4, August 10, August 17, and October 26, 1934; September 25 and October 9, 1936; *San Francisco Examiner*, April 7, 1936; interview with María Velásquez, San José, December 17, 1995; Derby, "Diaries," July 31–August 1, 1931, in Derby Papers, box 1, folder 9.

21. *Union Gazette*, October 26, 1934; *Oakland Tribune*, April 19, 1933.

22. *Hispano-America,* June 23, 1933; *Agricultural Worker,* February 20, 1934; interview with Lydia Ramírez, San José, May 9, 1995. For labor recruiters looking for "Mexican families" in Santa Clara County, see *San José Mercury,* April 19, 1929; Manuel Ramírez interview, June 12, 1996; *Union Gazette,* March 5 and 19, 1937; *Mefistófeles* (San Francisco), March 23, 1918, See the discussion of unionization in the 1930s in Chris Friday, *Organizing Asian American Labor: The Pacific Coast Canned-Salmon Industry, 1870–1942* (Philadelphia: Temple University Press, 1990).

23. Gutiérrez interview, March 12, 1995; *Lucha Obrera,* June 1934. For coverage of a similar strike, see *Union Gazette,* August 18, 1933. See Weber, *Dark Sweat, White Gold,* 79–111; and Daniel, *Bitter Harvest,* 141–221, on the strikes of 1933 and 1934.

24. Manuel Ramírez interview, November 3, 1995; Weber, *Dark Sweat, White Gold,* 79–136; Daniel, *Bitter Harvest,* 249–57. The *San José Mercury* approved of these anti-union activities by local police and vigilantes. Christensen et al., *Reflections of the Past,* 164; *Union Gazette,* December 2, 1938; December 22, 1939; *UCAPAWA News,* December 1939.

25. Montalvo, *Memoir,* 15; Gutiérrez interview, March 12, 1995.

26. Studies of UCAPAWA include Ruiz, *Cannery Women, Cannery Lives*; Weber, *Dark Sweat, White Gold,* 164–199; Gutiérrez, *Walls and Mirrors,* 110–175; Camarillo, *Chicanos in California,* 56–57; García, *Mexican Americans,* 145–174. For an excellent survey of left-union politics during this period, see Robert H. Zieger, *The CIO: 1935–1955* (Chapel Hill: University of North Carolina Press, 1995). Shevlin's interest in a CIO charter for his union increased when AFL locals and San Francisco-based Teamsters made new efforts to organize cannery and field workers in Northern California after early 1937. Manuel Ramírez interview, June 9, 1996; *Union Gazette,* May 17 and November 1, 1935; and March 5, 1937.

27. Quoted in *UCAPAWA News,* December 1939. See also *UCAPAWA News,* July 1939.

28. Interviews with Leo Vargas, San José, March 8, 1995; Manuel Ramírez, June 9, 1996; Santana, May 8, 1995.

29. Gutiérrez interview, March 12, 1995; Ruiz, *Cannery Women, Cannery Lives.*

30. *Union Gazette,* June 18, June 4, and December "Yearbook," 1937; January 21, 1938; April 18, 1941; *UCAPAWA News,* July 1939; interviews with María Velásquez, San José, December 17, 1995; Manuel Ramírez, June 9, 1996.

31. Vargas interview, March 8, 1995; *Proceedings of the 16th Convention of the International Brotherhood of Teamsters, October 13–17, 1954* (New York, 1955), 94; Gutiérrez, *Walls and Mirrors,* 110; Manuel Ramírez interview, June 9, 1996; *UCAPAWA News,* July–August 1940; November 15, 1942.

32. Interviews with Vargas, March 1 and March 8, 1995; Manuel Ramírez, June 9, 1996. In California's Central Valley, as well, UCAPAWA organizers lobbied government officials to address local discrimination. The union local in Shafter attempted to persuade post office employees to remove a sign at their delivery window that read "L to Z and Mexicans," while Local 254 in Fresno protested the segregation of African Americans in the U.S. Armed Forces, for example. See *UCAPAWA News,* July 1939; December 1939; February 23, 1942.

33. Interviews with Salazar, October 22, 1995; Lydia Ramírez, May 9, 1995; Rendón, April 1, 1996. On the Mexican consulate and labor issues during the 1930s, see Francisco Balderrama, *In Defense of La Raza: The Los Angeles Mexican Consulate and*

the Mexican Community (Tucson: University of Arizona Press, 1982), chap. 6, and Gilbert González, *Mexican Consuls and Labor Organizing: Imperial Politics in the American Southwest* (Austin: University of Texas Press, 1999). Similar union organizing also occurred in other locales on the *fiestas patrias*. In 1942 a group of Mathis, Texas, spinach workers in UCAPAWA Local 87 sponsored a Cinco de Mayo celebration, the first in that area since 1918. *UCAPAWA News*, May 28, 1942.

34. See, for example, *Semanario Imparcial* (San Francisco), September 24, 1938; *UCAPAWA News*, February 1943; March 1943; *F.T.A. News*, January 15, 1945.

35. Leo Vargas recalled that UCAPAWA members "went to the San Francisco office two times. Both times the man in charge turned us right away when we started talking about cops beating people up in Santa Clara County and about living conditions around [the] Mayfair [district]. The Mexican government didn't want to hear it." Vargas interview, March 8, 1995. Ramírez remembers that union officials in the 1930s and 1940s used the phrase "sentimental patriotism" to refer to Mexican nationalism that seemed unconnected, or antithetical, to labor organizing. Manuel Ramírez interview, June 12, 1996. *Lucha Obrera*, January 1935.

36. *La Prensa de Hoy*, August 26, 1940. On "working-class Americanism," see Gary Gerstle, *Working-Class Americanism: The Politics of Labor in a Textile City, 1914–1960* (New York: Cambridge University Press, 1989).

37. *UCAPAWA News*, March 1, 1942.

38. *San José Mercury*, April 25, 1941. *Union Gazette*, May 25, 1941; May 28, 1943. See Anzalone, "'From Chisler to War Work to Excess Labor,'" 54–55; San José Chamber of Commerce, *San José Data Sheet* (ms., 1949), in California Room, Martin Luther King, Jr. Public Library, San José. On the "second Gold Rush," see Marilynn S. Johnson, *The Second Gold Rush: Oakland and the East Bay in World War II* (Berkeley: University of California Press, 1993).

39. *Union Gazette*, March 20 and 27, 1942. U.S. Employment Service officials found that most returning veterans avoided the cannery jobs that they had held before entering the armed services, preferring instead to move into new industrial employment. *San José Mercury*, July 6, 1944; "Final Disposition Report, Ship Service Laundry," and "Final Disposition Report, Eckham Seed Company," October 4, 1944, and February 16, 1945, in FEPC records; *Union Gazette*, December 19, 1941; January 9 and March 27, 1942; "Racial Prejudices in San José, California," 13.

40. *Union Gazette*, May 7, April 30, and June 11, 1943; January 21, 1944.

41. *With the Mexican Laborers in the United States: Address Delivered on May 13 in the City of San José, California* (Mexico City: Department of Foreign Affairs, 1945), 3, 7; *Report of Activities of the California Farm Production Council* (Sacramento: Farm Production Council, 1945); *San José Mercury*, June 5 and August 10, 1943; May 4, June 21, and July 7, 1944.

42. *San José Mercury*, June 5, August 10, and August 21, 1943; June 21, July 7, July 8, and August 10, 1944.

43. *San José Mercury*, August 21, 1943; May 30, July 22, August 7, and August 10, 1944; *Union Gazette*, January 14, 1944.

44. Vargas interview, March 8, 1995; *UCAPAWA News*, February 23 and November 15, 1942; *Union Gazette*, May 21, 1943; *FTA News*, May 15, 1945. In a parable about the power of organized labor, unionists in Santa Cruz and Santa Clara counties also told the story of the muleskinner "Rastus Sambo Smith," a rough Southern type

who knew the power of a union. When his boss urged Rastus to take his whip to a nearby hornet's nest, Smith refused because "Them hornets is organized!" *Union Gazette*, February 16, 1940. Whites working at the Hendy machine plant in the county donned blackface and performed their own minstrel show to benefit the USO in 1942. *Union Gazette*, September 18, 1942. Teamsters in nearby Redwood City emphasized that wise African Americans would not cross picket lines or compete with union workers. According to union members, when a group of white Teamsters encountered a group of nonunion truckers, an African American resident left shaking his head. "White boy sure put me out of business in a hurry!" it was said he told onlookers. *Union Gazette*, April 11, 1941.

45. Patricia Zavella, *Women's Work and Chicano Families: Cannery Workers of the Santa Clara Valley* (Ithaca: Cornell University Press, 1987); *San José Mercury*, July 30, 1944; August 29, 1945; H. J. Flannery, "Street Lights for 100 New Residents a Day," *The American City* (August 1960), 129, 131.

46. Margaret Clarke, *Health in the Mexican-American Culture: A Community Study* (Berkeley: University of California Press, 1959, 1970), 23.

47. Fights between zoot suiters "were turf wars from down south," García remembers. "It was one L.A. neighborhood against another among the kids up here, and sometimes they saw themselves protecting a girlfriend or sister from another group of boys." Interview with Gilbert García, San José, July 8, 1996. *San José Mercury*, June 12 and 22, 1943; July 19, 1944; July 4 and 23, and August 25, 1945; Clarke, *Health in the Mexican American Culture*, 71.

48. *San José Mercury*, August 17, 1943; May 6 and 17 and June 4, 1944.

49. Ibid., July 30, 1945.

Chapter 6
Braceros and Business Machines

1. Frank J. Taylor, "Factory in the Country," *Saturday Evening Post* 218 (April 13, 1946), 20. The county's extensive program of adult education helped train the postwar workforce. For the development of adult education, see *Union Journal of Santa Clara County*, July 31, 1925; *Union Gazette* (San José), September 16, 1927; *San José Mercury-Herald*, January 4, 1930; June 20, 1943; May 14 and June 14, 1944; January 3, 1954; "Democracy at Work Solving Its Problems," *Scholastic* 38 (April 21, 1941), 6–7; and the annual *Handbook of Adult Education* (San José: Department of Adult Education, 1941–1963) at the California State Library in Sacramento.

2. "The Saga of San Jose: Santa Clara County Shows How to Balance Farms with Factories," *Fortnight* (February 18, 1949), 10; John W. Haanstram, "Sunlight, Roses, and Jukebox Genius," *Saturday Review* 39 (April 21, 1956), 48; Findlay, *Magic Lands*, 117–159. The low tabulation for "nonwhites" resulted in part from the Census Bureau's decision to label ethnic Mexicans "whites of Spanish surname." *Census of Housing: 1950*, vol. 1: *General Characteristics*, part 2, *Alabama-Georgia* (Washington, D.C.: Government Printing Office, 1953), table 1.

3. *San José Mercury-News*, July 31, 1995.

4. Clarke, *Health in the Mexican-American Culture*, 12; Galarza, "Marchise Camp-Santa Clara" (handwritten notes), October 3, 1955, in Galarza Papers, box 3, folder 1;

Galarza to Mitchell, June 3, 1953, in Southern Tenant Farmers Union (STFU) Papers, reel 37; Santa Clara County Planning Commission, *Master Plan of the City of San José, California* (San Jose: Santa Clara County, 1958), 13–14; State of California Department of Employment, *Labor Requirements for California Crops, 1948* (Sacramento: Farm Placement Service, 1948), 8. Frances Palacios remembered that "we worked the fields every summer to get our school clothes and get the things that we needed." Catherine N. Villarreal, "An Oral History on Frances 'Pancha' Palacios," May 29, 1989, in the Chicano Studies Library, San Jose State University. See also Varden Fuller, John W. Wamer, and George L. Viles, *Domestic and Imported Workers in the Harvest Labor Market: Santa Clara County, California, 1954* (Berkeley: Giannini Foundation of Agricultural Economics California Agricultural Experiment Station, 1956).

5. U.S. Commission on Civil Rights, "The Spanish-American Community of the San Francisco Bay Area," (unpublished staff report to the Commissioners, April 28, 1967), 16. Margaret Clarke reported in 1955 that, among Sal Si Puedes residents over twenty-five years of age, some 35 percent had never attended school, another 37 percent had never made it past the sixth grade, less than 10 percent had made it into the eighth, and just 1 percent had graduated from high school. Clarke, *Health in the Mexican-American Culture*, 61, 67, 74–75, 92.

6. *El Excéntrico*, December 1949; Clarke, *Health in the Mexican-American Culture*, 18–19.

7. Clarke, *Health in the Mexican-American Culture*, 32.

8. Margaret L. Sumner, "Mexican-American Minority Churches, USA," *Practical Anthropology* (May–June 1963), 117; "Protestant Spanish-Speaking Churches in the San Jose Area," (ms., April 1958), Father McDonnell Papers, box 2, file "1958," in the San Francisco Chancery Archives, Menlo Park, California; *El Excéntrico*, November 20, 1951; Clarke, *Health in the Mexican-American Culture*, 83, 88.

9. Clarke, *Health in the Mexican-American Culture*, 21.

10. Ibid., 108–109; *San José Mercury-Herald*, September 20, 1951.

11. Clarke, *Health in the Mexican-American Culture*, 23; *El Excéntrico*, December 1949 and February 1950.

12. *El Excéntrico*, April, May, July, November, and December 1949; César Chávez, Activity Report, April 2, 1956, in Ross Papers, Wayne State University, box 1, folder 27. According to one local researcher, fewer than 46 percent of Sal Si Puedes residents could read or write in Spanish in the mid-1950s. Clarke, *Health in the Mexican-American Culture*, 59.

13. Clarke, *Health in the Mexican-American Culture*, 26; *El Excéntrico*, February and December 1950; January 20, 1952; and January 5 and March 5, 1958; César Chávez, Activity Report, April 20, 1956, in Ross Papers, box 1, folder 31; June 21, 1956, in box 1, folder 39.

14. *San José Mercury-Herald*, September 16, 1951. In 1950 Virginia Armenta tallied 40,089 votes to beat her four competitors and win the title of "Queen" at the Cinco de Mayo celebrations. *El Excéntrico*, May 5, 1950; October 5, 1951.

15. *El Excéntrico*, February 1950. Young women formed the Venus Club in 1958, promising new members "skating and bowling parties." *El Excéntrico*, January 5, 1958.

16. Galarza to William Becker, October 9, 1950, in Galarza Papers, box 1, folder 3. On Galarza, see Stephen Pitti, "Ernesto Galarza, Mexican Immigration, and Farm

Labor Organizing in Postwar California," in *The Countryside in the Age of the Modern State*, ed. Catherine McNicol Stock and Robert D. Johnston (Ithaca: Cornell University Press, 2001), 161–188; Joan London and Henry Anderson, *So Shall Ye Reap: The Story of Cesar Chavez and the Farm Workers' Movement* (New York: Thomas Y. Crowell, 1970), 115–140. Galarza's approach to politics breaks from the mold that most historians have used to characterize the era's dominant style of political organizing. See García, *Mexican Americans*, 231.

17. Ernesto Galarza, [untitled,] June 12, 1942, in Galarza Papers, box 62, folder 3; "Ernesto Galarza, Director of Research and Education," (biographical sketch), at end of 1951, in STFU Papers, University of North Carolina, Chapel Hill, (on microfilm) reel 36; Mitchell to Milton Plumb, August 9, 1957, in STFU Papers, reel 40; Grubbs, "Prelude to Chavez," 454–455. For an introduction to the spirit of reformism during these years, see George Lipsitz, *Rainbow at Midnight: Labor and Culture in the 1940s* (Chicago: University of Illinois Press, 1994).

18. Galarza to Mitchell, July 26, 1948, in STFU Papers, reel 34. In Los Angeles in 1948, Galarza reported that he had met a lawyer "who just lost out in an election for superior court judge. He is particularly interested in fighting police brutality in LA county, concerning which he is going to send me material. I'm convinced that a persistent job with this type of person is quite necessary and not too difficult to get going." Galarza to Mitchell, July 26, 1948, in STFU Papers, reel 34.

19. Clarke, *Health in the Mexican-American Culture*, 78.

20. R. V. Heredia to Galarza, May 29, 1950, in Galarza Papers, box 50, folder 3; Galarza to Mitchell, July 26, 1948, in STFU Papers, reel 34; Galarza to Mitchell, August 7, 1948, in STFU Papers, reel 34; Galarza to Mitchell, July 5, 1948, and Galarza to Mitchell, July 18, 1948, in STFU Papers, reel 34.

21. Ruíz, *Cannery Women, Cannery Lives*, 103–123; "Activity Report, April 4, 1956," in Fred Ross Papers, box 1, folder 27; interview with Ray Salazar, San José, October 22, 1995; Galarza to Mitchell, July 26, 1948, in STFU Papers, reel 34.

22. Jim Wrightson to Mitchell, March 5, 1948, in STFU Papers, reel 32; *DiGiorgio Strike Bulletin #20*, March 20, 1948, in STFU Papers, reel 32; F. R. Betton to Arthur C. Churchill, October 16, 1948, in STFU Papers, reel 34; "Memorandum—Plans for Organization of Agricultural Labor," 1947, in STFU Papers, reel 33; transcript of interview by Anne Loftis with Hank Hasiwar, November 25, 1975, in Anne Loftis Papers, box 1, folder 8, Department of Special Collections, Stanford University; Galarza to Mitchell, October 31, 1949, in Galarza Papers, box 7, folder 6; Ernesto Galarza, "Mexican-United States Labor Relations and Problems," in Galarza Papers, box 1, folder 8; Galarza to Mitchell, July 18, 1948, in STFU Papers, reel 34; Ernesto Galarza, "Big Farm Strike: A Report on the Labor Dispute at the DiGiorgio's," *Commonweal*, June 4, 1948, 182; Galarza to Mitchell, January 19, 1949, in STFU Papers, reel 34; Ernesto Galarza, "American and Foreign Farm Workers in California," statement to the President's Commission on Migratory Labor, August 12, 1950, in Galarza Papers, box 1, folder 8. While unionists primarily expressed fear of job competition with Mexicans, they also worried about Asian American workers. According to the *DiGiorgio Strike Bulletin*, "Rumors are prevalent that workers of Japanese ancestry are being recruited to work behind the picket lines, and that workers of Mexican descent, from as far off as El Paso, Texas, are being urged to break the picket line." The California State Federation of Labor reported that "Numerous rumors have been

afloat that efforts were being made to recruit Japanese, Mexicans and Filipinos" as strikebreakers. *DiGiorgio Strike Bulletin* 3 (November 13–15, 1947), in STFU Papers, reel 33. "DiGiorgio Strike Faces Crucial Development," *Weekly Newsletter from California State Federation of Labor*, November 19, 1947, in STFU Papers, reel 33.

23. Galarza, "Personal and Confidential Memorandum," in Galarza Papers, box 1, folder 8; Galarza, "Without Benefit of Lobby," in Galarza Papers, box 1, folder 8.

24. "Atenta Invitación," [flier,] August 11, 1951, Galarza Papers, box 8, folder 5; "Anuncio Oficial de la Union de Trabajadores de Rancho A.F. of L. No Sea Usted Esquirol!!!" (December 2, [1948?]), in Galarza Papers, box 8, folder 5; H. L. Mitchell to SANTA, March 16, 1949, in STFU Papers, reel 34; interviews with Manuel Hurtado, April 2, 1996; Castro, May 14, 1996; Luis Manríquez, May 12, 1996.

25. Galarza to Mitchell, February 11, 1950, in STFU Papers, reel 35; Galarza to Mitchell, July 5, 1948, in STFU Papers, reel 34; "Anuncio Oficial," in Galarza Papers, box 8, folder 5; "Triunfos de la Unión," [flier printed in the Imperial Valley in 1951 or 1952,] in Galarza Papers, box 8, folder 5; "Ahora es Cuando Los Trabajadores Agrícolas de California Deben Entrar en el Sindicato Americano Nacional de Trabajadores Agrícolas," in Galarza Papers, box 8, folder 5; Galarza, [report to Mitchell,] February 11, 1950, in STFU Papers, reel 35. Galarza found that braceros spent much of their leisure time in bars "exchang[ing] gossip on wages, chances for a transfer to a better job, possible contact with some 'good' farmer, help in 'fixing immigration papers' for permanent residence." Braceros interviewed October 1 and 14, 1955, in Galarza Papers, box 18, folder 7.

26. Luis Manríquez interview, May 12, 1996.

27. Gutiérrez, *Walls and Mirrors*, 152–160; Galarza, "Supplementary [report]," December 24, 1949, in STFU Papers, reel 34; Galarza to Mitchell, July 5, 1948; Galarza and Hasiwar, "Confidential Memo," February-May 1951, in STFU Papers, reel 35.

28. Interview with Lupe Castro, San José, May 14, 1996; Galarza to Mitchell, July 5, 1948, in STFU Papers, reel 34; Galarza to Mitchell, July 18, 1948, in STFU Papers, reel 34; Luis Manríquez interview, May 12, 1996. As San José's Father Donald McDonnell, discussed in the following chapter, and other Catholic priests in California became interested in the economic problems of farmworkers in the late 1950s, Galarza reported that "I have meetings scheduled in three areas [around California] next week to discuss organization. The pressure from Catholic priests particularly is very insistent." Galarza to Dorothy, June 23, 1948, in STFU Papers, reel 34; Galarza to Mitchell, June 6, 1957, in STFU Papers, reel 39.

29. "El Valle Imperial" (pamphlet), in Galarza Papers, box 8, folder 5; interviews with Castro, May 14, 1996; Hurtado, April 2, 1996; Galarza to Mitchell, June 9, 1950, in STFU Papers, reel 35; Galarza to Mitchell, March 11, 1949, in STFU Papers, reel 34.

30. "Resolution Calling for an Investigation of Income Tax Evasion by Foreign Nationals Employed on American Farms," December 13, 1947, in STFU Papers, reel 33; interview with Ray Salazar, San José, October 22, 1995; Galarza to Mitchell, October 31, 1949, in Galarza Papers, box 7, folder 6. On Mexican American reactions to the immigration debate during this period, see Gutiérrez, *Walls and Mirrors*, 117–178.

31. "Corrido del Valle Imperial," in Galarza Papers, box 19, folder 6.

32. Galarza, interview with nine nationals in Terminous, October 20, 1955, in Galarza Papers, box 18, folder 7; Galarza quoted in Sam Kushner, *Long Road to Delano* (New York: International Publishers, 1975), 101; Galarza to Mitchell, June 22, 1957, in STFU Papers, reel 39. Regarding bracero opinions of U.S. unions, see Galarza's interview with bracero at Cal Pack, October 13, 1955, in Galarza Papers box 18, folder 6. A former union secretary in Mexico told him that "Here we [braceros] could not have a committee. Some would be afraid [of deportation]." Galarza, interview with braceros, November 16, 1955, in Galarza Papers, box 18, folder 7. The California press did make its way into bracero camps. "*La Opinión* sometimes circulates" among braceros, noted Galarza, as did "old copies of Mexican newspapers." Workers shared news of Mexico with one another, and a major flood in Tampico in 1955 prompted all of the workers in one camp to volunteer $2 for the relief effort. Interview with a bracero in Tracy, September 20, 1955, in Galarza Papers, box 3, folder 1. Interview in Santa Paula, November 28, 1955, in Galarza Papers, box 18, folder 7. Galarza, "Personal and Confidential Memo," in Galarza Papers, box 1, folder 8.

33. Galarza interview with Fr. McDonald [*sic*] in San José, September 24, 1955, in Galarza Papers, box 3, folder 1; Galarza to Dawes, October 2, 1951, in STFU Papers, reel 36.

34. Galarza to Mitchell, May 29, 1954, in STFU Papers, reel 37; minutes of the First California Council of Agricultural Unions Meeting, September 14–15, 1951, in STFU Papers, reel 36. See the extensive correspondence regarding the Alianza in the Galarza Papers, box 50, folder 3; Galarza to Dawes, October 2, 1951, in STFU Papers, reel 36.

35. Castro interview, May 14, 1996; Galarza to Bob Jones, November 28, 1950, in STFU Papers, reel 35. In 1952 Galarza wrote Mitchell from the Imperial Valley that "We are keeping up a running fire on the Mexican consuls and Alemán." Galarza to Mitchell, January 19, 1949, in STFU Papers, reel 34. Galarza to Mitchell, May 26, 1952, in Galarza Papers, box 7, folder 6. Throughout the 1950s, Galarza expressed anger that in the negotiation of the international labor agreement, "the fact that the Mexican constitution states categorically that worker's [*sic*] rights are inalienable has not been taken very seriously." "Statement of the National Farm Labor Union on the Importation of Agricultural Workers from Mexico," June 4, 1948, in STFU Papers, reel 32. Galarza also wrote Mitchell in 1951 that "I have been in touch with several [Mexican] deputies (congressmen) some are old friends. . . . We can have some speeches in Congress if we want them." Galarza to Mitchell, February 4, 1951, in STFU Papers, reel 35. Galarza to Bob Jones, November 28, 1950, in STFU Papers, reel 35. NFLU Press Release, June 4, 1948, in STFU Papers, reel 33.

36. Espinosa interview, May 30, 1996; "A $10 dólares por cabeza!," "En Hermosillo están Contratando Braceros," and "Detrás de la Cortina de Humo, Miguel Alemán," [fliers from 1951 or 1952,] Galarza Papers, box 8, folder 5; *El Organizador del Campo*, March 3, 1951; Statement of the Sindicato Americano Nacional Agrícolas, AFL, Bakersfield, January 21, 1949, in Galarza Papers, box 8, folder 5; Galarza to Mitchell, May 8, 1951, in STFU Papers, reel 35; Galarza to Mitchell, January 17, 1951; Galarza to Mitchell, September 11, 1952, in STFU Papers, reel 36. On the Mexico City press, see Galarza to Mitchell, January 1954, in STFU Papers, reel 37.

37. "Supplementary Report, 1954–1955," in STFU Papers, reel 39; see also the

letters written in January 1949, in STFU Papers, reel 34; Galarza to Mitchell, April 29, 1953, in STFU Papers, reel 37; Galarza to Mitchell, June 17, 1953, in STFU Papers, reel 37; Galarza to Frank Noakes, June 3, 1956, in STFU Papers, reel 39; Galarza to Mitchell, March 11, 1957, in STFU Papers, reel 42; Joe García, "Solidarity Forever. . . . Report on the Conference of the Mexican and American Union Leaders Held in Mexico City, December 14, 15, 16, 1953, Extracts from *The Industrial Worker*," in STFU Papers, reel 37; "Talk by Dr. Ernesto Galarza at UFW Boycott Office," in Anne Loftis Papers, box 1, folder 10.

38. Manuel Hurtado interview, April 2, 1996; Sal Ortega to Galarza, March 11, 1950, in Galarza Papers, box 10, folder 4. On Luis Juárez, see *San José Mercury-News*, October 28, 1979.

39. Galarza to Beth Biderman, July 25, 1950, in Galarza Papers, box 12, folder 4; blank letter on NFLU stationary (n.d.), in Galarza Papers, box 8, folder 5. The best general study of the deportations of the 1950s remains Juan Ramón García, *Operation Wetback: The Mass Deportation of Mexican Undocumented Workers in 1954* (Westport, CT: Greenwood Press, 1980).

40. Discussing union "abuse" of California farmworkers, Galarza criticized "labor men at the top" who wanted to help Mexicans by adopting what Galarza called "secondary remedies." "Local industrial and service unions don't look beyond the town boundaries to find out why the minority groups are so prolific [as] scabs" and had little interest in joining unions, he wrote H. L. Mitchell. Central Labor Councils in urban California "know all about bandages and nothing at all, apparently, about tourniquets. They have plenty of jobs to offer applying iodine but none at all finding who beat up the victim." Galarza to Mitchell, September 29, 1954, in STFU Papers, reel 38.

Chapter 7
Political Power

1. Interview with Mary San Miguel, San José, October 27, 1995. Estimates on population figures are largely derived from census tract information. The 1950 census lists 1,413 "foreign-born Mexicans" in the city of San Jose and 6,180 "Spanish-surnamed residents." The Census Bureau tabulated these numbers by counting only residents of tracks in which there were "at least 200" Spanish-surnamed residents and clearly did not count at least 523 foreign-born Mexicans scattered throughout the city. To estimate the number of "Spanish-surnamed residents" in those tracts not counted by the bureau, I have used the following method: Since 1,413 "foreign-born Mexicans" yielded 6,180 Spanish-surnamed residents, a similar conversion from 523 "foreign-born Mexicans" would yield an additional 2,380 "Spanish-surnamed residents."

2. *El Excéntrico*, May 5, 1950.

3. Ibid., February 1950.

4. "Minutes of the Founding Convention," in Asilomar, California, March 20, 1954, in Gallegos Papers, box A-16, file "Letter from Marion Graff," Special Collections, Green Library, Stanford University; typed notes [1960] and "It Occurs to Me" (pamphlet) in the Fred Ross Papers, box 10, folder 12. The Arizona CSO chapters

were founded in the communities of Avondale, Casa Grande, Chandler, Coolidge, Eloy, Glendale, Mesa, Phoenix, Scottsdale, and Tempe in 1954. "National Executive Board Members and Addresses," in Gallegos Papers, box A-14. While the CSO helped change the shape of Latino politics in California, it has received little scholarly attention, in part because César Chávez' biographers have treated the CSO as a mere stepping stone in the development of the United Farm Workers, and in part because scholars have not had access to records of the CSO or leading individuals in the organization until very recently. For the most extensive history of the CSO, see Gutiérrez, *Walls and Mirrors*, 168–172. Mario García's *Mexican Americans*, while claiming to be a comprehensive survey of Mexican politics in the United States between 1930 and 1960, covers the CSO in less than three pages. On Chávez, see, for example, Richard Griswold del Castillo and Richard A. García, *César Chávez: A Triumph of Spirit* (Norman: University of Oklahoma, 1995).

5. Interview with Leonard Ramírez, San José, September 20, 1996; Herman Gallegos, "The Saga of Sal Si Puedes" (ms., n.d.), in Gallegos Papers, box A-13; "A History of the Northern Region AFSC Branch" (ms., n.d.), in Josephine Duveneck Papers, Hoover Archives, Stanford University, box 4; *Palo Alto Times*, October 22, 1953. Settles had been active in Japanese American "resettlement" in the area since 1945. JACL attorney Wayne Kanemoto praised Settles in 1955 for having worked "unfailingly and relentlessly . . . combating discrimination and prejudice" in the county. Letter from Kanemoto to Hector Moreno, June 10, 1955, in Gallegos Papers, box A-14. Throughout the 1950s the AFSC continued to work with "the settled or settling migrants" in rural California who "have demonstrated a certain degree of personal responsibilities." "Report on Agricultural Labor Project" (ms., 1956), in Josephine Duveneck Papers, box 2. For a summary of the AFSC's work with Mexicans in Texas in the 1950s, see "One Out of Five" (statement of the Texas AFSC, n.d.) in the Galarza Papers, box 10, folder 9 (hereafter EGSU). The Los Angeles CSO formally affiliated with the Federation for Civic Unity in October 1949. Minutes of Los Angeles CSO Program Planning Committee, October 10, 1949, in Fred Ross Papers, box 5, folder 5. The Federation for Civic Unity in San José had in fact been offering an annual college scholarship for Mexican students in the area since 1950. *San José Mercury*, June 22, 1950; *San José Evening News*, May 19, 1954; César Chávez, Activity Report, February 15, 1956, in Ross Papers, Walter Reuther Archives, Wayne State University, box 1, folder 21. While the Jewish community in Los Angeles had played an important role in the CSO's development there, their small number in Santa Clara County in part explains why the organization in the South Bay did not work closely with Jewish residents in Santa Clara County. Stephen D. Kinsey has estimated that by 1972 there were only approximately 2,500 Jewish residents in Santa Clara County. Stephen D. Kinsey, "They Called It Home: The Development of the Jewish Community of San José, California, 1850–1910" (M.A. thesis, San José State University, 1975), 2–10.

6. "A History of the Northern Region AFSC Branch," 8; interviews with Gallegos, Palo Alto, September 20, 1996; Ramírez, September 20, 1996; "The Saga of Sal Si Puedes," in Gallegos Papers, box A-13. On the "Bloody Christmas" case, see the letter from Tony Ríos to Roger Baldwin [n.d. 1953?], in Fred Ross Papers, box 5, folder 1. Mexicans in San José during this period patronized newsstands that sold Spanish-

language newspapers such as *La Opinión*, which published extensive accounts of racial discrimination in the Los Angeles area. See *El Excéntrico*, February 1950.

7. "The Saga of Sal Si Puedes," in Gallegos Papers, box A-13; *The Monitor* (San Francisco), January 25, 1957; Gallegos interview, September 20, 1996; Santa Clara County CSO Chapter Report, January 1, 1956–June 30, 1956, in Gallegos Papers, box A-16; Minutes of the Founding Convention, March 20, 1954, in Gallegos Papers, box A-16, file "Letter from Marion Graff"; McDonnell to John J. Mitty, February 15, 1951, in McDonnell Papers, Archives of the San Francisco Archdiocese, box 2, file "Reports: Missionary Apostolate"; Gallegos to Duggan, August 5, 1982, in Gallegos Papers, box 14, unfiled material. Some members of the Catholic clergy openly involved themselves in the strikes of the immediate postwar period. One Church handbill announced that "We ask that every Catholic working in the canneries speak with their priest and learn from him the dangers of voting for the union controlled by the Communist Party and Russia." The flier then informed Mexicans that the CIO union had promised that all Mexican immigrants would be "removed from their jobs immediately" if the FTA won the contest, warning "this is the protection you have under the CIO Tobacco [FTA] Union." "La Verdad" (pamphlet, [1947?]), in Ernesto Galarza Papers, box 13, folder 7. In San José most clergy remained ignorant or indifferent to the growing Latin American presence around the Bay, and the twentieth-century Catholic Church had done little to serve local Latino parishioners, concentrating instead on the area's Portuguese and Italian communities. At the national level, the work of the Bishops' Committee for the Spanish Speaking was a driving force in the Church's new interest in Mexican parishioners, and in the local Archdiocese McDonnell was one of a small group of priests calling themselves "the Mission Band for the Spanish Speaking" who reached out to Mexicans in Stockton, Oakland, Decoto, and San José after 1950. *Catholic Council for the Spanish Speaking Newsletter*, November 11, 1948; report of Monsignor Edward Maher, in McDonnell Papers, box 2. See also Gina Marie Pitti, "'A Ghastly International Racket': The Catholic Church and the Bracero Program in Northern California, 1942–1964" (South Bend: Working Paper Series, Cushwa Center for the Study of American Catholicism, University of Notre Dame, forthcoming), and Gina Marie Pitti, "'To Hear about God in Spanish': Ethnicity, Church and Community Activism in Northern California's Mexican American Colonias, 1942–1964" (Ph.D. dissertation, Stanford University, 2003).

8. Interviews with Gallegos, September 20, 1996; Ramírez, September 23, 1996; Santa Clara County Chapter of Community Service Organization, "Help Us Build This Bridge" (pamphlet, 1957), 3, in Ernesto Galarza Papers, box 13, file 8; "Saga of Sal Si Puedes," in Gallegos Papers, box A-13; Cabrera to Chávez, July 30, 1954, in United Farm Workers, Office of the President Collection, Wayne State University, box 2, folder 7 (hereafter UFW-PP); César Chávez, Activity Reports, February 26 and July 22, 1956, in Ross Papers, box 1, folders 22 and 41, and box 2, folder 4; Santa Clara County CSO Chapter Report, January 1–June 30, 1956, in Gallegos Papers, box A-16; Santa Clara County CSO Chapter Report, January 1–June 11, 1960, in Gallegos Papers, box 29. Attendance at San José CSO meetings varied during the 1950s. In September 1956, for instance, only forty-nine members appeared for the general assembly meeting, although between January and June approximately one hundred San José residents attended those meetings. By early 1960 the chapter reported that over two

hundred residents of the area were active in the local CSO. César Chávez, Activity Report, September 7, 1956, in Ross Papers, box 1, folder 44.

9. "A History of the Northern Region AFSC Branch," 10; Minutes of the Founding Convention, March 20, 1954, in Gallegos Papers, box A-16, file "Letter from Marion Graff"; *Convention Special!* [newsletter], 1955, in Fred Ross Papers, box 11, folder 10; "Tentative Program for CSO Founding Convention, March 20–21, 1954," in Gallegos Papers, box A-1. Mexicans "from as far as Lodi and Watsonville" wrote the San José chapter in 1954 to inquire "about CSO." Santa Clara County CSO, 1954, in Gallegos Papers, box A-13. César Chávez's familiarity with the semirural East Side of San José also contributed to his ability to organize similar areas in the Central Valley. In Tulare County, Ross Papers advised Chávez in 1954 that the census figures probably did not report the correct number of Mexicans in the area because, "as you know, there are large concentrations of Spanish-speaking people living right on the edge of the city (as in Sal Si Puedes for instance)." Ross to Chávez, May 10, 1954, in UFW-PP, box 2, folder 7.

10. "What Is the CSO?" (pamphlet, Monterey County, 1957), in Gallegos Papers, box A-13; Herman E. Gallegos, "Get Out if You Can . . . Community Organization among Mexican-Americans in a Northern California Community" (ms., fall 1957), in Gallegos Papers, box A-13; Gallegos interview, September 20, 1996; Piñon interview, September 23, 1996. Leaders of the San José chapter worried about suspected Communists, but many CSO leaders throughout the state also argued that the United States should not continue its witch hunts against suspected subversives. The CSO in San José and Los Angeles declared that red-baiting threatened their efforts to "integrate" Mexicans and non-Mexicans into common organizations. And at a meeting of the Personnel Committee at the home of Luis Zárate in 1957, members discussed whether the organization should have a "loyalty oath" similar to the one required of union leaders after the Taft-Hartley Act passed in 1947. Zárate and others argued that such a provision was unnecessary and "ridiculous." César Chávez, Activity Reports, March 21, 1956, and January 9, 1957, in Ross Papers, box 1, folder 25, and box 2, folder 8; *CSO Reporter*, February 28, 1952, in Fred Ross Papers, box 10, folder 12.

11. Interview with Al Piñon, San José, September 23, 1996; "Help Us Build This Bridge."

12. Minutes of the Founding Convention, March 20, 1954, in Gallegos Papers, box A-16, file "Letter from Marion Graff."

13. Galarza to Mitchell, May 29, 1954, in STFU Papers, reel 37; Gallegos interview, September 20, 1996; César Chávez, Activity Report, May 4, 1956, in Ross Papers, box 1, folder 33; Minutes of the Founding Convention, Asilomar, California, March 20, 1954, in Gallegos Papers, box A-16, file "Letter from Marion Graff." In Santa Clara County only Laborers Local 270 offered the CSO consistent support, a tribute, no doubt, to growing ethnic Mexican dominance of the Valley's construction trade. *El Excéntrico*, October 21, 1955; César Chávez, Activity Reports, April 26 and August 29, 1956, in Ross Papers, box 1, folders 31 and 43. The CIO Council of Los Angeles was the state's only Central Labor Council to note the establishment of the National CSO at its 1954 convention. Minutes of the Founding Convention, Asilomar, California, March 20, 1954, in Gallegos Papers, box A-16, file "Letter from Marion Graff."

14. César Chávez, Activity Reports, March 7–8 and May 23, 1956, in Ross Papers,

box 1, folders 23, 25, 26, and 35. Writing in 1951, San José State College student Elida Coronado noted that "San José State had never been so crowded with [Mexican veterans] as it is this year." *El Excéntrico*, December 5, 1951.

15. César Chávez, Activity Reports, February 17, March 8, April 7, and May 3, 1956, in Ross Papers, box 1, folders 21, 23, 28, and 35; Salcido to Chávez, n.d., in UFW-PP, box 2, folder 3; Delgadillo to Chávez, n.d., in UFW-PP, box 2, folder 2; *San José Mercury*, March 15, 1954, and August 2, 1956; interviews with Ramírez and Gallegos, September 20, 1996. Herman Gallegos remembered that César Chávez, a young lumber handler, "had a very deep-rooted suspicion of [the] middle class." Interview with Herman Gallegos by Laurie Coyle, San Francisco, n.d., in author's possession. Membership committee chair Isabel Medina and other officials were among those Eastsiders with little formal education. Chávez noted in 1957 that Medina "can't speak, read, or write English, doesn't know how to read or write Spanish. Despite all this he can lead his committee into doing the work." César Chávez, Activity Report, April 4 and May 2, 1956, in Ross Papers, box 1, folders 25 and 32.

16. Piñon interview, September 23, 1996; César Chávez, daily reports, January 10 and 16, 1957, in Ross Papers, box 1, folder 18.

17. Interview with Luis Zárate, San José, September 22, 1996; César Chávez, Activity Reports, February 15 and 24, March 23, 1956, and May 3, 1957, in Ross Papers, box 1, folders 21, 25, and 32; *El Excéntrico*, October 1951; "Conference on the Education of Spanish-Speaking People" (program, n.d.); Minutes of the San José CSO Education Committee, March 17, 1959, in Fred Ross Papers, unfiled material; "Senate Resolution No. 204," June 11, 1957, *State Journal*, in Gallegos Papers, box A-13; Ed Levin "to whom it may concern," n.d., in UFW-PP, box 2, folder 2; William Broom to Hector Moreno, June 10, 1955, in Gallegos Papers, box A-14. The Adult Education Department announced in 1952 that its purpose was "to assimilate into one dynamic whole the various cultures which make up America." "Adult Education Department Schedule, 1952–1953" (pamphlet, 1952), in California State Library, Sacramento.

18. Fred Ross, *Conquering Goliath: Cesar Chavez at the Beginning* (Keene, CA: El Taller Gráfico Press, 1989), 2; Santa Clara County Chapter Report, January–June 1956, in Gallegos Papers, box A-16; Aurelio N. Ramírez to all CSO chapters (n.d.), in UFW-PP, box 2, folder 5. Gallegos recalls that, despite the rhetoric of personal transformation at the heart of the CSO's promotion, "for each one of us who became involved in the CSO, there was already some steering in the individual [towards political action]. It's too easy to say, 'Well, I had a transformation when I got involved in the organization.'" Gallegos interview, September 20, 1996.

19. Albert Camarillo, "Mexican Americans in a San Jose High School, 1940–1980," (ms., January 1986); "Emphasize" [notes for presentation], in Gallegos Papers, box A-13; Edward Roybal, text of speech in the Minutes of the Founding Convention, Community Service Organization, March 20, 1954, in Gallegos Papers, box A-16, folder "letter from Marion Graff"; *El Excéntrico*, December 1949. A statewide convention of CSO chapters in 1957 emphasized that two members, Rudy Hernández and Felipe Rubio, had won the Congressional Medal of Honor. Hanford's Peter B. García spoke "with pride of service with the infantry in the Southwest Pacific during World War II, covering the area from New Caledonia to Japan." García stressed that "he was with the first unit in Japan" and had been "twice wounded in action." But the armed services also removed potential organizers from California. Bernie Frausto, a young

employee at the Ford Motor Company in Milpitas and a gifted organizer of Mexican teenagers in East San José, would have taken over the San José chapter in 1956 if he had not been drafted into the armed services. *CSO Reporter*, April 1, 1957, in Ernesto Galarza Papers, box 13, folder 7; Ed Laubengayer, "It Occurs to Me," *Valley's News Press* [Santa Barbara, n.d.], in Gallegos Papers, box A-16; *San José Mercury*, August 2, 1956.

20. Interview with Hector Moreno, San José, September 18, 1996; CSO Training Program, June-August 1957, in Fred Ross Papers, box 10, folder 15; application for Aid to the Ford Motor Company [1956], Gallegos Papers, box A-13.

21. *El Excéntrico*, January 5, 1952; CSO Training Program, June–August 1957, in Fred Ross Papers, box 10, folder 15; Minutes of the San José CSO Education Committee, June 16, 1959, in Fred Ross Papers, unfiled materials; Santa Clara County CSO Chapter Report, January 1–June 30, 1956, in Gallegos Papers, box A-16. Hector Moreno and Albert Piñon remember this period as one of enormous sacrifice for their families, as they maintained their right to remain active in the organization while their spouses did not. Interviews with Piñon, September 23, 1996, San José; Moreno interview, September 18, 1996.

22. Interview with Edith Moreno, San José, September 18, 1996; César Chávez, Activity Reports, April 2, March 7, September 12, and November 15, 1956, in Ross Papers, box 1, folders 23, 27, and 44, and box 2, folder 4; Santa Clara County CSO Chapter Report, July 15, 1960, in Gallegos Papers, box A-14; "Membership List, 1956," in Community Service Organization Offices, San José, California, file 3. For similar work performed by women in the Hanford local, see the *Hanford Sentinel*, July 24, 1959. See also Cynthia E. Orozco, "The Origins of the League of United Latin American Citizens (LULAC) and the Mexican American Civil Rights Movement in Texas with an Analysis of Women's Political Participation in a Gendered Context, 1910–1929" (Ph.D. dissertation, University of California, Los Angeles, 1993).

23. César Chávez, Activity Reports, January 4 and 18, 1956, in Ross Papers, box 2, folder 7; "Conference on the Education of Spanish-Speaking People" (program), in Gallegos Papers, box 14.5; Report of the San José CSO Chapter, in Gallegos Papers, box A-16; *Bakersfield Press*, February 24, 1955; *La Opinión*, March 15, 1955.

24. *El Excéntrico*, December 5, 1951; Gutiérrez, *Walls and Mirrors*, 152–178; "CSO Training Program," in Fred Ross Papers, box 4, unfiled material; César Chávez, daily report, January 1 and 9, 1957, Ross Papers, box 2, folder 8. CSO organizers encountered many ethnic Mexicans in the area who remained closely tied to their home country, including "Mr. Hernández [who] told us that his wife has been going to Mexico ever since he can remember" and Mercedes Montoya, who spent her vacations during these years visiting "all the brothers and sisters of her parents who lived in Sonora, Mexico." César Chávez, Activity Report, May 3, 1956, in Ross Papers, box 1, folder 32. Lino Covarrubias remembers that while the Oakland CSO chapter did decide to limit membership to U.S. citizens, organization leaders in San José "did not agree with the proposal." Interview with Lino Covarrubias, San José, October 15, 1995. The presence of Mexican immigrants demanded that CSO meetings in Los Angeles and San José be conducted in both languages. Members also translated the proceedings of the National CSO's 1954 founding convention into Spanish. See the minutes of the Lincoln Heights CSO General Meetings, in Fred Ross Papers, box 5, folder 11; *Help Us Build This Bridge!* (pamphlet); Minutes of the Founding Conven-

tion, March 20, 1954, in GPSU, Box A-16, file "Letter from Marion Graff"; César Chávez, Activity Report, March 12, 1956, in Ross Papers, box 1, folder 23. Proposals in San José to limit membership to U.S. citizens were first defeated by "a healthy majority" in 1956. Santa Clara County Chapter Report, January 1–June 30, 1956, in Gallegos Papers, box A-16; César Chávez, Activity Report, January 18, 1956, in Ross Papers, box 1, folder 18.

25. *El Excéntrico*, January 20, 1952; César Chávez, Activity Reports of March 20 and 29, April 20, and June 21, 1956, in Ross Papers, box 1, folders 26, 29, and 31; "Chávez diary" entry of August 26, 1956, in Ross Papers, box 1, folder 43. Long the most visible Spanish-speaking activist in the county, CSO organizers later overheard a group of Mexicans in the city commenting that José J. Alvarado was the "only man who has helped" Mexicans in the area. César Chávez, Activity Report, April 2, 1956, in Ross Papers, box 1, folder 27.

26. "Saga of Sal Si Puedes," in Gallegos Papers, box A-13; Loretta Shea and Nancy Delaney, "Spanish-Speaking Protestant Churches of the Mayfair Area" (ms., San José State University, 1978), in Antonio Soto Papers, Special Collections, Green Library, Stanford University, box 2; San José Chapter, "CSO Training Program," June–August 1957, in Ross Papers, box 10, folder 15; Phil Buskirk to Gallegos, August 21, 1957, in Gallegos Papers, box A-14; Minutes of San José CSO House Meeting, November 30, 1955, in UFW-PP, box 2, folder 8; Clarke, *Health in the Mexican-American Culture*, 12; Report of the Santa Clara County CSO Chapter, January 1–June 30, 1956, in Gallegos Papers, box A-16; César Chávez, Activity Report, April 21, May 8, and June 27, 1956, in Ross Papers, box 1, folders 31, 33, and 39. CSO officers stressed that their organization was committed to "assur[ing] justice and a voice in the government" in order to allow men to guarantee the "protection of [their] home and family." Community Service Organization, "Help Us Build This Bridge," Ernesto Galarza Papers, box 14, folder 8. On the cooperation of Protestant churches with the CSO, see César Chávez, Activity Reports, March 8 and 29, and April 5, 1956, in Ross Papers, box 1, folders 23, 26, and 27.

27. *El Excéntrico*, December 5, 1951; Ross to Alinsky, February 20, 1948, in Fred Ross Papers, Folder "Alinsky, Early Correspondence"; César Chávez, Activity Reports, March 21, April 2 and 23, May 2, 1956, in Ross Papers, box 1, folders 25, 27, and 32; "National CSO Seeks Ouster of Selma Officials," *Fresno Bee* (1960?), clipping in Gallegos Papers, box A-13; Jack D. Forbes, "Uncle Tony: A Legend in His Own Time," *Ventura County Star-Free Press Magazine* (August 8, 1964), 3–4; Minutes of the Special Executive Board Meeting, Report of Cruz Reynoso, September 23, 1962, in Burciaga Papers, Walter Reuther Archives, Wayne State University, box 1.

28. César Chávez, Activity Reports, November 19, 1954, February 15, March 20, April 4, 11 and 29, May 10 and 21, 1956, in Ross Papers, box 1, folders 6, 21, 27, 29, 30, 33, and 35. Dan Fernández, the chair of the Immigration Committee in 1956, believed that "the most important service performed has been to prevent many of these people from being taken by the so-called immigration counselor (*coyote*)." Santa Clara County CSO Chapter Report, January 1–June 30, 1956, in Gallegos Papers, box A-16.

29. César Chávez, Activity Reports of May 7, October 31, and November 8, 1956, in Ross Papers, box 1, folders 22 and 33.

30. "Notes on the house meeting at 2223 Kammerer," December 6, 1955, in

UFW-PP, box 2, folder 8; "Minutes of the Founding Convention," March 20, 1954, in Gallegos Papers, box A-16, file "Letter from Marion Graff"; César Chávez, Activity Reports of March 21 and May 12, 1956, in Ross Papers, box 1, folders 25 and 34; letter to Chet Holifield, author unknown, February 17, 1955, in Fred Ross Papers, box 11, folder 10; Report of the Santa Clara County CSO Chapter, January 1–June 30, 1956, in Gallegos Papers, box A-16. Elderly residents who took their citizenship exam in a language other than English were required to prove they had resided in the United States for twenty years or more. Writing several years before, the journalist Humberto García had emphasized that local Mexicans could not allow their "sentimental" love of Mexico to inhibit their political involvement in American society. "It is appropriate, natural, and necessary to have affection for our native land," he wrote "but we have to see things as they are and not with a delirious mind. The hypocritical patriotism of lifting a bottle of liquor and shouting 'Viva Mexico!' to a country which we deserted will . . . improve nothing. It is a thousand times more glorious for Mexico if her sons, once they leave their paternal hearth, adopt another land as their own, becoming an integral part of it, and taking interest in civic activities. . . . It is best to demonstrate that Mexico produces the best sort . . . [since] if we do not accept the United States and we are not actually in Mexico, we find ourselves in the middle of nowhere, wishing to go who knows where." *El Excéntrico*, February 1950.

31. Minutes of the San José CSO Education Committee, March 17, 1959, Gallegos Papers, box A-16; interviews with Gallegos, September 20, 1996; Moreno, September 18, 1996; Minutes of the General Meeting, August 20, 1952, in Ross Papers, box 5, folder 7; "Committee Functions," in UFW-PP, box 2, folder 1; Helen Valenzuela, Minutes of the Youth and Education Committee, n.d., in Gallegos Papers, box A-13; "What Is CSO?" (pamphlet), in Gallegos Papers, box A-13; Minutes of the San José CSO Education Committee, April 14, 1959, in Fred Ross Papers, unfiled material; César Chávez, Activity Report, February 15, 1957, in Ross Papers, box 1, folder 21. The Alameda chapter, established with the help of San José residents such as César Chávez, successfully lobbied the Decoto School Board in 1953 and 1954 to hire two "Spanish-speaking teachers in the schools." Also with help from San José members, CSO members in Kings County protested in early 1957 when their local School Board expelled a group of Mexican students. Minutes of the Founding Convention, March 20, 1954, in Gallegos Papers, box A-16, file "Letter from Marion Graff"; Minutes of the Los Angeles CSO General Meeting, June 16, 1952, in Fred Ross Papers, box 5, folder 7; *CSO Reporter*, April 1, 1957.

32. "A History of the Northern Region AFSC Branch," 10; "CSO, Santa Clara County Report" [1955?], in Gallegos Papers, box A-13; César Chávez, Activity Report, March 12 and 29, 1956, in Ross Papers, box 1, folders 23 and 26; Santa Clara County CSO Chapter Report, January 1–June 30, 1956, in Gallegos Papers, box A-16. The first chapter in Los Angeles had confronted similar problems of urban underdevelopment in Mexican East Side barrios, and Southern California members had rallied residents of Bernal Street to address the flooding in their neighborhood. "Program of the Industrial Areas Foundation," 1949; Minutes of the Los Angeles CSO Program Planning Committee, January 2, 1950, in Fred Ross Papers, box 5, folder 5. Foreshadowing many later political struggles over equitable urban growth, members also met with the Los Angeles Housing Authority to protest rent increases in the region. CSO activists even approached government officials about the increase in bus fares in

their city. Minutes of the Los Angeles Program Planning Committee, July 25, 1949, and March 13, 1950, in Fred Ross Papers, box 5, folders 5 and 7; Minutes of the Los Angeles CSO Executive Committee, October 8, 1951, in Fred Ross Papers, box 5, folder 6; Minutes of the Los Angeles CSO General Meeting, March 19, 1952, in Fred Ross Papers, box 5, folder 7.

33. "CSO Chapters Mobilize Drive for New Voters," *San José News* [n.d., 1954?], in Gallegos Papers, box 8, unfiled material; Leo Sánchez to César Chávez, n.d., in UFW-PP, box 2, folder 3; "Letter to _____ CSO," n.d., in UFW-PP, box 2, folder 3; "The CSO Story" (pamphlet); Santa Clara County Chapter Report, January 1–June 30, 1956, in Gallegos Papers, box A-16; *Oakland CSO Newsletter* (August 1957), in Gallegos Papers, box A-13. Because of widespread ethnic Mexicans interest in this campaign, CSO members in 1954 resolved to support legislation granting pensions to noncitizens who had "lived in the [United] States for twenty-five years or more." Minutes of the Founding Convention, in Fred Ross Papers, box 10, folder 12. See also the Minutes of the Executive Board of the Monterey Chapter of the CSO, July 16–17, 1955, in Gallegos Papers, box A-13.

34. Fred Ross, "work diary," July 11, 1957, in Fred Ross Papers, box 5, folder 1; CSO Training Program," June–August 1957, in Fred Ross Papers, box 10, folder 15. When the California legislation finally passed in 1961, the *Los Angeles Mirror* called the bill "a just and humane measure" and wrote that "much of the credit goes to the CSO." *Los Angeles Mirror*, July 21, 1961.

35. Santa Clara County CSO Chapter Report, 1954, in Gallegos Papers, box A-13; César Chávez, Activity Report, March 7, 1956, in Ross Papers, box 1, folder 23; *El Excéntrico*, February 5, 1958. Instances of police harassment of Mexican youths contributed to the growth of the CSO in other parts of the state as well. In King City, for example, when two teenagers were killed in a fight, "the police and the press presumed that the Mexican boys [accused of the crime] were guilty." Outraged adults protested the detention of the Mexican suspects and eventually succeeded in having the boys released from jail. Local residents maintained their loose organization to continue to monitor race relations in the area and contacted Fred Ross, who arrived to establish the Monterey County CSO in 1954. "Minutes of the Founding Convention," March 20, 1954, in Gallegos Papers, box A-16, file "Letter from Marion Graff." See also the *Hanford Sentinel*, July 15, 1963. Many teenagers were attracted to the CSO because of the organization's concern about community-police relations. Mexicans in the Los Angeles Harbor Area CSO reported in 1955 that "teenagers were more active . . . than the older people" in their chapter. Minutes of the Executive Board Meeting, October 29, 1955, in Fred Ross Papers, box 5, folder 4. For a summary of San José Mexican residents' impressions of the local police force, see Barbara Joan Oskoui, "Police, the Public, and the Mass Media: A Ghetto/Barrio Study" (M.A. thesis, San José State University, 1980); Stella Estrada to San José Community Service Organization, November 13, 1955, in UFW-PP, box 2, folder 8; *El Excéntrico*, November 5, 1951; Minutes of the Executive Board Meeting, October 29, 1955, in Fred Ross Papers, box 5, folder 4; "Outline of Facts Supporting Request of Funds for CSO," August 27, 1956.

36. Juvenile Probation Department, County of Santa Clara, *Annual Report* (1957), in the Hoover Library, Stanford University; César Chávez, Activity Report, March 4, 1956, in Ross Papers, box 1, folder 23; *CSO Reporter*, April 1, 1957. In 1951 the Los

Angeles chapter had protested to the editors of the city's *Eastside Journal* when a journalist wrote about "so-called rat packs, hoodlums, [and] gangs" of Mexicans in East Los Angeles. Minutes of the Los Angeles CSO Executive Committee, September 24, 1951, in Fred Ross Papers, box 5, folder 6; Minutes of the San José CSO Education Committee, June 9 and 16, 1959, in Fred Ross Papers, unfiled material; San José Community Service Organization to Mayor of San José, the San José City Council, and San José Chief of Police, August 18, 1960, in Agricultural Workers Organizing Committee (AWOC) Papers, Walter Reuther Archives, Wayne State University, box 2, folder 19.

37. Minutes of the Founding Convention, Asilomar, California, March 20, 1954, in Gallegos Papers, box A-16, file "Letter from Marion Graff"; "History of the Northern Region AFSC Branch," 9; César Chávez, Activity Reports, February 17 and August 2, 1956, in Ross Papers, box 1, folders 21 and 25; Gallegos interview, September 20, 1996; "Saga of Sal Si Puedes," in Gallegos Papers, box A-13. Fred Ross told CSO members at the Asilomar national convention in 1954 that "The CSO has found the answer for the betterment of the Chicano. . . . It's simple—register and vote!" "Grass-Roots Group Forms," *San José News*, n.d. [1954], in Gallegos Papers, box 8, unfiled material. The national office sent all members a list of the voting records of every California Assemblyman in 1960, suggesting that Mexican Americans push for a broad approach to civil rights that would include raising the minimum wage, reforming the Bracero Program, establishing laws banning discrimination in public housing, and developing new safeguards against false arrest by local police. "Index, 1960," in Gallegos Papers, box A-16.

38. The voter registrar in Santa Clara County finally relented to CSO demands because Los Angeles unionists successfully pressured the Santa Clara County Central Labor Council to give its support. Minutes of the 1956 National Convention, in Gallegos, A-14; Fred Ross, "You've Heard About It!"; "The Saga of Sal Si Puedes," in Gallegos Papers, box A-13; *San José Evening News*, November 5, 1952; Moreno interview, September 18, 1996; Chávez diary, August 26, 1956, in Ross Papers, box 1, folder 43; César Chávez, Activity Report, 11 March 1956, in Ross Papers, box 1, folder 24. During this same period, Hope Mendoza of the Los Angeles CSO reported registering Mexicans to vote at churches in the San Fernando Valley. Minutes of the Los Angeles CSO General Meeting, April 2, 1952, in Fred Ross Papers, box 5, folder 7.

39. "The Saga of Sal Si Puedes," in Gallegos Papers, box A-13; Chávez to Governor Edmund G. Brown, November 13, 1952, in UFW-PP, box 2, folder 2.

40. *CSO Reporter*, November 1958.

41. *El Excéntrico*, September 1950; "The CSO Story." As Ramírez remembers, the electoral success of "Edward Roybal was the inspiration for us to start the CSO here." Ramírez interview, September 20, 1996. When Mexicans in Fresno and Oakland began to work to establish chapters of the organization in 1954, they spent their energies on voter registration campaigns before writing chapter constitutions. Minutes of the Founding Convention, in Fred Ross Papers, box 10, folder 12. See also Charles F. B. Roeth, State Department of Employment Area Manager, to Gallegos, March 27, 1956, in Gallegos Papers, box A-16; and *San José Mercury*, January 21, 1959.

42. Activity Report, March 23, 1956, in Ross Papers, box 1, folder 25; Santa Clara County Chapter Report, April 22, May 22, and January 1–June 30, 1956, in Gallegos Papers, box A-16; Moreno interview, September 18, 1996. The organization empha-

sized that leaders did "not endorse candidates or political parties, and is adamantly opposed to any form of totalitarianism whether it be Communism or Fascism." "What Is the CSO?" (pamphlet), in Gallegos Papers, box A-13. Despite such moderation, the *Oxnard Press-Courier* and other newspapers still criticized the organization for seeming to endorse only "candidates with Mexican names." *Oxnard Press-Courier,* November 26, 1958.

43. Minutes of the general meeting of the Fresno CSO, n.d., in Fred Ross Papers, box 10, folder 12; Santa Clara County Chapter Report, April 6, 1956, in Gallegos Papers, box A-16; Fred Ross and Gene Lowry to Gallegos, November 18, 1954, in Gallegos Papers, box A-13; César Chávez, Activity Reports, March 23 and April 26, 1956, in Ross Papers, box 1, folders 25 and 31.

44. Some members of the organization believed the CSO's failure to endorse candidates only confused Mexican American voters. To increase their candidate's relative number of votes, the Sánchez campaign had encouraged voters to mark their ballots only once instead of checking the names of four candidates, but the local Spanish-language radio announcer José Alvarado told listeners on the day before the election that residents were "required" to vote for four individuals. Activity Reports, April 10, 1954, in Ross Papers, box 1, folder 28.

45. César Chávez to Anthony Ríos, February 8, 1956, in UFW Office of the President Collection, box 2, folder 8; Herman Gallegos, "Voter Registration Report," in AWOC Collection, box 2, folder 19.

46. *El Excentrico,* August 20, October 5, and December 5, 1962.

47. Minutes of the Department of Migrant Ministry Meeting, February 3, 1964; *El Excéntrico,* April 5, 1962.

48. See the advertisement in *El Excéntrico,* October 5, 1962; Inter-Agency Conference on Services for Farmworkers in Santa Clara County, "Conference Summary" (ms., April 19, 1958), National Farm Workers Ministry Collection, Part 1, Office Files, R-ST, Wayne State University Archives, box 8, folder.

49. San Jose Model Cities Application, 1968 (ms.), Part 1–B, 7–9.

Chapter 8
Silicon Valley

1. Findlay, *Magic Lands,* 145. Since the mid-nineteenth century, ethnic Mexicans overwhelmingly predominated that population (making up 22 percent of the city) but were joined by scattered numbers of Puerto Ricans, Central Americans, and South Americans as well. City of San José, Department of City Planning and Building, *San José: Immigration, Ancestry and Education* (pamphlet, September 1992). Paralleling a process witnessed elsewhere in California and the Southwest, the Santa Clara Valley's "Hispanic origin" population therefore has became considerably more ethnically diverse since the mid-1960s.

2. Catherine N. Villarreal, "An Oral History on Frances 'Pancha' Palacios," May 29, 1989, Chicano Studies Library, San Jose State University. See Joséph A. Rodríguez, "Ethnicity and the Horizontal City: Mexican Americans and the Chicano Movement in San José, California" *Journal of Urban History* 21:5 (July 1995), 597; *The Forumeer* (San José), October 1969. As one local ethnic Mexican explained, "Principal objec-

tions to the San Jose celebration by the chicano organizations was that the 'cultural heritage' extolled by the Fiesta is that of the Spanish Conquistador and the early Californiano. The contemporary Mexican-American argues that these men were the agents of oppression in the subjugation of his Indian ancestors. They question why Mexican Americans should commemorate an historical situation that has prevented them from taking pride in their Indian and Mestizo origin and, therefore, from finding a true individual and social identity." "Fiesta de las Rosas," *Bronze* 1:4 (June 1969), 4–5; "Las Rosas Parade Attracts 75,000," *San José Mercury News*, June 2, 1969; "30 Charge 'Brutality' in Arrests," *San Francisco Examiner*, June 2, 1969.

3. Transcript of the Superior Court of the State of California in and for the County of Santa Clara Juvenile Division, Honorable Gerald S. Chargin, Judge, September 2, 1969, in United Farm Workers Office of the President Collection, box 25, folder 18. Despite these incredible pronouncements, Fred Lucero, the attorney for the defense in the case, remembered that Chargin did not punish the Mexican youth, instead choosing to separate the siblings and send the boy home with his grandmother. Interview with Fred Lucero, San José, November 2, 1995.

4. Armando Morales, *Ando Sangrando (I Am Bleeding): A Study of Mexican American-Police Conflict* (Fair Lawn, NJ: R. E. Burdick, 1972), 12.

5. *Specified Minorities and Poverty, Santa Clara County* (San José: Economic and Social Opportunities, 1978), tables 22–24.

6. Y. Arturo Cabrera, "Spanish-Surname Students at San José State College: A Comparison of 1963–1964 and 1966–1967" (ms. in author's possession), 2. Postgraduation employment patterns of Mexican American high school students are discussed in William P. Baker and Henry C. Jensen, *Mexican American, Black, and Other Graduates and Dropouts* (San José: East Side Union High School, 1971), in Papers of the Santa Clara County Planning Department, Special Collections, Green Library, Stanford University, box 2; Villarreal, "An Oral History on Frances 'Pancha' Palacios"; Roland M. Wagner and Diane M. Schaffer, "Social Networks and Survival Strategies: An Exploratory Study of Mexican American, Black, and Anglo Female Family Heads in San Jose, California," in *Twice a Minority: Mexican American Women*, ed. Margarita B. Melville (St. Louis: C. V. Mosby Company, 1980), 174; Santa Clara Valley Employment and Training Board, *The People We Serve* (San Jose, 1975); Zavella, *Women's Work and Chicano Families*.

7. Christian Zlolniski, "The Informal Economy in an Advanced Industrialized Society: Mexican Immigrant Labor in Silicon Valley," *Yale Law Journal* 103:2289 (June 1994), 2308; Karen Hossfield, "Divisions of Labor, Divisions of Lives: Immigrant Women Workers in Silicon Valley" (Ph.D. dissertation, University of California at Santa Cruz, 1988); *San José Mercury News*, June 2, 1991; Jesús Martínez Saldaña, "At the Periphery of Democracy: The Binational Politics of Mexican Immigrants in Silicon Valley," 80.

8. Rodríguez, "Horizontal City," 597; Baker and Jenson, *Mexican American, Black, and Other Graduates and Dropouts*.

9. Gascon interview, Chicano Studies Resource Library, SJSU.

10. Minutes of the Department of Migrant Ministry Meeting, February 3, 1964, in the National Farm Workers Ministry Collection, Part 1, Office Files, R-ST, Wayne State University Archives, box 10, folder 9; *San José News*, July 19, 1967; *La Palabra de MASC*, May 1968.

11. Oliverez, "Chicano Student Activism at San Jose State College," 36–37. *Spartan Daily*, October 26, 1967.

12. *Spartan Daily*, November 2, 1967.

13. *Bronze* (Oakland), January 1969; *San Francisco Chronicle*, May 14, 1972; Juan Olivérez, "Chicano Student Activism at San José State College, 1967–1972: An Analysis of Ideology, Leadership, and Change" (Ph.D. dissertation, University of California at Berkeley, 1991).

14. *El Grito* (Berkeley), Summer 1968; *La Palabra de MASC*, May 1968; *The Spartan* (San José State University), September 23, 1968; *San José Mercury-News*, December 13, 1968, and May 29, 1988; interview with Villarreal, November 2, 1995; Juan Olivérez, "A Chicano Commencement," *San José Studies* 19:1 (Winter 1993), 104–121.

15. *Adelante* 1:1 (San José), April 1968; "The Community Speaks," transcript of public hearings held by the San José Goals Committee, January 17–18, 1968, in the Social Sciences Library, San José State University; *El Andar* (Santa Cruz) Winter 1999; Mexican Heritage Plaza, *1999–2000 Premier Season* (published program).

16. *El Chisme* 1:2–3 (February 1970); *La Palabra de MASC* (San José), March 1968. On the visit of Corky González to the San José area in 1968, see *La Palabra de MASC*, December 18, 1968. First National Chicano Youth Liberation Conference, "El Plan Espiritual de Aztlán," in *Aztlán: An Anthology of Mexican American Literature*, ed. Luis Valdez and Stan Steiner (New York: Alfred A. Knopf, 1972), 403–404. The Plan de Aztlán was reprinted in a number of Chicano newspapers and magazines published in the San José area as well. See, for instance, *Trucha* (June 1970).

17. *People's World* (San Francisco), May 13, 1967; *The Forumeer*, August 1971.

18. "Porque nos oponemos a la guerra en Indochina" (flyer, 1971), in "San José State Folder," Cambodia-Kent State Strike Collection, Bancroft Library; *La Palabra de MASC*, December 18, 1968; *El Vocero* (San José), April 1972, May 1972.

19. *The Forumeer*, August 1971. On Henry B. González, see Gutiérrez, *Walls and Mirrors*, 186–187.

20. *San José News*, March 9, 1973; *El Vocero* (April 1972). See also the article on Santa Clara County's Silvia Torres, the American G.I. Forum member of the month in December 1964, in *The Forumeer*, December 1964; *San José Mercury-News*, November 17, 1964.

21. Oliverez, "Chicano Student Activism at San Jose State College," 86–87; letter from Armando Valdez to Pat Vasquez, July 1, 1966, in Valdez Papers, box 1, folder 1; Gascon interview, Chicano Studies Resource Library, SJSU. A small number of local college students who affirmed cultural nationalism's central importance established a short-lived group known as Los Estudiantes de Aztlán in the summer of 1972. Oliverez, "Chicano Student Activism at San Jose State College," 101.

22. *Teen Angels* (Milpitas), March 1982; interview with José R. Villarreal, San José, November 2, 1995. One such organization was the Community Action Patrol (CAPS), an effort to monitor police officers responding to reported crimes in Mexican barrios.

23. Armando Valdez to Pat Vásquez, July 1, 1966, in Valdez Papers, box 1, folder 9; "Sí—The Accent Is on Initiative" (pamphlet), in Valdez Papers, box 1, folder 14; Isabel Durón to Al Piñon, July 28, 1966, in Valdez Papers, box 1, folder 9. Later organizations did the same. MAYO, the MACSA-sponsored "Mexican American Youth Organization," also visited local high schools in the late 1960s to "provide the

Mexican American youth with a situation where he can develop some of the leadership characteristics that are so important for success." *Adelante* 1:1 (San Jose), April 1968. See also Villarreal, "An Oral History on Frances 'Pancha' Palacios."

24. *Adelante* 1:1 (San José), April 1968.

25. Interview with José Villa, Chicano Resource Library, San José State University.

26. An organization called Raza Sí, composed of mostly Mexican American professionals, helped undocumented residents defend their East Side residency during the 1980s, and other groups such as the Immigration Counseling Center, run by Catholic Social Services, followed the CSO's example in criticizing the gouging practices of other notary publics in the city. *San José Mercury-News*, October 9, 1989; *Groundswell* (San Jose), October 1978.

27. *Boletín de la Confederación de la Raza Unida*, November 14, 1976; *San José Mercury-News*, October 10, 1989; *San José Community News*, May 29–June 11, 1973.

28. San José Model Cities Program, *First Annual Report* (San José: Model Cities Program, 1970).

29. "Sí Initiates Proposal for a Community Action Program," in Valdez Papers, box 1, folder 13; *The Forumeer*, July 1971; *San José Mercury-News*, February 2, 1973; interview with Coronado.

30. *San José Mercury-News*, July 2, 1966; *La Palabra* (San José), November 1, 1969; *The Forumeer*, January 1969; *El Boletín* (San José), September 1969, October 1971, November 1971; *San José Mercury-News*, November 7, 1971, and April 15, 1972; Constitution of the Confederación de la Raza Unida Condado de Santa Clara" and "Organizational List," in "Ernestina García" file, Chicano Studies Library, San José State University. On job-training programs designed by Mexican American residents of the area, see Galarza Papers, box 62, folder 1.

31. *San José Mercury-News*, November 21, 1993; *Voz del Frente Estudiantil Chicano*, January 21, 1981; "Raza Day Brings Students to SJSU," *Spartan Daily*, March 9, 1984.

32. Martínez Saldaña, "At the Periphery of Democracy," 127–128; *San José Mercury-News*, July 27, 1977, November 1, 1979, October 10, 1989, and May 1, 1995; *Trucha* (San José), June 1970.

33. Martínez Saldaña, "La Frontera del Norte," 380; José David Saldívar, *Border Matters: Remapping American Cultural Studies* (Berkeley: University of California Press, 1997), 4; Sam Quiñones, "Tiger Tales," *Metro* (San José), December 31, 1997.

34. Gascon interview, Chicano Studies Resource Library, SJSU; *El Paladin* (San José), May 3, 1964, April 23, 1964; Martínez Saldaña, "At the Periphery of Democracy," 223–287.

35. *Sin Fronteras* (Los Angeles), August 1977; interview with Mary San Miguel, San José, October 27, 1995. See Zavella, *Women's Work and Chicano Families* for a general discussion of these processes.

36. Quoted in Martínez Saldaña, "At the Periphery of Democracy," 115.

37. *San José Mercury-News*, September 12, 1990, and May 3, 1994; *The Leader* (Newsletter of the American G.I. Forum, San José Chapter), April 1991.

38. *RazaTeca* 2:4 (San José), August 1997, 34.

39. Ibid.

Epilogue
Devil's Future

1. The scholarly and popular literature on Mexican immigration, Latino culture, and anti-immigrant sentiment during the 1980s and 1990s is vast. See, in particular, Douglas S. Massey and Kristen E. Espinosa, "What's Driving Mexico-U.S. Migration? A Theoretical, Empirical, and Policy Analysis," *American Journal of Sociology* 102:4 (January 1997), 991–992.

2. "Fortune San Jose," *Fortune Magazine* (June 5, 1989), quoted in Jesús Martínez Saldaña, "La Frontera del Norte," in *Over the Edge: Remapping the American West* ed. Valerie J. Matsumoto and Blake Allmendinger (Berkeley: University of California Press, 1999), 375.

3. Jesús Martínez Saldaña, "At the Periphery of Democracy: The Binational Politics of Mexican Immigrants in Silicon Valley" (Ph.D. dissertation, U.C. Berkeley, 1993), 187.

4. Lorna Dee Cervantes, *Emplumada* (Pittsburgh: University of Pittsburgh Press, 1981), 35–37.

Bibliography

Published Sources

Abbot, Carl. "The Metropolitan Region: Western Cities in the New Urban Area." In *The Twentieth-Century West: Historical Interpretations.* Edited by Gerald D. Nash and Richard W. Etulain. Albuquerque: University of New Mexico Press, 1989.

———. *The New Urban America: Growth and Politics in Sunbelt Cities.* Chapel Hill: University of North Carolina Press, 1981.

———. "Southwestern Cityscapes: Approaches to American Urban Environment." In *Essays on Sunbelt Cities and Recent Urban America.* Edited by Robert B. Fairbanks and Kathleen Underwood. College Station: Texas A & M Press, 1990.

Achor, Shirley. *Mexican Americans in a Dallas Barrio.* Tucson: University of Arizona Press, 1978.

Acuña, Rodolfo F. *A Community under Seige: A Chronicle of Chicanos East of the Los Angeles River, 1945–1975.* Los Angeles: Chicano Studies Research Center Publications, UCLA, 1984.

———. "La Generación de 1968: Unfulfilled Dreams." *Corazón de Aztlán* 1 (January–February 1982): 6–7.

———. *Occupied America: A History of Chicanos,* 3d edition. New York: Harper and Row, 1988.

Adult Education Department [San José] Schedule, 1952–1953. Pamphlet, California State Library, 1952.

Adult Education Department Schedule, 1957–1958. Pamphlet, California State Library, 1957.

Adult Education Department Schedule, 1961–1962. Pamphlet, California State Library, 1961.

Alesch, Daniel J., and Robert A. Levine. *Growth in San Jose: A Summary Policy Statement.* Santa Monica: Rand Corporation, 1973.

Allsup, Carl. *The American G.I. Forum: Origins and Evolution.* Austin: University of Texas, Center for Mexican American Studies, 1982.

Almaguer, Tomás. *Racial Fault Lines: The Historical Origins of White Supremacy in California.* Berkeley: University of California Press, 1994.

Alvirez, David, Marta Tienda, and Dudley L. Posten, Jr. "Earning Differences between Anglo and Mexican American Male Workers in 1960 and 1970: Changes in the 'Cost' of Being Mexican American." *Social Science Quarterly* 57:3 (December 1976): 618–631.

American G.I. Forum of Texas and Texas State Federation of Labor. *What Price Wetbacks?* Austin: American G.I. Forum of Texas and Texas State Federation of Labor, AFL, 1953.

Anaya, Rudolfo A., and Francisco Lomeli, eds. *Aztlán: Essays on the Chicano Homeland.* Albuquerque: University of New Mexico Press, 1989.

Anderson, Benedict. *Imagined Communities: Reflections on the Origin and Spread of Nationalism.* New York: Verso Press, 1983.

Anderson, Dewey. *Always to Start Anew: The Making of a Public Activist.* New York: Vantage Press, 1970.

Anderson, Henry P. *The Bracero Program in California, with Particular Reference to Health Status, Attitudes, and Practices.* New York: Arno Press, 1976.

Apostle, Richard A., Charles Y. Glock, Thomas Piazza, and Marijean Suelzle. *The Anatomy of Racial Attitudes.* Berkeley: University of California Press, 1983.

Arbuckle, Clyde, and Ralph Rambo. *Santa Clara County Ranchos.* San Jose: Rosicrucian Press, 1968.

Armitage, Katie H. "'This Far Off Land': The Overland Diary, June–October, 1867, and California Diary, January–March, 1868, of Elizabeth 'Bettie' Duncan." *Kansas History* 12:1 (1989): 13–27.

Arroyo, Luis L. "Chicano Participation in Organized Labor: The CIO in Los Angeles, 1938–1950." *Aztlán* 6:2 (1976): 277–303.

———. "Notes on Past, Present and Future Directions of Chicano Labor Studies." *Aztlán* 6:2 (1976): 137–149.

Baker, Bonnie Lea, Richard A. Wald, and Rita Zamora. *Economic Aspects of Mexican and Mexican-American Urban Households.* San Jose: Institute for Business and Economic Research, San Jose State University, 1971.

Baker, William P., and Henry C. Jensen. *Mexican American, Black, and Other Graduates and Dropouts.* San José: East Side Union High School, 1971.

Balderrama, Francisco. *In Defense of La Raza: The Los Angeles Mexican Consulate and the Mexican Community.* Tucson: University of Arizona Press, 1982.

Bannon, John Francis. *The Spanish Frontier Borderlands Frontier, 1513–1821.* New York: Holt, Rinehart and Winston, 1970.

Barrera, Mario. *Beyond Aztlán: Ethnic Autonomy in Comparative Perspective.* Notre Dame: University of Notre Dame Press, 1988.

———. *Race and Class in the Southwest: A Theory of Racial Inequality.* Notre Dame: University of Notre Dame Press, 1979.

Beechey, Frederic W. *Narrative of a Voyage to the Pacific and Bering's Strait.* London: Henry, Colburn, and Richard Bentley, 1831.

Bell, Marjorie, ed. *Delinquency and the Community in Wartime. Yearbook National Probation Association 1943.* New York: National Probation Association, 1944.

Belser, Karl. "The Making of Slurban America," *Cry California* 5 (Fall 1970): 5.

Benjamin, Walter. *Illuminations,* ed. Hannah Arendt. New York: Schocken Books, 1968.

Berger, Bennett M. *Working-Class Suburb: A Study of Auto Workers in Suburbia.* Berkeley: University of California Press, 1960.

Bergquist, Charles. *Labor in Latin America: Comparative Essays on Chile, Argentina, Venezuela, and Colombia.* Stanford: Stanford University Press, 1986.

Bernard, Richard M., and Bradley R. Rice, eds. *Sunbelt Cities: Politics and Growth Since World War II.* Austin: University of Texas Press, 1983.

Bethell, Leslie, ed. *Mexico since Independence.* New York: Cambridge University Press, 1991.

Bisceglia, Louis R. "Primary Sources of Anti-English Activities in California, 1916– 1936: The John Byrne Collection." *Southern California Quarterly* 64:3 (1982): 227–237.

Blauner, Robert. *Racial Oppression in America.* New York: Harper and Row, 1972.

Blum, Linda M. "Possibilities and Limits of the Comparable Worth Movement." *Gender & Society* 1:4 (1987): 380–399.

Boyden, Richard. "Where Outsized Paychecks Grow on Trees": War Workers in San Francisco Shipyards." *Prologue* 23:3 (1991): 253–259.

Bradshaw, Ted K. "Trying Out the Future," *Wilson Quarterly* 4 (Summer 1980): 66– 82.

Briggs, Vernon M., Walter Fogel, and Fred H. Schmidt. *The Chicano Worker.* Austin: University of Texas Press, 1977.

Brody, David. *In Labor's Cause: Main Themes on the History of the American Worker.* New York: Oxford University Press, 1993.

Broek, Jan Otto Marius. *The Santa Clara Valley, California: A Study in Landscape Changes.* Utrecht: Uitgevers, 1932.

Broussard, Albert S. *Black San Francisco: The Struggle for Racial Equality in the West, 1900–1954.* Lawrence: University Press of Kansas, 1993.

———. "Oral Recollection and the Historical Reconstruction of Black San Francisco, 1915–1940." *Oral History Review* 12 (1984): 63–80.

Browning, Rufus P., Dale Rogers Marshall, and David H. Tabb. *Protest Is Not Enough: The Struggle of Blacks and Hispanics for Equality in Urban Politics.* Berkeley: University of California Press, 1984.

Broyles-Gonzalez, Yolanda. *El Teatro Campesino: Theater in the Chicano Movement.* Austin: University of Texas Press, 1994.

Bullock, Paul. "Combating Discrimination in Employment." *California Management Review* 3:4 (Summer 1961): 18–32.

———. "Employment Problems of the Mexican-American." *Industrial Relations* 3:3 (May 1964): 37–50.

Cabrera, Yisidro Arturo. "A Follow-Up Study of Bilingual Education Emphasis Teacher Graduates from a Three-Year Federal Title VII Project Conducted at San Jose State University." Ms., 1980.

Calavita, Kitty. *Inside the State: The Bracero Program, Immigration, and the I.N.S.* New York: Routledge Press, 1992.

California Canning Bartlett Pear Statistics, 1938–1947 Inclusive. Sacramento: California State Department of Agriculture, 1947.

California State Department of Industrial Relations. *Californians of Spanish Surname: Population, Education, Employment, Income.* San Francisco: Fair Employment Practice Commission, Division of Fair Employment Practices, 1965.

California State Department of Industrial Relations. *Californians of Spanish Surname:*

Population, Education, Employment, Income: A Summary of Changes between 1960 and 1970—Based on U.S. Census of Population. San Francisco: State of California Agriculture and Services Agency, Fair Employment Practice Commission, Division of Fair Employment Practices, 1976.

Calles, Rudy. *Champion Prune Pickers: Migrant Worker's Dilemma.* Los Alamitos, CA: Hwong Publishing Company, 1979.

Camarillo, Albert. *Chicanos in a Changing Society: From Mexican Pueblos to American Barrios in Santa Barbara and Southern California, 1848–1930.* Cambridge: Harvard University Press, 1979.

———. *Chicanos in California: A History of Mexican Americans in California.* San Francisco: Boyd & Fraser, 1984.

Canclini, Néstor García. *Transforming Modernity: Popular Culture in Mexico,* trans. Lidia Lozano. Austin: University of Texas Press, 1993.

Cardoso, Lawrence A. *Mexican Emigration to the United States, 1897–1931.* Tucson: University of Arizona Press, 1980.

Carpenter, Niles. *Immigrants and Their Children, 1920.* Washington, D.C.: Government Printing Office, 1927.

Carson, Clayborne. *In Struggle: SNCCC and the Black Awakening in the 1960s.* Cambridge: Harvard University Press, 1981.

Castillo, Pedro. "The Making of the Mexican Working Class in the United States: Los Angeles, California: 1820–1920." In *El Trabajo y los Trabajadores en la Historia de México.* Edited by Elsa Cecilia Frost, Michael C. Meyer, and Josefina Zoraida-Vasquez. Mexico City: Colegio de México, 1979.

Chabram-Dernersesian, Angie. "I Throw Punches for My Race, but I Don't Want to Be a Man: Writing Us- Chica-nos (Girl,Us)/Chicanas-into the Movement Script." In *Cultural Studies.* Edited by Lawrence Brossberg, Cary Nelson, and Paula A. Treichler, 81–95. New York: Routledge, 1992.

Chacón, Ramón D. "Labor Unrest and Industrialized Agriculture in California: The Case of the 1933 San Joaquin Valley Cotton Strike." *Social Science Quarterly* 65 (June 1984): 336–353.

Chapman, Paul Davis. "Schools as Sorters: Testing and Tracking in California, 1910–1925." *Journal of Social History* 14:4 (1981): 701–717.

Chávez, Leo R. *Shadowed Lives: Undocumented Immigrants in American Society.* San Diego: Harcourt Brace Jovanovich College Publishers, 1992.

Chávez, John R. *The Lost Land: The Chicano Image of the Southwest.* Albuquerque: University of New Mexico Press, 1984.

"Chicano Labor History." *La Raza.* 2:1 (February 1974): 48–53.

"Chicano Workers." *La Raza.* 1:8 (1972): 18–23.

City of San José, Department of City Planning and Building. *San José: Immigration, Ancestry, and Education.* San Jose: City of San José, 1992.

Clark, Margaret. *Health in the Mexican-American Culture: A Community Study.* Berkeley: University of California Press, 1959.

Clayton, James L. "Defense Spending: Key to California's Growth," *Western Political Quartlerly* 15 (June 1962): 280–293.

Cleland, Robert Glass. *March of Industry.* Los Angeles: Powell Publishing Company, 1929.

Cockcroft, James D. *Outlaws in the Promised Land: Mexican Immigrant Workers and America's Future.* New York: Grove Press, 1986.

Cohen, Gaynor. "Alliance And Conflict Among Mexican Americans." *Ethnic and Racial Studies* 5:2 (1982): 175–195.

Cohen, Lisbeth. *Making a New Deal: Industrial Workers in Chicago, 1919–1939.* New York: Cambridge University Press, 1990.

Cohen, Robin. *Contested Domains: Debates in International Labour Studies.* London: Zed Books, 1991.

Colton, Walter. *Three Years in California.* New York: A. S. Barnes, 1851.

Commonwealth Club of California, Research Advisory Council. *The Population of California.* San Francisco, Commonwealth Club, 1946.

Conmy, Peter T. "Historical Development of San José, the Native Sons' 1938 Parlor City." *The Grizzly Bear* (May 1938): 6.

Copp, Nelson G. *'Wetbacks' and Braceros: Mexican Migrant Laborers and American Immigration Policy, 1930–1960.* San Francisco: R and E Research Associates, 1971.

"Correcting San Jose's Boomtime Mistakes." *Business Week,* September 19, 1970, 74–76.

Cortés, Carlos E., ed. *Mexican Labor in the United States.* New York: Arno Press, 1974.

Couto, Richard A. *Ain't Gonna Let Nobody Turn Me Around: The Pursuit of Racial Justice in the Rural South.* Philadelphia: Temple University Press, 1991.

Coy, Owen Cochran. *Gold Days.* San Francisco: Powell Publishing Company, 1929.

———. *The Great Trek.* San Francisco: Powell Publishing Company, 1931.

Craig, Richard B. *The Bracero Program: Interest Groups and Foreign Policy.* Austin: University of Texas Press, 1971.

Crawford, Vicki L., Jacqueline Anne Rouse, and Barbara Woods. *Women in the Civil Rights Movement: Trailblazers and Torchbearers, 1941–1965.* Bloomington: Indiana University Press, 1990.

Cull, John Augustine. *The Bride of Mission San Jose.* New York : The Abingdon Press, 1920.

D'Antonio, William V., and Julian Samora. "Occupational Stratification in Four Southwestern Communities: A Study of Ethnic Differential Employment in Hospitals." *Social Forces* 41:1 (October 1962): 17–25.

Daniel, Cletus E. *Bitter Harvest: A History of California Farmworkers, 1870–1941.* Ithaca: Cornell University Press, 1981.

Daniels, Douglas Henry. *Pioneer Urbanites: A Social and Cultural History of Black San Francisco.* Philadelphia: Temple University Press, 1980.

Daniels, Roger. *The Politics of Prejudice.* Berkeley: University of California Press, 1962.

———. *Prisoners without Trial: Japanese Americans in World War II.* New York: Hill and Wang, 1993.

DaVanzo, Julie. *U.S. Internal Migration: Who Moves and Why?* Santa Monica: Rand Corporation, 1978.

Davis, Marilyn P. *Mexican Voices/American Dreams: An Oral History of Mexican Immigration to the United States.* New York: Henry Holt, 1990.

Davis, Mike. *City of Quartz: Excavating the Future in Los Angeles.* New York: Vintage Press, 1990.

Davis, Wiliam Heath. *Sixty Years in California.* San Francisco: A. J. Leary, 1889.

Department of Commerce. *Census of Manufactures, 1905: California, Oregon, and Washington,* Bulletin 49. Washington, D.C.: Government Printing Office, 1906.

Department of Commerce. *Population: 1920, Occupations.* Washington, D.C.: Department of Commerce, 1923.

———. *United States Census of Agriculture, 1925. Report for States, Part III, Western States.* Washington, D.C.: Government Printing Office, 1927.

———. *United States Census of Agriculture, 1935. Report for States with Statistics for Counties,* vol. 1. Washington, D.C.: Government Printing Office, 1936.

———. *United States Census of Agriculture, 1945,* vol. 1, part 33. Washington, D.C.: Government Printing Office, 1946.

Detzer, Karl. "Father and Mother Sharpen Their Wits." *School and Society* 52:1336 (August 3, 1940): 65–67.

di Leonardo, Micaela. *The Varieties of Ethnic Experience: Kinship, Class, and Gender among California Italian-Americans.* Ithaca: Cornell University Press, 1984.

Division of Labor Statistics and Research, State of California. *Work Injuries in Agriculture, 1950.* San Francisco: Government Printing, 1951.

———. *Work Injuries in Agriculture, 1951.* San Francisco: Government Printing, 1952.

———. *Work Injuries in Agriculture, 1957.* San Francisco: Government Printing, 1958.

———. *Work Injuries in Agriculture, 1959.* San Francisco: Government Printing, 1960.

Draper, Alan. "A Sisyphean Ordeal: Labor Educators, Race Relations and Southern Workers, 1956–1966." *Labor Studies Journal* 16:4 (1991): 3–19.

DuBois, Ellen Carol, and Vicki L. Ruiz. *Unequal Sisters: A Multicultural Reader in U.S. Women's History.* New York: Routledge, 1990.

Duflot de Mofras, Eugene. *Duflot de Mofras' Travels on the Pacific Coast.* 2 vols. Trans. and ed. Marguerite Wilbur. Santa Ana: The Fine Arts Press, 1937.

Eakins, David W., ed. *Businessmen and Municipal Reform: A Study in Ideals and Practice in San Jose and Santa Cruz, 1896–1914.* San José: Sourisseau Academy for California State and Legal History, San José State University, 1976.

Escobar, Edward J. "The Dialectics of Repression: The Los Angeles Police Department and the Chicano Movement, 1968–1971." *Journal of American History* 79:4 (March 1993): 1483–1514.

Fallows, Marjorie. "The Mexican American Laborers: A Different Drummer?" *Massachussetts Review* 8:1 (Winter 1967): 166–176.

Farquhar, Francis P. *Up and Down California in 1860–1864: The Journal of William H. Brewer.* Berkeley: University of California Press, 1966.

Faue, Elizabeth. "Paths of Unionization: Community, Bureaucracy, and Gender in the Minneapolis Labor Movement of the 1930s." In *Work Engendered: Toward a New History of American Labor.* Edited by Ava Baron, 296–319. Ithaca: Cornell University Press, 1991.

Findlay, John M. "Far Western Cityscapes and American Culture since 1940," *Western Historical Quarterly* 22 (February 1991): 19–23.

———. *Magic Lands: Western Cityscapes and American Culture after 1940.* Berkeley: University of California Press, 1992.

Flammang, Janet A. "Effective Implementation: The Case of Comparable Worth in San Jose." *Policy Studies Review* 5:4 (1986): 815–837.

Flannery, H. J. "Street Lights for 100 New Residents a Day." *The American City* (August 1960): 129–131.

Fogel, Walter. *Education and Income of Mexican-Americans in the Southwest.* Los Angeles: Mexican American Study Project, Graduate School of Business, University of California, Los Angeles, 1965.

Foote, H. S. *Pen Pictures from the Garden of the World.* Chicago: Lewis Publishing Company, 1888.

Forbes, Jack D. "Hispano-Mexican Pioneers of the San Francisco Bay Region: An Analysis of Racial Origins." *Aztlán* 14:1 (Spring 1983): 175–189.

Fox, Richard Wightman, and T. J. Jackson Lears, eds. *The Culture of Consumption: Critical Essays in American History, 1880–1980.* New York: Pantheon Books, 1983.

Frank, Dana. *Purchasing Power: Consumer Organizing, Gender, and the Seattle Labor Movement, 1919–1929.* New York: Cambridge University Press, 1994.

Fraser, Steven, and Gary Gerstle. *The Rise and Fall of the New Deal Order, 1930–1980.* Princeton: Princeton University Press, 1989.

Fredrickson, George M. *The Arrogance of Race: Historical Perspectives on Slavery, Racism, and Social Inequality.* Middletown, CT: Wesleyan University Press, 1988.

———. *The Black Image in the White Mind.* New York: Harper & Row, 1971.

Fremont, John C. *Memoirs of My Life.* Chicago: Belford and Clarke, 1887.

Friday, Chris. *Organizing Asian American Labor: The Pacific Coast Canned-Salmon Industry, 1870–1942.* Philadelphia: Temple University Press, 1990.

Friedman, Ralph. "Booming California," *Frontier* 8 (April 1957): 10–11.

Frisch, Michael. *A Shared Authority: Essays on the Craft and Meaning of Oral and Public History.* Albany: State University of New York, 1990.

Fuller, Varden, John W. Warner, and George L. Viles. *Domestic and Imported Workers in the Harvest Labor Market: Santa Clara County, California, 1954.* Berkeley: University of California, California Agricultural Experiment Station, Giannini Foundation of Agricultural Economics, 1956.

Gabin, Nancy. "Time Out of Mind: The UAW's Response to Female Labor Laws and Mandatory Overtime in the 1960s." In *Work Engendered: Toward a New History of American Labor.* Edited by Ava Baron, 351–374. Ithaca: Cornell University Press, 1991.

Gagnier, Regenia. "The Two Nations: Homelessness as an 'Aesthetic Issue' Past and Present." *Stanford Humanities Review* 3:1 (Winter 1993): 34–53.

Galarza, Ernesto. *Barrio Boy.* Notre Dame: University of Notre Dame Press, 1971.

———. *Farm Workers and Agri-business in California, 1947–1960.* Notre Dame: University of Notre Dame Press, 1977.

———. "Life in the United States for Mexican People: Out of the Experience of a Mexican." In *Proceedings of the National Conference of Social Work,* 399–404. Chicago: University of Chicago Press, 1930.

———. "Mexicans in the Southwest: A Culture in the Process." In *Plural Society in the Southwest.* Edited by Edward Spicer. New York: Interbook, 1972.

———. "Pan-American Union Chief Speaks." *The Pan-American* (February 1945): 12–14.

Galarza, Ernesto. *The Roman Catholic Church as a Factor in the Political and Social History of Mexico*. Sacramento: The Capital Press, 1928.

———. *Spiders in the House and Workers in the Field*. Notre Dame: University of Notre Dame, 1970.

Gamboa, Erasmo. *Mexican Labor and World War II: Braceros in the Pacific Northwest, 1942–1947*. Austin: University of Texas Press, 1990.

Gamio, Manuel. *The Life Story of the Mexican Immigrant*. New York: Dover Publications, 1971.

———. *Mexican Immigration to the United States: A Study of Human Migration and Adjustment*. New York: University of Chicago Press, 1939.

Garcia, Alma M. "The Development of Chicana Feminist Discourse." In *From Different Shores: Perspectives on Race and Ethnicity in America*, ed. Ronald Takaki, 175–183. New York: Oxford University Press, 1994.

García, Mario T. *Desert Immigrants: The Mexicans of El Paso, 1880–1920*. New Haven: Yale University Press, 1981.

———. *Memories of Chicano History: The Life and Narrative of Bert Corona*. Berkeley: University of California Press, 1994.

———. *Mexican Americans: Leadership, Ideology, and Identity, 1930–1960*. New Haven: Yale University Press, 1989.

García, Richard. "The Making of the Mexican American Mind." In *History, Culture and Society: Chicano Studies in the 1980s*. Ypsilanti, MI: Bilingual Press, 1983.

Garr, Daniel J. "A Frontier Agrarian Settlement: San José de Guadelupe [*sic*], 1777–1850." *San José Studies* 2:3 (November 1976).

Gecas, Viktor. "Self-Conceptions of Migrant and Settled Mexican Americans." *Social Science Quarterly* 54:3 (December 1973): 179–195.

Genovese, Eugene D. "Black Nationalism and American Socialism: A Comment on Harold Cruse's *Crisis of the Negro Intellectual*." In *In Red and Black: Marxian Explorations in Southern and Afro-American History*. New York: Vintage Books, 1971.

Gerstle, Gary. *Working-Class Americanism: The Politics of Labor in a Textile City, 1914–1960*. New York: Cambridge University Press, 1989.

Gilroy, Paul. *Small Acts: Thoughts on the Politics of Black Cultures*. New York: Serpent's Tail, 1993.

———. *'There Ain't No Black in the Union Jack': The Cultural Politics of Race and Nation*. Chicago: University of Chicago Press, 1987.

Goldschmidt, Walter. *As You Sow: Three Studies in the Social Consequences of Agribusiness*. Montclair, N.J.: Allanhead, Osmun, 1978.

Gómez-Quiñones, Juan. *Chicano Politics: Reality and Promise, 1940–1990*. Albuquerque: University of New Mexico Press, 1990.

Gómez-Quiñones, Juan, and Luis Leobardo Arroyo. "On the State of Chicano History: Observations on Its Development, Interpretations, and Theory, 1970–1974." *Western Historical Quarterly* 7 (April 1976): 155–185.

Gómez-Quiñones, Juan, and David Maciel. *Al Norte del Río Bravo: Pasado Lejano (1600–1930)*. Mexico City: Siglo Veintiuno Editores, 1981.

González, Gilbert G. *Labor and Community: Mexican Citrus Worker Villages in a Southern California County, 1900–1950*. Chicago: University of Illinois Press, 1994.

González, Kathleen Ann. "That Was Living." *San Jose Studies* 19:1 (Winter 1993): 46–52.

González, Luis. *San José de Gracia: Mexican Village in Transition,* trans. John Upton. Austin: University of Texas Press, 1972.

Gordon, Avery F., and Christopher Newfield, eds. *Mapping Multiculturalism.* Minneapolis: University of Minnesota Press, 1996.

Governor C.C. Young's Fact-Finding Committee. *Mexicans in California.* San Francisco: R and E Research Associates, 1970.

Green, James R. *The World of the Worker: Labor in Twentieth-Century America.* New York: Hill and Wang, 1990.

Gregor, Howard F. "Spatial Disharmonies in California Population Growth." *Geographical Review* 53 (January 1963).

Gregory, James N. *American Exodus: The Dust Bowl Migration and Okie Culture in California.* New York: Oxford University Press, 1989.

Grele, Ronald J., ed. *International Annual of Oral History, 1990: Subjectivity and Multiculturalism in Oral History.* New York: Greenwood Press, 1992.

Grele, Ronald J., with Studs Terkel, Jan Vansina, Dennis Tedlock, Saul Benison, and Alice Kessler-Harris. *Envelopes of Sound: The Art of Oral History.* New York: Praeger, 1991.

Griffin, Paul F., and Ronald L. Chatham. "Urban Impact on Agriculture in Santa Clara County, California." *Annals of the Association of American Geographers* 48 (September 1958): 195–208.

Griswold del Castillo, Richard. *La Familia: Chicano Families in the Urban Southwest, 1848 to the Present.* Notre Dame: University of Notre Dame Press, 1984.

Grossman, James R. *Land of Hope: Chicago, Black Southerners, and the Great Migration.* Chicago: University of Chicago Press, 1989.

Gutiérrez, David G. "An Ethnic Consensus? Mexican American Political Activism since the Great Depression." *Reviews in American History* 19 (Summer 1991): 289–295.

———. *Between Two Worlds: Mexican Immigrants in the United States.* Wilmington: Jaguar Books, 1996.

———. *Walls and Mirrors: Mexican Americans, Mexican Immigrants, and the Politics of Ethnicity.* Berkeley: University of California, 1995.

Gutiérrez-Jones, Carl. *Rethinking the Borderlands: Between Chicano Culture and Legal Discourse.* Berkeley: University of California Press, 1995.

Haas, Lisbeth. *Conquests and Historical Identities in California, 1769–1936.* Berkeley: University of California Press, 1995.

Hadley, Eleanor M. "A Critical Analysis of the Wetback Problem." *Law and Contemporary Problems* 21 (Spring 1956): 334–357.

Hallagan, William S. "Labor Contracting in Turn-of-the-Century California Agriculture." *Journal of Economic History* 40:4 (December 1980): 757–776.

Hamburger, Philip. "Notes for a Gazetteer: XLI—San Jose, Calif.," *New Yorker* 39 (May 4, 1963): 148–154.

Handbook of Adult Education, 1941–1942. Pamphlet, California State Library, 1941.

Handbook of Adult Education, 1943–1944. Pamphlet, California State Library, 1943.

Handbook of Adult Education, 1944–1945. Pamphlet, California State Library, 1944.

Handbook of Adult Education, 1945–1946. Pamphlet, California State Library, 1945.

Handbook of Adult Education, 1946–1947. Pamphlet, California State Library, 1946.

Handbook of Adult Education 1948–1949. Pamphlet, California State Library, 1948.

Handbook of Adult Education, 1949–1950. Pamphlet, California State Library, 1949.

Hansen, L. O. "The Political and Socioeconomic Context of Legal and Illegal Mexican Migration to the United States (1942–1984)." *International Migration* (Switzerland) 26:1 (1988): 95–107.

Hansen, Niles M., and William C. Gruben. "The Influence of Relative Wages and Assisted Migration on Locational Preferences: Mexican Americans in South Texas." *Social Science Quarterly* 52:1 (June 1971): 103–114.

Harrington, Michael. *The Other America: Poverty in the United States.* Baltimore: Penguin Press, 1962.

Harris, William H. "Federal Intervention In Union Discrimination: FEPC and West Coast Shipyards During World War II." *Labor History* 22:3 (1981): 325–347.

Hawley, Ellis W. "The Politics of the Mexican Labor Issue, 1950–1965." *Agricultural History* 40:3 (July 1966): 157–176.

Hayne, F. Bourn. "A Boy's Voyage to San Francisco, 1865–1866: Selections from the Diary of William Bowers Bourn Ingalls." *California Historical Society Quarterly* 36:4 (December 1957).

Healey, Dorothy, and Maurice Isserman. *Dorothy Healey Remembers A Life in the American Communist Party.* New York: Oxford University Press, 1990.

Helpland, Kenneth I. "McUrbia: The 1950s and the Birth of the Contemporary American Landscape," *Places: A Quarterly Journal of Environmental Design* 5:2 (1988): 40–49.

Hernández, José. "Foreign Migration into California." In *California's Twenty Million: Research Contributions to Population Policy.* Edited by Kingsley Davis and Frederick G. Styles. Population Monograph Series no. 10. Berkeley: University of California, 1971.

Hernández, José Amaro. *Mutual Aid For Survival: The Case of the Mexican Americans.* Malabar, FL: Robert Krieger Publishers, 1983.

Herrera-Sobek, María. *The Bracero Experience: Elitelore versus Folklore.* Los Angeles: UCLA Latin American Center Publications, 1979.

———. *Northward Bound: The Mexican Immigrant Experience in Ballad and Song.* Bloomington: Indiana University Press, 1993.

Herzog, Lawrence A. *Where North Meets South: Cities, Space, and Politics on the U.S.-Mexico Border.* Austin: Center for Mexican American Studies, 1990.

Higham, John. *Send These to Me: Immigrants in Urban America.* Revised edition. Baltimore: The Johns Hopkins University Press, 1984.

Hinga, D. "Rio Grande, River of Death." *Collier's* 118 (August 17, 1946): 24.

Hobsbawm, E. J. *Nations and Nationalism since 1780: Programme, Myth, Reality.* New York: Cambridge University Press, 1990.

Hoffman, Abraham. *Unwanted Mexican Americans in the Great Depression: Repatriation Pressures, 1929–1939.* Tucson: University of Arizona Press, 1974.

Hondagneu-Sotelo, Pierrette. *Gendered Transitions: Mexican Experiences of Immigration.* Berkeley: University of California Press, 1994.

Hoover, Robert L. "Notes and Documents: The Death of Yóscolo." *Pacific Historical Review* 51:3 (August 1982).

Horowitz, Daniel. *American Social Classes in the 1950s: Selections from Vance Packard's The Status Seekers.* New York: Bedford Books of St. Martin's Press, 1995.

Horowitz, Ruth. *Honor and the American Dream: Culture and Identity in a Chicano Community.* New Brunswick: Rutgers University Press, 1983.

Huerta, Jorge A. *Chicano Theater: Themes and Forms.* Ypsilanti, MI: Bilingual Press/Editorial Bilingue, 1982.

Hurtado, Albert L. *Indian Survival on the California Frontier.* New Haven: Yale University Press, 1988.

In the Valley of Heart's Delight, San Jose/Santa Clara County, California. Souvenir Program of the Fiesta de las Rosas. San José: Hillis-Murgotten, 1931.

Jackson, Kenneth T. *Crabgrass Frontier: The Suburbanization of the United States.* New York: Oxford University Press, 1985.

Jackson, W. Turrentine. "Mazatlán to the Estanislao: The Narrative of Lewis Richard Price's Journey to California in 1849." *California Historical Society Quarterly* 39:1 (March 1960).

Jacobson, Yvonne. *Passing Farms, Enduring Values: California's Santa Clara Valley.* Los Altos, CA: William Kaufmann, 1984.

James, William F., and George H. McMurry. *History of San Jose, California.* San José: Smith Printing Company, 1933.

"Jones' Pantoscope of California," *California Historical Society* 6:3 (September 1927): 250–253.

Jones, Robert C. *Mexican War Workers in the United States: The Mexico-United States Manpower Recruiting Program, 1942–1944.* Washington, D.C.: Pan-American Union, 1945.

Kane, Tim D. "Structural Change and Chicano Employment in the Southwest, 1950–1970: Some Preliminary Observations." *Aztlán* 4:2 (Fall 1973): 383–398.

Kasinitz, Philip, ed. *Metropolis: Center and Symbol of Our Times.* New York: New York University Press, 1995.

Kelley, Robin D. G. *Hammer and Hoe: Alabama Communists During the Great Depression.* Chapel Hill: University of North Carolina Press, 1990.

Kellogg, Josephine D. "Priests in the Field: The San Francisco Mission Band, 1950–1961." *U.S. Catholic Historian* 8:3 (1989): 215–230.

Kerber, Linda K., Alice Kessler-Harris, and Kathryn Kish Sklar, eds. *U.S. History as Women's History: New Feminist Essays.* Chapel Hill: University of North Carolina Press, 1995.

Kessler-Harris, Alice. *Out to Work: A History of Wage-Earning Women in the United States.* Ithaca: Cornell University Press, 1979.

Kibbe, Pauline R. *Latin Americans in Texas.* Albuquerque: University of New Mexico Press, 1946.

Kingsolver, Barbara. *Holding the Line: Women in the Great Arizona Mine Strike of 1983.* Ithaca: ILR Press, Cornell University, 1989.

Kirstein, Peter N. *Anglo over Bracero: A History of the Mexican Worker in the United States from Roosevelt to Nixon.* San Francisco: R and E Research Associates, 1977.

Kiser, George C. "Mexican American Labor before World War II." *The Journal of Mexican American History* 2 (Spring 1972): 122–142.

Knight, Robert. *Industrial Relations in the San Francisco Bay Area, 1900–1918.* Berkeley: University of California Press, 1960.

Kroeber, Alfred L. *Handbook of the Indians of California.* Berkeley: California Book Co., 1953.

Kusmer, Kenneth L. *A Ghetto Takes Shape: Black Cleveland, 1870–1930.* Chicago: University of Illinois Press, 1976.

Landis, John D. "Land Regulation and the Price of New Housing: Lessons from Three California Cities." *Journal of the American Planning Association* 52:1 (1986): 9–21.

Langum, David J. *Law and Community on the Mexican California Frontier: Anglo-American Expatriates and the Clash of Legal Traditions, 1821–1846.* Norman: University of Oklahoma Press, 1987.

Lapham, Macy H. *Soil Survey of the San Jose Area, California.* Washington, D.C.: Government Printing Office, 1904.

Levy, Jacques E. *César Chávez: Autobiography of La Causa.* New York: W.W. Norton, 1975.

Lichtenstein, Nelson. "The Making of the Postwar Working Class: Cultural Pluralism and Social Structure in World War II." *Historian* 51:1 (1988): 42–63.

———. *The Most Dangerous Man in Detroit: Walter Reuther and the Fate of American Labor.* New York: Basic Books, 1995.

Limón, José E. *Mexican Ballads, Chicano Poems: History and Influence in Mexican-American Social Poetry.* Berkeley: University of California Press, 1992.

Lipsitz, George. *Time Passages: Collective Memory and American Popular Culture.* Minneapolis: University of Minnesota Press, 1990.

Locke, Delia M., and Marcella Thorp Emerick, eds. "Hi-Ho! Come to the Fair!": Early California Fairs." *Pacific Historian* 29:1 (1985): 22–29.

London, Joan, and Henry Anderson. *So Shall Ye Reap: The Story of Cesar Chavez and the Farm Workers' Movement.* New York: Thomas Y. Crowell, 1970.

Loomis, Charles P., and Nellie H. Loomis. "Skilled Spanish-American War-Industry Workers from New Mexico." *Applied Anthropology* 2 (October–December 1942): 3–36.

Lotchin, Roger W. "The City and the Sword through the Ages and the Era of the Cold War." In *Essays on Sunbelt Cities and Recent Urban America.* Edited by Robert B. Fairbanks and Kathleen Underwood, 87–124. College Station: Texas A & M Press, 1990.

Lukes, Timothy J., and Gary Y. Okihiro. *Japanese Legacy: Farming and Community Life in California's Santa Clara Valley.* Cupertino: California History Center, De Anza College, 1985.

Lyle, Jerolyn R. "Factors Affecting the Job Status of Workers With Spanish Surnames." *Monthly Labor Review* 96:4 (April 1973): 10–16.

Lyman, Chester Smith. *Around the Horn to the Sandwich Islands and California.* New Haven: Yale University Press, 1924.

Maciel, David. *Al Norte del Río Bravo: Pasado Inmediato (1930–1981).* Mexico City: Siglo Veintiuno Editores, 1981.

McWiliams, Carey. *California: The Great Exception.* Westport, CT: Greenwood Press, 1971.

———. *Ill Fares the Land.* Boston: Little, Brown, 1944.

———. *North from Mexico.* Westport, CT: Greenwood Press, 1968.

———. *Southern California: An Island on the Land* (Santa Barbara: Peregrine Smith, 1979.

Malone, Michael P., and Richard W. Etulain. *The American West: A Twentieth-Century History.* Lincoln: University of Nebraska Press, 1989.

Marable, Manning. *Race, Reform, and Rebellion: The Second Reconstruction in Black America, 1945–1990* Second edition. Jackson: University Press of Mississippi, 1991.

Marin, Marguerite V. *Social Protest in an Urban Barrio: A Study of the Chicano Movement, 1966–1974.* Lanham, MD: University Press of America, 1991.

Márquez, Benjamin. *LULAC: The Evolution of a Mexican American Political Organization.* Austin: University of Texas Press, 1993.

Matthews, Glenna. "The Community Study: Ethnicity and Success in San José." *Journal of Interdisciplinary History* 7:2 (Summer 1976): 305–318.

———. "The Fruit Workers of the Santa Clara Valley: Alternative Paths to Union Organization during the 1930s." *Pacific Historical Review* 54, no. 1 (1985): 51–70.

Mazón, Mauricio. *The Zoot-Suit Riots: The Psychology of Symbolic Annihilation.* Austin: University of Texas Press, 1984.

Meinig, D. W. "American Wests: Preface to a Geographical Interpretation." *Annals of the Association of American Geographers* 62 (June 1972): 159–184.

Menchaca, Martha. *The Mexican Outsiders: A Community History of Marginalization and Discrimination in California.* Austin: University of Texas Press, 1995.

Mendel-Reyes, Meta. *Reclaiming Democracy: The Sixties in Politics and Memory.* New York: Routledge Press, 1995.

Mercer, Kobena. "'1968': Periodizing Postmodern Politics and Identity." In *Cultural Studies.* Edited by Lawrence Brossberg, Cary Nelson, and Paula A. Treichler, 424–437. New York: Routledge Press, 1992.

"Mexican vs. Negro Workers." *Regeneración* 1:2 (July 7, 1970): 2.

Meyers, Fredric. "Employment and Relative Earnings of Spanish-Name Persons in Texas Industries." *Southern Economic Journal* 19:4 (April 1953): 494–507.

———. *Spanish-Name Persons in the Labor Force in Manufacturing Industry in Texas.* Austin: University of Texas Press, 1951.

Michaels, Walter Benn. "Race into Culture: A Critical Genealogy of Cultural Identity." *Critical Inquiry* 18:4 (Summer 1992): 655–685.

Millard, Bailey. *History of the San Francisco Bay Region.* San Francisco: American Historical Society, 1924.

Miller, Karen K. "Race, Power and the Emergence of Black Studies in Higher Education." *American Studies* 31:2 (1990): 83–98.

Monkkonen, Eric H. *America Becomes Urban: The Development of U.S. Cities & Towns, 1780–1980.* Berkeley: University of California Presss, 1988.

Monroy, Douglas. "An Essay on Understanding the Work Experience of Mexicans in Southern California, 1900–1939." *Aztlán* 12:1 (1981): 59–74.

———. "La Costura en Los Angeles, 1933–1939: The ILGWU and the Politics of Domination." In *Mexican Women in the United States: Struggles Past and Present.* Edited by Magdalena Mora and Adelaida R. Del-Castillo. Los Angeles: University of California, Chicano Studies Research Center, 1980.

Montejano, David. *Anglos and Mexicans in the Making of Texas, 1836–1986.* Austin: University of Texas Press, 1987.

Montgomery, David. *Citizen Worker: The Experience of Workers in the United States with Democracy and the Free Market during the Nineteenth Century.* New York: Cambridge University Press, 1993.

———. *The Fall of the House of Labor.* New York: Cambridge University Press, 1987.

Montoya, Velma. "Mexican Americans and Negroes and Los Angeles Labor Unions." *The Journal of Mexican American Studies* 1:2 (Winter 1971): 84–90.

Moody, J. Carroll, and Alice Kessler-Harris. *Perspectives on American Labor History: The Problems of Synthesis.* DeKalb: Northern Illinois University Press, 1990.

Moore, Shirley Ann. "Getting There, Being There: African-American Migration to Richmond, California, 1910–1945." In *The Great Migration in Historical Perspective: New Dimensions of Race, Class, and Gender.* Edited by Joe William Trotter, Jr. Bloomington: Indiana University Press, 1991.

Moquin, Wayne, with Charles Van Doren, eds. *A Documentary History of the Mexican Americans.* New York: Bantam Books, 1971.

Morales, Armando, *Ando Sangrando (I Am Bleeding): A Study of Mexican American-Police Conflict.* Fair Lawn, NJ: R. E. Burdick, 1972.

Morefield, Richard. *The Mexican Adaptation in American California, 1846–1875.* San Francisco: R and E Research Associates, 1971.

Morrison, Peter A. "The Role of Migration in California's Growth." In *California's Twenty Million: Research Contributions to Population Policy.* Edited by Kingsley Davis and Frederick G. Styles, 33–34. Population Monograph Series no. 10. Berkeley: University of California, 1971.

Morrow, William W. *Spanish and Mexican Private Land Grant Cases.* San Francisco: Bancroft-Whitney, 1923.

Munro-Fraser, J. P. *History of Santa Clara County, California.* San Francisco: Alley, Bowen, 1881.

Muñoz, Carlos, Jr. *Youth, Identity, Power.* New York: Verso Press, 1989.

Nasatir, Abraham P. "The French Consulate in California, 1843–1856." *The Quarterly of the California Historical Society* 12:1 (March 1933).

Navarro, Armando. *Mexican American Youth Organization: Avant-Garde of the Chicano Movement in Texas.* Austin: University of Texas, 1995.

North, David S. *Seven Years Later: The Experiences of the 1970 Cohort of Immigrants in the U.S. Labor Market.* Washington, D.C.: Linton and Company, 1978.

Northrup, Herbert R. "Race Discrimination in Trade Unions. The Record and the Outlook." *Commentary* 2:2 (August 1946): 124–131.

Orsi, Robert Anthony. *The Madonna of 115th Street: Faith and Community in Italian Harlem, 1880–1950.* New Haven: Yale University Press, 1985.

Otero, J. F., and Michael D. Boggs. "A New Awareness for Latino Workers." *The American Federationist* 81:5 (May 1974): 1–5.

Pagden, Anthony. *Lords of All the World: Ideologies of Empire in Spain, Britain and France, 1500–1800.* New Haven: Yale University Press, 1995.

Palermo, Joe. "Black Power on Campus: The Beginnings." *San Jose Studies* 14:2 (1988): 31–48.

Paul, Rodman W., ed. *A Victorian Gentlewoman in the Far West: The Reminiscences of Mary Hallock Foote.* San Marino, CA: Huntington Library, 1972.

Pedelty, Mark. "The New California Mission System: Museums, Gift Shops, and Historical Archaeologists." *Kroeber Anthropological Society Papers* 73–74 (1992): 80–91.

Peña, Manuel H. *The Texas-Mexican Conjunto: History of a Working Class Music.* Austin: University of Texas Press, 1985.

Pfeffer, Max J. "Industrial Farming." *Democracy* 3:2 (1983): 37–49.

Pitt, Leonard. *The Decline of the Californios.* Berkeley: University of California Press, 1966.

Polk's City Directory, 1900, 1910, 1920, and 1930. San Jose, California.

Portelli, Alessandro. *The Death of Luigi Trastulli and Other Stories: Form and Meaning in Oral History.* Albany: State University of New York Press, 1991.

Proceedings of the 16th Convention of the International Brotherhood of Teamsters, October 13–17, 1954. New York, 1955.

Proceedings of the Third Annual Convention of the ILWU, April 1–11, 1940. North Bend: Coos Bay Harbor Press, 1940.

Rafael, Vicente L., ed. *Discrepant Histories: Translocal Essays on Filipino Cultures.* Philadelphia: Temple University Press, 1995.

Raphael, Edna E. "Working Women and Their Membership in Labor Unions." *Monthly Labor Review* 97:5 (May 1974): 27–33.

Rawls, James. *Indians of California: The Changing Image.* Norman: University of Oklahoma, 1984.

Redfield, Robert. *Tepoztlán, A Mexican Village: A Study in Folk Life.* Chicago: University of Chicago Press, 1930.

Reinhardt, Richard. "Joe Ridder's San Jose," *San Francisco Magazine* 7 (November 1965): 70.

Rendon, Gabino. *Prediction of Adjustment Outcomes of Rural Migrants to the City.* San Francisco: R and E Research Associates, 1976.

Report of Activities of the California Farm Production Council. Sacramento: Farm Production Council, 1945.

Rickard, Judy. *Media Habits of Mexican-Americans in Eastside San Jose.* San Jose: Institute for Business and Economic Research, San Jose State University, 1976.

Ritchie, Donald A. *Doing Oral History.* New York: Twayne Publishers, 1995.

Roediger, David R. *Towards the Abolition of Whiteness.* New York: Verso Press, 1994.

———. *The Wages of Whiteness: Race and the Making of the American Working Class.* New York: Verso Press, 1992.

Romero, Mary. *Maid in the U.S.A.* New York: Routledge Press, 1992.

Romo, Ricardo. *East Los Angeles: History of a Barrio.* Austin: University of Texas Press, 1983.

Rosaldo, Renato. *Culture and Truth: The Remaking of Social Analysis.* Boston: Beacon Press, 1989.

Ross, Fred. *Conquering Goliath: Cesar Chavez at the Beginning.* Keene, CA: El Taller Gráfico Press, United Farm Workers, 1989.

Ross, Stanley R., ed. *Views Across the Border: The United States and Mexico.* Albuquerque: University of New Mexico Press, 1978.

Rouse, Roger. "Mexican Migration and the Social Space of Postmodernism." *Diaspora* 1:1 (Spring 1991): 8–23.

Ruíz, Vicki L. *Cannery Women, Cannery Lives: Mexican Women, Unionization, and the California Food Processing Industry, 1930–1950.* Albuquerque: University of New Mexico Press, 1987.

Saldívar, José David. *Border Matters: Remapping American Cultural Studies.* Berkeley: University of California Press, 1997.

Saldívar, Ramón. "Bordering on Modernity: Américo Paredes' *Between Two Worlds* and the Imagining of Utopian Social Space." *Stanford Humanities Review* 3:1 (Winter 1993): 54–66.

———. *Chicano Narrative: The Dialectics of Difference.* Madison: University of Wisconsin Press, 1990.

Samora, Julian, Jorge A. Bustamante, and Gilbert Cardenas. *Los Mojados, the Wetback Story.* Notre Dame: University of Notre Dame Press, 1971.

San Jose, California, City Planning Commission. *Master Plan of the City.* San Jose: City of San Jose, 1958.

San Jose: Design for Tomorrow. San Jose: City of San Jose, 1960.

San Jose Model Cities Program, *First Annual Report.* San Jose: Model Cities, 1970.

San Juan, E., ed. *On Becoming Filipino: Selected Writings of Carlos Bulosan.* Philadelphia: Temple University Press, 1995.

Sánchez, Armand J., and Roland M. Wagner. "Continuity and Change in the Mayfair Barrios of East San Jose." *San José Studies* 5:2 (May 1979): 6–19.

Sánchez, George J. *Becoming Mexican American: Ethnicity, Culture and Identity in Chicano Los Angeles, 1900–1945.* Berkeley: University of California Press, 1993.

Sánchez, Nellie Van de Grift. *Spanish Arcadia.* San Francisco: Powell Publishing Company, 1929.

Sánchez, Rosaura. *Telling Identities: The* Californio *Testimonies.* Minneapolis: University of Minnesota Press, 1995.

Sánchez-Tranquilino, Marcos, and John Tagg. "The Pachuco's Flayed Hide: Mobility, Identity, and *Buenas Garras.*" In *Cultural Studies,* eds. Lawrence Brossberg, Cary Nelson, and Paula A. Treichler, 556–565. New York: Routledge, 1992.

Santa Clara County Planning Department. "Components of Yearly Population Increase, 1950–1976, Santa Clara County." *Info.* 576 (July 1976): 1–2.

———. *Eastside Interim General Plan.* Santa Clara County Planning Department pamphlet, 1956.

———. *Land Use Issues in Santa Clara County.* San Jose: City of San José, 1963.

Santa Clara Valley Employment and Training Board. *The People We Serve.* San Jose: County of Santa Clara, 1975.

Saragoza, Alex M. "The Significance of Recent Chicano-Related Historical Writings: An Appraisal." *Ethnic Affairs* 1 (Fall 1987): 24–62.

Sassen, Saskia. *Cities in a World Economy.* Thousand Oaks: Pine Forge Press, 1994.

Saunders, Lyle, and Olen F. Leonard. *The Wetback in the Lower Rio Grande Valley of Texas.* Austin: Inter-American Education Occasional Papers no. 7, University of Texas, 1951.

Sawyer, Eugene Taylor. *The History of Santa Clara County, California.* Los Angeles: Historic Record Company, 1922.

Schneider, Jimmie. *Quicksilver: The Complete History of Santa Clara County's New Almadén Mine.* San José: Zella Schneider, 1992.

Sears, Mary. "The Flat-Tired, Flat-Tired-People." *Californians* 7:2 (1989): 14–17, 58.

Seaton, Douglas P. *Catholics and Radicals.* Lewisburg: Bucknell University Press, 1981.

Segura, Denise A. "Chicana and Mexican Immigrant Women at Work: The Impact of Class, Race, and Gender on Occupational Mobility." *Gender & Society* 3:no. 1 (1989): 37–52.

———. "Inside the Work Worlds of Chicana and Mexican Immigrant Women." In *Women of Color in U.S. Society.* Edited by Maxine Baca Zinn and Bonnie Thornton Dill, 95–112. Philadelphia: Temple University Press, 1994.

Seventh Annual Fiesta de las Rosas of Santa Clara County, San Jose, California, May 21, 1932. San José: Hillis-Murgotten Co., 1932.

Sitkoff, Harvard. *A New Deal for Blacks: The Emergence of Civil Rights as a National Issue.* Volume 1: *The Depression Decade.* New York: Oxford University Press, 1978.

Smith, Henry Nash. *Virgin Land.* Cambridge: Harvard University Press, 1950.

Sommers, Laurie Kay. "Inventing Latinismo: The Creation of 'Hispanic' Panethnicity in the United States." *Journal of American Folklore* 104:411 (1991): 32–53.

Souvenir of the First Annual Santa Clara Valley Fiesta de las Rosas. San José: Hillis-Murgotten, Co., 1926.

Souvenir of the Santa Clara County Fourth Annual Fiesta de las Rosas, 1929. San José: Hillis-Murgotten Co., 1929.

Specified Minorities and Poverty, Santa Clara County. San José: Economic and Social Opportunities, 1978.

Spivak, Gayatri Chakravorty. *In Other Worlds: Essays in Cultural Politics.* New York: Routledge Press, 1987.

Squires, Gregory D. *Capital and Community in Black and White: The Intersections of Race, Class, and Uneven Development.* Albany: State University of New York, 1994.

Stanford Environmental Law Society. *San Jose, Sprawling City: A Report on Land Use Policies and Practices in San Jose, California.* Stanford: Stanford University Press, 1971.

Starr, Kevin. *Americans and the California Dream, 1850–1915.* New York: Oxford University Press, 1973.

State of California. *Aerospace Employment, California and Metropolitan Areas, 1949–69.* Sacramento: Government Printing Office, 1970.

State of California, Department of Employment. *Labor Requirements for California Crops, 1948.* Sacramento: Farm Placement Service, 1948.

Steinberg, Stephen. *The Ethnic Myth: Race, Ethnicity, and Class in America.* Boston: Beacon Press, 1989.

Stern, Norton B., and William M. Kramer. "The Silk Man of San Jose: An Episode in California Economic Development." *Western States Jewish History* 21:2 (1989): 166–170.

"Story of Mexican-Born Boy Shows American Assimilation." *The Christian Science Monitor,* July 24, 1944.

Takaki, Ronald T. *Iron Cages: Race and Culture in Nineteenth-Century America.* New York: Alfred A. Knopf, 1979.

Taylor, Frank J. "Factory in the Country." *Saturday Evening Post,* April 13, 1946, 20, 133–134.

Taylor, Paul S. *Mexican Labor in the United States.* 7 vols. Berkeley: University of California Press, 1930.

Taylor, Paul S., and Tom Vasey, "Historical Background of California Farm Labor." *Rural Sociology* 1 (September 1936): 401–419.

Texas State Unemployment Compensation. *Origins and Problems of Texas Migratory Farm Labor.* Report Prepared by the Farm Placement Service, Austin, State Publishing Office, 1940.

Tiano, Susan. *Patriarchy on the Line: Labor, Gender, and Ideology in the Mexican Maquila Industry.* Philadelphia: Temple University Press, 1994.

Todd, Arthur Cecil. *The Cornish Miner in America.* Glendale: Arthur H. Clark Company, 1967.

Treviño, Roberto R. "Prensa y Patria: The Spanish-Language Press and the Biculturation of the Tejano Middle Class, 1920–1940." *The Western Historical Quarterly* 22:4 (November 1991): 451–472.

Trounstine, Philip J., and Christensen, Terry. *Movers and Shakers: The Study of Community Power.* New York: St. Martin's Press, 1982.

Tuck, Ruth. *Not with the Fist.* New York: Harcourt and Brace, 1946.

U.S. Bureau of the Census, *Fifteenth Census of the United States: 1930. Population. Vol. 3, Part 1: Alabama-Mississippi.* Washington, D.C.: Government Printing Office, 1932.

———. *U.S. Census of Population: 1960. Subject Reports. Mobility for Metropolitan Areas,* Final Report PC(2)-2C. Washington, D.C.: Government Printing Office, 1963.

U.S. Congress, House of Representatives. Committee on Agriculture. *Mexican Farm Labor.* Hearings on H.J. Res. 355. 83d Congress, 2d Session. Washington, D.C.: Government Printing Office, 1954.

Ueda, Reed. *Postwar Immigrant America: A Social History.* New York: Bedford Books of St. Martin's Press, 1994.

Ullman, Edward L. "Amenities as a Factor in Regional Growth," *Geographical Review* 44 (January 1954): 119–132.

United States Immigration and Naturalization Service. *Annual Report of the United States Immigration and Naturalization Service.* Washington, D.C.: Government Printing Office, 1966.

———. *Report of Field Operations of the Immigration and Naturalization Service.* Washington, D.C.: Government Printing Office, 1967–68.

Urban Economics Division, Larry Smith & Company. *Mexican Trade and Cultural Center Financial Feasibility Evaluation, Prepared for the Mayor's Committee for the Mexican Trade and Cultural Center.* San Francisco: Larry Smith, 1972.

Valdés, Dennis Nodín. *Al Norte: Agricultural Workers in the Great Lakes Region, 1917–1970.* Austin: University of Texas Press, 1991.

Valdez, Armando, Albert Camarillo, and Tomás Almaguer, eds. *The State of Chicano Research on Family, Labor, and Migration: Proceedings of the First Stanford Symposium on Chicano Research and Public Policy.* Stanford: Stanford Center for Chicano Research, 1983.

Valdez, Armando. "Insurrection in New Mexico—Land of Enchantment." *El Grito* 1:1 (Fall 1967): 15–24.

Valdez, Luis, and Stan Steiner, eds. *Aztlán: An Anthology of Mexican American Literature*. New York: Alfred A. Knopf, 1972.

Vance, James E., Jr. *Geography and Urban Evolution in the San Francisco Bay Area*. Berkeley: Institute of Governmental Studies, University of California, 1964.

Vargas, Zaragosa. *Proletarians of the North: A History of Mexican Industrial Workers in Detroit and the Midwest, 1917–1933*. Berkeley: University of California Press, 1993.

"Views of a Mexican Worker on His Return from the United States." *Inter-American* 3:2 (February 1944): 37–38.

Villarreal, Arturo. "Lowriders." *The West* supplement to *San José Mercury-News*, October 10, 1993.

Wagner, Roland M., and Diane M. Schaffer. "Social Networks and Survival Strategies: An Exploratory Study of Mexican American, Black, and Anglo Female Family Heads in San Jose, California. In *Twice a Minority: Mexican American Women*. Edited by Margarita B. Melville. St. Louis: C. V. Mosby Company, 1980.

Walker, Richard A., and Williams, Matthew J. "Water from Power: Water Supply and Regional Growth in the Santa Clara Valley." *Economic Geography* 58:2 (1988): 95–119.

Weber, Devra. *Dark Sweat, White Gold: California Farm Workers, Cotton, and the New Deal*. Berkeley: University of California Press, 1994.

Weber, Francis J., ed. *The Patriarchal Mission: A Documentary History of San Jose*. Los Angeles: Libra, 1986.

"Wetbacks, Cotton, and Korea." *Nation* 172 (May 21, 1951): 408.

"Wetbacks Swarm in." *Life* 30 (May 21, 1951): 33–37.

Winther, Oscar Osburn. *The Story of San Jose, California's First Pueblo*. San Francisco: California Historical Society, 1935.

With the Mexican Laborers in the United States: Address Delivered on May 13 in the City of San José, California. Mexico City: Department of Foreign Affairs, 1945.

Wollenberg, Charles. "*James vs. Marinship*: Trouble On The New Black Frontier." *California History* 60:3 (1981): 262–279.

Woolsey, Ronald C. "Pioneer Views and Frontier Themes: Benjamin Hayes, Horace Bell, and the Southern California Experience." *Southern California Quarterly* 72:3 (1990): 255–274.

Yans-McLaughlin, Virginia. "Metaphors of Self in History: Subjectivity, Oral Narrative, and Immigration Studies." In *Immigration Reconsidered: History, Sociology, and Politics*. Edited by Virginia Yans-McLaughlin. New York: Oxford University Press, 1990.

Young, Robert. *White Mythologies: Writing History and the West*. New York: Routledge, 1990.

Yu, Connie Young. "John C. Young, a Man Who Loved History." *Chinese America: History and Perspectives* (1989): 3–14.

Zamora, Emilio. *The World of the Mexican Worker in Texas*. College Station: Texas A & M Press, 1993.

Zavella, Patricia. "*Mujeres* in Factories: Race and Class Perspectives on Women, Work, and Family." In *Gender at the Crossroads of Knowledge: Feminist Anthropol-*

ogy in the Postmodern Era. Edited by Micaela di Leonardo. Berkeley: University of California Press, 1991.

Zavella, Patricia. *Women's Work and Chicano Families: Cannery Workers of the Santa Clara Valley.* Ithaca: Cornell University Press, 1987.

Zieger, Robert H. *The CIO: 1935–1955.* Chapel Hill: University of North Carolina Press, 1995.

Zlolniski, Christian. "The Informal Economy in an Advanced Industrialized Society: Mexican Immigrant Labor in Silicon Valley." *Yale Law Journal* 103:2289 (June 1994), 2305–2335.

Unpublished Sources

Abrahams, Yolanda. "The Mexican American Population of San José, 1924–1926." Research paper, Stanford University, Winter 1976.

Akers, Elizabeth. "Mexican ranchos in the vicinity of Mission San Jose." M.A. thesis, University of California, Berkeley, 1931.

Akulicz de Santiago, Anne M. "Residential Segregation of Spanish Origin Populations: A Study of Recent Trends in a Sample of U.S. Cities." Ph.D. dissertation, University of Wisconsin-Milwuakee, 1984.

Anthony, Donald. "Labor Conditions in the Canning Industry in the Santa Clara Valley of the State of California." Ph.D. dissertation, Stanford University, 1928.

Archibeque, Criz R. "Ethnic Minority Membership in the Building and Construction Trades Unions in the Phoenix Metropolitan Area." M.A. thesis, Arizona State University, 1941.

Bale, Cynthia M. "Chicano History in the Twenties in San Jose, California, 1927–1929." Research paper, Stanford University, June 2, 1976.

Brookshire, Marjorie S. "The Industrial Pattern of Mexican-American Employment in Nueces County, Texas." Ph.D. dissertation, University of Texas, 1954.

Bullock, Paul. "Occupational Distribution by Major Ethnic Groups and by Labor Market Areas, Selected Government Contractors, Los Angeles Metropolitan Area." Ph.D. dissertation, University of California, Los Angeles, 1963.

Cabrera, Y. Arturo. "Spanish-Surname Students at San José State College: A Comparison of 1963–1964 and 1966–1967." Ms., n.d.

California State College, San José. "Racial Prejudices in San José, California as Observed by a College Class in Race Relations." Ms. San José, California, 1948.

Camarillo, Albert. "Mexican Americans in a San Jose High School, 1940–1980." Ms., January 1986.

Chávez, Roberta Marguerite. "Intimate Alliances: Intermarriage between Mexicanns and Anglos in Nineteenth-Century San José, 1820–1880." Paper presented at the Pacific Coast Branch of the American Historical Association, August 7, 1995.

Clark, Margaret. "Sickness and Health in Sal Si Puedes; Mexican-Americans in a California Community." Ph.D. dissertation, University of California, Berkeley, 1957.

Corden, Barry B. "A Sketch of the Chicano Community of San Jose, 1920–1923." Research paper, Stanford University, June 11, 1976.

Dar, Rodrigo Antonio. "Language Usage among Multilingual Filipino High School Students in San Jose, California." Ph.D. dissertation, University of San Francisco, 1981.

Datel, Robin Elisabeth. "Historic Districts in Three American and Two Western European Cities: A Geographical Study." Ph.D. dissertation, University of Minnesota, 1983.

de Luna Martinez, Yaya. "A five-year study of Chicano educational opportunity program students at a California State University." Ph.D. dissertation, University of Southern California, 1976.

Department of Industrial Relations. "Filipino Study and Immigration Summary, 1919–1928." Ms. California State Archives, Sacramento, 1929.

Eversole, Robert Wayne. "Towns in Mexican Alta California: A Social History of Monterey, San Jose, Santa Barbara, and Los Angeles, 1822–1846." Ph.D. dissertation, University of California, San Diego, 1989.

Faltis, Christian Jan. "A study of Spanish and English Usage among Bilingual Mexican Americans Living in the Las Calles Barrio of San Jose, California." M.A. thesis, San Jose State University, 1976.

Federal Manuscript Census. Santa Clara County, California, 1900, 1910, 1920.

Flores, William Vincent. "The Dilemma of Survival: Organizational Dependence, Conflict and Change in a Chicano community." Ph.D. dissertation, Stanford University, 1987.

Geilhufe, Nancy LaNelle. "Ethnic Relations in San José: A Study of Police-Chicano Interaction." Ph.D. dissertation, Stanford University, 1972.

Gómez, Laura E. "From Barrio Boys to College Boys: Ethnic Identity, Ethnic Organizations, and the Mexican American Elite, the Cases of Ernesto Galarza and Manuel Ruiz, Jr." Stanford Center for Chicano Research Working Paper no. 25, May 1989.

Gray, James. "The American Civil Liberties Union of Southern California and Imperial Valley and Agricultural Labor Disturbances, 1930–1934." Ph.D. dissertation, University of California, Los Angeles, 1966.

Greenbert, Jaclyn. "Industry in the Garden: A Social History of the Canning Industry and Canning Workers in the Santa Clara Valley, California, 1870–1920." Ph.D. dissertation, University of California, Los Angeles, 1985.

Halstead, Donna Jean. "Culture on Trial? A Case Study of Dispute." Ph.D. dissertation, University of California, Berkeley 1983.

Hernández, Guadalupe D. "A Case Study of Four Generations of Mexican Women." Undergraduate thesis, San José State University, 1972.

Huszar, Paul Conrad. "On the Rationale of Urban Growth: A Behavioral Study of San Jose, California." Ph.D. dissertation, University of California, Berkeley, 1972.

Jones, Lamar B. "Mexican American Labor Problems in Texas." Ph.D. dissertation, University of Texas, 1965.

Keller, John Frederick. "The Production Worker in Electronics: Industrialization and Labor Development in California's Santa Clara Valley." Ph.D. dissertation, University of Michigan, 1981.

Kinsey, Stephen D. "They Called It Home: The Development of the Jewish Community of San José, California, 1850–1910." M.A. thesis, San José State University, 1975.

Leonard, Kevin Allen, "Years of Hope, Days of Fear: The Impact of World War II on Race Relations in Los Angeles." Ph.D. dissertation, University of California, Davis, 1992.

Llamas, Carmen Mandy. "Attitudes of Chicana women in the San Jose area towards the Equal Rights Amendment (ERA)." M.S.W thesis, San José State University, 1986.

Lockhart, Katharine Meyer. "A Demographic Profile of an Alta California Pueblo: San Jose de Guadalupe, 1777–1850." Ph.D. dissertation, University of Colorado, Boulder, 1986.

McBroome, Delores Nason. "Parallel Communities: African-Americans in California's East Bay, 1850–1963." Ph.D. dissertation, University of Oregon 1991.

Mayfield, David W. "Ecology of the Pre-Spanish San Francisco Bay Area." Master's thesis, San Francisco State University, 1978.

Miller, Robert. "A Comparative Study of the Phonetic Problems of Anglo and Mexican-American Poor Readers in the East Side Union High." M.A. thesis, San José State University, 1973.

Moss, Richard L. "Earnings of Spanish-Origin and Non-Spanish-Origin Males in 1969, in Five Southwestern States." Ph.D. dissertation, University of New Mexico, 1973.

Navarro, Richard Arthur. "Identity and Consensus in the Politics of Bilingual Education: The Case of California, 1967–1980." Ph.D. dissertation, Stanford University, 1984.

Olivérez, Juan. "Chicano Student Activism at San José State College, 1967–1972: An Analysis of Ideology, Leadership, and Change." Ph.D. dissertation, University of California at Berkeley, 1991.

Orozco, Cynthia E. "The Origins of the League of United Latin American Citizens (LULAC) and the Mexican American Civil Rights Movement in Texas with an Analysis of Women's Political Participation in a Gendered Context, 1910–1929." Ph.D. dissertation, University of California, Los Angeles, 1993.

Oskoui, Barbara Joan. "Police, the Public, and the Mass Media: A Ghetto/Barrio Study." M.A. thesis, San José State University, 1980.

Rankin, Jerry L. "Mexican-Americans and Manpower Policy." Ph.D. dissertation, University of Arizona, 1971.

Reynolds, Diane Adele Trombetta. "Economic Integration and Cultural Assimilation: Mexican-Americans in San Jose." Ph.D. dissertation, Stanford University, 1974.

Ribera, Anthony David. "The Proactive Model of Police Administration: A Study of Urban Police Department Administration Illustrating How a Proactive Approach Can Improve Efficiency and Effectiveness." Ph.D. dissertation, Golden Gate University, 1987.

Richardson, Al. "The Chicano and the American school system: A Case Study." Ms. University of California, Santa Cruz, 1972.

Rodríguez, Anita. "The Operational Beginning of the Eastside Drug Abuse Center: A

Study Presented to the Faculty of the New College." Undergraduate thesis, San José State University, 1975.

Rodríguez, Consuelo G. "A Study in the Perceptions of High School Chicanas of Their Counselors." Research paper presented to the School of Education, San José State University, 1970.

Rusmore, Jay Theodore, and Sandra L. Kirmeyer. "Family Attitudes among Mexican-American and Anglo-American Parents in San Jose, California." Paper presented at the Western Psychological Association meetings in Los Angeles, April 1976.

Saldaña, Jesús Martínez. "At the Periphery of Democracy: The Binational Politics of Mexican Immigrants in Silicon Valley." Ph.D. dissertation, University of California, Berkeley, 1993.

Sánchez, Alfredo. "El Barrio Summer School." Undergraduate thesis, San José State University, 1973.

Sánchez, George J. "Adaptation to Conquest: The Mexican Community of San José, 1845–1880." Working Papers series no. 4, Stanford Center for Chicano Research, Stanford University, 1984.

San José Police Department. "Collected Statistics, 1959." Unpublished booklet, California State Library, Sacramento, 1959.

Santa Clara County Marriage Records, 1930, 1935, and 1940. Office of the Santa Clara County Recorder, San José, California.

Shea, Loretta, and Nancy Delaney. "Spanish-Speaking Protestant Churches of the Mayfair Area." Ms., San José State University, 1978.

Silva, Raymond J. "Evaluation of Preschool Programs for Disadvantaged Mexican-American Children in Terms of Kindergarten and First Grade Readiness." Undergraduate thesis, San José State University, 1969.

Thompson, John M. "Mobility, Income and Utilization of Mexican American Manpower in Lubbock, Texas, 1960–1970." Ph.D. dissertation, Texas Technical University, 1972.

Torres, Gregorio Mora. "Los Mexicanos de San Jose, California: Life in a Mexican Pueblo, 1777–1846." Paper presented at the Pacific Coast Branch of the American Historical Association, August 11, 1994.

Torres, María E. "Participatory Democracy and Bilingual Education: The Case of San Jose, California." Ph.D. dissertation, Stanford University, 1982.

Torres-Gil, Manuel. "Political Behavior a Study of Political Attitudes and Political Participation among Older Mexican-Americans." Ph.D. dissertation, Brandeis University, 1976.

Tulledo, Stan. "Mexican-American News in the San Jose Mercury News: A Content Analysis." M.S. thesis, San José State University, 1981.

United States Commission on Civil Rights. "The Spanish-American Community of the San Francisco Bay Area." Staff report, April 28, 1967.

Valencia, Francisco. "New Almadén and the Mexican." M.A. thesis, San Jose State University, 1977.

Villareal, Roberto M. "Illusions of Progress, Chicano Labor Activity in Texas, 1940–1970." M.A. thesis, University of Texas, 1973.

Villarreal, Arturo. "Black Berets For Justice." M.A. thesis, San José State University, 1991.

Waddell, Jack C. "Value Orientations of Young Mexican-American Males as Reflected in Their Work Patterns and Employment Preferences." M.A. thesis, University of Texas, 1962.

Yarmus, Marcia Dorothy. "The Hispanic World of John Steinbeck." Ph.D. dissertation, New York University, 1984.

Primary Sources

Newspapers

Adelante
The Agricultural Worker
Alta California
Bronze
The Californian
Catholic Council for the Spanish Speaking Newsletter
Catholic Rural Life
CSO Reporter
El Andar
El Boletin
El Chisme
El Clamor Público
El Defensor
El Excéntrico
El Grito
El Machete
El Malcriado
El Nuevo Mundo
El Paladin
El Porvenir
El Vocero
Farm Labor Newsletter
The Forumeer
FTA News
Groundswell
Hispano-America
Hormiga
La Crónica
La Raza Magazine
La Reforma
The Leader
Lucha Obrera
Mefistófeles
Oakland CSO Newsletter
Organizador del Campo
People's World
Que Tal

RazaTeca
San Francisco Bulletin
San Francisco Chronicle
San Francisco Examiner
San José Community News
San José Mercury Herald
San José Mercury-News
San José News
San José Pioneer
San José Telegraph
Santa Clara Register
Sin Fronteras
Spartan Daily
Teen Angels
Trailblazer: California Pioneers of Santa Clara County
UCAPAWA News
Union Gazette
Union Journal of Santa Clara County
Voz del Campo
Voz del Frente Estudiantil Chicano

Legal Documents

United States vs. Castillero
Santa Clara County Petitions for Naturalization 1900–1945. 47 volumes. Santa Clara
        Courthouse, San José, California.

Interviews

José Aldama, San José, October 5, 1996
Dolores Andrade, San José, October 17, 1996
Joaquin Andrade, San José, November 5, 1995
Lorena Castillo, Santa Clara, August 7, 1996
Lupe Castro, San José, May 14, 1996
Mary Contreras, San José, May 8, 1995
Lino Covarrubias, San José, October 15, 1995
Mario Espinosa, Santa Clara, May 30, 1996
Claude Fernández, Palo Alto, April 2, 1995
Josefina Fierro, Palo Alto, March 22, 1995
Gustavo Flores, San José, March 30, 1996
Dolores Fuentes, Santa Clara, April 27, 1996
Mae Galarza, Palo Alto, May 2, 1995
Herman Gallegos, San José, September 20, 1996
Gilbert García, San José, July 8, 1996
Federico Garza, San José, June 28, 1995; October 2, 1995
Eulalio Gutiérrez, San José, March 12, 1995
Manuel Hurtado, San José, April 2, 1996
Nellie Hurtado, San José, April 11, 1996
Adelaida Lucero, San José, May 9, 1996

Fred Lucero, San José, November 2, 1995
Frances Maldonado, San José, September 3, 1995
Luis Manríquez, San José, May 12, 1996
Ray Morelos, Santa Clara, August 2, 1996
Edith Moreno, San José, September 18, 1996
Hector Moreno, San José, September 18, 1996
Ana Ortega, San José, December 2, 1996
Lucinda Otero, San José, May 12, 1995
Frances "Pancha" Palacios, by Catherine N. Villarreal, May 29, 1989, in Chicano
        Studies Library, San José State University
Al Piñon, San José, September 23, 1996
Estela Ramírez, San José, November 3, 1995
Harry Ramírez, San José, November 3, 1995
Leonard Ramírez, San José, September 20, 1996
Lydia Ramírez, San José, May 9, 1995
Manuel Ramírez, San José, June 9, 1996
Luz Rendón, San José, April 1, 1996
Cecilia Romero, Santa Clara, June 11, 1996
Ray Salazar, San José, October 22, 1995
Mary San Miguel, San José, October 27, 1995
María Santana, Santa Clara, May 8, 1995
Henry Santiestevan, Washington D.C., November 3, 1995
E. David Sierra, San José, February 3, 1995
María Soto, Sunnyvale, California, May 11, 1996
Dora Stroud, Menlo Park, October 2, 1996
Leo Vargas, San José, March 8, 1995
María Velásquez, San José, December 17, 1995
Omar Velásquez, San José, June 23, 1995
José R. Villarreal, San José, November 2, 1995
Luis Zárate, San José, September 22, 1996

Other Oral Narratives

"Relacion de Secundino Robles," Bancroft Library.
"Recollections of Mary A. Jones, 1825–1918" (typescript), Bancroft Library.
Gallegos, Herman E. "Equity and Diversity: Hispanics in the Nonprofit World," oral
        history conducted in 1988 by Gabrielle Morris, Regional Oral History Of-
        fice, Bancroft Library, University of California, Berkeley, 1989.

Manuscript and Archival Collections

Agricultural Workers Organizing Committee (AWOC) Collection. Walter Reuther Ar-
        chives, Wayne State University, Detroit, Michigan.
Tony Burciaga Papers. Walter Reuther Archives, Wayne State University, Detroit,
        Michigan.
Cambodia-Kent State Strike Collection. Bancroft Library, University of California,
        Berkeley.
César Chávez Papers. Walter Reuther Archives, Wayne State University, Detroit,
        Michigan.

Community Service Organization Records. San Jose Chapter, CSO Chapter Office, San José, California.

Josephine Duveneck Papers. Hoover Archives, Stanford University, Stanford, California.

Ernesto Galarza Papers. Department of Special Collections, Green Library, Stanford University, Stanford, California.

Herman Gallegos Papers. Department of Special Collections, Green Library, Stanford University, Stanford, California.

Manuel Gamio Papers. Bancroft Library, University of California, Berkeley.

Anne Loftis Papers. Department of Special Collections, Green Library, Stanford University, Stanford, California.

Donald McDonnell Papers. Archdiocese of San Francisco Chancery Archives, Menlo Park, California.

National Association for the Advancement of Colored People Papers. Microfilm copy, Green Library, Stanford University, Stanford, California.

New Almadén Mine Papers. Department of Special Collections, Green Library, Stanford University, Stanford, California.

Fred Ross Papers. Department of Special Collections, Green Library, Stanford University, Stanford, California.

Fred Ross Papers. Walter Reuther Archives, Wayne State University, Detroit, Michigan.

Manuel Ruíz Papers. Department of Special Collections, Green Library, Stanford University, Stanford, California.

Santa Clara County Juvenile Delinquency Department Collection. Hoover Archives, Stanford University, Stanford, California.

Santa Clara County Planning Department Records. Department of Special Collections, Green Library, Stanford University, Stanford, California.

Selected Documents of Records of the Committee on Fair Employment Practice, 1941–1946. Microfilm copy, Stanford University, Stanford, California.

Southern Tenant Farmers Union Papers. Microfilm copy, Stanford University, Stanford, California.

United Farmworkers Organizing Committee Papers. Walter Reuther Archives, Wayne State University, Detroit, Michigan.

United Farmworkers President's Collection Papers. Walter Reuther Archives, Wayne State University, Detroit, Michigan.

Armando Valdez Papers. Department of Special Collections, Stanford University, Stanford, California.

Earl Warren Papers. California State Archives, Sacramento, California.

Index

Page numbers followed by *f* or *t* indicate the presence of figures or tables, respectively.